It's Velocity, Stupid!
Is The Velocity Of Money The Forgotten Variable Of Macroeconomics?

Harrison C. Hartman

INFINITY
PUBLISHING

It's Velocity, Stupid! Is the Velocity of Money the Forgotten Variable of Macroeconomics?

ISBN 978-1-4958-0426-7 Paperback
ISBN 978-1-4958-0427-4 Hardback
ISBN 978-1-4958-0442-7 eBook
Library of Congress Catalog Card Number: 2015936319

Published March 2015

INFINITY PUBLISHING
1094 New DeHaven Street, Suite 100
West Conshohocken, PA 19428-2713
Toll-free (877) BUY BOOK
Local Phone (610) 941-9999
Fax (610) 941-9959
Info@buybooksontheweb.com
www.buybooksontheweb.com

PREFACE

THE TITLE AND INTRODUCTORY REMARKS

Many people are wondering why the recovery from the most recent recession in the United States is 'dragging on'. They can find part of the answer in the pages of this book, and its focus on the recent shocking and alarming plunge in the velocity of money in the U.S. Readers can consider failing to maintain values of the velocity of money in the U.S. closer to its value in the fourth quarter of 2007 as similar to missing an important piece of a puzzle or missing a key ingredient in a recipe.

Did the title get your attention? Let me make some clarifying remarks. For those not familiar, the velocity of money is an average – the average number of times that a unit of currency trades per time period (for example, how many times the United States dollar trades in a year). As Mishkin (2004, p. 518) and likely many others point out, the average is calculated by dividing a measure of spending by the number of dollars in circulation. When the measure of spending is the total amount spent on the goods in gross domestic product, the main measure of production in the U.S. and other economies, the measure of velocity is called income velocity, as noted by Dornbusch, Fischer, and Startz (2008, p. 386) and others. The income velocity of money in the U.S. has fallen most quarters after the fourth quarter of 2007, and it has fallen sharply. Hereafter, use of the term 'velocity' will usually refer to income velocity.

The velocity of money fell by more than thirty-seven per cent after the fourth quarter of 2007 through the first quarter of 2013 based on data from www.economagic.com, and in the year 2014 it appears that velocity is still falling further! Unemployment rates jumped up in the Great Recession and have been declining but at a tortoise-esque pace in the Not-So-Great Recovery. Lives have been disrupted, if not devastated. Are these events related?

Readers may come away from this book with the sense that the suffering and hardships that many have endured as the result of the economic downturn could have been reduced, if not prevented, with improved policy. Unfortunately, without a better understanding of the velocity of money, the lackluster recovery could continue to be lackluster. Fortunately, remedies should be readily available. If a lack of spending is the problem, stabilization policies provide the solution, so that optimism and solid growth would replace despair and near stagnation. An improved understanding of why this downturn is different than most, combined with appropriate fiscal (and perhaps monetary) policies could restore income and jobs for those tragically deprived for far too long.

Regarding the first part of the title, Stokes (2012) and others note that James Carville's original quote was "The economy, stupid!" Galoozis (2012) and others point out that although the utterance of those words by Carville was to people working on the Clinton campaign for the United States Presidency in 1992, a variation of Carville's words became widely and famously used in the campaign. Thus, the variation of the quote may have taken on much greater significance.

I am referring to myself, if anyone, when using the word 'stupid.' What took me so long to realize (at least consciously), as Hansen (2009) and others had already pointed out, that the velocity of money in the United States, meaning the number of times on average that each U.S. dollar trades in a GDP transaction per year, has been falling precipitously?

If macroeconomics has a list of forgotten or underemphasized variables, then the velocity of money would likely rank at or near the top of the list, in my opinion, as of this writing. I would also add that I did not sufficiently appreciate the need to study and monitor the velocity of money at least until around the time when I was watching Darda and Keene (2011) on Surveillance Midday in August 2011. That (and perhaps a few other things) led me to work on Hartman (2011), Hartman (2013), and this book.

While Carville's original words were spoken to focus attention on the condition of the U.S. economy during a campaign, I hope that the pages that follow will draw some attention to an underemphasized macroeconomic statistic and provide much-needed relief for so many. What does the rapid decline in the velocity of the U.S. dollar in recent years imply about the ability of different forms of economic policies to lift the U.S. economy out of the doldrums? Textbook-style macroeconomic theory will help us to answer that question. A review of economic data will also help to make points and raise questions.

BACKGROUND

To provide some context about the economic environment that gave rise to this book, first consider that calculations using data that were available at www.economagic.com on July 20, 2013 indicate that real GDP in the U.S. economy, the main measure of production in the United States (further defined in Chapter 1), has been increasing since the third quarter of the year 2009. However, the pace of growth in real GDP has been slower than during many other economic recoveries, and real GDP fell sharply during the so-called 'Great Recession' in 2008 and early 2009.

Many accounts, for example Morici (2013) and Krugman (2013), indicate that an overwhelming majority of the economic gains generated in this Not-So-Great Recovery have gone to a very small percentage of the population. Therefore, it seems all the more crucial to note that recent fiscal policies of increasing taxes and reducing government spending contradict textbook macroeconomic prescriptions for increasing economic growth in the short term. Does this mean that the U.S. economy must rely primarily on expansionary monetary policy going forward to try to stimulate additional growth in real GDP and employment? And what does this imply about the economic prospects for most people in the United States if economic growth does not pick up soon? What policies would most likely lead to faster growth for the U.S. economy?

A theme in this book will be that the money supply, meaning the number of dollars circulating in the economy, can potentially have an important impact on the velocity of money. For those not familiar, M1 and M2 are two measures of the money supply, which will be discussed in more detail in Chapter 1 and other chapters. For now, suffice it to say that M1 includes only highly liquid assets such as currency and checking account deposits with no limit on the number of checks that can be written per period, while M2 includes all components of M1 plus some less liquid assets such as savings accounts that pay a higher expected interest rate than the assets in M1. Does a limit ever exist as to how large the money supply can grow before velocity begins to decrease?

An improved understanding of the velocity of money is extremely helpful for understanding one of the reasons why the current economic recovery has not been more robust. The velocity of the M1 measure of the money supply in the United States has decreased nearly every quarter after the fourth quarter of the year 2007, as shown by data found on www.economagic.com on July 20, 2013, and the overall decline has been rather steep, falling by more than thirty-seven per cent from its peak in the fourth quarter of 2007 of approximately 10.37 times per year through the first quarter of 2013 when it was around 6.47 times per year. How helpful will increasing the money supply be at stimulating GDP spending in the economy when the average number of times that each dollar trades in GDP transactions keeps falling? Should policymakers at the Federal Reserve (and elsewhere) incorporate explicit forecasts of velocity into policy deliberations?

A diagram in Baumol and Blinder (2012, p. 298) indicates that from 1929 through 2010, the velocity of M1 in the United States was greater than two times per year in every year except one. Another diagram in Baumol and Blinder (2012, p. 298) illustrates that the velocity of the M2 measure of the U.S. money supply exceeded 1.5 times per year every year from about 1950 through 2010. Values of velocity greater than one indirectly imply that the U.S. economy did not have enough dollars to buy all of the goods and services produced in any of the years from 1929 through 2010, at least at prevailing prices, *without at least some of the dollars trading more than once each year*. To state it somewhat differently, the level of spending in a year in the economy has been greater than the number of dollars circulating in the economy each year for at least eighty years (and perhaps a lot longer). This makes clear how important the exchange of dollars for goods and services is to the health of the U.S. economy.

In recent years, the M1 money supply has been growing at a faster rate than the M2 money supply (although M2 has experienced a greater increase than M1 in terms of the number of 'dollars' in the M2 measure of the money supply). Moreover, the M1 money supply has grown at a much faster rate than total spending on real GDP goods. Why are people holding so many more dollars in forms that pay little or no interest if they are not going to spend the dollars when they could receive a higher rate of interest by holding the buying power in M2 forms not part of M1?

The questions raised above in this Preface are some of the issues that this book begins to address. At this point, completely satisfactory answers to at least some of the questions may be elusive. However, working toward answers to these questions could yield great benefits in terms of increasing living standards and better utilizing scarce resources.

AUDIENCES AND CHAPTERS

This book is written with the goal of providing value to audiences with different levels of expertise in macroeconomics and also different areas of interest. Those with less experience in macroeconomics may have their interest piqued by seeing the velocity of money within the context of a recession and a sluggish recovery precipitated by the most recent financial crisis in the U.S. For them, the introductory material presented here will help to make the more advanced material easier to comprehend. On the other hand, economists may instead find the introductory material to be a useful, refreshing but optional review. They may also find some of the questions raised stimulating.

While some may find all that they want to know about the velocity of money in this book (and thus may view this book as 'an end'), others may come away wanting to learn more. For those in the latter group, this book is closer to 'a beginning' than 'an end.' I have tried to write this book with both of these groups in mind.

The chapters in this book may seem like essays, except that at least some of the material in the later chapters builds upon some of the material from the earlier chapters. Some of the textbook-style organization in this book where concepts are developed over multiple chapters is done for the benefit of a general audience. Although economists may prefer that topics would be covered concisely in as few chapters as possible, I hope and ask that they will bear with this format. I also hope that everyone will be able to find the information that they seek.

Economists may prefer to read the first part of Chapter 1 (before the crash course in macroeconomics), at least parts of Chapters 2, 3, and 4, and then skip ahead to Chapter 8 which sums up the work presented in the first seven chapters and discusses some of the work remaining. They may then refer back to earlier chapters to see how this book culminates with Chapter 8. Those with less expertise in economics may benefit from reading the chapters in an order closer to, if not exactly the same as, the order in which they appear.

Those seeking an overview of financial crises, as they appear related to declines in the velocity of money, may want to read Chapter 5. Some may want a quantitative and descriptive analysis of factors that may impact velocity. They may find Chapter 6 and the 'In-Chapter Appendix' in Chapter 8 useful. Those who want to learn more about the money multiplier model and the money supply process may find Chapter 7 helpful. A further overview of this book appears in Chapter 1.

BUYER BEWARE

While I have taken considerable steps to eliminate errors of commission (and omission) in editing this book, it is highly likely that some errors will remain. However, please bear with me in the interest of making this book available and its drawing attention to velocity as soon as possible. I make no warranty that this book is free of errors, and I apologize for any and all errors. Should this book reach a revised edition or a second edition, I hope to correct as many errors as possible, as well as make other revisions such as extending the sample period. I cannot assume liability should users of any material in this book incur damages.

Please keep in mind that, in some cases in this book, I have not read the original source material of works referenced, and I am relying on the descriptions of others (whose works are referenced). Further, my referencing of other works in this book does not imply that I agree or disagree with these works. Also, I may not have read referenced works in their entirety. I cannot assume liability for any resulting damages. In the interest of making this available to readers as soon as possible, I am publishing this work with these caveats.

THANKS AND ACKNOWLEDGMENTS

I want to thank my parents for all of the love and support that they have generously provided. The hours that they have spent making suggestions and providing guidance, and that my father has spent editing, merit special acknowledgment and thanks. They have made this book a reality. I also thank my father for suggesting the 'forgotten variable' part of the title. I am glad that James Carville made his remark in the 1992 campaign.

My thanks go to the staff of Infinity Publishing for making this book available and to others for offering guidance and suggestions. I would also like to thank the teachers, professors, and others who helped to shape my learning, writing, and research. You have also made a highly significant contribution toward the completion of this book.

Harrison C. Hartman

REFERENCES FOR PREFACE

Baumol, W. J. and Blinder, A. S. (2012) *Macroeconomics: Principles and Policy*, twelfth edition. South-Western Cengage Learning, Mason, Ohio.

Darda, M. and Keene, T. (2011) on Surveillance Midday, Bloomberg TV, August 19, 2011.

Dornbusch, R., Fischer, S., and Startz, R. (2008) *Macroeconomics*, tenth edition. McGraw-Hill Irwin, Boston, Massachusetts.

Galoozis, C. (2012) "It's the Economy, Stupid." October 17, 2012, accessed October 9, 2013; available online at: harvardpolitics.com/united-states/its-the-economy-stupid/

Hansen, S. (2009) "Scary Drop in Velocity of Money: Is Deflation Knocking?" September 3, 2009, accessed September 25, 2011; available online at: seekingalpha.com/article/159814-scary-drop-in-velocity-of-money-is-deflation-knocking

Hartman, H. C. (2011) "The Decrease in the Velocity of Money in the United States: Some Possible Causes and Some Implications." *International Journal of Accounting Information Science and Leadership*, vol. 4, iss. 11, pp. 15-27.

Hartman, H. C. (2013) "More about the Decrease in the Velocity of Money in the United States: Some Potential Causes and Policy Implications." *Journal of International Business Management and Research*, vol. 3, iss. 10, pp. 116-138.

Krugman, P. (2013) "Plutocrats Feeling Persecuted." September 26, 2013, accessed October 9, 2013; available online at: www.nytimes.com/2013/09/27/opinion/krugman-plutocrats-feeling-persecuted.html?_r=0

Mishkin, F. S. (2004) *The Economics of Money, Banking, and Financial Markets*, seventh edition. Pearson Addison Wesley, Boston, Massachusetts.

Morici, P. (2013) "Obama Policies Increasing Inequality." September 16, 2013, accessed October 9, 2013; available online at: www.breitbart.com/Big-Government/2013/09/16/Obama-Policies-Make-Inequality-a-lot-Worse

Stokes, B. (2012) "Is it the Economy, Stupid?" October 3, 2012, accessed October 9, 2013; available online at: globalpublicsquare.blogs.cnn.com/2012/10/03/is-it-the-economy-stupid/

www.economagic.com

TABLE OF CONTENTS

CHAPTER 1
INTRODUCTION

GETTING STARTED

THE RECENT DECLINE IN THE VELOCITY OF MONEY

As I mentioned in the Preface, I am talking to myself when using the word 'stupid.' It took me a while to realize what Hansen (2009), Darda and Keene (2011), and others had pointed out -- the recent decrease in money velocity in the United States. After my realization, I pointed out the plummeting velocity of money in the U.S. in Hartman (2011) and Hartman (2013). From the perspective of the United States, the velocity of money refers to how many times on average people spend each U.S. dollar each year in a transaction that counts toward gross domestic product (GDP). Although some others may have focused on a broader measure of the money supply (M2) than the one used more often in this book (M1), the fact remains that the velocities of both of these measures of the money supply have fallen.

The rapid decrease in the velocity of M1 in the United States that started in the year 2008 provides what is likely one of the most stupefying, attention-grabbing statistics illustrating the Great Recession and the subsequent Not-So-Great Recovery in recent years. Much of the data in this book was found through www.economagic.com on July 20, 2013 and July 31, 2013. Using data from www.economagic.com as of July 20, 2013, in the fourth quarter of 2007, each dollar that was part of the (quarterly average) M1 money supply traded on an annualized basis roughly 10.37 times per year on average. However, by the first quarter of 2013, the velocity of M1 had fallen to roughly 6.47 times per year, on average: a decline of more than 37 per cent! Further, velocity continues to decline into the year 2014. This decline appears near the right edge of Figure 1.1, a graph of velocity data from the first quarter of 1959 through the first quarter of 2013 with quarters of years on the horizontal axis and the velocity of M1 on the vertical axis.

What could have caused this – the largest percentage decline in U.S. M1 velocity since the Great Depression and World War II era? Although this recent startling drop in velocity in the U.S. screams for attention, have few heard the cries?

Does the decline in the velocity of M1 indicate that insufficient spending is a major problem, if not the main problem, in the U.S. economy today? While the recovery was plodding along, at a nearly listless pace, people may have been clamoring, with considerable justification, for better economic prospects as denial turned to dejection and frustration, if not sorrow and anger. Could the ability to stimulate spending provide much needed and deserved relief to those struggling for so long? Could more spending stimulate growth and jobs? Could an improved understanding of velocity help?

OVERVIEW OF THE BOOK

This book strives to provide something for everyone, and this goal has influenced the writing and organization of the book. Those familiar may enjoy a refresher on the velocity of money and the increased attention devoted to velocity and some concepts that may not be getting appropriate attention. Some may come away with a slightly different perspective of velocity. Newcomers could benefit from an overview of some of the insights provided by macroeconomic analysis and money and banking. Those less familiar could also benefit from looking at the current sub-par performance of the U.S. economy through the lens of the velocity of money. As noted in the Preface, some material in later chapters builds upon some of the material in earlier chapters.

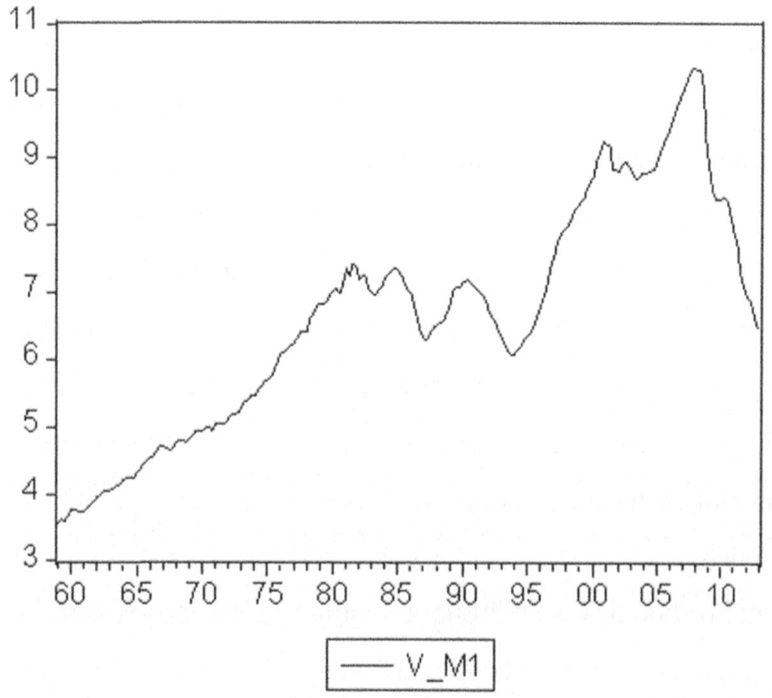

Figure 1.1 The Velocity of M1 in the U.S. Using Quarterly Data
1959q1 through 2013q1
Source: www.economagic.com

The present chapter offers a more detailed overview than the one in the Preface. After the overview, the current chapter provides a review of some introductory material from undergraduate macroeconomics and money and banking courses.

In terms of the chapters to follow, the next chapter, Chapter 2, discusses the implication of relying solely upon increases in the money supply to stimulate the present-day U.S. economy, complete with intuitive analogies for beginners. It also introduces the role of already low interest rates in the lackluster economy. In so doing, the chapter contrasts how the current U.S. economy differs from many other economies (including the U.S. economy at earlier points in time) emerging from recession. The second chapter additionally discusses some other policy options geared toward increasing real GDP growth. Further, Chapter 2 draws a distinction between the ability to spend versus the desire to spend, and it introduces the velocity of money as a function of the money supply as a topic for further discussion. Additionally, the chapter reviews four reasons why people hold money. The second chapter also begins a discussion of three main schools of macroeconomic thought and the behavior of velocity within the three schools. Because Chapter 2 deals with at least some of the topics covered in later chapters, all readers are encouraged to read at least part of the second chapter.

Chapter 3 considers further the velocity of money as a function of the money supply. Related to that, the chapter also asks whether a limit could exist at least at some points in time where an increase in the money supply would automatically lead to a reduction in velocity. It presents sub-divisions of the full sample period of quarterly data running from the first quarter of 1959 through the first quarter of 2013. The subdivisions are based largely on whether velocity is generally increasing or generally decreasing so that the ending quarters of sub-sample periods are usually either local maxima or local minima. It also considers data (including velocity data) from the Great Depression and World War II era in the U.S. Additionally, Chapter 3 further discusses the velocity of money in the major schools of macroeconomic thought.

Due to the importance of liquidity traps (if liquidity traps exist) and economies near liquidity traps in terms of the consequences for the velocity of money when the money supply increases further, Chapter 4 further discusses liquidity traps. If liquidity traps exist, interest rates in such economies would be low compared to normal values. A critical feature of a liquidity trap is that increases in the money supply fail to spark increases in spending on GDP items. If a money supply level exists beyond which further increases in the money supply would lead to decreases in velocity and if liquidity traps exist, then a liquidity trap would certainly be a case where a higher money supply would reduce velocity. People could sense that dollars are being held rather than being spent. Thus, Chapter 4 also presents a simple example to help illustrate why corporations may have been holding greater money balances recently in the U.S.

Because financial crises in the United States have often been associated with decreases in the velocity of money, Chapter 5 discusses some features of financial crises. Further, it presents a timeline of some of the events leading up to the most recent financial crisis in the United States and the Great Recession.

Chapter 6 furthers the discussion of velocity as a function of the money supply. It presents diagrams and regressions showing velocity determined by a single variable considered for each regression or diagram (with one of those variables being the money supply) and a constant term over the sub-sample periods introduced in Chapter 3. The purpose of the regressions and diagrams is to show the importance of money supply growth in determining velocity, at least at some points in time. During some of the sub-sample periods, the money supply is the best 'predictor' of the velocity of money of the variables considered.

Chapter 7 discusses the money multiplier model and the expansion of credit. Both of these related topics also relate to the velocity of money as they help to explain the 'money supply,' which is in the denominator of the equation used to calculate the velocity of money. In discussing the money supply process, the chapter identifies some of the major recent changes in quantities of funds that are part of M1 (and also M2) and funds that are part of M2 but not M1 (with Burton and Lombra (2006, p. 29) considering the former as 'money' and the latter as 'near money') and how these movements could help to explain why the velocity of M1 is falling much more rapidly (both in terms of the number of times per year each dollar on average is spent and in percentage terms) than the velocity of M2.

The last chapter of the book, Chapter 8, reviews the material presented to that point and discusses some of the work remaining. In so doing, the chapter poses questions about the velocity of money in some Keynesian analysis and in some monetarist analysis. The three motives for holding money in most textbooks may not be sufficient to explain the recent surge in M1 in the U.S., and a possible fourth motive is discussed. Factors potentially impacting velocity are further discussed. An 'In-Chapter Appendix' presents what may be the first step in finding the money supply level in the short term beyond which further money supply growth forces velocity to fall. (Although the material in this 'In-Chapter Appendix' may better lend itself to presentation in an Appendix at the end of a chapter, I wanted this material to appear before the conclusion of Chapter 8 (and the book). Thus, I placed this material as an 'In-Chapter Appendix' rather than as an Appendix at the end of the chapter.)

I 'tell the story' about the recent decrease in velocity in the U.S. with words, graphs, tables, and regressions. But before we go much further, let's make sure that everyone has some familiarity with some macroeconomic concepts often covered in undergraduate macroeconomics courses. Readers not familiar with these concepts would likely benefit from continuing to read, and readers looking for a quick review may also benefit from reading this information. On the other hand, readers already familiar may wish to skip ahead to the next chapter.

BRIEF REVIEW OF SOME IMPORTANT MACROECONOMIC CONCEPTS, OR A CRASH COURSE IN MACROECONOMICS

GROSS DOMESTIC PRODUCT OR OUTPUT

Gross domestic product, or GDP, provides a measure of the production of many of the goods and services part of reported market trades inside a nation's borders within a specific time period. 'Output' is a term synonymous with GDP. Some production, such as production for family members for free, is not included in GDP. Also, do-it-yourself production is not included. Charitable contributions and government transfer payments such as social security payments are not included because no good or service was produced in exchange for that payment. The production of imported items is not included in the GDP of the importing country because the production of those items was already counted toward the GDP of the country in which the items were produced. Counting the full value of imported items toward the GDP of the importing country and toward GDP in the country that produced the items would be double-counting. If an item was produced only one time, then it should count only once. By similar reasoning, the sale of pre-owned items does not count toward GDP if the sale goes directly from the former owner to the new end-user.

In the United States, GDP is measured in the dollars that people spent buying the goods produced to combine the productive activity of millions of different categories of goods into one number. How else could we compare, with considerable ease, the relative production value of a new home versus a pack of chewing gum? In other countries, GDP is measured in units of money in those countries. However, when prices change, the buying power of a dollar or of another currency changes and creates a problem with comparing unadjusted spending in two different periods to determine whether production has increased, decreased, or stayed the same between those two periods. More about this appears in the next section dealing with nominal GDP and real GDP.

Years ago, the main measure of production was Gross National Product (GNP) rather than Gross Domestic Product (GDP). The main difference between GNP and GDP is that GNP measures the production of all citizens of a nation regardless of where they reside during the measurement period, while GDP measures the production of all people living in a nation's borders.

One way of calculating GDP is to sum up the quantities bought by the four different categories of those who demand goods produced in a country. One group would be households who buy consumption goods. A second group would be firms (i.e., businesses) which buy new buildings, new machines, and inventories of items not yet sold to the final consumer. These three expenditures by businesses comprise investment in physical capital. The government sectors, a third group, make expenditures, some of which are specifically made in exchange for production. Those in other countries also buy goods made in a particular country and comprise the fourth group. Thus, from the perspective of the United States, the sum of consumption spending by households, investment spending on physical capital by firms, government purchases by the government sectors, and net exports (or exports minus imports) by those in other countries gives U.S. GDP. The sum of these four components, $C + I + G + NX$, is sometimes called 'aggregate demand.'

TWO MEASURES OF GDP: NOMINAL GDP AND REAL GDP

People spend much more on newly produced goods and services in the United States today (in the year 2014) than they did in the year 1959, the first year in the sample period for some of the analysis in this study based on quarterly data being readily available. (Although some of the data analyzed predates 1959 by decades, the earlier data may be available only on an annual basis). Of course, part of the increase in total spending on goods produced today is due to a greater level of production by the U.S. economy today versus in the year 1959. However, part of the increase in spending on newly made goods is due to a weighted average of prices of goods being more expensive today than it was in the year 1959 and thus has nothing to do with a greater level of production.

This illustrates an important difference in economics between nominal variables and real variables. Nominal variables in the United States are measured in dollars that have the buying power of a dollar in the period in which the nominal variable is being measured. On the other hand, real variables in the U.S. are measured in dollars that have constant buying power. So, U.S. nominal GDP measures the production of each good or service counted as part of GDP by using the actual price that some person, group, or organization paid for the item when the item was purchased. By contrast, U.S. real GDP measures the production of an item in GDP at the price of that particular item in an arbitrarily chosen period, usually a year, in which case the period is called 'the base year.' For example, if the base year is the year 2005, then the production of each pack of chewing gum in the year 2005, 1995, 1985, 1975, 1965, 1959, 2012, or any other year would be measured in real GDP in the year in which it was produced at however much the pack of gum cost in the year 2005. If the pack of gum cost one dollar in the year 2005, then the production of a pack of gum in the year 1959 would count as one constant-buying-power dollar toward real GDP in the year 1959 (even though the actual price paid for the pack of gum may have been much less than one dollar in that year). Likewise, the production of a pack of chewing gum in the year 2012 would contribute one constant-purchasing-power dollar toward real GDP in the year 2012 although the price of a pack of gum may have increased between the year 2005 and the year 2012.

Thus, an increase in real GDP between two different time periods automatically implies an increase in production by the economy between those two periods, while a decrease in real GDP between two periods implies a decrease in production. This follows because the prices used to compute real GDP cannot change unless the base year changes. An increase in nominal GDP between two periods could be due to an increase in production, but it could have also resulted from an increase in prices in the economy while actual production in the economy either did not change or decreased (the latter case assuming that the size of the increase in prices in the economy was large enough to outweigh the size of the decrease in production in the economy). Moreover, a decrease in nominal GDP could be due to a decrease in production but it could occur when the prices of goods in the economy decrease and there is either no change in production or an increase in production (the latter case assuming that the decrease in prices dominates the increase in production).

PRICE LEVELS AND INFLATION

The reader can see the importance of prices. Economists and others often want to know whether the cost of buying a particular bundle of goods (perhaps as large as the bundle of goods in gross domestic product) is increasing, decreasing, or staying the same. If the cost of the bundle is either increasing or decreasing, how rapidly or how slowly are prices changing? To address these questions, economists use price indexes as measures of the 'price level' in an economy. Price indexes such as the implicit GDP deflator (also called the implicit deflator or the GDP deflator or the deflator), the consumer price index (CPI), and the producer price index (PPI) are weighted averages of prices in the economy, each measuring the cost of a different bundle of goods. While the CPI measures the cost of a certain set of goods that a household may purchase and the PPI measures the cost of a different set of goods that producers may buy as inputs, the GDP deflator measures the cost of all items that are part of GDP. The percentage change in the price level is often called the inflation rate.

NOMINAL INTEREST RATES AND REAL INTEREST RATES

Just as there was an important difference between nominal GDP and real GDP, an important difference between nominal interest rates and real interest rates merits discussion. The reader can consider the interest rate as the cost of borrowing one dollar for one year. Lenders often grant loans only on the condition that the lenders will be repaid more total dollars than they initially lent (assuming no defaults) to compensate the lenders for sacrificing liquidity.

However, even if the borrower repays the lender in full on time, the lender does not necessarily gain purchasing power from the loan. When a lender receives more in repayment in terms of dollars than the lender originally granted in a loan to the borrower, the nominal interest rate for the loan is positive. But, over the course of the loan, many prices in the economy may have increased, which could have implied an increase in the price level. An increase in the price level can also be considered as a positive rate of inflation. If the inflation rate is greater than zero, the buying power of the dollars repaid by the borrower have less purchasing power than they would have had if prices remained exactly the same (or if prices had actually decreased).

If positive inflation has occurred, does the borrower have to pay the lender a sum great enough so that the lender enjoys a net gain in purchasing power when repaid? To offer a quick answer to the question, when the nominal interest rate is greater than the rate of inflation, the lender will enjoy a net increase in purchasing power as a result of having granted the loan and having been repaid. When a lender benefits from a net increase in purchasing power as a result of being repaid, the real interest rate is positive. On the other hand, if the lender suffers a loss in buying power from a loan, then the real interest rate is negative. The latter case (a real interest rate less than zero) can result even when a borrower repays a loan in full with interest, but the nominal interest rate agreed upon when the loan was granted by the lender is less than the rate of inflation over the time of the loan. If a lender has neither a gain nor a loss in buying power from a loan (when the nominal interest rate equals the rate of inflation), then the real interest rate equals zero.

EQUILIBRIUM, AGGREGATE DEMAND, AND AGGREGATE SUPPLY

An equilibrium in economics can be considered as a stable situation in an economy in that the equilibrium is sustainable unless something changes. In an equilibrium in economics, no active or potential participant in the market has a reason to change behavior. At a macroeconomic equilibrium point, all participants in the economy are doing the best that they can given what others are doing. Therefore, if an economy is not at the equilibrium, then at least one person or organization in the economy can make an adjustment to improve his, her, or its position in light of what others are doing. We would expect, then, that if an economy is not in equilibrium, then the economy would be heading toward the equilibrium (unless something was blocking such movement) as people would make adjustments that are clearly in their best interests. If an economy is in equilibrium, then we would expect the economy to remain in equilibrium unless something changes because everyone would already be doing the best possible given the choices made by others.

Often in macroeconomics, we want to understand past and current real GDP, and past and current price levels in an economy. We also often want to predict what will happen to real GDP and price levels in the future. The concept of an equilibrium will be very helpful to this end, as the equilibrium point in a model sometimes called the Aggregate Demand-Aggregate Supply model will help in understanding changes in real GDP and changes in the price level – past, present, and future – in an economy.

Aggregate demand (AD), loosely speaking, deals with the total quantity of newly made goods (part of GDP) that people in the economy are willing and able to buy. Often, AD is shown as a function of the price level. In the context of a model used to find equilibrium real GDP levels and equilibrium price levels, the AD function shows the quantity of GDP goods, measured in constant buying power U.S. dollars (or units of another currency if AD is measured for another country), that people will buy at various price levels. Textbook models assume that the AD function is downward-sloping because (1) at higher price levels, people can afford to buy less, all other things the same, and (2) at higher domestic price levels (and assuming no change in price levels in other countries), people domestically and abroad will substitute more goods produced in other countries for goods produced domestically, resulting in a decrease in the quantity of domestically-made goods demanded (measured in constant-buying-power currency), all other things equal. Conversely, at a lower domestic price level, all other things constant, (1) people can afford to buy more, and (2) people will buy more domestically-made items and buy fewer goods made in other countries. This represents an increase in the quantity of domestically-made goods demanded *ceteris paribus* (meaning all other things constant or all other things equal) at the lower domestic price level. In sum, from a demand perspective, the various demanders are willing and able to buy fewer goods at higher price levels and more goods at lower price levels, all other things constant. Figure 1.2 below shows an aggregate demand function.

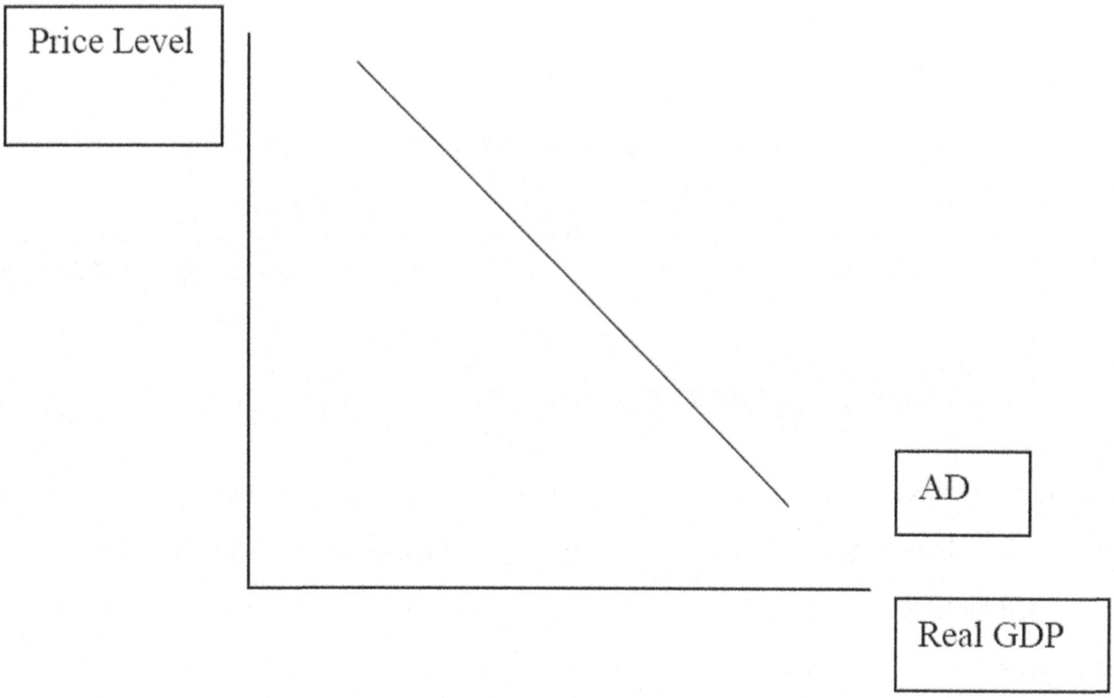

Figure 1.2 An Aggregate Demand (AD) Function

Aggregate supply (AS) shows the total quantity that suppliers are willing and able to sell at various price levels. While the AD function is downward-sloping, the slope of the AS function depends on the time horizon in textbook analysis. In a time horizon known as the long run, people and organizations have had the full opportunity to adjust to changes in the economy. (As we will see soon, it is reasonable to assume that in the short run and in an economy like the United States economy, some 'things' in the economy do not necessarily rapidly adjust following changes.) Textbook macroeconomic analysis assumes that when all prices and other factors are flexible, the relevant AS function is a vertical line at a level of real GDP sometimes called the long-run equilibrium level of real GDP. Figure 1.3 below shows the vertical long-run aggregate supply function.

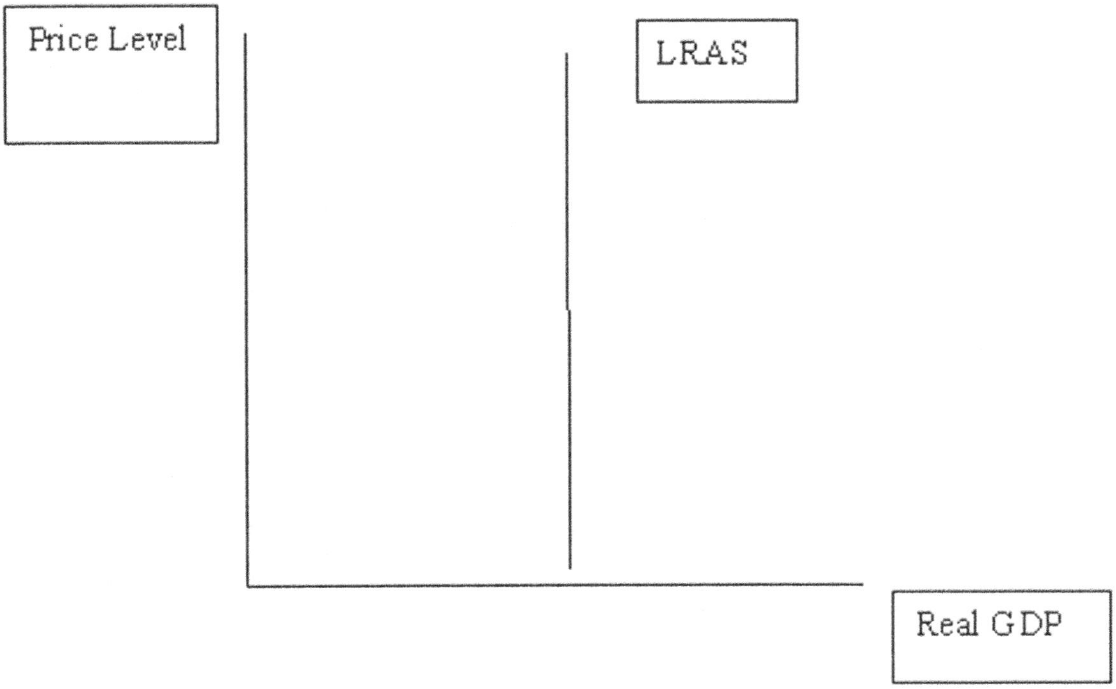

Figure 1.3 A Long-Run Aggregate Supply Function

However, over shorter time horizons, some factors prevent at least some prices from rapidly adjusting to their long-run equilibrium levels following changes in the economy. Contracts often prevent immediate price adjustments. Wages and salaries are often determined for at least one year at a time based on terms agreed upon by employers and employees. Sometimes businesses that produce items used by other businesses as inputs or materials also sign contracts agreeing to a set price for an input while the contract is in effect.

Further, considerations known as menu costs prevent some prices from adjusting. Coming from the example of a restaurant needing to print new menus when it changes prices, some businesses incur costs when they change prices, and the costs may not be trivial. For example, consider the cost that a major retailer with many stores would face to implement an across-the-board price change. The cost of changing prices would include the cost of printing new price tags and/or new signs showing the new prices. Some research also suggests that price inertia may result from some businesses reluctant to raise prices due to concern over losing customers if competitors do not also change prices and hesitant to reduce prices if competitors also as a result reduce prices. (Refer to Dornbusch, Fischer, and Startz (2008, pp. 130-134, 167, 555) for additional background information on why some prices may not adjust rapidly to changes.) The point is that in an economy like the U.S. economy where inflation is relatively low, it seems reasonable to assume that following a change in AD, some prices adjust quickly in the short run but some do not.

How does this impact the slope of the short-run aggregate supply (SRAS) function? One way to think about the SRAS function is first to think that a rising price level implies that the prices of at least some goods in the economy are rising. Assuming no change in the per unit production cost, producers have an incentive to produce a greater quantity at a higher price level. Another way to think about SRAS in the short run is to realize that when people in the economy want to buy more than before, at least *some* producers have higher per unit production costs for a greater production quantity. Businesses and other producers may need to bid resources away from other uses. Thus, per unit production costs may rise. To keep the same level of profitability, businesses must pass the price increases onto customers. Whether thinking about SRAS the first way in this paragraph or the second way, there is a positive relationship in the short run between real GDP supplied and the price level. Figure 1.4 shows an upward-sloping SRAS function.

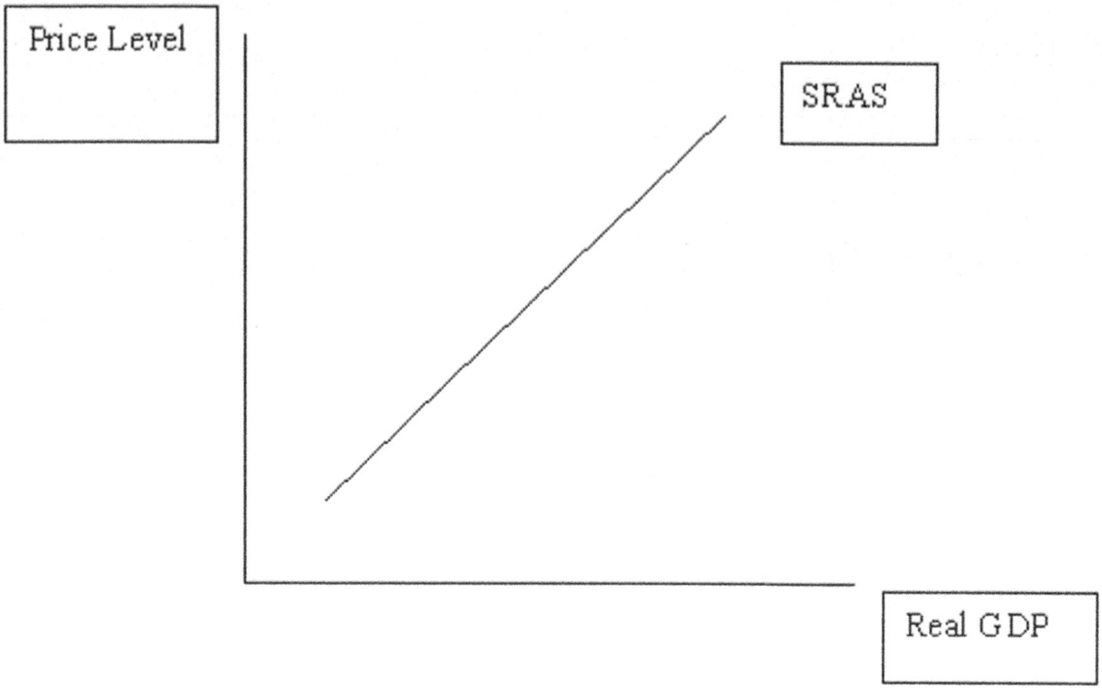

Figure 1.4 A Short-Run Aggregate Supply Function

Where is the equilibrium real GDP and the equilibrium price level in the Aggregate Demand-Aggregate Supply (AD-AS) model? We find the short-run equilibrium real GDP level and the short-run equilibrium price level in this model where the downward-sloping AD function intersects the upward-sloping SRAS function. In Figure 1.5, P_1 is the equilibrium price level and Y_1 is the equilibrium level of real GDP because it is the only point in the diagram where no one in the economy has an incentive to change behavior.

If the price level happened to be less than P_1, people in the economy would want to buy more than producers in the economy would be willing and able to produce. In this case, producers have incentives to increase prices, which would increase the price level and lead to an increase in the quantity supplied in the aggregate and a decrease in the quantity demanded in the aggregate.

If the price level was greater than P_1, the quantity supplied in the aggregate would exceed the quantity demanded in the aggregate. Producers would have incentives to reduce prices, leading to lower price levels and increasing the quantity demanded in the aggregate, while reducing the quantity supplied in the aggregate. The combination of a price level equal to P_1 and the level of real GDP equal to Y_1 is the only combination in Figure 1.5 in which no one in the economy has an incentive to change behavior.

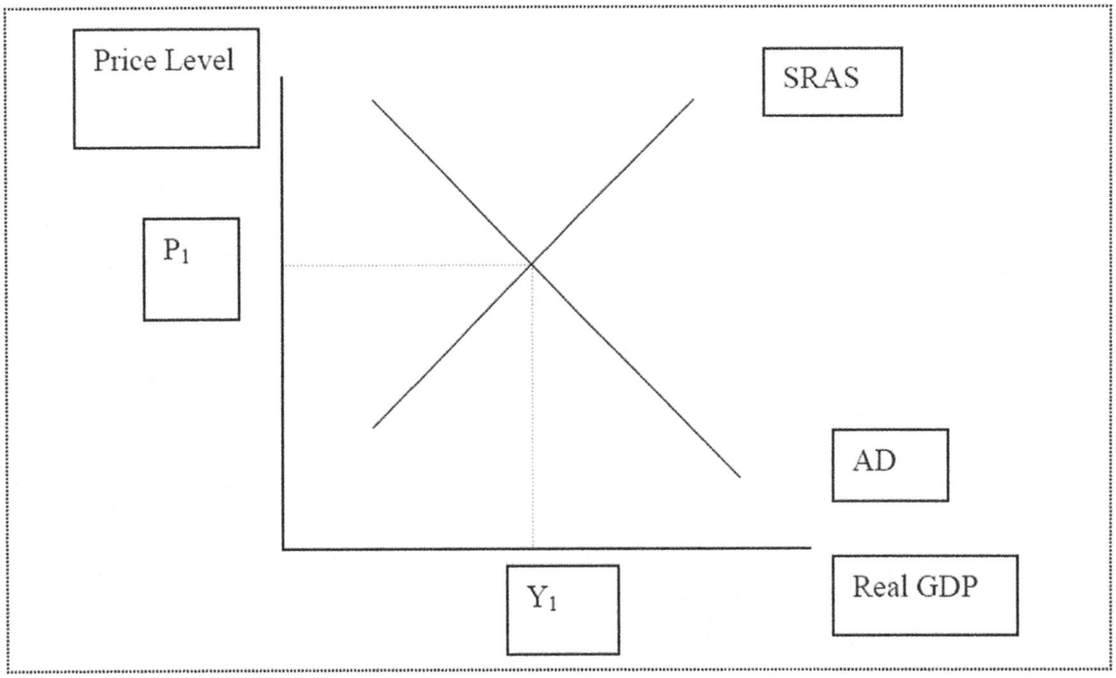

Figure 1.5 Short-Run Equilibrium in the AD-AS model

CHANGES IN REAL GDP AND CHANGES IN THE PRICE LEVEL IN THE SHORT RUN

What is the impact of a change or a shock that hits the economy on price levels and real GDP in the short run? Textbook analysis often suggests that four main types of shocks shift the aggregate supply function: changes in productivity or technology, changes in the availability of labor, changes in input prices, and changes in producers' expectations of future prices. Changes in these factors have their main impact, if not an exclusive impact, on aggregate supply. Changes in other factors such as changes in interest rates, changes in consumption plans, changes in businesses' purchases of machinery, changes in government spending, changes in exchange rates, and changes in income taxes have their main impact (if not the sole impact) on aggregate demand.

All other things equal, if technology or productivity improves, if labor becomes more available, if input prices decrease, or if producers expect lower selling prices in the future; SRAS shifts right leading to a decrease in equilibrium price levels and an increase in equilibrium real GDP. Figure 1.6 illustrates this change in equilibrium. Note that P_2, the new equilibrium price level, is less than P_1, and Y_2, the new equilibrium real GDP, is greater than Y_1. (To explain the shift in SRAS for the fourth shock, realize that if producers think that the price of the good that they sell will be lower in the future, then they will be willing to sell more today at each and every price level. This represents a rightward shift in aggregate supply.) Changes in the direction opposite of those listed in this paragraph would, all other things equal, shift aggregate supply left and lead to an increase in the equilibrium price level and a decrease in equilibrium real GDP, as shown in Figure 1.7.

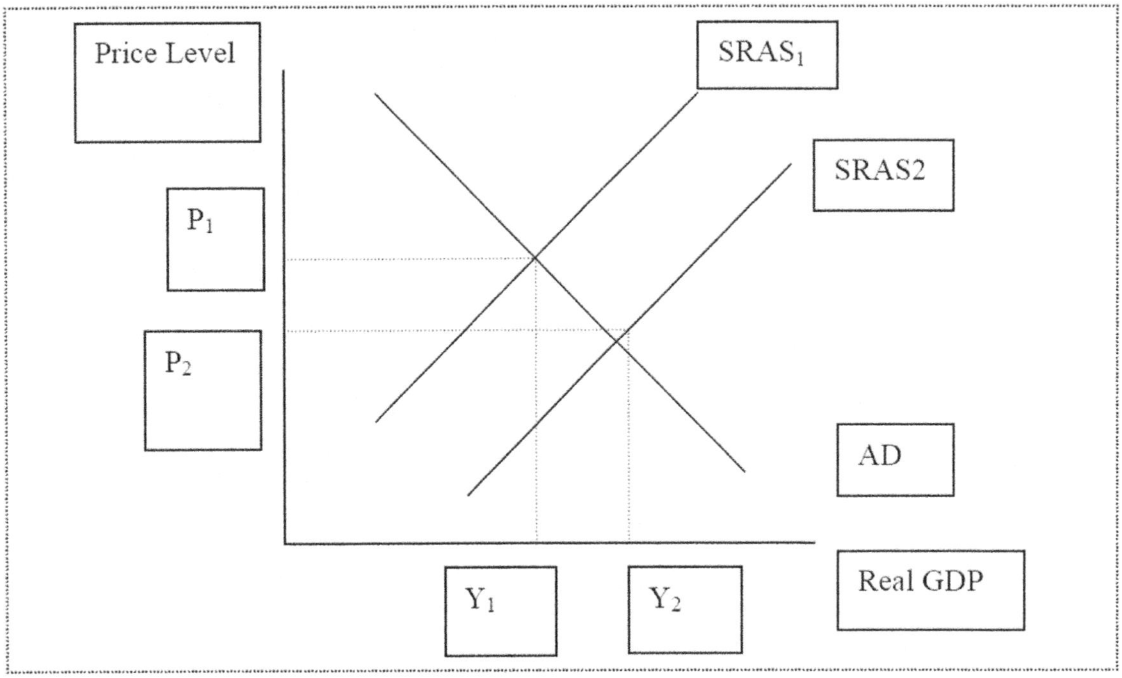

Figure 1.6 The Impact of an Increase (Rightward Shift) in SRAS

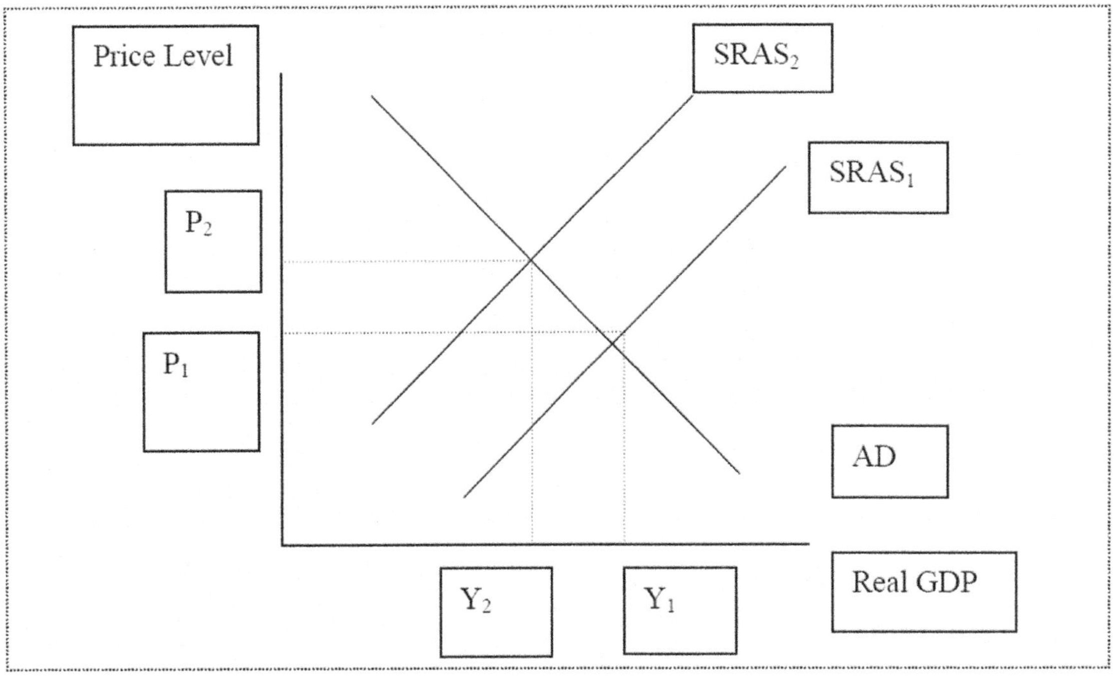

Figure 1.7 The Impact of a Decrease (Leftward Shift) in SRAS

All other things equal, an increase in the desire to spend on domestically-made items by households, businesses (on machines, buildings, and inventories), government sectors, or those in other countries would cause aggregate demand to shift right. Also, *ceteris paribus*, an increase in population or money supply (outside of a theoretical concept known as a liquidity trap discussed further in later chapters), or a decrease in income taxes or interest rates, would shift AD right. The result would be an increase in the equilibrium price level and an increase in equilibrium real GDP in the short run, as shown in Figure 1.8. Shocks that are the opposite would lead to a decrease in the equilibrium price level and a decrease in equilibrium real GDP in the short run resulting from a decrease in AD. This case is shown in Figure 1.9.

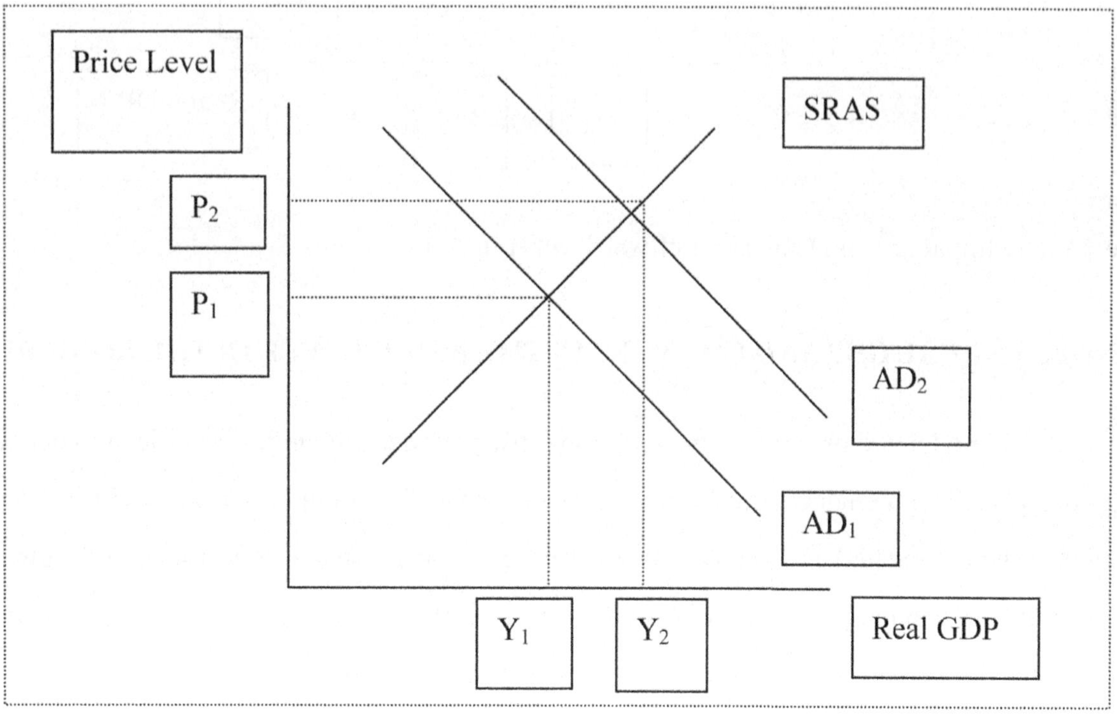

Figure 1.8 The Impact of an Increase (Rightward) Shift in AD

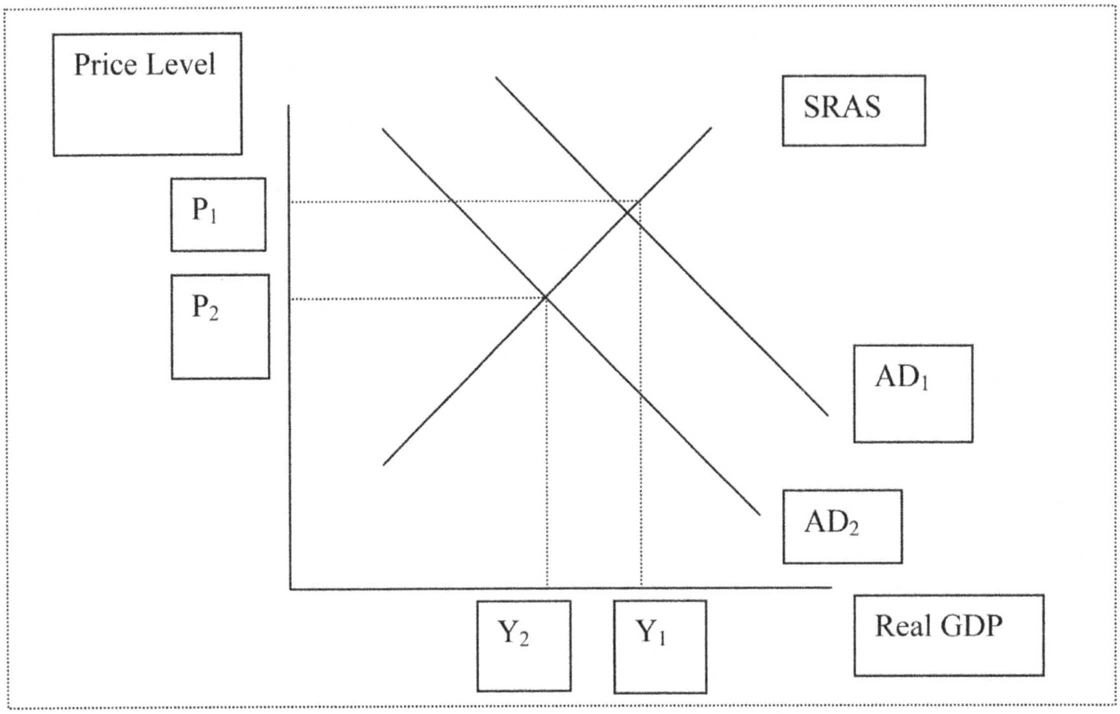

Figure 1.9 The Impact of an Decrease (Leftward) Shift in AD

CHANGES IN REAL GDP AND CHANGES IN THE PRICE LEVEL IN THE LONG RUN

The textbook model assumes that in the long run, only permanent changes in AS lead to permanent changes in real GDP. A permanent improvement in technology, for example, shifts LRAS right, leading to lower price levels and higher real GDP, all other things equal, at the new long-run equilibrium point.

Suppose that an economy is initially at the long-run equilibrium level of real GDP producing the maximum that it can sustain year after year after year with the presently available resources and technology. Following an increase in AD after initially being in long-run equilibrium, although real GDP can increase above the long-run equilibrium real GDP in the short run, it is because not all prices were able to adjust in the short run. When all prices adjust, the textbook model assumes that if AD remains at its higher level, price levels will rise even further than they rose in the short run, and real GDP will fall back to the long-run equilibrium real GDP.

Additionally, over short intervals, people can work more to produce a greater quantity than they can sustain indefinitely in the long term. This helps to explain how an increase in aggregate demand can lead to an increase in real GDP above the long-run equilibrium real GDP in the short run. However, people will tire if they keep working more than they can sustain indefinitely, resulting in a decrease in the amount they can produce compared with the short term, helping to explain the return to the long-run equilibrium real GDP following an increase in aggregate demand. (Further, the textbook model assumes that not all workers get higher pay to go along with producing more at the short-run equilibrium, and not all non-labor input prices were flexible in the short run. After all workers receive higher wages and higher salaries to keep up with rising price levels (and higher production in the short term) following an increase in aggregate demand, and after the prices of all non-labor inputs have also fully adjusted, real GDP will again return to the original level before the increase in aggregate demand, all other things equal, assuming that the economy started at the long-run equilibrium level of real GDP before the increase in aggregate demand occurred.) Figure 1.10 shows the difference between the short-run response and the long-run response.

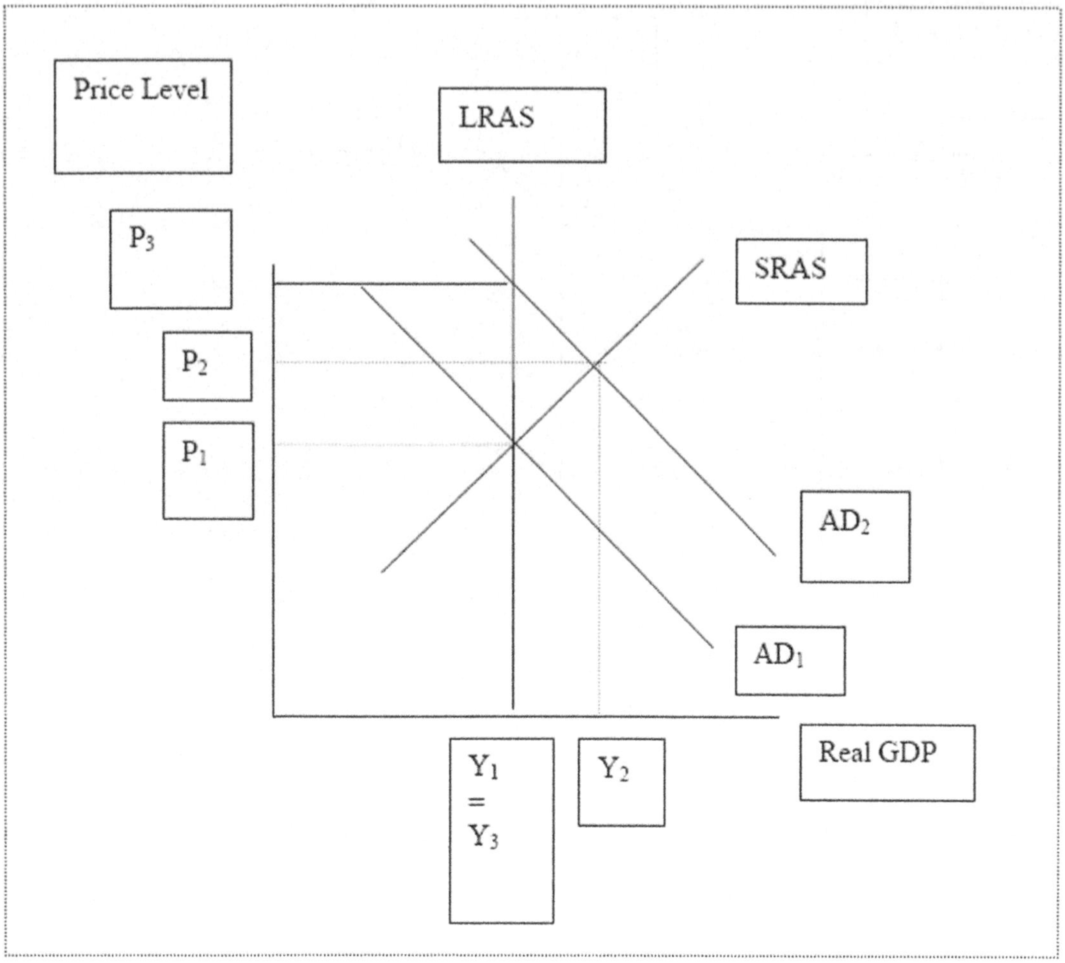

Figure 1.10 The Short-Run Impact and the Long-Run Impact of an Increase in AD Assuming the Economy Begins in Long-Run Equilibrium

On the other hand, after a decrease in aggregate demand, all other things equal, real GDP and the price level decrease at the short-run equilibrium. In the long run, as price levels fall further (given that some prices cannot adjust in the short run), the quantity of real GDP demanded in the aggregate increases while price levels fall further if aggregate demand remains at its reduced level. When price levels have had the full opportunity to adjust to the decrease in aggregate demand, the level of real GDP will be equal to the long-run equilibrium level, at a price level even lower than in the short run. If the economy was at the long-run equilibrium level of real GDP before the decrease in AD, the economy will return to the long-run equilibrium level of real GDP in the long run in the textbook model. This is shown in Figure 1.11.

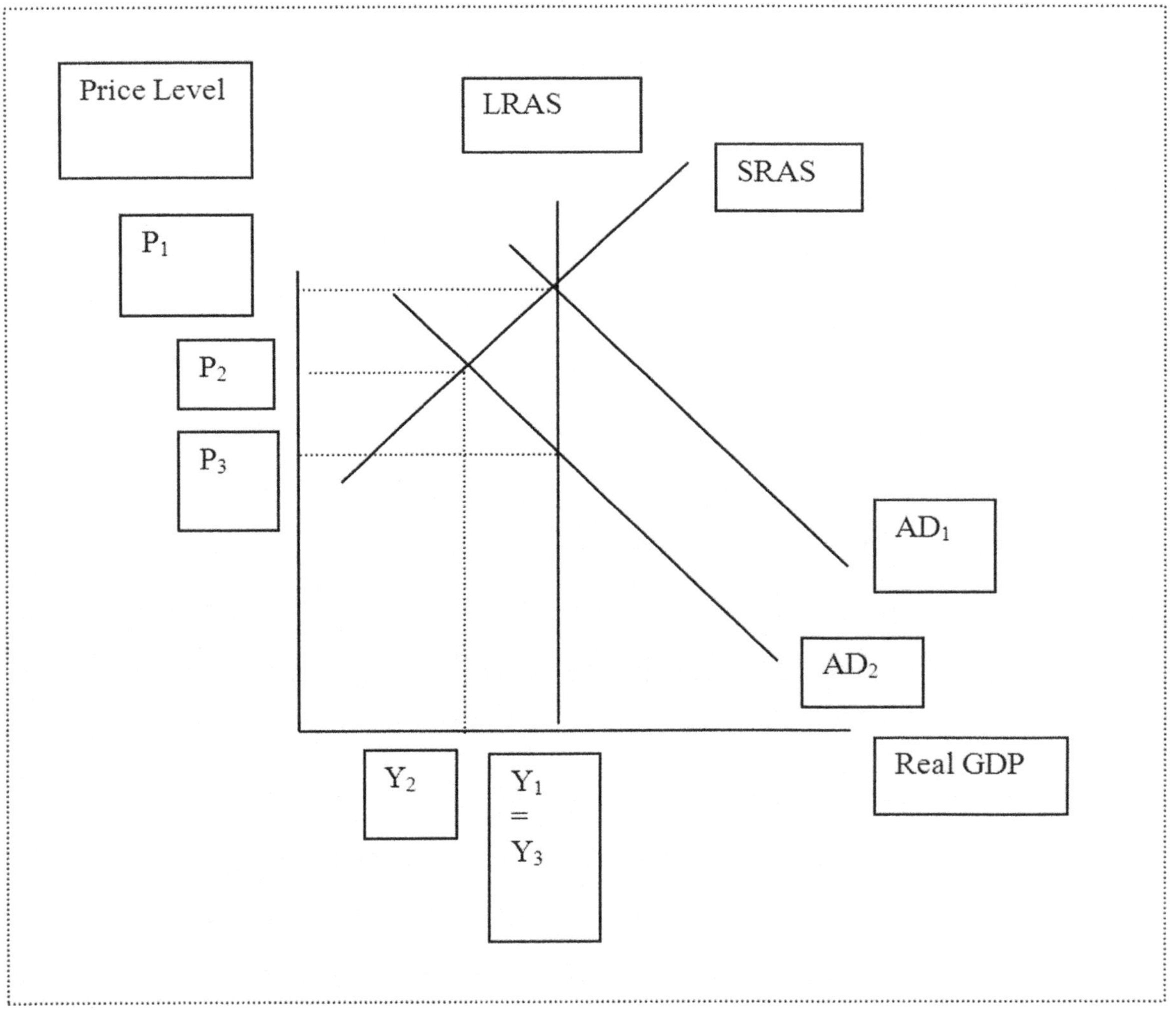

Figure 1.11 The Short-Run Impact and the Long-Run Impact of a Decrease in AD Assuming the Economy Begins in Long-Run Equilibrium

Note that in both Figure 1.10 and Figure 1.11, Y_3, the long-run equilibrium level of real GDP, is equal to the initial level, Y_1. However, in Figure 1.10, P_3, the long-run equilibrium price level is greater than not only P_1 but also P_2, the short-run equilibrium price level; while in Figure 1.11, P_3, again the long-run equilibrium price level, is less than not only P_1 but also P_2, also the short-run equilibrium price level.

If the economy is always heading back to the long-run equilibrium level of real GDP, how can we explain real GDP growing most years? That is, how can we explain economic growth? Factors such as improvements in technology and increases in population lead to an increase in the amount that an economy can produce each year. Thus, the vertical long-run AS function shifts to the right. You can see this in Figure 1.12. All other things constant, equilibrium price levels decrease and the long-run equilibrium level of real GDP rises.

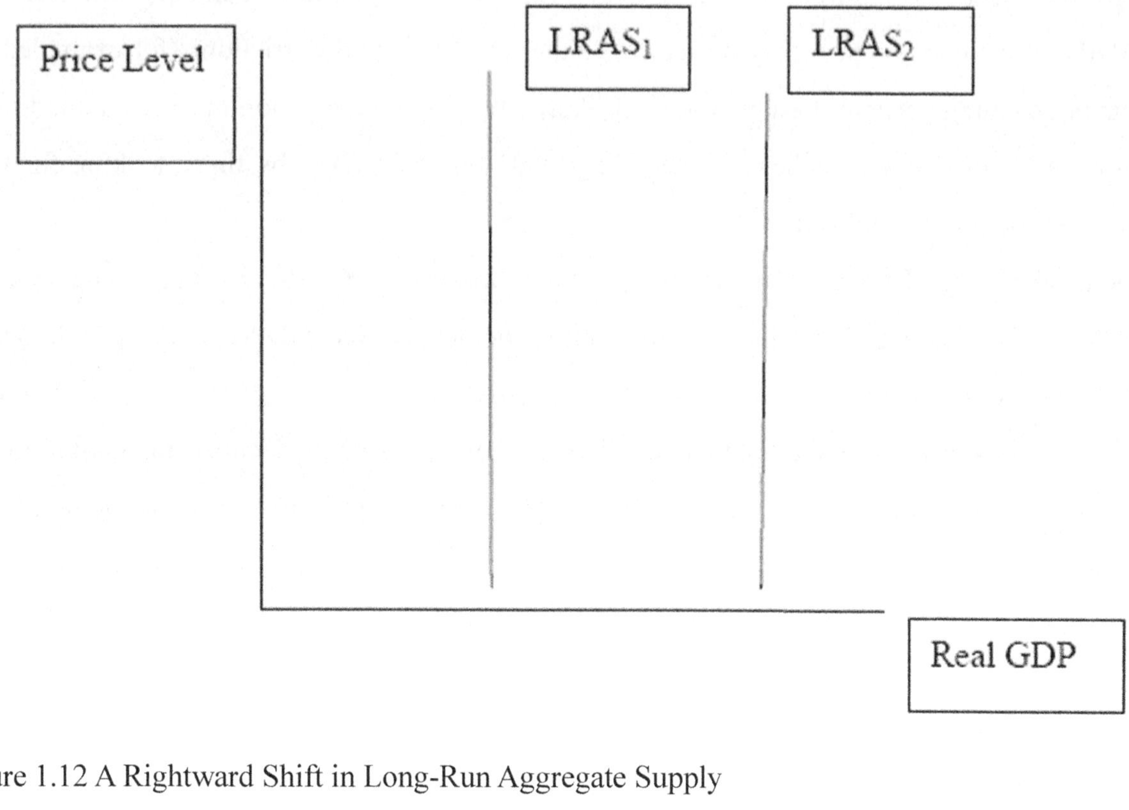

Figure 1.12 A Rightward Shift in Long-Run Aggregate Supply

Recall that above, we discussed factors that would, all other things equal, either increase the price level or decrease the price level. Some, however, use the rate of inflation (which is the percentage change in the price level) on the vertical axis rather than the price level in the AD-AS framework. Because of factors such as a money supply that usually increases and some employers and employees agreeing to wage and salary increases for two or more years at a time, a positive inflation rate may be, in a sense, 'built into' the price level generating process. Thus, it may better match the data to assume that a decrease (leftward shift) in AD or an increase (rightward shift) in AS would lead to a decrease in *inflation* but not necessarily a decrease in the *price level*. An increase in AD or a decrease in AS would lead, *ceteris paribus*, to both an increase in the price level and the rate of inflation.

UNEMPLOYMENT

The term 'full employment' as it is often used may be somewhat of a misnomer, because at the full employment level of real GDP (or the long-run equilibrium level of real GDP), unfortunately some people will be unemployed. People who are unemployed at the long- run equilibrium level of real GDP are unemployed primarily because of either (1) labor market frictions (for example, new entrants or re-entrants where these people will likely find employment soon but need some time to look for work), or (2) mismatches between skills and abilities offered by those looking for work versus those sought by employers.

If the level of real GDP is less than the long-run equilibrium real GDP, some may be unemployed mainly for cyclical reasons, but at the long-run equilibrium level of real GDP, cyclical unemployment equals zero. The unemployment rate in the economy that exists when the level of real GDP equals the full-employment level or the long-run equilibrium level is sometimes called the natural rate of unemployment, and it is equal to the frictional unemployment rate plus the structural unemployment rate. During a boom, some who would normally be unemployed mainly for either frictional reasons or structural reasons find work much faster as firms try to keep up with their customers. In this case, the actual unemployment rate would be *less* than the natural rate of unemployment.

THE SIMPLE MULTIPLIER

Sometimes, another model rather than the AD-AS model is used to find the equilibrium real GDP in an economy in the short run. This model distinguishes between two different types of spending. Let's consider a simple version of this model where we ignore taxes, interest rates, and price levels and assume a closed economy to see some important relationships as clearly as possible.

Recall that gross domestic product (GDP) depends in part on *spending*. While other factors such as productive capability impact gross domestic product, the reader should realize that for an economic transaction to be counted as part of GDP, one of the criteria for the transaction is that it must have been a part of *spending*. A well-established simple model in many textbooks for determining equilibrium GDP in the short run notes that (1) people would spend (by borrowing and/or using savings) in the short-term to buy necessities (and other goods) even if their incomes in the short-term were zero, but that (2) spending tends to increase in the short-term as incomes also increase, with the increase in spending amounting to less than one hundred cents per dollar of additional income. The first part of spending is sometimes called autonomous spending or autonomous expenditures because it is completely independent of short-term income. The model also incorporates the observation that spending for one person or group in the economy creates income (or at least gross income before taxes) for another person or group in the economy.

When additional money is spent, for example due to an increased desire to spend, the increase in income for at least one person in the model leads to a second increase in spending, but this second increase in spending is less than the initial increase in spending in the model given the assumption that a fraction of each dollar of income is saved and a fraction is spent in the current period. The second increase in spending creates a second increase in income in the model for at least one person. In turn, this leads to a third increase in spending where the third increase in spending is less than the second increase in spending, and the third increase in spending increases income for at least one person. Similar to previous rounds, the third increase in income increases spending, but by less than the previous round of additional income, the second increase in income. In each round, the increase in income is less than the previous increase in income, and the increase in spending each time gets smaller and smaller.

In this simplified version of the model, the reason why additional income and additional spending keep getting smaller each time is due to the assumption that a fraction of each dollar of income is saved for spending at some later point. This simplified version ignores complicating factors. In reality, taxes owed and increases in interest rates can also cause each additional increase in after-tax income and each subsequent increase in spending to diminish each time. For the present discussion, we do not need to complicate the analysis with factoring either interest rates or taxes into the model. The reader can refer to Dornbusch, Fischer, and Startz (2008, Chapters 9 and 10) or another textbook for more information about how the model can be modified to incorporate interest rates and taxes into the analysis. Higher price levels can also slow down the growth of spending in real terms. According to Baumol and Blinder (2012, pp. 189-191), factoring imports into the analysis implies less growth in spending on domestically produced goods and real GDP compared with a closed economy. These factors are not critical at this point.

The fraction of each additional dollar of income going toward spending is called the marginal propensity to consume, often abbreviated as the *mpc*, and the *mpc* is assumed to be greater than zero but less than one at the economy-wide level. The equilibrium level of GDP can be found by multiplying the total spending in the economy that does not depend on income in the current period by [1/(1 – *mpc*)] or [1/*mps*], where the *mps* equals the marginal propensity to save, or the fraction of each additional dollar of income that is saved. The *mps* is equal to 1 - *mpc*. The fraction [1/(1 – *mpc*)] or [1/*mps*] is often called the simple multiplier. Thus, in this simple model, the equilibrium real GDP equals the part of spending invariant to income, or autonomous spending, times the simple multiplier. Figure 1.13 shows this equilibrium as the intersection between the aggregate expenditure function with a slope of less than one and the 45-degree line with a slope of one.

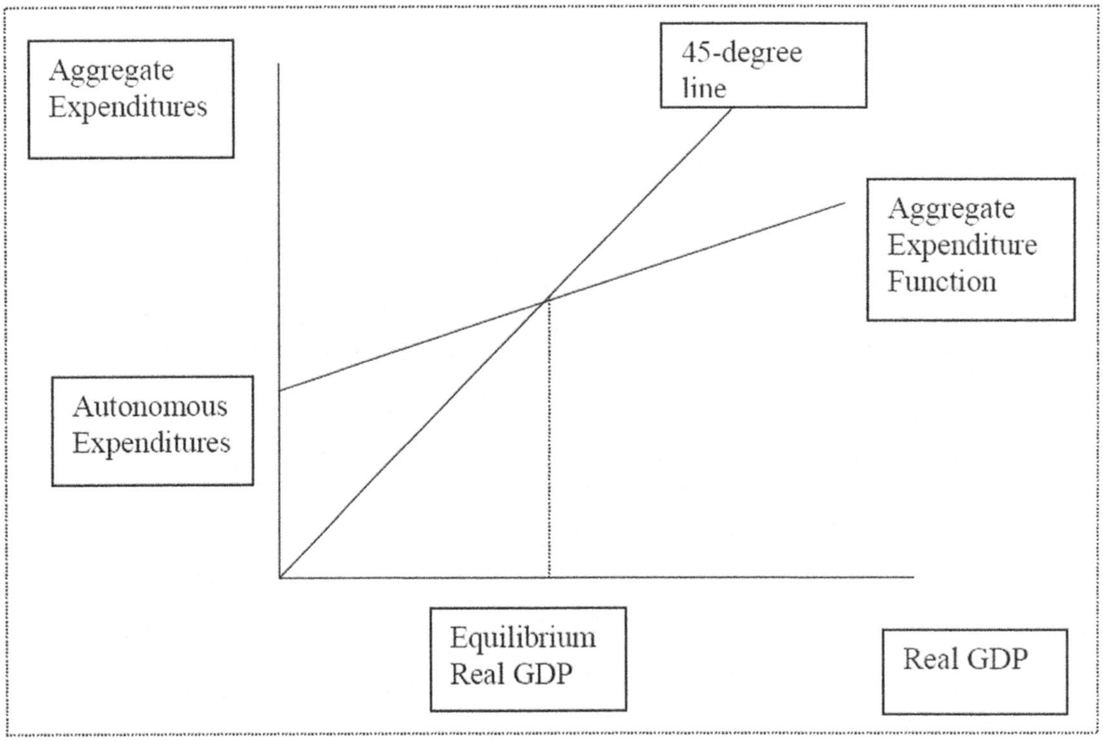

Figure 1.13 Equilibrium in the Aggregate Expenditure and Real GDP Diagram

No one in the economy has an incentive to change behavior at the equilibrium based on what others in the economy are doing. At the equilibrium, the total planned spending on the goods and services counted as part of GDP equals the total gross income generated from producing the goods and services that are part of GDP, and no person or group has an incentive to change behavior given what others are doing. The focus of incentives to change is on whether firms have either produced too much inventory and thereby have an incentive to reduce production (because sales were less than expected) or produced too little inventory and thus have an incentive to increase production (because sales were greater than anticipated). At the points along the 45-degree line, firms do not have an incentive either to increase production or to decrease production because sales were as expected and they have the inventory that they want.

Suppose that autonomous spending increased. Thus, the greater spending had nothing to do with an increase in income. Assuming all other things equal, the increase in equilibrium GDP in the simplified model can be found by multiplying the increase in autonomous spending by the simple multiplier above. The increase in equilibrium GDP must be greater than the size of the initial increase in spending as long as the *mps* is less than one implying that the *mpc* is greater than zero. The intuition to help explain how GDP can increase by more than the initial increase in spending has already been discussed above. To summarize quickly, increases in spending on the goods and services part of GDP lead to increases in income, which in turn lead to increases in spending on GDP goods by less than the previous increase in spending and income (assuming both the *mpc* and the *mps* are greater than zero), which in turn further increases income and spending (by a smaller amount) and so on. Thus, the thinking is that spending stimulates production (and potentially further spending and production). Figure 1.14 illustrates the increase in equilibrium real GDP due to an increase in autonomous expenditures. Note that decreases in spending that have nothing to do with changes in income can cause equilibrium real GDP to fall by more than the initial decrease in spending.

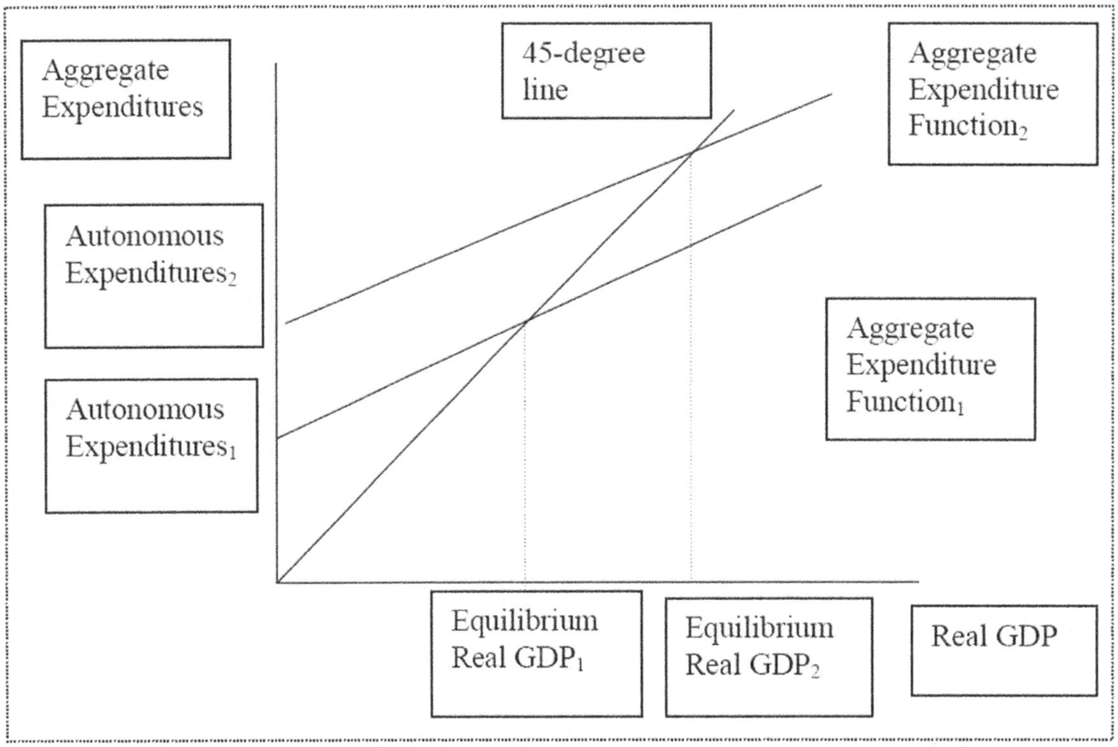

Figure 1.14 The Impact of an Increase in Autonomous Expenditures on Equilibrium Real GDP

All other things equal, an increase in the *mpc* (which implies a decrease in the *mps*) reduces the denominator of the simple multiplier, the fraction [1/(1 – *mpc*)]. This then increases the size of the multiplier so that all other things equal, an increase in the marginal propensity to consume leads to an increase in the equilibrium GDP. To the extent that spending stimulates production, when households spend a greater fraction of each dollar of income, the greater proportion of income going to spending leads to more income for at least one other person and stimulates more production.

THE FEDERAL FUNDS RATE

The federal funds rate represents the interest rate that one bank pays to another bank for a short-term loan. Banks often borrow from other banks to ensure that they have sufficient reserves to meet the Federal Reserve's reserve requirements. The Federal Reserve requires banks to hold a small fraction of some types of deposits so that if, unexpectedly, a surge in withdrawals occurs, the bank has enough liquid funds to remain solvent. Returning to the federal funds rate, currently the Federal Open Market Committee (FOMC) of the Federal Reserve is responsible for setting monetary policy and announces a target range for the federal funds rate and allows the federal funds rate to fluctuate within the range. Many believe that the federal funds rate has an important impact on economic activity.

MONEY

Some economic analysis finds a relationship between interest rates and money supply. Textbooks today often offer a functional definition of money, describing money as anything circulating in an economy that (1) is nearly universally accepted for making payments, (2) provides a standard measurement quantity, and (3) retains a substantial portion of its value over years.

Burton and Lombra (2006, p. 29) note that the smallest quantitative measure of money that is closest to the definition of money is the monetary aggregate M1. According to Burton and Lombra (2006, pp. 28, 29, 39), the components of M1 are funds in checking accounts where the owner or owners can write as many checks drawn on the account as they desire per month (provided that the account has sufficient funds for any checks written to clear), currency (probably including coins) held by the general public, and traveler's checks. For something to be part of M1, that item must be in the control of the general non-bank public. Bank reserves, including currency held in vaults by banks, do not count toward M1. Thus, the public wants to hold as part of M1 all of the dollars that are part of M1.

The M2 monetary aggregate consists of all components of M1 plus some assets less liquid than those in M1 (meaning assets less readily available for spending) such as time deposits, money market deposit accounts, savings deposit accounts, and money market mutual fund accounts held by individuals (where the first three categories may be capped at $100,000 for inclusion in M2), as noted by Burton and Lombra (2006, pp. 28). To compensate for reduced liquidity, the non-M1 parts of M2 pay a higher expected nominal interest rate to the owner or owners than the expected nominal interest rates of either zero per cent (in the case of cash and some checking accounts sometimes called 'demand deposits') or a very small positive rate (in the case of other checking accounts).

THE EQUATION OF EXCHANGE

Let's return attention to the velocity of money, the average number of times that a dollar is spent per year in a GDP transaction. It turns out that velocity can be calculated from data on real GDP, the GDP deflator, and the money supply. Through an old equation, Mishkin (2004, p. 518) and many others note that the money supply multiplied by the velocity of money equals the price level times real GDP (or algebraically, $M*V=P*Y$, where M is the money supply (M1 in this case), V is the velocity of M1, P is the price level (the deflator divided by 100), and Y is real GDP). The equation $M*V=P*Y$ is called the equation of exchange. After rearranging the equation of exchange, velocity equals the deflator (divided by 100) multiplied by real GDP divided by the money supply (or $V = P*Y/M$). In the equation of exchange, $P*Y$ equals nominal GDP. Thus, velocity equals nominal GDP divided by the money supply.

ADDITIONAL READING

Readers seeking more background information about nominal GDP and real GDP, price indexes, nominal interest rates and real interest rates, the short run versus the long run in the AD-AS model, the simple multiplier, and other topics covered before the federal funds rate in this short introduction to macroeconomics (beyond the works directly referenced); may refer to pages 26 through 28, 371 through 374, and Chapters Five, Six, Ten, and Fifteen in Mankiw (2007), Chapters Five, Six, Eight, Nine, and Ten in Baumol and Blinder (2012), Chapters Six, Seven, Eight, Eleven, and Twelve in Krugman and Wells (2009), and other relevant material in these books or other principles of macroeconomics textbooks or intermediate macroeconomic texts or perhaps material from a money and banking book such as Chapter 23 from Burton and Lombra (2006). Those seeking more about the federal funds rate, money, and the equation of exchange may want to consult Chapters Three and Twenty-Two and page 393 in Mishkin (2004), Chapter Two and pages 263, 516, and 517 in Burton and Lombra (2006), or another money and banking textbook or look for information in a principles of macroeconomics or intermediate macroeconomics book.

CHAPTER ONE REFERENCES

Baumol, W. J. and Blinder, A. S. (2012) *Macroeconomics: Principles and Policy*, twelfth edition. South-Western Cengage Learning, Mason, Ohio.

Burton, M. and Lombra, R. (2006) *The Financial System and the Economy: Principles of Money and Banking*, fourth edition. Thomson South-Western, Mason, Ohio.

Darda, M. and Keene, T. (2011) on Surveillance Midday, Bloomberg TV, August 19, 2011.

Dornbusch, R., Fischer, S., and Startz, R. (2008) *Macroeconomics*, tenth edition. McGraw-Hill Irwin, Boston, Massachusetts.

Hansen, S. (2009) "Scary Drop in Velocity of Money: Is Deflation Knocking?" September 3, 2009, accessed September 25, 2011; available online at: seekingalpha.com/article/159814-scary-drop-in-velocity-of-money-is-deflation-knocking

Hartman, H. C. (2011) "The Decrease in the Velocity of Money in the United States: Some Possible Causes and Some Implications." *International Journal of Accounting Information Science and Leadership*, vol. 4, iss. 11, pp. 15-27.

Hartman, H. C. (2013) "More about the Decrease in the Velocity of Money in the United States: Some Potential Causes and Policy Implications." *Journal of International Business Management and Research*, vol. 3, iss. 10, pp. 116-138.

Krugman, P. and Wells, R. (2009) *Macroeconomics*, second edition. Worth Publishers, New York, New York.

Mankiw, N. G. (2007) *Brief Principles of Macroeconomics*, fourth edition. Thomson South-Western, Mason, Ohio.

Mishkin, F. S. (2004) *The Economics of Money, Banking, and Financial Markets*, seventh edition. Pearson Addison Wesley, Boston, Massachusetts.

www.economagic.com

CHAPTER 2

WHAT DOES PLUMMETING VELOCITY TELL US? EXPANSIONARY MONETRY POLICY VERSUS EXPANSIONARY FISCAL POLICY WHEN INTEREST RATES ARE EXTREMELY LOW

IS MONETARY POLICY PUSHING ON A STRING?

As noted in the Preface and in Chapter 1, the velocity of money, or the number of times per year (on average) that each U.S. dollar has changed hands in real GDP transactions, has decreased substantially starting in early 2008. If each dollar is spent fewer times, adding dollars to the economy will not necessarily lead to an increase in real GDP, with increasing real GDP being one of the goals of the recent expansionary monetary policy. Some analogies may help to illustrate the difficulty of relying excessively on monetary policy to stimulate real GDP when velocity is falling.

Imagine an automobile that is not running properly. The car has been taken to a service station by its owner, who wonders why its performance is sub-par. If the automobile has only been driven a few miles since its tank was last filled with gasoline, then a lack of fuel is not the problem (assuming that the car has not developed a leak and assuming that the gasoline is the correct fuel for the vehicle). Obviously, filling the tank again would help the automobile be able to travel a few more miles because the tank is not absolutely full, but the additional fuel would be of limited help, given that a lack of fuel is not the main reason why the car is not running properly. Another measure, such as replacing the engine oil, adjusting the carburetor, or replacing a worn out part, would likely be much more helpful if one of those other measures solved the problem that was hindering the performance of the automobile.

Burton and Lombra (2006, pp. 13-15) compare the U.S. economy to a human body. To extend their analogy a bit, consider a person with sufficient nutrition but suffering from a serious illness. Giving someone who is sick additional food could help the ill person somewhat by giving the person additional energy to combat the illness, but we would not expect giving the person additional food to help much unless the person were tragically suffering from hunger or lack of nutrition. Other treatments would likely be more helpful in this person's recovery.

In some ways, the United States economy is similar to the car at the service station or the person suffering from an illness. With millions of people unemployed in the U.S. as of this writing, the U.S. economy is performing sub-optimally at least insofar as the economy is capable of producing more goods and services each quarter than the economy is currently producing, just as the automobile is capable of performing better. As others have pointed out, given that (1) resources are scarce, (2) not all wants can be satisfied, and (3) a day when a potential worker wants to work but is unable to find work cannot be recouped in a finite lifetime, unemployment presents a problem not only for those unemployed but also for the overall economy in part due to the additional goods that society loses that the unemployed could have produced.

Presumably in an effort to reduce unemployment rates and increase real GDP in the United States, the Federal Reserve Bank, the central bank of the United States, has been taking steps to increase the monetary base (total reserves held by banks plus currency held by the public outside of the banking system). These steps have led to an increase in the money supply. Yet, many would likely agree that the recent increases in the money supply in response to the recent U.S. financial crisis and recession have been at best only modestly successful at spurring economic growth (although the expansionary monetary policy may have been quite beneficial for other reasons). But, many might also agree that increases in the money supply were more successful at stimulating the U.S. economy during previous recessions and recoveries, when velocity may have decreased during or around the time of past recessions, but by a much smaller percentage.

Compare money injected into the U.S. economy in response to the recent financial crisis and recession with filling the gasoline tank of the automobile not running properly but already with enough fuel or giving food to an ill person who already has sufficient nutrition. Additional dollars injected into the U.S. economy as of this writing will likely help economic growth somewhat, just as additional fuel will help the automobile to travel farther than would be otherwise possible and additional food would give the patient more energy. I want to emphasize that the expansionary monetary policy implemented recently in the U.S. may have been extremely beneficial, if only for reasons discussed in the next paragraph. But the main problem with the U.S. economy at the present is not insufficient dollars in circulation or excessively high interest rates that discourage spending by households on consumption and spending by businesses on new buildings and new machinery. Likewise, the main problem with the car was not insufficient fuel. Moreover, the patient was not ill due to a lack of food.

Other economic policies would likely be more helpful at stimulating growth, just as other service measures would likely be more helpful at improving the performance of the car and the right medicine or the right treatment would be more useful in healing the patient. As it turns out, the expansionary monetary policy implemented by the Federal Reserve in recent years has probably been extremely helpful. But recalling the decrease in velocity, this expansionary policy may possibly have been more helpful in reducing the interest cost of the federal debt and in preventing a much larger economic downturn than in directly stimulating growth. In a frequently given example, economists have often compared expansionary monetary policy in this type of environment with pushing on a string. The thinking is that tighter monetary policy, akin to pulling on a string, may be more successful in reducing aggregate demand than expansionary monetary policy at increasing aggregate demand when interest rates are already quite low.

Given the recent recession and slow recovery and what has become the largest cumulative percentage decrease in the velocity of M1 since the Great Depression and World War II era, which policy measures would likely be most helpful in stimulating the U.S. economy? Why is monetary policy likely to be less successful today than it was during many previous downturns? And how did the U.S. economy get into this situation?

LOW INTEREST RATES AND REAL GDP GROWTH – THE RELATIONSHIP OR LACK THEREOF

Given the complexity of the questions raised, this study aims to offer partial answers. In so doing, we must pay attention to interest rates. Textbook policy recommendations to stimulate economic growth in the short term during either a period of contraction, no growth, or slow growth often include increasing the money supply to reduce interest rates to stimulate spending. However, the percentage increase in nominal GDP spending in the Not-So-Great Recovery has been rather modest given the relatively rapid increase in the money supply, and perhaps not what one would normally expect. Obviously, the U.S. economy over the last six or seven years is not what I would consider a 'normal economy.'

Readers may have noticed that many interest rates in the U.S. are currently (in mid-2014) rather low, with the federal funds rate close to zero per cent. Such low interest rates provide an important piece of the puzzle. Many (for example, Dornbusch, Fischer, and Startz (2008, p. 254)) discuss a zero interest rate bound. It is highly likely that nominal interest rates agreed upon by lenders and borrowers at the time when a loan is made cannot be less than zero per cent, assuming that lenders are seeking financial gain by lending. If this were not the case, then borrowers could repay loans in full without defaulting by giving lenders fewer dollars than they borrowed. If loans could be repaid before maturing, borrowers could make vast sums of money by borrowing at a negative interest rate, repaying the loan early (and pocketing the negative interest payment which would not need to be repaid), and then borrowing again at a negative interest rate and repaying early, and so on. (I think I gave this example in Hartman (2010)). This would amount to essentially 'free money' for borrowers.

Thus, any loans made at a negative nominal interest rate *ex ante* (meaning an interest rate in nominal terms less than zero agreed upon by the lender and the borrower before the borrower receives the funds) would have to be limited because under the scenario just described, a borrower could exhaust the financial resources of *any* lender except for a central bank capable of creating new money. In a sense, a lender who grants a loan at a nominal interest rate less than zero is paying the borrower for borrowing money. Hence, in light of the implications for lenders if nominal interest rates are less than zero, economists normally ignore the possibility of lenders seeking financial gain through loans agreeing to grant loans with negative nominal interest rates.

((Mishkin (2004, p. 69) offers a brief description of a case where interest rates on six-month Treasury bills in Japan were slightly less than zero (-0.004 per cent). But, as Mishkin (2004, p. 69) points out, this is clearly the exception rather than the rule, and apparently, these negative nominal interest rates did not last very long. Many (for example, David Jolly (2014) have noted that the European Central Bank recently began to 'pay' a negative interest rate on banks' deposits at the ECB to try to increase bank lending. This just illustrates the reason why gain-seeking lenders usually do not agree to lend at a negative nominal interest rate.)

Data from www.economagic.com accessed February 27, 2013 indicate that the daily ten-year Treasury constant maturity rate had fallen to 1.44 per cent on July 25, 2012. The ten-year rate increased to 2.05 per cent on February 13, 2013 before falling to 1.88 per cent on February 25, 2013. These interest rates seem quite low. At least some doubt whether expansionary monetary policy could have reduced the nominal ten-year Treasury interest rate much further below where it was in late July 2012.

So what happens when the money supply expands if interest rates are already close to zero per cent? In the extreme case where interest rates have already reached some low level that is the minimum rate feasible (perhaps zero per cent), one economic theory predicts that people in the economy will voluntarily hold any dollars newly added into the economy, without spending the additional dollars. In that extreme case, the quantity of money demanded (or the number of dollars that people want to hold where the dollars include coins and funds in checking accounts without limits on checks) becomes infinitely large at some low interest rate. The incentive to lend (with the possible exception of 'lending' to depository institutions such as commercial banks by storing funds in liquid deposit forms that are protected by deposit insurance) may be greatly reduced when interest rates reach some extremely low level, and many may believe that, from their perspective, the reward for lending is dominated by the risks that the borrower may default or that the lender will want to cash out early. Furthermore, it is almost certain that interest rates will be higher in the future when interest rates are at an extremely low level in the present.

In that environment, a controversial economic theory known as the speculative demand for money predicts that people would prefer to hold cash rather than to purchase bonds (and possibly other financial assets) because if interest rates rise in the future, the resale value of the bonds (and perhaps other assets as well) will decrease, all other things constant. It could be advantageous for those with extra cash to hold the cash rather than lend the cash (by purchasing new bonds) until the interest rate rises. Readers can consult Mishkin (2004, pp. 527-528), who attributes the speculative motive for holding money to Keynes, to learn more about the speculative motive. An asset motive for holding money is discussed briefly at the end of this section. Keynes' other two motives for holding money are discussed in the section 'Aggregate Demand and Money Demand.'

But, even if the speculative motive for holding money does not hold, an increased desire by people and organizations not including the banking system to hold money likely exists. From a list of the components of M1, the narrowest monetary aggregate, as in Mishkin (2004, p. 53), Burton and Lombra (2006, pp. 28, 29, 39), and elsewhere, for a dollar to be counted as a part of the money supply in the U.S., the dollar must be held as either cash or a travelers' check by a person or an organization outside of the banking system, or be part of a checking account with no limits on check-writing privileges per month. Mishkin (2004, p. 53) points out that travelers' checks originating from banks are categorized as checkable deposits when calculating M1, with only travelers' checks not originating from banks categorized separately in M1 calculations. Currency held in the banking system counts toward reserves but does *not* count toward the money supply. (If the bank reserves (which appear on the asset side of a bank's balance sheet) are associated with customers' deposits (which are liabilities on the other side of a bank's balance sheet), then the deposit liabilities do count toward the money supply if the accounts satisfy the requirements although the reserves do not).

Data accessed July 20, 2013 from www.economagic.com show that between December 2007 and December 2012, M1 increased by approximately 78 per cent. This indicates a rather rapid increase in the quantity of money demanded over a short span of time. Given that data accessed the same day from www.economagic.com and the author's calculations show that nominal GDP has increased by only approximately eleven per cent from the fourth quarter of 2007 through the fourth quarter of 2012, why are people and organizations holding so many dollars as 'money' rather than putting the dollars to work as a part of nominal GDP spending? This may be particularly puzzling given that people could receive a higher rate of interest (with almost no additional risk) by holding some of these dollars in assets such savings account deposits that pay a higher interest rate. Laidler (1993, p. 182) and others have discussed an asset motive for holding money (attributed by Laidler (1993, p. 182) to Marty (1961) and Cagan and Schwartz (1975)), and this may be at least part of the answer.

STIMULATING ECONOMIC GROWTH IN OR NEAR A LIQUIDITY TRAP

The U.S. economy is in a situation that, in my view, is near a liquidity trap, although it does not appear that the U.S. economy is in a complete liquidity trap as of this writing. A tell-tale sign of a liquidity trap is the presence of extremely low interest rates. This certainly seems to describe the U.S. economy right now. In short, when interest rates become extremely low and approach minimum feasible levels (perhaps equal to zero), the quantity of money demanded approaches infinity as it must to ensure that interest rates are greater than or equal to zero. In this case, many of the extra dollars demanded by people and organizations in the economy are held rather than being spent, assuming that additional spending requires a reduction in interest rates as an inducement. If that is the case, then further increases in the money supply, all other things equal, would lead only to a small increase in spending because the additional dollars would do little to drive nominal interest rates down further. In a complete liquidity trap, none of the newly added dollars are spent because the newly added dollars fail to reduce nominal interest rates. Thus, in a complete liquidity trap, increases in the money supply fail to cause increases in either real GDP or spending (including nominal GDP) in the economy. If nominal GDP fails to increase despite an increase in the money supply, then the velocity of money *must* fall.

During a more typical downturn, the Federal Reserve (or the Fed) can buy U.S. government Treasury bills (or T-bills) to reduce interest rates. The purchase of the T-bills by the Fed increases the supply of reserves in the banking system, thus creating pressure on the federal funds rate to fall. (Intuitively, with more reserves in the banking system, all other things constant, the cost of borrowing reserves would likely decrease.) Often, other longer-term interest rates follow suit, and this reduces the cost of borrowing to fund additional household consumption and business expenditures on new buildings, new machinery, and new inventory (the three components of business investment in physical capital). It also reduces the incentive to postpone consumption and investment in physical capital today by lowering the expected return of lending. Responding to reduced interest rates, all other things equal, businesses buy more physical capital and consumers may also respond by increasing consumption, but many economists focus on the increase in investment in physical capital as being particularly sensitive to interest rates. Thus, real GDP begins to grow again. This seems largely consistent with material in Mishkin (2004, pp. 398, 616-625), except Mishkin (2004, pp. 616-625) may place more confidence than some economists in the ability of lower interest rates to stimulate increases in consumer durable purchases and net exports.

One of the important differences between the current economic environment in the United States and a more 'normal' downturn is that the Federal Reserve has already been implementing monetary policy aggressive enough to drive the federal funds rate to less than one-quarter-of-one per cent. Many have noted that so-called conventional monetary policies are approaching a limit on their effectiveness, given that the federal funds rate cannot go much lower assuming a zero bound. The Federal Reserve has responded to the most recent U.S. recession and sluggish recovery by implementing three phases of quantitative easing, or buying assets with longer terms to maturity, to reduce further longer-term interest rates, and perhaps reduce them faster. Other interest rates may be more important for determining investment in physical capital by firms and consumption by households, but these interest rates could also be getting near minimum feasible values. The quantitative easing measures likely have also further increased the quantity of money in circulation. Given a relatively sharp and deep decline in the velocity of M1, it is unclear how effective the increases in money supply have been in stimulating growth in real GDP.

VELOCITY DURING RECESSIONS

Mishkin (2004, pp. 520-521) notes that velocity frequently decreases during recessions. Thus, the recent decrease in the velocity of M1 in the United States (without considering the *magnitude* of the decrease in the velocity of M1) is similar to many, if not most, recessions in the U.S. One of the important differences between the recent U.S. recession and sluggish recovery compared with many other downturns, however, is the *size* of the decrease in M1 velocity. Based on data on www.economagic.com accessed July 20, 2013, the author calculates that the velocity of M1 decreased by roughly 37.5 per cent between the fourth quarter of 2007 and the first quarter of 2013.

The second largest percentage decline in M1 velocity in the United States after the Great Depression/World War II era from the peak to the trough is roughly 18.4 per cent between the third quarter of 1981 and the fourth quarter of 1993. This time span of more than a decade includes two periods of at least six consecutive quarters when the velocity of M1 *in*creased and spans multiple periods later called 'sub-sample periods,' with each sub-sample period determined based mainly on whether velocity is trending upward or downward. The period from the third quarter of 1981 through the fourth quarter of 1993 includes part of a recession in the early 1980s and a recession in the early 1990s, but more factors than these recessions likely contributed to the decrease in M1 velocity from the early 1980s to the mid-1990s. For comparison purposes, from the fourth quarter of 2000 through the second quarter of 2003, M1 velocity decreased by only approximately 6 per cent. Why has M1 velocity decreased so rapidly during the Great Recession and its aftermath?

The sharp decline in the velocity of M1 in the United States should lead policymakers to question whether monetary policy alone in the present economy can achieve the goals of increasing real GDP growth rates and reducing unemployment rates to pre-recession levels at a much faster pace. Expansionary monetary policy can increase the money supply and reduce interest rates to encourage spending and create less of a reward for saving. But, monetary policy *cannot guarantee* that newly added dollars will be spent, particularly in an economy like the present U.S. economy which is either on the brink of a liquidity trap or in a liquidity trap. With the M1 money supply having increased by roughly 78 per cent over a five year span, the U.S. economy has plenty of dollars. Now it is time for policymakers to find ways to get those dollars moving faster again! After all, for an activity to be part of U.S. gross domestic product, the activity had to result in certain types of *spending*, which implies a movement of dollars as part of a trade. By providing dollars and at times reducing interest rates in an effort to stimulate spending when the performance of the economy appears sub-par, the Federal Reserve can merely 'lead horses to water,' as the saying goes.

FISCAL POLICY

Given that monetary policy may have approached the limit of its ability to stimulate economic activity in the U.S. (if monetary policy has not already reached the limit), what policy measures would likely be best suited for spurring growth in the U.S.? The answer may be surprising.

By way of analogy, let's consider a different situation. For those not familiar, when driving on ice and the car begins to slide out of control, the advice is to 'steer into the slide.' It probably seems counterintuitive, but that is the best way to regain control of the vehicle. Steering in the opposite direction of the slide can cause the car to spin around. Turning into the slide can stop the vehicle from spinning and help the car to regain traction.

At least some economists recommend greater government deficit spending to stimulate an economy that is either contracting or growing slowly (or not at all), particularly when interest rates are extremely low. Just as is the case with steering into the slide, it may seem counterintuitive to increase deficit spending in order to stimulate the economy when interest rates are quite low. People may feel that the U.S. cannot afford such measures when the economy is not performing well and budget deficits had increased substantially during the Great Recession. However, periods of high unemployment and real GDP below its potential are perhaps the *best* times for deficit spending. By increasing government spending and reducing tax revenue, both of which individually would lead to a larger budget deficit, households and firms will have more available to spend, all other things equal. Policymakers would expect that people will spend at least part of the additional after-tax income, creating additional income for others in the economy.

Additionally, at least some economists would suggest combining expansionary monetary policy with expansionary fiscal policy in the U.S. economy. A disadvantage of expansionary fiscal policy is that, all other things equal, the budget deficit increases. A cost of the budget deficit is higher interest rates, which can slow down future growth by making it harder for firms to borrow for building new buildings and buying new machines. But in an economy like the U.S. economy today, interest rates are already low, and expansionary monetary policy could help to keep interest rates low in the short term. Thus, the deficits would not substantially reduce firms' additions of new machines and buildings. In fact, some economists suggest that fiscal policy is at its greatest effectiveness compared with monetary policy when interest rates are extremely low and the economy is in or close to a liquidity trap. Moreover, with so many in the United States seeking employment, it is difficult to see how further fiscal expansion could displace the productive efforts of those looking for work and companies seeking more customers. For additional information, refer to Dornbusch, Fischer, and Startz (2008, p. 263).

Another possible drawback of expansionary fiscal policy is that, all other things equal, inflation or an increase in the price level would occur. However, although the money supply in the U.S. has grown very rapidly after the fourth quarter of 2007 while at the same time inflation has been relatively subdued, is higher inflation a major concern right now in the U.S., particularly if expansionary fiscal policy could create growth and reduce cyclical and perhaps other forms of unemployment?

However, when recovering from other downturns, monetary policy could be more effective than fiscal policy for several reasons. As implied above, the deficits associated with expansionary fiscal policy could increase interest rates. Further, the approval process for fiscal policy could take weeks or months, while it is shorter for monetary policy. Also, in an open economy, expansionary fiscal policy in the U.S. could cause the U.S. dollar to appreciate and cause the U.S. trade deficit to widen. (Readers can find more in Chapters 11, 12, and 17 of Dornbusch, Fischer, and Startz (2008).) But again, many, if not all, of these features fail to describe accurately the recent if not present U.S. economy.

RECENT STIMULUS PACKAGES IN THE U.S.

The situation in the U.S. economy in early 2014 may have many questioning the ability of fiscal policy to stimulate the economy given the relatively small increase in real GDP relative to its pre-recession levels following the stimulus measures passed in 2008 and 2009. The first stimulus, the Recovery Rebate and Stimulus for the American People Act, according to Krugman and Wells (2009, pp. 351, 362-363) passed in early February 2008 and was largely a tax rebate. The subsequent stimulus in 2009, Baumol and Blinder (2012, p. 222) point out, was divided in roughly equal percentages to

(1) support for local and state governments, (2) increases in federal government expenditures, and (3) reductions in taxes. Data from www.economagic.com accessed July 20, 2013 and the author's calculations show that real GDP in the U.S. rose temporarily in the second quarter of 2008, which followed the passage of the first stimulus measure. Moreover, data from www.economagic.com show that real GDP started to grow again in the third quarter of 2009, relatively soon after the passage of the second stimulus.

Recalling the analogy of the U.S. economy to a human, giving a patient a treatment or a medicine does not always lead to an instant cure. In the case of the common cold where no known cure currently exists, there are methods of providing at least partial relief from the symptoms. However, someone with a cold is still 'sick' after taking cold medicine. A patient with a curable illness often needs at least a few days before recovering to normal health. A patient with an injury instead of an illness who begins a rehabilitation procedure cannot expect immediate full recovery when just beginning the rehabilitation.

During the Great Depression (which was associated with a major financial crisis in the U.S.), the author's calculations using data in Dornbusch, Fischer, and Startz (2008, p. 582) (complied by the Bureau of Economic Analysis) show that it took the U.S. economy roughly eight years from the trough of the depression in 1933 to return to potential real output in 1941. (This assumes a three per cent growth rate in potential real output each year after 1929. Real output fell each year from 1929 through 1933 and again in 1938. The trend calculation, however, assumes a constant growth rate.) Given that the recovery from the most recent recession began in the third quarter of 2009, the U.S. economy has been recovering for more than four years. Assuming that the economy does not enter a 'double dip' (which is not necessarily a safe assumption given tighter fiscal policy, the possibility of problems in the European Union and elsewhere spilling over into the U.S., and the fact that some economic data suggest that the U.S. recovery may be weakening), the recovery might have a considerable way to go.

The reader should also realize that some economists with different views had at least slightly similar criticisms about the likely results of the second stimulus. To simplify, in a *Wall Street Journal* blog titled "Economists Debate: Diverse Perspectives on Stimulus" with Phil Izzo (2009) as the complier, J. Bradford DeLong felt that the stimulus was too small, while Martin Feldstein may have felt that the stimulus was improperly structured to be effective. Regarding the size of the stimulus, the reader should remember that if this criticism does not seem valid, then recall that most of the stimulus funds were spread out over three years and that the total dollar value of the second stimulus (roughly $800 billion) was still less than ten per cent of nominal gross domestic product for a year. Much truth may exist in the criticism over how the stimulus funds were spent. But that criticism does not imply that the general idea of a stimulus package was inappropriate. Returning to the analogy of the ill patient, it helps to give the patient not only the correct medicine, but also a sufficient amount of medicine.

In addition to the problems of the stimulus being too small and possibly poorly targeted, a further problem is that the fraction of each additional dollar of disposable income (or after-tax income) that goes toward consumption may have decreased during the recession and the recovery. This potential decrease may be showing up in the decrease in the velocity of the M1 money supply. A greater increase in after-tax income may be necessary to reach a targeted increase in spending (and gross domestic product) if people are spending fewer dollars of additional income that they receive.

GOVERNMENT SPENDING AND VELOCITY

Wiseman (2012) and perhaps others have noted that between the second quarter of 2009 and the second quarter of 2012, a measure of *total* government spending decreased by an estimated 4.5 per cent. The reduction in *total* government spending could be slowing the economic recovery. Textbook-style arguments analyzing the short-term impact of an increase in government spending during a downturn would likely assume that total government spending has increased. For example, they may assume that federal government spending has increased while state and local government spending have remained constant, thus leading to an increase in total government spending. Further, Wiseman (2012) notes that during the U.S. recovery in the 1980s, a measure of government spending increased by fifteen per cent over a similar timespan, and it increased in many other recoveries in contrast with the recovery that began in 2009.

Although many policymakers deciding on government spending and taxes may not be thinking directly about the velocity of money, the decline in money velocity may help to guide them in trying to return the economy to full employment. Government purchases, one category of government expenditures, could be particularly helpful in stimulating real GDP because the expenditures are made by the government in exchange for production that counts toward GDP. With government purchases, the dollars exchange hands at least once in GDP transactions.

As noted in the Preface, graphs in Baumol and Blinder (2012, p. 298) show that the velocities of both M1 and M2 have exceeded one time per year in the U.S. for decades. Values of velocity greater than one imply that dollars must trade more than one time each year in order to finance the level of spending on production in a year. Because the U.S. did not have enough dollars to sustain levels of spending in previous years without the dollars in both M1 and M2 trading on average more than once per year, the exchange of at least some dollars more than one time per year was critical in maintaining production levels and living standards. Of course, the exchange of dollars contributes to velocity. Thus, velocity merits attention.

Increasing government purchases (and other expansionary fiscal policies) could be a way of countering the sharp downward trend in the velocity of money that began in the first quarter of 2008. Unlike other forms of expansionary fiscal policy, namely tax reductions and increases in government transfer payments, dollars that are part of increases in government purchases must be exchanged for the production of goods and services at least once. The decline in velocity that has been concomitant with the rapid increase in the M1 money supply recently in the U.S. not only helps to make a case for expansionary fiscal policy (particularly increases in government purchases), but it also highlights an important difference between the ability of an economy as a whole to spend versus actual spending in the economy.

SPENDING CAPACITY

Economists often note a strong positive correlation between the money supply and the price level in the economy, particularly in the long run. Economists also would likely agree that, assuming that an economy produces at 'full employment,' when the money supply increases at a faster rate than the production capacity in the economy, price levels in the economy will increase faster than they would if the percentage increase in the money supply is slower than the growth rate of production capacity, all other things equal. Similarly, when an economy produces at less than 'full employment,' price levels would likely rise more slowly following an increase in the money supply of a certain percentage, all other things equal, than price levels would rise if the economy were already producing at full employment and the money supply would increase by the same percentage.

This probably helps in explaining why the M1 money supply has increased by approximately 78 per cent from December 2007 through December 2012, using data from www.economagic.com

accessed July 20, 2013, but the deflator has increased only about 8.5 per cent from the fourth quarter of 2007 through the fourth quarter of 2012. In short, although the money supply has increased by a large percentage over the last few years in the United States, the U.S. economy has been operating at considerably less than full employment and therefore, output can expand without a large increase in the price level as producers can acquire more inputs without having to pay prices that are much higher.

Note that the money supply growth rate has exceeded the growth rate in aggregate demand as measured by nominal GDP in the economy. The ability to spend, or spending capacity, in an economy is at least somewhat analogous to production capacity except that it deals with the ability of households, firms, the government sectors, and perhaps those in other countries to spend on goods (produced in the U.S.) rather than the ability of producers to make goods. Just because an economy has the ability to produce a certain sustainable maximum quantity of goods in the aggregate in a given time period does not mean that the economy will produce that quantity of goods in that time period. Likewise, the ability of the various groups who demand goods produced in the United States to spend a certain amount in a certain time period does not ensure that they will spend that amount. Spending capacity depends in part on the nominal money supply. With more dollars in circulation, a greater amount of total spending in the economy can be facilitated with the same velocity. (To simplify, I assume that velocity is equal to the maximum velocity to that point when thinking about the spending capacity in the economy in a period. Barring a major disturbance to the payments system, it should be possible for each dollar to trade on average at least as many times in the next quarter as it traded in a previous quarter. Future work can adjust the concept of spending capacity as needed.)

In lieu of a formal definition for spending capacity, can we think about spending capacity for a quarter as the money supply in that quarter multiplied by the maximum velocity of that monetary aggregate up to that point in time? If the velocity of money reaches a new 'all-time high' in a quarter, then that is the velocity value to use in this informal formulation of spending capacity. The state of the application of technology to the payments system may constrain the number of times that dollars can, on average, trade per time period. This is the main reason why I suggest using the maximum velocity up to a point in time for estimating spending capacity in this 'working definition,' because the fact that dollars traded a certain number of times per period in the data proves that it was technically possible. Another approach would be to use the maximum of the velocity from the previous quarter or the current quarter (rather than over the full sample period) when estimating the spending capacity for a quarter.

It may not be completely clear how to define spending capacity, particularly precisely. What is completely clear, though, is that the U.S. economy has enough dollars to maintain a much higher level of spending than is currently occurring. Barring a major increase in the price level, how many jobs could be created with more spending? How many more goods and services could be produced with more spending, assuming no major increase in prices? If prices remain in check, how much higher could real profits for companies be with greater spending? But until spending picks up, we will not be able to reach those goals.

As noted above, when the money supply growth rate exceeds the production capacity or growth in production capacity in the economy, price levels increase more rapidly and sooner than they would if the money supply growth rate had not exceeded the growth rate in production capacity. Likewise, when spending capacity grows rapidly due to a rapid increase in the money supply, spending capacity growth can far outpace growth in aggregate demand (which represents actual spending on GDP items). If the growth in spending capacity is much larger than the growth in aggregate demand as measured by nominal GDP, then the velocity of money must decrease.

Despite rapid growth in the money supply in the United States beginning in the year 2008, aggregate demand appears to have grown by a comparatively small amount, as evidenced by nominal GDP growing by a much smaller percentage than the money supply. (Baumol and Blinder (2012, pp. 296-299) note that some have considered aggregate demand and nominal GDP as essentially the same. Due to the desire to use readily available data and the desire for analytical simplicity, this study will focus on nominal GDP as a proxy for total spending. This is despite the fact that not all spending is included in nominal GDP.) If a large increase in spending on items not included in GDP within the last few years has not occurred, then the total spending on both GDP items and non-GDP items has failed to keep up with a measure of spending capacity broader than the one in this book which is based on income velocity rather than transactions velocity.

AGGREGATE DEMAND AND MONEY DEMAND

What seems to be holding growth in aggregate demand in the United States back? Problems in the labor market appear to be one factor. Unemployment rates in the U.S. jumped up following the most recent financial crisis and have been slow to decline. Some of those who lost jobs, but were able to find work, were able to do so only for much lower pay. With so many impacted by lengthy spells of unemployment and others accepting much lower wages and salaries just to find work, it should be no surprise that aggregate demand has grown little.

Reduced asset values present another problem. The decrease in the value of houses and many equity shares as the financial crisis unfolded reduced the ability of people in the economy to buy goods, and it took years for the value of many assets that suffered a steep loss to come close to recovering.

The financial system presents further problems. In the aftermath of the financial crisis, financial organizations may be more hesitant about granting loans. Some households and some businesses require access to credit in order to buy. Further, some small businesses in particular need access to credit in order to pay employees and suppliers and to make other payments. Therefore, a reduction in lending could curb growth in aggregate demand.

Additionally, uncertainty about the economic prospects for the future could be slowing down the growth in aggregate demand. Pessimism regarding future income prospects and future economic stability in light of the factors discussed above and other factors combined with potential financial problems in Europe and elsewhere and tighter fiscal policy noted by Wiseman (2012) and others could be causing some who are fortunate enough to have additional funds to hold the dollars rather than spend the dollars.

For those who remain unconvinced, consider the reasons that Keynes listed as to why people hold money, including highly liquid bank deposits. Above, we already discussed one of Keynes' motives for money demand. To help make a point, let's consider all three motives. According to Mishkin (2004, p. 521-522), Keynes stated that one of the reasons why people hold money is due to the transactions motive for holding money. These are funds held as money to finance planned expenditures. Mishkin (2004, p. 522) further stated that Keynes also discussed a precautionary motive for holding money. These are funds held for unplanned or emergency expenditures. Keynes further discussed a third motive, the speculative motive for holding money.

Of Keynes' three motives, the speculative motive is the least agreed upon motive for holding money regarding whether the motive actually exists. In the speculative motive, Mishkin (2004, p. 522) noted that Keynes stated that people hold money if they expect interest rates to be higher in the future. Thus, they expect that the prices of previously issued bonds will be lower. People are holding money rather than bonds or other assets (if they hold money due to the speculative motive) because they do not want to incur a capital loss. Also recall the asset motive for holding money that Laidler (1993, p. 182) credits to Marty (1961) and Cagan and Schwartz (1975). The takeaway from this is that with the precautionary motive, the speculative motive, and the asset motive (if the latter two exist), people in the economy may hold dollars in forms that fit the definition of M1 for reasons other than for planned expenditures. Thus, it is possible for the percentage growth of the quantity of money in circulation to exceed the percentage growth in aggregate demand, at least in the short term. A simple example in Chapter 4 will help to explain why some banks and some corporations may want to hold dollars.

But, if it is possible for the growth rate in the money supply, a determinant of spending capacity, to exceed the growth rate in aggregate demand (taken to be the growth rate in nominal GDP in this case), then from the algebraic definition of the velocity of money, the velocity of money must fall. Given that the growth rate of nominal GDP can be surpassed by far by the growth rate of the money supply, could a limit exist, at least at some points in time, as to how large nominal GDP can grow in a limited time period despite the growth in the money supply? Perhaps more importantly, does a money supply level exist, at least at some points in time, beyond which further increases in the money supply will automatically lead to a decrease in the velocity of money?

To address that question, it will be helpful to think about the velocity of money as a function of the money supply. A graph will show this. Based on a scatter graph plot with the quarterly average seasonally-adjusted M1 money supply on the horizontal axis and the velocity of M1 on the vertical axis, the sample period with quarterly data for the velocity of M1 (beginning with the first quarter of 1959 and running through the first quarter of 2013) will be divided into ten sub-sample periods based on whether velocity is usually, if not always increasing or whether velocity is usually, if not always decreasing. Discussion of the velocity of money as a function of the money supply and the possibility of a money supply level beyond which further monetary expansion will result in a decrease in velocity will continue in the next chapter.

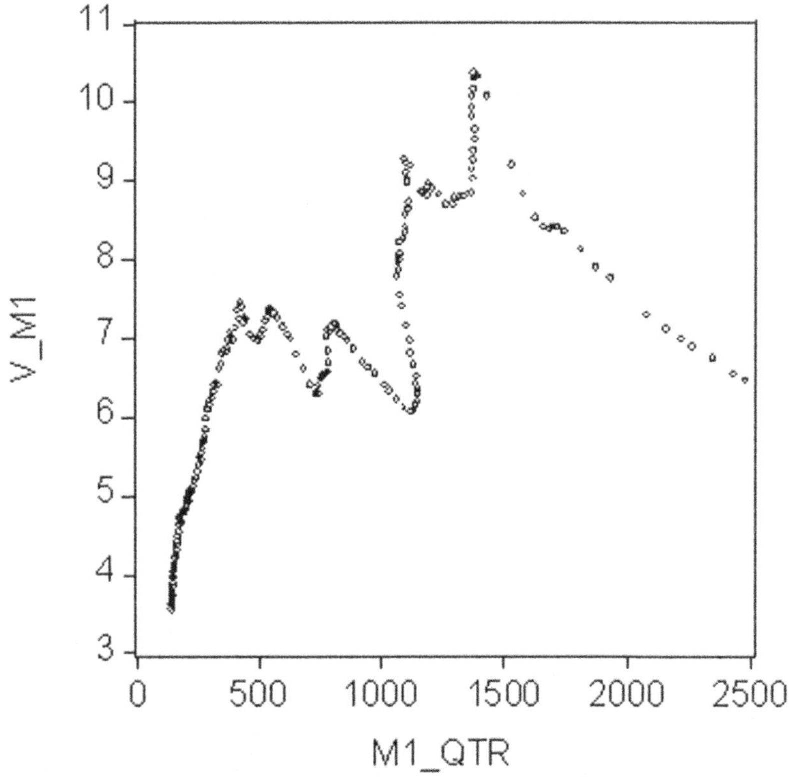

Figure 2.1 M1 Money Supply (quarterly) and the Velocity of the M1 Money Supply
1959 quarter one through 2013 quarter one, quarterly data
Source: www.economagic.com and the author's calculations

AN INTRODUCTION TO THE THREE MAJOR MACROECONOMIC SCHOOLS OF THOUGHT

Before concluding, let's review some basics about the major schools of macroeconomic thought. We will consider the classical school of macroeconomic thought, the Keynesian school of macroeconomic thought, and the monetarist school of macroeconomic thought. (For our purposes, we need not worry about either the neoclassical school or the new Keynesian school. We can assume that the neoclassical school of macroeconomic thought would likely have views on velocity similar to the classical school, while the new Keynesian school would probably view the velocity of money similarly to the Keynesian school.)

Of the three schools of thought considered, the classical school is the only one that clearly predates the Great Depression. In a sense, the Great Depression gave rise to both the Keynesian and monetarist schools of thought as many were not satisfied with the ability (or inability) of the classical school to offer a satisfactory explanation for the Great Depression. One of the critical assumptions of the classical school of macroeconomic thought is that prices and other factors adjust very rapidly following changes in aggregate demand. In the most extreme interpretation of the classical school of macroeconomic thought, prices and other factors adjust so rapidly that changes in real output in the economy are due only to changes in aggregate supply because changes in aggregate demand affect only the price level in the most extreme version of the classical school. This implies that in the most extreme interpretation of the classical school (and perhaps more extreme than classical economists actually believed), the economy is always getting the maximum production out of the resources and technology available.

In an interpretation of the classical school not quite as extreme, in the event of an economic downturn (due to a drop in demand), the best policy is simply to wait for the price level (i.e. the implicit deflator) to adjust downward because it is assumed that the price level will adjust very rapidly. Upon the completion of the speedy price adjustment process, the economy will once more be producing optimally, or the maximum sustainable quantity of output per quarter or per year.

The most extreme interpretation of the classical school of macroeconomic thought would also suggest that the unemployment rate as measured by the Bureau of Labor Statistics (BLS) must be zero per cent because in the most extreme version of the classical school, wages and salaries and other factors related to jobs adjust so quickly that everyone who wants a job can find employment. (People who are not employed and who have not sought employment within the last four weeks and are not laid off workers waiting to be recalled are counted by the BLS as not being part of the labor force rather than being counted as unemployed.)

The tragic and unfortunate experience of the Great Depression, which in the United States brought years of double-digit unemployment rates and real output levels below the real output level in 1929 in the United States, seems to have led to people looking for answers. People probably questioned whether economies were producing the most possible given constraints of resources and technology. Trying to figure out what went wrong led to the Keynesian and monetarist schools of macroeconomic thought.

Krugman and Wells (2009, p. 156) state that in Keynesian analysis, an economic downturn arises due to insufficient demand. In the most extreme interpretation of the Keynesian school (and likely more extreme than Keynes wrote), prices in the economy do not rise following an increase in aggregate demand. Thus, the policy recommendations following a downturn would include reducing taxes and increasing government spending to give households and firms more money to spend. The result in this extreme view of the Keynesian school of macroeconomic thought would be an increase in real output (as measured by real GDP or real GNP) but no change in the price level. In a less extreme interpretation of the work of Keynes, price levels would rise following the tax cuts and increases in government spending, but only after the economy had reached full employment. According to Mishkin (2004, p. 608), Keynesian economists originally thought that expansionary monetary policy could increase real output only by reducing interest rates and inducing spending. Changes in the money supply alone, according to Mishkin (2004, p. 608), did not lead to increases in real output unless interest rates fell in original Keynesian analysis. This view could have led to Keynesian economists forgetting the potential importance of monetary policy.

This could also have opened the door for the monetarist school of thought. According to Burton and Lombra (2006, pp. 516-517), in the monetarist school of thought, changes in the money supply were the main cause of business cycle fluctuations. The monetarists would likely point to a large decrease in the money supply between 1929 and 1933 when explaining the severity of the Great Depression.

VELOCITY IN THE THREE MAIN SCHOOLS OF MACROECONOMIC THOUGHT

Suppose that we consider as did Mishkin (2004, pp. 518-524, 528-532) the velocity of money in the three major schools of macroeconomic thought: the classical school, the Keynesian school, and the monetarist school. The discussion of the velocity of money in these three schools of macroeconomic thought will be in very broad brush strokes just so that everyone reading has some familiarity.

According to Mishkin (2004, pp. 518-519), the classical school of thought assumed that the velocity of money was usually roughly constant over the short term. This view was the original interpretation of the quantity theory of money. Many (for example, Burton and Lombra (2006, pp. 516-517)) have pointed out that the quantity theory of money converts the equation of exchange ($M*V = P*Y$) into a theory of aggregate demand if we think of nominal GDP as representing aggregate demand.

Mishkin (2004, p. 521) stated that economists may have realized during the Great Depression (perhaps for the first time) that the velocity of money can fall substantially during sharp economic downturns. Thus, according to Mishkin (2004, p. 523), Keynes (at least implicitly through the demand for money) assumed that the velocity of money can vary based on factors such as real output in the economy and interest rates. Higher real output (at least implicitly) would lead to greater velocity, all other things equal, while lower real output would reduce velocity in Keynesian analysis, all other things constant.

Likewise, higher real interest rates would increase velocity in Keynesian analysis, all other things equal, and lower real interest rates would reduce velocity in the Keynesian view, all other things the same. Regarding real interest rates and velocity, the thinking is that higher real interest rates, all other things constant, reduce the quantity of purchasing power that people want to hold in the most liquid forms (for example, forms that would be considered money). The reward of more interest earnings from lending one dollar for one year rather than holding the dollar is assumed to compensate for the liquidity risk, where people may have unplanned expenditures and are forced to try to liquidate assets that are not in a form ready for spending, perhaps at a capital loss. As a result of people holding fewer dollars, all other things the same, when interest rates rise, people would spend the smaller quantity of dollars that they did hold more frequently, on average, leading to an increase in velocity.

Mishkin (2004, pp. 523, 531) noted that while interest rates impact the velocity of money in Keynesian analysis, interest rates impact the velocity of money little, if at all, in the work of Milton Friedman, the most well-known of the monetarists. According to Mishkin (2004, p. 531), permanent income was the main factor driving money demand in the work of Friedman. However, Laidler (1993, pp. 143-144) states that (1) Allan Meltzer (1963) found that the quantity of money demanded would decrease as the interest rate on a twenty-year bond increased, all other things equal, and that (2) Karl Brunner and Allan Meltzer (1963) found that interest rate data helped to forecast future velocity values within the sample period. (Dornbusch, Fischer, and Startz (2008, p. 473) list Brunner and Meltzer as being well-known monetarists.) Baumol and Blinder (2012, p. 298) and Burton and Lombra (2006, pp. 516-517) stated that monetarists interpreted velocity as being perhaps sufficiently predictable to guide monetary policy. This view, with velocity predictable but not necessarily constant, was a second interpretation of the quantity theory of money.

Further discussion of the velocity of money in the classical, Keynesian, and monetarist schools of thought follows in the next chapter. This discussion will in part be related to the Great Depression and the Great Recession and sluggish recovery.

CHAPTER TWO REFERENCES

Baumol, W. J. and Blinder, A. S. (2012) *Macroeconomics: Principles and Policy*, twelfth edition. South-Western Cengage Learning, Mason, Ohio.

Brunner, K. and Meltzer, A. H. (1963) "Predicting Velocity: Implications for Theory and Policy." *Journal of Finance*, vol. 18, May, pp. 319-354.

Burton, M. and Lombra, R. (2006) *The Financial System and the Economy: Principles of Money and Banking*, fourth edition. Thomson South-Western, Mason, Ohio.

Cagan, P. and Schwartz, A. J. (1975) "Has the Growth of Money Substitutes Hindered Monetary Policy?" *Journal of Money, Credit, and Banking*, vol. 7, May, pp. 137-160.

Dornbusch, R., Fischer, S., and Startz, R. (2008) *Macroeconomics*, tenth edition. McGraw-Hill Irwin, Boston, Massachusetts.

Hartman, H. C. (2010) "The Effectiveness of Fiscal Policy in (Near) Liquidity Traps." *International Journal of Accounting Information Science and Leadership,* vol. 3, iss. 7, pp. 1-10.

Izzo, P. compiler. (2009) "Economists Debate: Diverse Perspectives on Stimulus." January 29, 2009, accessed January 17, 2014; available online at: blogs.wsj.com/economics/2009/01/29/economists-debate-diverse-perspectives-on-stimulus

Jolly, D. (2014) "European Central Bank Holds Interest Rates Steady." July 3, 2014, accessed July 22, 2014; available online at: www.nytimes.com/2014/07/04/business/international/ecb-holds-interest-rates-steady.html?_r=0

Krugman, P. and Wells, R. (2009) *Macroeconomics*, second edition. Worth Publishers, New York, New York.

Laidler, D. E. W. (1993) *The Demand for Money: Theories, Evidence, and Problems*, fourth edition. Harper Collins College Publishers, New York, New York.

Marty, A. (1961) "Gurley and Shaw on Money in a Theory of Finance." *Journal of Political Economy*, vol. 69, February, pp. 56-62.

Meltzer, A. H. (1963) "The Demand for Money: the Evidence from the Time Series." *Journal of Political Economy*, vol. 71, June, pp. 219-246.

Mishkin, F. S. (2004) *The Economics of Money, Banking, and Financial Markets*, seventh edition. Pearson Addison Wesley, Boston, Massachusetts.

Wiseman, P. (2012) "Weak Recovery Marked." *Atlanta Journal-Constitution*, August 16, 2012, p. A8.

www.economagic.com

CHAPTER 3

VELOCITY AS A FUNCTION OF MONEY SUPPLY (AND AN ECONOMIC OVERVIEW OF THE GREAT DEPRESSION/WORLD WAR II ERA): DOES A LIMIT EXIST AS TO HOW MUCH THE MONEY SUPPLY CAN GROW BEFORE A FURTHER INCREASE IN THE MONEY SUPPLY CAUSES VELOCITY TO FALL?

AN INTRODUCTION TO VELOCITY FUNCTIONS

Why should we even consider the possibility of the velocity of money depending in part on the level of the money supply? The short answer to the question is that without this consideration, we may be missing something. But what could we be missing?

Baumol and Blinder (2012, p. 298) suggest that a higher money supply level probably increases nominal GDP by a smaller percentage than the percentage increase in the money supply because the greater money supply, all other things equal, leads to lower interest rates, which in turn reduce velocity, all other things equal. As we shall see, this reasoning fits at least fairly well the present situation in the U.S. after the fourth quarter of 2007 (through the first quarter of 2013 and perhaps beyond). It may also fit part of the Great Depression and World War II era in the U.S. and maybe also the U.S. in the mid-1980s. But what about the period that began no later than the first quarter of 1959 and ran through the third quarter of 1981 when both the M1 money supply and the velocity of M1 were simultaneously *increasing* most of the time? What could help us to understand the difference between these different time periods when the M1 money supply and its velocity sometimes moved together in the same direction and at other times moved in opposite directions?

Hartman (2011) estimated a velocity function for money in the United States where the change in the velocity of M1 in the U.S. is a function of lagged changes in real GDP, current and past federal funds rates, and lagged changes in velocity. Hartman (2013) estimated VAR models and VEC models with different versions of M1 velocity, real GDP, the federal funds rate, and the ten-year Treasury rate in the U.S. Earlier, some other studies estimated velocity functions for the United States and/or other countries with varying specifications, such as velocity depending on one or more of the following time series variables on the right side of the equation: lagged values of velocity and/or current and/or past values of interest rates, permanent income, temporary income shocks, and/or inflation, with the time series variable or variables on the right side of the equation either in level form or first difference form. Two such studies are Duczynski (n.d.) and Omer (2010). The estimation of velocity functions is certainly not new. Laidler (1993, p. 144) lists Meltzer (1963) and Brunner and Meltzer (1963) as estimating velocity functions, although I have not consulted the original sources in writing in this book.

But in my aforementioned studies, the money supply does not appear, at least directly, on the right side of the regression equations for the velocity of money on the left side of the equations. Thus, these studies may not capture a possible direct impact (at least in full) of the money supply on the velocity of money within the same period. In my earlier studies, by having the money supply in regressions only through its potential impact on other variables in the equations such as velocity and interest rates, did I overlook something? This could be a weakness or an area for further improvement of my earlier studies on velocity.

THE IMPACT OF THE MONEY SUPPLY ON VELOCITY, ALL OTHER THINGS EQUAL

Readers should remember that the money supply level in a particular period appears directly in the algebraic definition of the velocity of money within the same period. From a rearranged version of the equation of exchange, the velocity of money in a period equals nominal GDP (which is real GDP multiplied by the implicit GDP deflator divided by 100) in that period divided by the money supply in the same period. As Mishkin (2004, p. 518) and many others have noted, algebraically, the equation can be written as $V = (P*Y)/M$, where V is the velocity of money, P is the implicit GDP deflator (representing the price level) divided by 100, Y is real GDP, and M is the money supply. Thus, for any particular level of nominal GDP (which is $P*Y$), a greater money supply (assuming that the increase in the money supply does not lead to an increase in nominal GDP within the same period) implies a smaller velocity. This situation occurs if and when an increase in the money supply fails to spark an increase in GDP spending and leaves nominal GDP unchanged. (Dornbusch, Fischer, and Startz (2008, pp. 421-422) note that an increase in the money supply often impacts spending only after a delay.) Data from www.economagic.com found July 20, 2013 and the author's calculations indicate that nominal GDP increased between the fourth quarter of 2007 and the fourth quarter of 2012 by approximately 11.3 per cent over that five year period while between December 2007 and December 2012, M1 increased by nearly 78 per cent.

Although in the short term an increase in the money supply, all other things equal, leads to a decrease in interest rates, is it sufficient to analyze velocity in terms of interest rates, real GDP, and past values of velocity as in the regressions of Hartman (2011) and Hartman (2013)? Should the implicit deflator and the contemporaneous money supply level be part of the analysis of the velocity of money? Can any insight be gained by viewing the velocity of money as a function of the money supply? Could the main reason why velocity has fallen so sharply be that the money supply has increased at a rapid rate while failing to spark an increase in GDP spending even close to the size of the increase in the money supply? Could the increase in the money supply be possibly more important than interest rates and real GDP individually in determining the recent decline in M1 velocity? Does a money supply level exist, at least at some times, beyond which a further increase in the money supply guarantees a decrease in velocity? Should such a level of the money supply exist, I refer to this money supply level, which would be likely to vary from one quarter to the next, as the Non-Decreasing-Velocity Money Supply Level (NDVMSL). It is the greatest money supply level consistent with at least a constant velocity. Readers may also think of it as the Maximum-Constant-Velocity Money Supply Level (MCVMSL).

A combination of at least four economic concepts leads to the possibility of such a money supply level existing, at least at times. First, in the short term, a limit exists as to how much an economy can produce. In the brief overview of some macroeconomic concepts in the first chapter, we saw that in the short run, it is possible for an economy to produce more in a given time period than the long-run equilibrium quantity. That is, in the short term, an economy can make more in a finite time period than would be possible for the economy to sustain in all subsequent time periods of the same length, all other things constant. However, in a quarter or a year, an economy can only produce so much real GDP with the resources and technology that it has in a finite time period, even if people would devote every second of the day to production. In that extreme case where all time is devoted to working, people will grow tired, thus limiting the amount that can be produced. If a limit regarding short-term production did not exist, we could produce any amount of real GDP by increasing aggregate demand and having people work more and adding any unutilized resources to have any quantity supplied in the aggregate including an infinite quantity.

Second, as we saw in the first chapter, in an economy like the U.S. where prices are relatively stable, factors such as contracts prevent some prices from increasing rapidly in response to an increase in aggregate demand. For example, an increase in the money supply could cause an increase in aggregate demand. But hypothetically, if the money supply would happen to increase by five per cent in a quarter, then contracts and other considerations would often result in the price level either rising by less than five per cent in the same quarter or not rising at all in the same quarter, *ceteris paribus*.

Third, the precautionary motive for holding money that Mishkin (2004, p. 522) and others attribute to Keynes, combined with some other possible motives, suggests that at least some people may consider increasing M1 balances, mainly of currency and funds in checking accounts where the owner or owners have unrestricted check-writing privileges, but not to be able to spend more on GDP items. My understanding is that people must decide to hold buying power in a form consistent with the definition of M1 in order for that buying power to count toward M1. But, what if not all M1 balances were held for planned spending purposes?

Fourth, given the three concepts above, it is possible that an increase in the money supply in a quarter may not result in an increase in nominal GDP within the same quarter by the same percentage. Although the reasoning may possibly be different regarding at least some of the three concepts above, is this not the point made by Baumol and Blinder (2012, p. 298)? With possible limits on the responsiveness of both real GDP and the price level to an increase in the money supply within the same quarter, the percentage increase in nominal GDP spending could be less than the percentage increase in M1 within the same quarter. It has already been noted above that the percentage increase in nominal GDP spending could be less than the percentage increase in M1 within the same quarter. It has already been noted above that nominal GDP has failed to increase by a percentage even close to the percentage increase in M1 in the U.S. starting in the year 2008. Does this suggest that a non-constant money supply level exists, at least at times, beyond which further increases in the money supply in effect 'push down' the velocity of money? If so, the maximum money supply level consistent with no change in velocity (from the previous quarter) would be the NDVMSL.

Further discussion of the theory of a NDVMSL appears later in this chapter and in other chapters in this book. For now, note that Figure 3.1 shows a scatter graph diagram for M1 and the velocity of M1 in the United States using data from www.economagic.com as of July 20, 2013. The M1 money supply is measured in billions of dollars and shows the quarterly average of the three months of seasonally adjusted data in the quarter. The quarterly velocity data are reported on an annualized basis. Each point shows the average M1 money supply for a quarter in the sample period and the velocity of M1 in that quarter. The sample period runs from the first quarter of 1959 through the first quarter of 2013. The same graph is Figure 2.1 in Chapter 2.

A relatively quick glance at Figure 3.1 reveals that the relationship between the level of M1 and the velocity of M1 appears to change over time. The relationship between M1 and its velocity seems to oscillate between periods when velocity was usually, if not always, increasing and periods when velocity was usually, if not always, decreasing. Calculating the quarterly percentage change in the money supply for each quarter shows that the quarterly average of M1 decreased only about thirty quarters during a sample period of more than 210 quarters. Of the quarters where M1 decreased, only five had a greater decrease than one percentage point (not on an annualized basis). Because the money supply increased most quarters, looking at the scatter graph points from left to right is similar to viewing the points in chronological order. The reader should realize, however, that equal distances from left to right on the graph do not necessarily represent equal time periods. They simply imply changes in the money supply of equal dollar amounts.

The discussion about velocity and the money supply that follows identifies sub-sample periods from the sample period running from the first quarter of 1959 through the first quarter of 2013 based largely on identifying local minimum points and local maximum points and whether velocity is for the most part increasing or decreasing during a sub-sample period (and the implication for the slope of the best-fit line). The reason for starting the sample period in 1959 is that 1959 is the first year when money supply data that was measured more frequently than annually was readily available. The sub-sample periods are then used in a later chapter as time periods for calculating the slopes of best-fit lines. Given that the task at hand in this chapter is to begin to look at the potential for a changing relationship between the M1 money supply and the velocity of money (particularly starting with the year 1959), much of the discussion of economic conditions possibly related to M1 and its velocity starting with the year 1959 will be tabled for now until Chapter 6.

Sub-sample Period	Beginning Quarter	Ending Quarter
first	1959q1	1981q3
second	1981q4	1983q2
third	1983q3	1984q4
fourth	1985q1	1987q2
fifth	1987q3	1990q2
sixth	1990q3	1993q4
seventh	1994q1	2000q4
eighth	2001q1	2003q2
ninth	2003q3	2007q4
tenth	2008q1	2013q1

Table 3.1 Sub-Sample Periods

M1 AND VELOCITY OVER THE SAMPLE PERIOD FROM THE FIRST QUARTER OF 1959 THROUGH THE FIRST QUARTER OF 2013

The data in this section are from www.economagic.com as of July 20, 2013. Revisions have been made to at least some of the data since then. However, (1) to make findings available as soon as possible, and (2) to use data that is either the same as or more similar to data available to people during the most recent financial crisis, recession, and much of the slow recovery in the U.S.; this study uses the data available as of July 20, 2013. Future work could use revised data and could extend the sample period.

The first sub-sample period runs from the first quarter of 1959 through the third quarter of 1981. M1 velocity in the U.S. increased in most quarters during this sub-sample period from about 3.56 times per year in the first quarter of 1959 to approximately 7.44 times per year in the third quarter of 1981. Over that time, the quarterly average of M1 increased from roughly 139 billion dollars to roughly 427 billion dollars.

Velocity then decreased for six out of the next seven quarters to roughly 6.98 times per year in the second quarter of 1983 while M1 continued to increase to roughly 499 billion dollars. Thus, the second sub-sample period begins in the fourth quarter of 1981 and goes through the second quarter of 1983. The endpoints for all of the sub-sample periods except for the last sub-sample period are quarters when velocity was either at a local maximum or a local minimum (if not a maximum or a minimum within the sample period). The last sub-sample period ended simply because of the end of the sample period for this study.

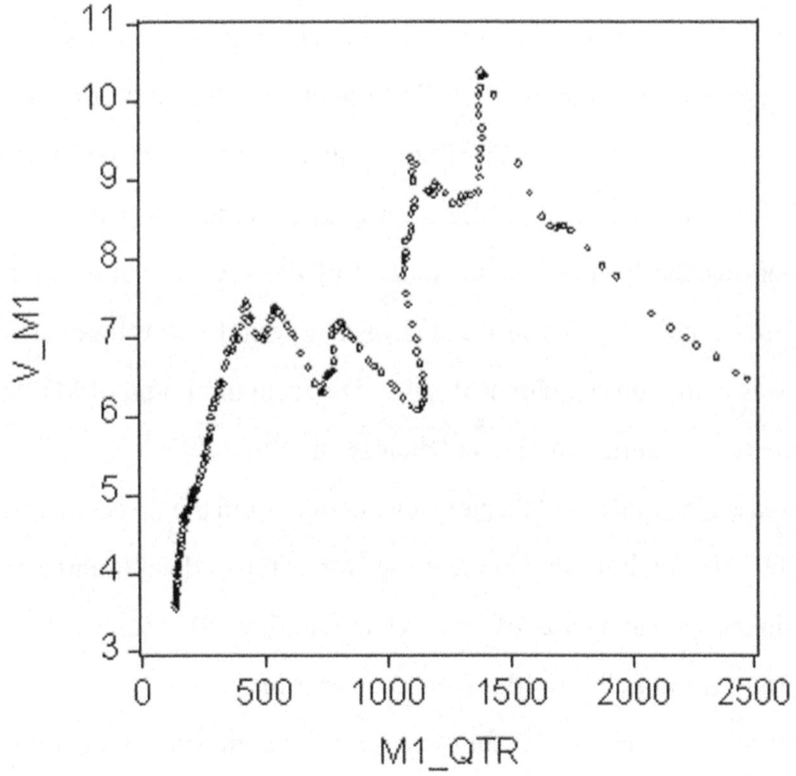

Figure 3.1 M1 Money Supply (quarterly) and the Velocity of the M1 Money Supply
1959 quarter one through 2013 quarter one, quarterly data
Source: www.economagic.com and the author's calculations

The velocity of M1 rebounded for six consecutive quarters starting in the third quarter of 1983, which started the third sub-sample period running through the fourth quarter of 1984 when M1 velocity was roughly 7.37 times per year, while quarterly average M1 continued to increase over this period, reaching approximately 548 billion dollars by the fourth quarter of 1984. Starting in the first quarter of 1985, marking the beginning of the fourth sub-sample period, M1 velocity began to decrease again, falling to slightly less than 6.30 times per year by the second quarter of 1987, the end of the fourth sub-sample period, but quarterly average M1 continued to increase to about 744 billion dollars over that time.

From the third quarter of 1987 through the second quarter of 1990, the fifth sub-sample period, velocity increased most quarters, reaching about 7.19 times per year by the second quarter of 1990. M1 increased most quarters during that interval, reaching about 806 billion dollars by the second quarter of 1990.

Then, velocity fell for fourteen consecutive quarters during the sixth sub-sample period (the third quarter of 1990 through the last quarter in 1993) to approximately 6.07 times per year, while M1 increased to roughly 1,122 billion (or 1.122 trillion) dollars during that period. In the first quarter of 1994, the velocity of M1 began a period of 28 consecutive quarters of increases, through the fourth quarter of 2000 (marking the beginning and the end of the seventh sub-sample period), reaching approximately 9.27 times per year. M1 at the end of that period was roughly 1.093 trillion dollars, slightly less than it was in the fourth quarter of 1993. The local minimum of M1 during that time was roughly 1.065 trillion dollars during the second quarter of 1997.

Velocity then decreased in eight out of the next ten quarters from the first quarter of 2001 through the second quarter of 2003 (the eighth sub-sample period), reaching a local minimum of approximately 8.70 times per year in the second quarter of 2003. Over that time, M1 increased almost every quarter, and was roughly 1.266 trillion dollars in the second quarter of 2003.

In the third quarter of 2003, velocity began to increase for eighteen consecutive quarters (the ninth sub-sample period), reaching a maximum of approximately 10.37 times per year in the fourth quarter of 2007. M1 increased in twelve of those eighteen quarters, with the quarterly average of monthly M1 data reaching roughly 1.375 trillion dollars in the fourth quarter of 2007 (but having reached roughly 1.381 trillion dollars in the first and second quarters of 2006).

Over the next twenty-one quarters, from the first quarter of 2008 through the first quarter of 2013 (the tenth sub-sample period), velocity decreased in eighteen of the twenty-one quarters, having fallen to roughly 6.99 times per year by the first quarter of 2012 and roughly 6.47 times per year by the first quarter of 2013. M1 increased in each quarter during that period, reaching roughly 2.47 trillion dollars by the first quarter of 2013. This represents an increase in the quarterly average of M1 data of roughly 79.6 per cent between the fourth quarter of 2007 and the first quarter of 2013. Using quarterly average data, the first quarter of 2013 was the seventh consecutive quarter in which the percentage increase in the M1 money supply was greater than fifty per cent from five years earlier. From the third quarter of 2011 through the first quarter of 2013, the percentage increases in the M1 money supply from five years earlier are approximately as follows: 51.9, 57.4, 61.9, 64.4, 70.7, 76.3, and 78.5.

The only other quarters in the sample period of quarterly data (which began with the first quarter of 1959) where the percentage increases in M1 from five years ago were greater than fifty per cent were from the first quarter of 1986 through the fourth quarter of 1988. The maximum of these was in the second quarter of 1987, when the percentage increase in M1 was approximately 66.5 per cent from the second quarter of 1982 through the second quarter of 1987. In the second quarter of 1987, the velocity of M1 reached a local minimum of approximately 6.297 times per year. Given that a relatively rapid increase in the M1 money supply in both the mid-1980s and the present time has accompanied a noticeable decrease in velocity, could increases in the money supply in some sense 'cause' decreases in velocity when money supply growth exceeds nominal GDP growth? Further, does this mean that a money supply level exists, at least some of the time, where further increases in the money supply would have to create a decrease in velocity? Has the U.S. economy already surpassed such a money supply level so that further increases in the money supply will be of limited benefit for a while in terms of *directly* spurring economic growth? More direct discussion of the possibility of such a money supply level continues in the next section which deals with the Great Depression and the World War II era.

VELOCITY IN THE GREAT DEPRESSION/WORLD WAR II ERA

As noted at the end of the previous section, another period of interest related to the velocity of M1 in the United States is the Great Depression and World War II era. This period is not included in the sample period mentioned earlier because quarterly or monthly data for at least some of the variables in this study are not readily available prior to 1959. Because this book emphasizes the period starting in 1959 and running through the first quarter of 2013 and particularly the most recent of those years, while the topic turns to the Great Depression and World War II era, more discussion of economic conditions possibly related to the M1 money supply and its velocity during the Great Depression and war period will be presented in the current chapter, while the discussion of economic conditions possibly related to changes in M1 and its velocity for the period beginning in 1959 will be presented in later chapters. (This is not to say, however, that economic conditions possibly related to M1 and its velocity in the Great Depression/World War II era will not be discussed further in other chapters.)

According to Burton and Lombra (2006, pp. 234, 485), the money supply initially decreased substantially during the Great Depression as thousands of banks failed. Until the Glass-Steagall Act, as Burton and Lombra (2006, pp. 287, 302) point out, no deposit insurance existed in the U.S. to protect depositors in the event of a bankruptcy. Thus, the passive allowance of bank failures by the Federal Reserve was probably largely responsible for a sharp decrease in the money supply between 1929 and 1933. Also, as Burton and Lombra (2006, p. 485) point out, an increase in the fraction of currency to bank deposits occurred (probably because many nervous depositors converted bank deposits to cash as bank failures surged in the absence of deposit insurance), and banks opted to increase dramatically their holdings of excess reserves to try to ensure solvency. Burton and Lombra (2006, p. 485) state that excess reserves skyrocketed from (approximately) $25 million in 1929 to surpass the $2 billion mark in 1933, and the fraction of cash to bank deposits nearly doubled over those years. For those not familiar with the money supply process, it turns out that both the surge in excess reserves and the surge in cash holdings relative to deposits would, all other things equal, lead to a decrease in the money supply. Chapter 7 has more information on the money supply process.

I have some data which I believe are from the *Statistical History of the United States from Colonial Times to the Present* (1976, pp. 224, 263, 992, 1105). (Assume that the data in this chapter on annual M1, nominal GDP, real GDP, the implicit deflator, and velocity in the U.S. for the years 1929 through 1950 are from the *Statistical History of the United States from Colonial Times to the Present* (1976, pp. 224, 263, 992, 1105) unless otherwise stated. Note that velocity from these years also comes from my calculations.) The data show a decrease in the money supply, as M1 fell by approximately twenty-five per cent from 1929 (when it was 26.64 billion dollars) through 1933 (when it reached 19.91 billion dollars), while nominal GNP fell from 103.1 billion dollars to 55.6 billion dollars between those years. Burton and Lombra (2006, p. 231) also point out that between September of 1929 and July of 1932, the Dow Jones Industrial Average plummeted from 381 to 41. Data from Dornbusch, Fischer, and Startz (2008, p. 462) show unemployment rates greater than 14 per cent from 1931 through 1939 (and perhaps beyond, but the data stop in 1939). At the depth of the Great Depression, the unemployment rate in the U.S. reached around 25 per cent for the year 1933. In light of these statistics, did a feeling of despair grip the U.S. economy? Figure 3.2 shows annual M1 and its velocity in the U.S. from 1929 through 1950, similar to the way Figures 2.1 and 3.1 show quarterly average M1 and its velocity from the first quarter of 1959 through the first quarter of 2013.

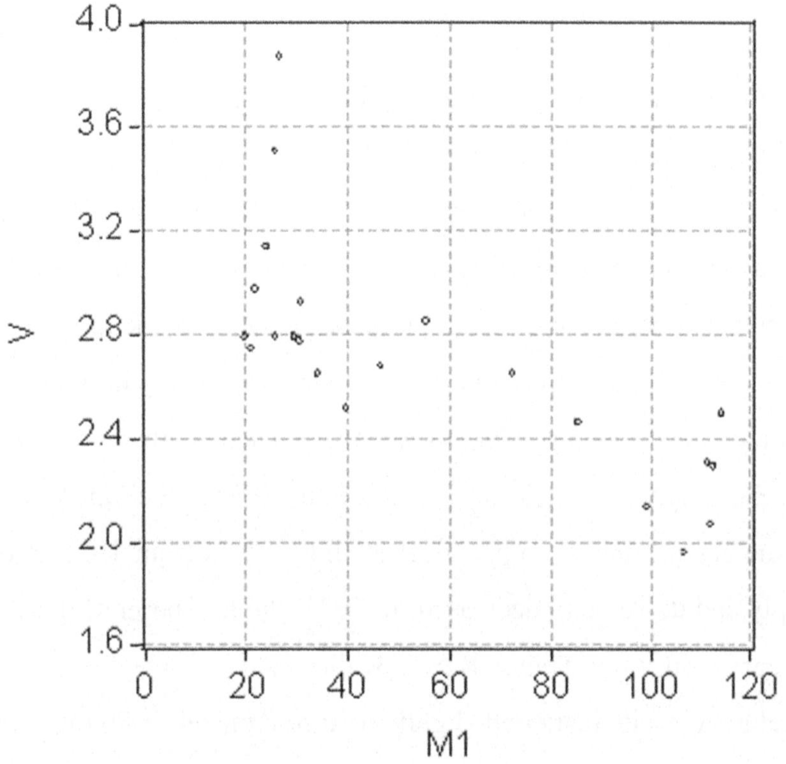

Figure 3.2 M1 Money Supply and the Velocity of the M1 Money Supply
1929 through 1950, annual data
Source: *Statistical History of the United States from Colonial Times to the Present (1976)*, and the author's calculations

Painting in relatively broad brush strokes, the velocity of M1 fell from around 3.87 times per year in 1929 to a local minimum in 1932 around 2.75 times per year, as real GNP, the implicit deflator, nominal GNP, M1, and its velocity all fell. Both real and nominal GNP, the deflator, and M1 all reached minimum values (at least from 1929 through 1950) in the year 1933, one year after the year for the local minimum for velocity. By the low point of the Great Depression in the U.S. in 1933, nominal GNP had decreased from about 103.1 billion dollars in 1929 to about 55.6 billion dollars in 1933, with real GNP decreasing from roughly 203.6 billion 1958-buying-power dollars to roughly 141.5 billion 1958-buying-power dollars between 1929 and 1933, and the implicit deflator declining from 50.6 to 39.3 between those years. As noted above, the M1 money supply had fallen from 26.64 billion dollars in 1929 to 19.91 billion dollars in 1933, with velocity falling from its 1929 level of about 3.87 times per year to around 2.75 times per year in 1932 before rebounding slightly to roughly

2.79 times per year in 1933. (Source: *Statistical History of the United States from Colonial Times to the Present* (1976) and the author's calculations) Also, data from Dornbusch, Fischer, and Startz (2008, p. 462) show that the unemployment rate skyrocketed between 1929 and 1933, rising from an estimated 3.2 per cent to an estimated 24.9 per cent during that period.

Recall that this was a period of numerous bank failures and a sharp decline in the stock market. Could it be that a confluence of events such as the stock market crash of 1929 and the subsequent downward trend in stock indexes, the wave of bank failures, a surge in unemployment, a decrease in confidence, and a decrease in wealth led to a decrease in the non-decreasing-velocity money supply level? If a non-decreasing-velocity money supply level (NDVMSL) existed at this time, then the NDVMSL had apparently fallen in part due to the bank failures and plummeting stock indexes to a money supply level smaller than the actual money supply level in those years from 1929 through 1932 as both the M1 money supply and its velocity decreased. In 1933, the low point of macroeconomic activity during the Great Depression in the United States, while real GNP, the deflator, nominal GNP, and M1 continued to decline, velocity increased slightly to approximately 2.79 times per year. Therefore, if a NDVMSL existed, then the further decrease in the M1 money supply from approximately 21.1 billion dollars to roughly 19.9 billion dollars between 1932 and 1933 likely brought the M1 money supply below the NDVMSL because the velocity of M1 increased slightly as the economy reached the bottom of the Great Depression.

M1 rebounded from its low around 19.9 billion dollars in 1933 so that it had increased by more than fifty per cent by 1937 and wound up increasing by more than five-fold from 1933 to 1946. From 1934 through 1946, the only year in which M1 decreased was 1938, when M1 fell by less than 1.3 per cent from its 1937 level. Information from Burton and Lombra (2006, pp. 231, 234, 236) suggests that the passage of the Glass-Steagall Act of 1933, among other things, established deposit insurance and was followed by a sharp drop in the number of bank failures in the United States. This could have accomplished much in terms of restoring confidence to a shaken economy.

Although the resemblance of the economy to a downward spiral without an end in the foreseeable future may have been over, there were likely some 'fits and starts' as the economy struggled to return to where it was before the collapse. In 1934 and 1935, the annual real GNP growth rates were between nine and ten per cent, and the unemployment rate fell both years from the 1933 peak of 24.9 per cent to 20.1 per cent in 1935. Then in 1936, the growth rate of real GNP accelerated to nearly fourteen per cent before slowing to about five per cent in 1937. The unemployment rate declined to 16.9 per cent in 1936 and 14.3 per cent in 1937. Real GNP in 1937 had nearly returned to its level in 1929. Attention turned to reducing the budget deficits that had increased during the Great Depression. An effort that nearly balanced the federal budget in 1938 was accompanied by a decrease in real GNP of about five per cent and a surge in the unemployment rate to nineteen per cent that year. Positive growth returned in 1939 and 1940, with real GNP increasing by roughly 8.5 per cent in each of those years. (Source: *Statistical History of the United States from Colonial Times to the Present* (1976), Dornbusch, Fischer, and Startz (2008, p. 462); and the author's calculations)

After falling sharply for three consecutive years from 1930 through 1932, the years 1933 through 1938 may have been somewhat erratic ones for finding a clear trend in the velocity of M1. The velocity of M1 fluctuated between 2.77 times per year and 2.98 times per year from 1933 through 1938. Velocity exhibited two short-term 'spike-ups' during this period in 1934 and 1937. In 1934, M1 velocity rose from roughly 2.79 times per year in 1933 to about 2.98 times per year, only to decrease to about 2.79 times per year the following year. In 1937, the velocity of M1 jumped up again, this time from around 2.79 times per year in 1936 to around 2.92 times per year, only to fall to about 2.78 times per year in 1938. The decrease in velocity in 1938 was likely the result of the noticeable decrease in nominal GNP mentioned above. While the M1 money supply decreased slightly between 1937 and 1938, real GNP decreased and the deflator declined slightly. The years 1939 and 1940 saw increasing money supply and increasing real GNP combined with declining velocity. The money supply growth was likely an important factor behind the decrease in velocity, given that nominal GNP increased in both of those years, implying an increase in total GNP spending. In 1940, nominal GNP was still below its level in 1929 (although real GNP surpassed its 1929-level by 1939). (Source: *Statistical History of the United States from Colonial Times to the Present* (1976) and the author's calculations) Thus, if a NDVMSL existed in the U.S. economy in 1939 and 1940, the increases in the money supply in these years could have pushed the money supply above that level.

The years 1941 and 1942 brought rising M1 and rising velocity to the U.S. economy. The increase in velocity was probably due to nominal GNP rising at a much faster rate in those years than it rose in 1939 and 1940. From 1942 through 1946, the M1 money supply in the United States nearly doubled, from about 55.36 billion dollars to roughly 106.46 billion dollars. In fact, the M1 money supply growth rate between 1942 and 1943 was roughly 30.5 per cent, clearly the largest annual growth rate between 1930 and 1950. Notice that it was in the year 1943 when the velocity of M1 started to decrease again. The three year span from 1942 through 1944 had the fastest growth rate of M1 of any three-year span in the Great Depression/World War II era in the U.S., with the last two of those years occurring during a period of declining M1 velocity. (Source: *Statistical History of the United States from Colonial Times to the Present* (1976) and the author's calculations)

It could be that the relatively rapid growth in M1 was the main factor behind the decrease in M1 velocity, as real GNP growth was quite rapid from 1941 through 1944, likely due largely to the increase in federal government spending that was part of the war effort. If a NDVMSL existed during this period, the rapid money supply growth could have driven the money supply level above the NDVMSL during the years in which velocity fell. The decline in M1 velocity in 1945 and 1946 is understandable given that real GNP fell during those years, slightly in 1945 and more rapidly in 1946, with velocity falling to about 1.96 times per year, while the M1 money supply continued to grow. (Source: *Statistical History of the United States from Colonial Times to the Present* (1976) and the author's calculations) A diagram in Baumol and Blinder (2012, p. 298) and subsequent data from www.economagic.com suggest that the velocity of M1 in the United States in the year 1946 is the minimum value for the velocity of M1 at any point from 1929 through 2012 (and beyond).

Based on data from the *Statistical History of the United States from Colonial Times to the Present* (1976) and my calculations, the U.S. economy experienced greater velocity of money each year starting in 1947 and running through 1950, while the M1 money supply increased each of those years except 1949, when it decreased by roughly one per cent. In the years when the money supply increased from 1947 through 1950, it increased at a slower rate than it had increased from 1939 through 1946.

Incomes grew during the war, but people in the U.S. probably wound up saving some of the additional income due in part to the war. After the war ended, it appears that pent-up demand was released, and people went out and spent. This could have caused an increase in the NDVMSL by a dollar amount greater than the increase in the actual money supply, so that although the money supply rose most years from 1947 through 1950, the actual money supply was below a possible NDVMSL during those years. This would have enabled growth in the velocity of money, particularly when the growth rate in the money supply level slowed down.

As implied above, the war efforts could also help to explain the decrease in the velocity of money from after 1942 through 1945 as the people who received new income did not have normal spending possibilities. After the end of the war, perhaps people in the U.S. economy were more ready, willing, and able to spend than during the Depression years. However, the large increase in real federal government expenditures (as I calculate from data in Baumol and Blinder (2012, last page (unnumbered before inside back cover))) in the early- and-mid-1940s, all other things equal, would have led to an increase in velocity. This last point shows the potential importance of the war reducing spending opportunities when trying to understand declining velocity after 1942 through 1945.

Regardless of whether the war effort had such effects on the velocity of money in the United States, the rapid increase in the money supply probably did have a negative impact on the velocity of money. In addition to the decrease in M1 velocity after 1942 through 1946, the velocity of M1 trended downward after 1934 through 1940 (despite increases in M1 velocity in 1936 and 1937). The M1 money supply nearly doubled between 1933 and 1940 and again between 1942 and 1946. By analogy, the rapid increase in the money supply in the U.S. economy after the fourth quarter of 2007, combined with sluggish growth in nominal GDP, explain the rapid decrease in the velocity of M1 since then. Although the growth rate of nominal GNP was faster between 1942 and 1946 (despite a slight decrease in nominal GNP between 1945 and 1946) than the growth rate of nominal GDP between the fourth quarter of 2007 and the fourth quarter of 2012, the money supply also grew at a faster rate from 1942 to 1946 than from the fourth quarter of 2007 to the fourth quarter of 2012, Similarly, despite the fact that nominal GDP increased by nearly eighty per cent from 1933 through 1940, the M1 money supply increased by an even larger percentage over that time, which explains the general decline in the velocity of the M1 money supply over that time despite some temporary upward spikes. (Source: *Statistical History of the United States from Colonial Times to the Present* (1976), www.economagic.com, and the author's calculations)

As noted earlier, this study relies mainly on M1 to represent the money supply because, as Burton and Lombra (2006, p. 29) suggest, M1 more closely matches the definition of money than M2. However, this study also considers M2 for possible insights. Data from the *Statistical History of the United States from Colonial Times to the Present* (1976) and my calculations indicate that in the Great Depression in the United States, M1 decreased less in percentage terms between 1929 and 1933 than did M2. M1 also increased more rapidly in percentage terms from its 1933 minimum than did M2, at least through 1950. For example, the average annual estimate for M1 in 1945 was about 4.98 times the size of M1 in 1933, while the average annual estimate for M2 in 1945 was roughly 3.93 times as large as the estimate for 1933. Does this finding impact velocity data? The velocity of M1 fell by roughly 23.5 per cent between 1933 and 1945, while the velocity of M2 fell by only about 3 per cent over that time. (Earlier, from 1929 to 1933, the velocity of M2 fell by roughly 22 per cent, while the velocity of M1 fell by nearly 28 per cent with the declines from 1929 through 1932 roughly 27 per cent for M2 velocity and approximately 29 per cent M1 velocity.) Given that the monetary aggregate (M1 or M2) is the only difference in the formula used to calculate the velocity of either M1 or M2, it appears that the level of the money supply can impact velocity. Do these facts about M1 versus M2 suggest that during the Great Depression and World War II era, a 'flight to quality' in money holdings by people in the United States (and perhaps in other countries) occurred, much in the same way that risk aversion in contemporary times could have caused M1 to increase by a higher percentage than M2 as the United States economy struggles to return to trend GDP? Could low interest rates have played a role? Are there other explanations?

INITIAL QUESTIONS ABOUT AND CRITICISMS OF THE NDVMSL THEORY

One of the reasons why to my knowledge relatively little, if any, attention has been given to the theoretical possibility of a money supply level beyond which the velocity of money must decrease and its implications for policy (although a passage in Baumol and Blinder (2012, p. 298) does point out a reason why increasing money supply could lead to lower velocity) is because much of the time, the money supply has been less than that level, and at times possibly far below that level, if the theory holds and the level exists. Over the full sample period of quarterly data from the first quarter of 1959 through the first quarter of 2013, both the M1 money supply and its velocity generally increased (despite some notable drops in velocity, especially the decline after the fourth quarter of 2007), and frequently both have increased the same quarter. If both the money supply and its velocity increase in the same quarter, then the money supply level after its increase could not have been greater than the NDVMSL for that quarter, if such a level existed.

In fact, one familiar with the 1970s through 1980 may think (without looking at the actual data) that while the money supply was increasing (often at a rate more rapid than in the 1960s), it may have been more likely that the U.S. economy found itself at a point where a negative AS shock resulted in lower real GDP but higher nominal GDP (due to higher inflation) and thus also an increase in velocity (despite an increase in the money supply most of these quarters) rather than finding itself at a point where increasing money supply growth was associated with decreasing velocity during those years. Again, if the money supply and velocity were both increasing, and if a NDVMSL existed at that time, then the money supply must have been less than the NDVMSL for velocity to have increased.

In the forty-four quarters of the years 1970 through 1980, the velocity of M1 decreased in only seven quarters, increasing every other quarter during this period. Thus, there were a maximum of seven quarters from 1970 through 1980 when the money supply could have been greater than the hypothesized NDVMSL. This is despite the fact that over the forty-four quarter period, the quarterly average M1 money supply increased each quarter except one, the second quarter of 1980 (when real GDP decreased but velocity increased and nominal GDP increased slightly).

This time period may bring to mind negative aggregate supply shocks, which were introduced in Chapter 1. If negative aggregate supply shocks such as energy crises dominate the impact of positive aggregate demand shocks (and perhaps also factors such as improvements in technology leading to positive aggregate supply shocks), then in the short term, data would show higher price levels (and usually higher inflation) but lower real GDP. The negative AS shocks could lead to higher nominal GDP if the increase in the price level dominates the decrease in real GDP in the calculation of nominal GDP.

Of the ten quarters when real GDP decreased but nominal GDP increased over the forty-four quarters beginning with 1970 and running through 1980, velocity increased in seven of those quarters and decreased in three. (The three quarters when velocity decreased during the negative AS shocks were among the seven quarters when the M1 money supply increased and its velocity decreased.) Thus, the number of quarters during this eleven-year period when real GDP decreased but nominal GDP increased was greater than the number of quarters when the money supply increased but velocity decreased. However, more related to the initial point about increasing velocity during negative AS shocks versus a possible NDVMSL, the number of quarters during this period when velocity increased during a negative AS shock (seven) was the same as the number of quarters when an increase in the money supply may have 'pushed down' velocity (seven). But, with rising inflation, energy crises, and other problems of the era, people at that time (and other times) may not have thought much about the relationship between velocity and the money supply.

The purpose of this book is not to offer definitive proof of the hypothesis that a non-decreasing-velocity money supply level exists. Rather, one of the goals of this work is to raise this hypothesis as a theoretical possibility and, if the hypothesis holds, then to point out that the hypothesis helps to explain the recent inability of monetary policy in the U.S. to stimulate a more robust recovery. Even if the hypothesis does not hold, then economists must attempt to explain the pronounced drop in the velocity of M1 while the nominal M1 money supply has increased rapidly.

Maybe the aforementioned periodic negative relationship between M1 and its velocity is coincidental because M1 has no impact on its velocity. However, given that (1) the money supply appears in the denominator of the formula used to calculate velocity, and (2) from the first quarter of 2008 through the first quarter of 2013 velocity decreased every quarter except for three quarters while the M1 money supply in the U.S. has increased at a rapid rate, does it make sense to argue that the velocity of money is unrelated to the supply of money?

The NDVMSL theory is at odds with the view that velocity is purely random. If a NDVMSL exists, and if the actual money supply level is greater than the cut-off point, then velocity must fall. Data from www.economagic.com and the author's calculations show that the rapid increase in the M1 money supply, by roughly 79.6 per cent (using the quarterly average of monthly data) from the fourth quarter of 2007 through the first quarter of 2013, has not been accompanied by a comparable increase in nominal GDP or its components, real GDP and the implicit GDP deflator (divided by 100). From the fourth quarter of 2007 through the first quarter of 2013, nominal GDP has increased by only approximately 12.1 per cent. (The reader should recall that from the equation of exchange, velocity equals nominal GDP divided by the money supply.)

Based on these observations from the fourth quarter of 2007 through the first quarter of 2013, why are people in the United States economy holding so many more dollars in a form liquid enough to be counted as part of M1 when many of the newly added dollars may not be held for spending on nominal GDP? Based on the information about the Great Depression and World War II era, could we also ask why people held nearly twice as many dollars in M1 forms in 1946 as they held in 1942 when nominal GNP increased by only about 32 per cent (a small corresponding increase compared to the percentage increase in the money supply)?

Perhaps extremely low interest rates in the early-to-mid-1940s and the modern-day U.S. economy help to explain the rapid increase in holdings of liquid assets, including the components of M1. (Readers should realize that growth in nominal output and real output was often relatively high in the early-to-mid-1940s, in contrast to the U.S. economy today.) In a sense, the rapid increase in the M1 money supply over both of those periods may have been 'pushing down' the velocity of money. That is, the money supply had increased more rapidly than the total output spending plans of the various spenders who purchased goods produced in the U.S. economy, such as U.S. households, U.S. firms, U.S. government sectors, and those in other countries who buy U.S.-made goods.

But, if the increase in the M1 money supply was in some sense responsible for causing the decrease in velocity, it is not a mere coincidence that increases in the money supply sometimes occur when the velocity of money falls. Velocity also appears *not* to be completely random given that velocity can be calculated from a formula which is comprised of components that are likely not completely random.

Classical macroeconomic analysis assumed that velocity was usually nearly constant in the short term. If velocity is constant, then it would make little sense, in my opinion, to ask whether a money supply level exists beyond which further increases in the money supply decrease velocity. Although the view that velocity is constant would qualify as criticism of NDVMSL theory, my reading of decades of data is that velocity is clearly not constant.

Some may feel that even if a NDVMSL exists, then its existence is trivial. However, given that the recent reliance on monetary policy rather than fiscal policy to complete the recovery in the U.S. has helped somewhat but has come up far short as of this writing of returning real GDP to its trend, is it trivial that millions of people in the U.S. are looking for jobs?! Is it trivial that so many do not have adequate nutrition?! Is it trivial that so many businesses have gone out of business?! Is it trivial that for years now the U.S. economy clearly has been capable of sustainably producing more goods with its resources and technology?! Of course, monetary policy could benefit from estimating where the NDVMSL lies and by how much velocity would decrease if the money supply would increase past the NDVMSL.

In my view, a better criticism of the theory of a non-decreasing-velocity money supply level than either suggesting that velocity is constant or that what seems to be a relationship between M1 and its velocity is merely a coincidence or is trivial or that velocity is random is that without the expansionary monetary policy implemented recently in the United States, a much deeper downturn in the U.S. would have occurred, and the deeper downturn would have resulted in a larger decrease in velocity. By providing liquidity and keeping interest rates low, perhaps the expansionary monetary policy prevented an even greater number of defaults from occurring and prevented an even larger decrease in aggregate demand and nominal GDP. (Nominal GDP decreased by approximately 3.7 per cent between the second quarter of 2008 (the local maximum) and the second quarter of 2009 (the local minimum) based on data from www.economagic.com and the author's calculations but conceivably could have decreased by more without the expansionary monetary policy.)

For a hypothetical example, suppose that if the U.S. quarterly average money supply had not changed since the fourth quarter of 2007, then U.S. nominal GDP would have decreased by fifty per cent from the fourth quarter of 2007 through the fourth quarter of 2012. (This is a hypothetical example for illustrative purposes and does not necessarily reflect what would have happened in the U.S. economy in the absence of a large increase in the money supply after the fourth quarter of 2007.) Assuming no change in the money supply from the fourth quarter of 2007 through the fourth quarter of 2012 but a fifty per cent decrease in nominal GDP, then the velocity of money would have fallen by fifty per cent. Given that the velocity of money in the actual data decreased by approximately 36.9 per cent rather than fifty per cent, the recent expansionary monetary policy in the U.S. *may* have actually *in*creased velocity compared with what the velocity of money would have been in the hypothetical scenario above even though looking at the actual economic data from quarter to quarter could lead to the conclusion that the greater money supply has caused the velocity of M1 to decrease nearly every quarter after the fourth quarter of 2007.

To sum up, two ways of viewing the impact of the recent expansionary monetary policy in the U.S. are that (1) increases in the money supply, combined with slow growth in nominal GDP, caused velocity to fall from quarter to quarter in the actual data, and (2) increases in the money supply prevented a larger downturn and may have increased velocity compared to what velocity would have been without the expansionary monetary policy. The former is clearly consistent with NDVMSL theory, while the latter could be viewed as a criticism. To avoid ambiguity, the theory of a non-decreasing-velocity money supply level deals with changes in observed data from one quarter to the next or from one year to the next rather than dealing with actual data versus hypothetical data.

Another question to consider is 'Does the theory of a non-decreasing-velocity money supply level assume that velocity would not decrease without a change in the money supply?' The answer to this question is somewhat complicated. During a period when the money supply is growing rapidly as is the case as of this writing in the United States, the theory suggests that if the money supply increases above (or is already above and remains above) a certain level which depends on several factors including spending plans, then velocity must fall. In turn, this implies that if the money supply remains below (or perhaps winds up at or below) that level, then velocity would either increase or perhaps remain unchanged. However, the recent financial crisis in the U.S. probably led to a decrease in the non-decreasing-velocity money supply level. Of course, if a non-decreasing-velocity level of money supply exists, and if it decreased recently in the U.S., then it is easier to recognize in hindsight that it may have decreased substantially as the U.S. economy has generated more than six years of data since the peak of M1 velocity.

Even if one takes the view that the velocity of money would have decreased in the U.S. after the fourth quarter of 2007 without an increase in the money supply, then this view would still be consistent with the NDVMSL theory. In NDVMSL theory, the reader should recall that the NDVMSL can decrease with no change in the money supply level, which in turn could lead to a decrease in velocity without an increase in the money supply. Additionally, the NDVMSL could potentially increase without a change in the money supply level and possibly lead to an increase in velocity without any change in the money supply.

If one wants to emphasize the comparison of actual velocity data to what would have happened hypothetically to velocity, then one should realize that, given the rapid increase in M1 recently in the U.S., nominal GDP spending would have grown much more rapidly (and may have returned real GDP to trend by now) had velocity not fallen. However, NDVMSL theory, if it holds, offers an explanation for the decrease in velocity in that money supply growth has placed the money supply beyond the NDVMSL almost every quarter in the U.S. after the fourth quarter of 2007, forcing velocity to fall.

In light of data from the U.S. early in the Great Depression when money supply, velocity, nominal GNP, real GNP, and the deflator all decreased for three consecutive years (with all of those variables except velocity continuing to decline for a fourth year); it is certain that velocity can decrease without an increase in the money supply. But again, the NDVMSL theory acknowledges that the NDVMSL can increase, decrease, or remain unchanged based on economic conditions. To give one example, if a NDVMSL existed just before the Great Depression, then various factors associated with a large decrease in aggregate demand led to a decline in the NDVMSL. For another example, if NDVMSL theory holds, then the fact that M1 growth has by far surpassed nominal GDP growth in the U.S. during the Great Recession and the Not-So-Great Recovery has an important impact on the policy responses most likely to stimulate growth in real GDP and to reduce unemployment rates.

More work remains to determine whether the NDVMSL actually exists. But, if it does exist, then what factors determine when it exists (if it exists only some of the time) and what factors impact the size of any such NDVMSL? The 'In-Chapter' Appendix in Chapter 8 discusses what may be the first step in estimating and forecasting any NDVMSL that may exist by looking at categories of possible relationships between nominal M1 growth and nominal GDP growth over a very short time horizon.

Additional work remains as to whether a NDVMSL exists in a hyperinflationary economy. General agreement may not exist as to what inflation rate would be the minimum rate of hyperinflation, but most if not nearly all would likely agree that the inflation rate would have to be at least 100 per cent per year to be considered hyperinflation, and many would likely say that the minimum inflation rate that is consistent with hyperinflation is much higher. At a 100 per cent inflation rate where prices on average double every year, the price level as measured by either the implicit deflator or the consumer price index could be so sensitive to changes in the money supply in the short term that a NDVMSL may possibly not exist in a hyperinflationary environment. (To my knowledge, hyperinflationary economies are always associated with very rapid money supply growth, although the timing of the rapid money supply growth may not be clear.) Data on the velocity of money in such economies could be illuminating.

MORE ABOUT VELOCITY IN THE SCHOOLS OF MACROECONOMIC THOUGHT

Mishkin (2004, pp. 518-519) traces the origins of the study of the velocity of money to the work of (1) Irving Fisher (in the United States) and (2) economists in England (more specifically, Cambridge). These works mentioned by Mishkin (2004, pp. 518-519) would fall in the classical school of macroeconomic thought. While Mishkin (2004, pp. 518-519) notes that in Fisher's work velocity was usually close to constant in the short term, Mishkin (2004, p. 518) also points out that Fisher studied transactions velocity and that Fisher's analysis stated that the money supply multiplied by transactions velocity equals the average price of total transactions multiplied by the total number of transactions in the economy per time period. Rather than transactions velocity, most analysis of velocity today including the current book emphasizes what Dornbusch, Fischer, and Startz (2008, p. 386) and many others call income velocity, which measures the number of times each unit of currency trades per period (on average) in GDP transactions.

In an extreme form, the classical school of macroeconomic thought assumes that prices and other factors adjust very rapidly to disturbances. Thus, if the economy is not performing optimally, the best option in an extreme view of classical macroeconomics is simply to wait while prices and other factors rapidly adjust to return the economy to the optimal outcome which has the greatest sustainable output level possible.

Dissatisfaction resulting from what seems to have been an extended departure of real output and employment from acceptable levels during the Great Depression perhaps gave rise to the Keynesian and monetarist schools of macroeconomic thought. The fact that the rapid decrease in the money supply and the Dow Jones Industrial Average and the surge in bank failures coincided with the Great Depression (Burton and Lombra (2006, pp. 231, 485)), helps to explain (1) why monetarists may have concluded (as may be implied by Burton and Lombra (2006, p. 516)) that the decrease in the money supply was perhaps the main cause of the Great Depression, and (2) why some may have concluded that factors such as the wave of bank failures and the stock market crash were the main culprits by leading to the Great Depression. The falling money supply, the plummeting DJIA, and the surging bank failures could have been related to explanations that Dornbusch, Fischer, and Startz (2008, p. 467) attribute to the Keynesian school of thought – those being (1) massive decreases in business' spending on new buildings, machines, and possibly also new inventories, and (2) perhaps also a sharp drop in consumption spending by households. Regarding the impact of the money supply on aggregate demand, Keynesian analysis, according to Mishkin (2004, pp. 585-586, 604, 607-608) focuses on the impact of the money supply on interest rates and then in turn on the impact of interest rates on investment in physical capital, although many early Keynesian economists may have disregarded the potential importance of monetary policy.

The reader should realize that a relationship probably existed between the decrease in the money supply and the bank failures, high real interest rates, and possibly also the stock market crash. Any of these events alone, all other things equal, would lead to a decrease in aggregate demand. To the extent that these events were interrelated, the contention of Dornbusch, Fischer, and Startz (2008, p. 469) that monetarist analysis and Keynesian analysis of the Great Depression are not mutually exclusive has merit. Mishkin (2004, p. 521) notes that during the Great Depression, economists for (perhaps) the first time understood that the velocity of money decreased during recessions and depressions. As noted above, both the money supply and velocity were simultaneously decreasing for the first few years in the Great Depression.

From a monetarist perspective, the substantial decrease in the U.S. money supply between 1929 and 1933 was likely the main reason for the severity of the Great Depression. Could it be that the rapid decrease in the money supply (from 26.64 billion dollars in 1929 to 19.91 billion dollars in 1933), by spurring a large economic downturn, was the main reason for the decrease in the velocity of M1, approximately twenty-eight per cent between 1929 and 1933 (and roughly twenty-nine per cent between 1929 and 1932)? (Source: *Statistical History of the United States from Colonial Times to the Present* (1976) and the author's calculations) A conclusive answer to this question may be elusive, but the view that a decrease in the M1 money supply was the main cause of the decrease in the velocity of M1 raises questions.

First, the NDVMSL theory as stated recognizes that if a NDVMSL exists, then this money supply level can decrease based on economic factors. Would not a NDVMSL, if it exists, have decreased as the result of a large decrease in aggregate demand? Second, monetarist economic analysis assumes that the velocity of money is predictable to some extent, according to Baumol and Blinder (2012, p. 298) and Burton and Lombra (2006, pp. 516-517). Would monetarist analysis have predicted that the velocity of M1 would have decreased by approximately twenty-nine per cent based on a decrease in the money supply of roughly twenty-five per cent? Additionally, the M1 money supply nearly doubled from 1942 through 1946, from approximately 55.36 billion dollars to 106.46 billion dollars. Yet, during those years, the velocity of M1 fell from roughly 2.85 times per year to roughly 1.96 times per year. (Source: *Statistical History of the United States from Colonial Times to the Present* (1976) and the author's calculations) If the decrease in the velocity of M1 by approximately twenty-nine per cent from 1929 through 1932 was mainly due to a decrease in the M1 money supply, then would not the rapid increase in the M1 money supply lead monetarists to a prediction of a higher velocity of money between 1942 and 1946 rather than the decrease as shown by the data?

However, the view that falling velocity early in the Great Depression in the U.S. was the result of falling money supply (leading to a much larger decline in nominal GDP) could be similar to the aforementioned view that much higher money supply levels recently in the U.S. led to velocity being much higher than it would have been without the expansionary policy. The latter is one of the criticisms of NDVMSL theory mentioned above. With the information available as of this writing, these alternative viewpoints should not be dismissed summarily.

From a different perspective, were the changes in the velocity of money during the Great Depression predictable enough to satisfy the monetarists' characterization of velocity as being predictable to some degree? What about what happened to the velocity of M1 in the United States starting in the early 1980s? Was the velocity of M1 predictable then? And why has the rapid increase in the money supply in the U.S. starting in 2008 not generated a much larger increase in nominal GDP? Despite these questions, if the large decrease in the United States money supply was the main reason why the Great Depression was so severe in the U.S., modern policymakers seem committed to preventing such a decrease in the money supply following a financial crisis from happening again in modern times. Thus, the rapid increase in the money supply starting in early 2008 could have helped prevent a downturn much worse.

In terms of questions for the Keynesian school of thought, why did velocity appear to follow fairly closely to a trend line (into the early 1980s) for more than twenty years? Doesn't that seem to be predictable? Why do so many Keynesian economists today, with the possible exception of those in monetary policy circles and those in some financial markets (and maybe a few academic circles), *seem* to *almost* forget about the velocity of money? While velocity is not constant, and some may argue that it is not predictable, the fact that the velocity of money depends on real output, the implicit deflator, and the money supply, all important macroeconomic variables, implies that velocity may also be an important macroeconomic variable. For example, changes in the velocity of money imply changes in the relationship between nominal output and the money supply. Information about this changing relationship could help improve our understanding of the economy.

A further question for the Keynesian school of thought is why haven't the increases in government spending and tax reductions, both of which would be stimulus measures, led to faster growth? The likely answer in the Keynesian school of thought is that the stimulus measures did help as the U.S. economy has been growing since 2009 (at least through the first quarter of 2013 based on data from www.economagic.com accessed July 20, 2013), but (1) the stimulus measures could have been comparable to trying to apply a small bandage to a gaping wound, and (2) a measure of total government expenditures (federal, state, and local) fell about 4.5 per cent from the second quarter of 2009 through the second quarter of 2012, as noted by Wiseman (2012), while they normally increase during other recoveries. The sharp decrease in the velocity of money starting in the first quarter of 2008 is perhaps most consistent with the Keynesian school of thought (unless the decrease has been predictable).

Supporters of the classical school of thought could point to falling home prices as an appropriate adjustment given the decrease in the demand for housing. Further, those working in the classical school of thought could suggest that after housing prices and other factors have adjusted to the drop in demand in the U.S. economy, the economy would return to the trend level of real GDP and the natural rate of unemployment. However, those in other schools of thought may wonder that if prices and other factors always adjust rapidly, then why has this process taken years? Further, has velocity been nearly constant?

Before turning to another topic, let's again view the notion that the velocity of money and also the change in the velocity of money are purely random and without significance, but this time also view it within the context of the three major schools of macroeconomic thought. Although there may be some randomness in velocity and the change in velocity, results from Hartman (2011) and Hartman (2013) lead me to believe that the change in the velocity of M1 is probably not completely random. In turn, the velocity of M1 is probably not completely random. If changes in velocity were completely random, a non-decreasing-velocity money supply level probably would not exist because the existence of such a money supply level would mean that if the money supply were greater than that particular level, then velocity must decrease, implying some degree of predictability. This explanation of velocity being completely random does not fit very well with any of the three main schools of macroeconomic thought. Originally in the classical school of macroeconomic thought, the velocity of money was approximately constant in the short-term in most instances, at least as described by Mishkin (2004, pp. 518-519). But, if velocity is roughly constant most of the time, then velocity is not purely random. According to Burton and Lombra (2006, p. 516-517) and Baumol and Blinder (2012, p. 298), in the monetarist school of macroeconomic thought, the velocity of money is predictable to some degree. But then the velocity of money cannot be totally random. Of the three major schools of macroeconomic thought, velocity is probably the least predictable in the Keynesian school of thought. Nonetheless, it may not be completely random. If, as Mishkin (2004, p. 523) notes, the velocity of money in the Keynesian school of thought can be written in terms of real output and real money demand (the latter of which is a function of interest rates and real income or real output), then velocity is random only insofar as there is no predictable relationship between those determinants.

CHAPTER THREE REFERENCES

Baumol, W. J. and Blinder, A. S. (2012) *Macroeconomics: Principles and Policy*, twelfth edition. South-Western Cengage Learning, Mason, Ohio.

Brunner, K. and Meltzer, A. H. (1963) "Predicting Velocity: Implications for Theory and Policy." *Journal of Finance*, vol. 18, May, pp. 319-354.

Burton, M. and Lombra, R. (2006) *The Financial System and the Economy: Principles of Money and Banking*, fourth edition. Thomson South-Western, Mason, Ohio.

Dornbusch, R., Fischer, S., and Startz, R. (2008) *Macroeconomics*, tenth edition, McGraw-Hill Irwin, Boston, Massachusetts.

Duczynski, P. (n.d.) "The Velocity of Money and Nominal Interest Rates: Evidence from Developed and Latin-American Countries." accessed September 25, 2011; available online at: duczynski.czweb.org/pdf/Velocity.pdf.

Hartman, H. C. (2011) "The Decrease in the Velocity of Money in the United States: Some Possible Causes and Some Implications." *International Journal of Accounting Information Science and Leadership*, vol. 4, iss. 11, pp. 15-27.

Hartman, H. C. (2013) "More about the Decrease in the Velocity of Money in the United States: Some Potential Causes and Policy Implications." *Journal of International Business Management and Research*, vol. 3, iss. 10, pp. 116-138.

Laidler, D. E. W. (1993) *The Demand for Money: Theories, Evidence, and Problems*, fourth edition. Harper Collins College Publishers, New York, New York.

Meltzer, A. H. (1963) "The Demand for Money: the Evidence from the Time Series." *Journal of Political Economy*, vol. 71, June, pp. 219-246.

Mishkin, F. S. (2004) *The Economics of Money, Banking, and Financial Markets*, seventh edition. Pearson Addison Wesley, Boston, Massachusetts.

Omer, M. (2010) "Velocity of Money Functions in Pakistan and Lessons for Monetary Policy." *State Bank of Pakistan Research Bulletin*, vol. 6, no. 2, pp. 37-55. Available online at: www.sbp.org.pk/research/bulletin/2010/Vol06No.2/Omar.pdf

Statistical History of the United States from Colonial Times to the Present. (1976) Introduction by Ben J. Wattenberg. Basic Books, New York, New York.

Wiseman, P. (2012) "Weak Recovery Marked." *Atlanta Journal-Constitution*, August 16, 2012, p. A8.

www.economagic.com

CHAPTER 4

VELOCITY DURING LIQUIDITY TRAPS, NEAR LIQUIDITY TRAPS, AND THE NDVMSL: WHY ARE CORPORATIONS (AND HOUSEHOLDS) HOLDING SUCH LARGE VOLUMES OF 'MONEY' (RATHER THAN OTHER ASSETS OFFERING A HIGHER RETURN)?

WHY IS THE GREAT RECESSION AND THE SUBSEQUENT RECOVERY ATYPICAL? INTEREST RATES AND THEIR EFFECTS

Readers may wonder why the U.S. economy seems to have been in something close to a morass for more than five years. Wading through the discussion in this chapter, part of which deals with liquidity traps (which may provide a rough approximation of the present U.S. economy), will help in better understanding the sub-par recovery. Interest rates play a major role in economies in a liquidity trap (if such economies exist) and economies close to a liquidity trap (my 'take' on the U.S. economy).

Interest rates can have a profound impact on economic activity. Many economists (for example, Dornbusch, Fischer, and Startz (2008, pp. 187-188, 224-228)) note that, all other things the same, higher interest rates discourage firms from investing in physical capital (i.e. new machines, buildings, and inventory). For firms needing to borrow funds to acquire additional physical capital, a higher interest rate on the loan makes it more costly for such firms to borrow. Thus, firms cannot afford to invest in as much capital as before. Higher interest rates on loans can also discourage firms with extra cash from investing in physical capital. More firms with extra cash prefer to lend money rather than buy new buildings and new machines when they can make more money by lending due to higher interest rates paid by loans, all other things the same.

Similarly, higher interest rates on loans make it more costly for consumers to borrow if consumers need access to credit to consume more. Even for consumers fortunate enough to have sufficient financial resources so that they do not need to borrow to consume more, a higher interest rate can discourage consumption by increasing the reward for lending today rather than spending today. While Dornbusch, Fischer, and Startz (2008, pp. 187-188) note that interest rates could affect consumption, Baumol and Blinder (2012, p.157) state that most studies find that interest rates have little impact on consumption.

During recessions, interest rates often decrease, although they usually remain well above zero. As implied by Burton and Lombra (2006, pp. 470-472, 612), the Federal Reserve can increase the growth rate of the money supply by purchasing Treasury bills to reduce the federal funds rate, which will, in turn, lower other interest rates in the economy, all other things equal. As a result, firms' purchases of physical capital (and perhaps also households' consumption) will increase all other things equal, and the economy will recover from the recession.

However, the Great Recession was not a normal downturn, and the Not-So-Great Recovery is an atypical recovery. The recent extended presence of very low interest rates in the United States may more closely resemble the U.S. during the Great Depression and World War II era than during any other time since then.

Extremely low interest rates bring up the possibility of a liquidity trap. If a liquidity trap exists, further increases in the money supply fail to reduce interest rates because they are already very low and could be close to zero. In this environment, dollars added to the money supply are held but not for the purpose of increasing GDP spending in the current period. Consequently, increases in the money supply fail to generate an increase in aggregate demand.

Some economists place *much* more emphasis on the liquidity trap as a theoretical possibility rather than as a practical reality, perhaps even discounting the latter. Dornbusch, Fischer, and Startz (2008, p. 253) who credit Keynes with coming up with the concept of a liquidity trap, also note that in Keynes' (1936) *The General Theory of Employment, Interest, and Money*, Keynes apparently did not know of the actual existence of such an economy. Krugman and Wells (2009, p. 476) credit Hicks (1937) with coining the name 'liquidity trap.' Readers can refer to Dornbusch, Fischer, and Startz (2008, pp. 253-254, 261) or other textbooks for additional information on liquidity traps.

Given the lack of consensus on whether liquidity traps can exist in actual economies, this book will often focus on economies that are close to being in a liquidity trap. Whether an economy is in a liquidity trap or near a liquidity trap, it is more important (at least at this point) to consider the behavior of lenders (and perhaps borrowers) when interest rates are quite low. It makes sense to assume that lenders seeking financial gain through lending would not agree to grant a loan at an interest rate less than zero per cent, thus creating a zero interest rate bound. As Krugman and Wells (2009, p. 463) and others point out, lenders would have more purchasing power by keeping money rather than lending the money at an interest rate less than zero. Hence, monetary policy may not be able to force interest rates below some level.

If liquidity traps do exist and if an economy is in a liquidity trap, further increases in the money supply in that economy *must* cause a decrease in the velocity of money. From the equation of exchange, the velocity of money can be calculated as the price level (the implicit GDP deflator divided by 100) multiplied by real GDP divided by the money supply. If the money supply increases but nominal GDP does not increase (because neither real GDP nor the price level would increase because of an increase in the money supply when the economy is in a liquidity trap), then velocity *must* decrease. Recall that in a liquidity trap, interest rates do not decrease following an increase in the money supply.

Another way to see this uses the realization that velocity is an average for all dollars in circulation. If the economy is in a liquidity trap (and not merely near a liquidity trap), then the velocity of each additional dollar added must be zero. If the velocity of all dollars in circulation was greater than zero before the increase in the money supply, then the additional dollars added which have a velocity of zero *at the margin* in a liquidity trap reduce the overall average velocity of all dollars in circulation including the newly added dollars.

This is like the frequently used example of softball and baseball players, basketball players, or football players. If a softball player or a baseball player has a batting average greater than 0.000 before an at bat but is retired in that at bat, the '0 for 1' of making an out at the margin lowers the player's overall average. The same is true for a basketball player with a free throw percentage greater than zero before attempting a free throw. If the player misses the free throw, the player's free throw percentage falls because of the '0 for 1' performance at the margin. Likewise, a quarterback in football with a completion percentage greater than zero before attempting a pass who throws an incomplete pass receives a reduced completion percentage due to the '0 for 1' incompletion at the margin. Similarly, newly added dollars in a liquidity trap in effect exchange hands zero times in a GDP transaction per period at the margin and bring down the overall velocity.

If liquidity traps do exist, they have clear implications for NDVMSL theory. Because increases in the money supply fail to increase GDP spending in liquidity traps, velocity must decrease following an increase in the money supply. That in turn implies that if the NDVMSL theory holds, the economy is above (or just at) the NDVMSL 'cut-off' before an increase in the money supply if it is in a liquidity trap.

Now suppose that the economy is not literally in a liquidity trap but that interest rates are very low and economic growth is sluggish. What would be the impact of an increase in the money supply in this situation? If the economy is not quite in a liquidity trap but interest rates are very low, an additional increase in the money supply could possibly further reduce interest rates slightly. Lower interest rates could lead to firms spending more buying new machines and building new buildings due to firms' ability to borrow more at a lower cost. Households may also be able to afford to consume more at a lower interest rate. If the velocity of dollars newly added to the money supply is not equal to zero, then the additional dollars added can still lead to higher spending, higher price levels, and higher real GDP.

But if interest rates are already very low and near minimum possible values, further expansionary monetary policy cannot lower interest rates much further assuming that nominal interest rates must be greater than or equal to zero. Thus, firms do not notice much of a reduction in borrowing costs for building new buildings and buying new machines. Households do not notice much of a reduction in the cost of borrowing for additional consumption. Thus, the velocity of newly added dollars *at the margin* would very likely be greater than zero, but it would likely be less than the average velocity of dollars in circulation before the additional increase in the money supply. Under these assumptions, the overall average velocity of money would probably fall, just as the overall average velocity of money would fall if the money supply increased during a time when the economy was in a liquidity trap. In either case, it is as if the additional money supply is driving down the velocity of money because the money supply is growing faster than the public's desire to increase spending. In short, growth in the money supply and growth in spending capacity, the latter introduced in Chapter 2, would be outpacing growth in aggregate demand.

If during an actual liquidity trap, velocity must decrease following an increase in the money supply, then when the economy is close to a liquidity trap but not actually in what is technically a liquidity trap, further increases in the money supply would probably still 'drive down' the velocity of money unless the velocity of money in circulation before the further increase in the money supply was already extremely low. Expansionary monetary policy in effect driving down the velocity of money seems to fit much of the data from the U.S. economy recently.

But, if this is the case, then is it possible that in at least some cases, the money supply in circulation and the capacity to spend could exceed aggregate demand as measured by nominal GDP spending (and perhaps also the total spending) in the economy at that time? This is an important possibility because, if money supply growth and spending capacity growth exceed growth in actual aggregate demand, then the impact of additions to the money stock would then reduce the velocity of money, and this result may not be restricted only to liquidity traps and economies close to being in a liquidity trap.

WHO HOLDS U.S. DOLLARS AND WHY?

The U.S. money supply, as measured by both M1 and M2, has been increasing rapidly recently, starting in the year 2008. Who is holding the newly added U.S. dollars, given that many of them do not seem to be increasing U.S. nominal GDP much? Are people in other countries holding more U.S. dollars, helping to explain the rapid increase in M1 and M2?

FOREIGN DEMAND

People in other countries sometimes want to hold units of currencies from other countries (i.e. people outside the U.S. holding U.S. dollars), as noted by Dornbusch, Fischer, and Startz (2008, p. 377) and others. This could be due to instability or the potential for instability in other countries. For example, in countries experiencing hyperinflation (or extremely high inflation rates), people may begin to use currencies from other countries as better stores of value and thus potentially better media of exchange. But, which country or countries are experiencing hyperinflation that would explain the rapid increase in demand for U.S. dollars so that the U.S. money supply increased by more than seventy per cent from December 2007 through December 2012, based on data from www.economagic.com? The threat of political instability in one country could also cause people to want to hold units of currency from other countries. But again, given that the U.S. is still the largest economy in the world, do political instability and hyperinflation, both in other countries, sufficiently explain the M1 money supply increasing by more than seventy per cent in less than five years?

Further, some from other countries may want to hold U.S. currency because they believe that the U.S. dollar will appreciate (relative to one or more other currencies) and give them capital gains. While the U.S. dollar may appreciate in value, could that explain such rapid growth in M1 in the U.S.? Before answering that question, I should point out that M1 is growing more rapidly than M2. The component parts of M1 either pay a zero nominal interest rate (i.e. currency, some checkable deposits) or a very low nominal interest rate (for example, other checkable deposits). The non-M1 parts of M2 are likely to pay a higher interest rate than the component parts of M1 and would thus give the holder a greater return than holding M1 (and also a greater capital gain if the U.S. dollar appreciates compared with other currencies). Therefore, if currency speculation by those in other countries is the main reason for the growth in the money supply in the United States, why is M1 growing at a faster rate than M2? Note that the fact that non-M1 parts of M2 usually pay a higher expected return than the components of M1 implies that if someone holds equal balances of M1 and non-M1 M2 assets, the latter will grow at a faster rate than M2. This suggests that an increased preference for M1 over non-M1 parts of M2 may have occurred.

Two further reasons why people in other countries may want to hold more dollars would be to purchase more goods produced in the United States and to buy more U.S. assets. Are U.S. exports increasing rapidly enough to suggest that the main reason for the rapid increase in M1 is due to an increase in the demand for U.S. exports? If the surge in the demand for U.S. dollars is primarily due to an increase in demand for U.S. assets, why are the sellers of the assets disproportionately (compared with some earlier times) keeping the proceeds from the asset sales in the form of M1 assets rather than converting the assets to M2-only forms or forms not part of either M1 or M2?

DOMESTIC DEMAND

It is highly likely that a substantial portion of the surge in the demand for U.S. dollars, particularly those that are assets liquid enough to be counted as part of M1, is demand from U.S. households and U.S. businesses. But why are they holding more dollars? Whether the rise in the demand for U.S. M1 is mainly by foreign or domestic entities, why is M1 growing at a faster rate than M2, according to data from www.economagic.com and the author's calculations (although the total growth of the number of dollars of M2 is greater than the growth in the number of dollars of M1)?

If my memory is correct, data from www.economagic.com indicate that checkable deposits have grown at a much faster rate than currency since December 2007, at least through the first quarter of 2013. Could it be that corporations (both financial and non-financial) are holding dollars on their balance sheets to increase the probability of solvency? Could people be concerned about not having liquidity in the future?

MORE ABOUT THE THEORY OF A NDVMSL

As noted earlier, assuming that an economy is in a liquidity trap, an increase in the money supply must lead to a decrease in the velocity of money. This follows because the greater money supply would fail to increase nominal output, the numerator in the fraction which algebraically defines velocity, while the denominator of the fraction, the money supply, rises. Thus, if an economy is in a liquidity trap, the money supply is already at or beyond the NDVMSL, and any further increase in the money supply would further reduce the velocity of money.

Because it is uncertain whether liquidity traps exist, let's also review what would likely happen to the velocity of money if an economy happened to be near a liquidity trap but not actually in a liquidity trap. An increase in the money supply would lead to a relatively small decrease in nominal interest rates, assuming that nominal interest rates would already be approaching the zero interest rate limit in an economy near a liquidity trap. Thus, nominal interest rates cannot fall much further. In turn, the cost to borrow falls little, leading to a small increase in nominal GDP. If interest rates are getting close to some minimum feasible level, then it is possible and perhaps likely that the percentage increase in the money supply will likely be greater than the percentage increase in nominal GDP if money supply growth is rapid. If the percentage increase in the money supply exceeds the percentage increase in nominal GDP, then the velocity of money must fall. Therefore, this analysis suggests that a NDVMSL likely exists for an economy close to a liquidity trap but not actually in a liquidity trap.

This brief review has reminded us that if a liquidity trap actually exists in an economy, then such an economy has a NDVMSL by the assumptions (and definition) of a liquidity trap, and the economy is already either at or beyond the NDVMSL. We are also reminded that if an economy is near a liquidity trap, a NDVMSL could exist, and the money supply in such an economy could be greater than or equal to the NDVMSL, implying that a further increase in the money supply would cause velocity to decrease.

But could the NDVMSL theory possibly apply not just to economies near liquidity traps (if they exist) but also more broadly to economies with interest rates higher than those that would normally be associated with approaching a liquidity trap? If a NDVMSL exists, then its existence implies that an increase in the money supply above the NDVMSL would reduce velocity as the percentage change in nominal GDP would be less than the percentage change in the money supply. Looking at the sample period using quarterly data which begins in the first quarter of 1959, there have been times when the money supply growth rate has exceeded the growth rate in nominal GDP. If a NDVMSL existed, these periods would have been consistent with the money supply surpassing that level.

One particular period of interest would be from the first quarter of 1985 through the second quarter of 1987. During this period, real GDP, the implicit deflator, and M1 all grew each quarter. The percentage growth rate in M1 exceeded the percentage growth in nominal GDP, causing the velocity of M1 to fall from roughly 7.37 times per year in the fourth quarter of 1984 to approximately 6.30 times per year in the second quarter of 1987, according to data from www.economagic.com.

This was a period when interest rates were relatively high, at least compared with interest rates in the U.S. economy to this point in the 2010s. The quarterly average of monthly federal funds rate data from www.economagic.com and the author's calculations was greater than six per cent each quarter from the first quarter of 1985 through the second quarter of 1987 (with the greatest value of nearly 8.5 per cent in the first quarter of 1985), while the quarterly average of the ten-year U.S. Treasury rate exceeded seven per cent each quarter from 1985q1 through 1987q2 (with a maximum of nearly 11.6 per cent in the first quarter of 1985). Interest rates in this range do not seem to be consistent with those of an economy either near or in a liquidity trap because the actual interest rates mentioned do not seem to be very low.

Moreover, both real GDP and the deflator grew during this period. Real GDP increased by almost 8.9 per cent from its value in the fourth quarter of 1984 through the second quarter of 1987, while the deflator increased by roughly 6.7 per cent over that period, as per the author's calculations using data from www.economagic.com. Thus, total GDP spending (or nominal GDP) increased by an amount over this ten-quarter period that appears very inconsistent with what would normally be considered a liquidity trap.

Yet, as noted above, the velocity of M1 fell by slightly more than one time per year during this period from approximately 7.37 times per year to approximately 6.30 times per year, according to www.economagic.com, because the quarterly average M1 money supply grew at a rate of roughly 36 per cent while nominal GDP grew by only roughly 16 per cent over this period. Thus, a NDVMSL could possibly exist in an economy during times not characterized as being near a liquidity trap or in a liquidity trap. The NDVMSL theory would explain the data discussed above from the first quarter of 1985 through the second quarter of 1987 as coming from an economy that had a NDVMSL and a more rapid money supply growth rate from the first quarter of 1985 through the second quarter of 1987 that pushed the actual money supply level above the NDVMSL.

Thus a NDVMSL could possibly exist outside of the confines of a liquidity trap. However, much more work remains before we can place much confidence in the theory of a NDVMSL. The theory may be of much less practical use if policymakers cannot forecast with some accuracy where the NDVMSL lies, and any NDVMSL that may exist can increase, decrease, or remain unchanged over time, making any forecasts more challenging.

MORE ABOUT LIQUIDITY TRAPS

A REVIEW

Because a NDVMSL exists during a liquidity trap (if a liquidity trap exists) essentially by the definitions of a liquidity trap and the velocity of money, we now explain a liquidity trap in more detail. Extremely low interest rates (such as in a liquidity trap) on loans often reflect extremely weak demand in an economy, particularly if the low interest rates persist. The intuition is that with more robust demand in the economy, firms and entrepreneurs would bid up interest rates by trying to borrow more so that their enterprises could keep pace with their expectations of demand. (During more robust economies, consumers may also bid up interest rates when buying houses, automobiles, and other 'big-ticket' items.) Weak demand is also consistent with either sluggish growth in real GDP, no growth in real GDP, or a reduction in real GDP in the economy. Also, if lenders attempt to add their inflation forecasts to a constant real interest rate as discussed by Irving Fisher and many others, the persistence of low interest rates on loans could signify low inflation expectations likely due to weak demand if the money supply is growing rapidly.

However, economies near liquidity traps if not in liquidity traps can experience vigorous growth in real output. As mentioned in Chapter 3, this could characterize the U.S. economy in the World War

II era, when interest rates were very low. It is likely that increases in government spending helped to fuel the rapid expansion in real output at that time.

If a liquidity trap exists, nominal interest rates in the economy must be at a point where the rates cannot go any lower. This brings up the aforementioned point about a possible minimum interest rate. As interest rates approach zero per cent, the general public absorbs additional dollars that are newly added to the money supply. But, when interest rates reach some minimum value, any further increase in the money supply fails to reduce nominal interest rates.

The assumption that interest rates cannot go any lower is critical for the possible occurrence of a liquidity trap. In a more normal economy, all other things equal, an increase in the quantity of money in circulation (that could arise in the case of the United States from the Federal Reserve buying U.S. government debt) leads to a decrease in the cost of borrowing a dollar for one year, which is the interest rate. A lower interest rate also creates less of a reward for lending a dollar, all other things equal. Therefore, all other things equal, in a more normal economy, many economists believe that lower interest rates stimulate firms' construction of new buildings, firms' purchases of new machines, and firms' manufacturing of new inventories, as firms needing to borrow to afford the new machines and new buildings and new inventories can more easily afford to borrow and firms fortunate enough to be able to buy without borrowing have less reason to try to increase profits by lending. Firms' purchases of new machinery, firms' construction of new buildings, and firms' production of inventory all count toward investment in national income accounting. Some economists believe that lower interest rates could also lead to greater consumption by households.

To recap, in a more normal economy, expansionary monetary policy decreases interest rates. Lower interest rates, in turn, could increase investment and perhaps consumption. With consumption and investment counting as two major components of aggregate demand, real GDP could increase, at least in the short-term, as the result of expansionary monetary policy. But again, at least in a model known as the IS-LM model, a key assumption in the analysis is that increases in the money supply reduce nominal interest rates, but interest rates would not fall following an increase in the money supply if liquidity traps exist and if the economy were in a liquidity trap. If an economy happened to be in a liquidity trap, expansionary monetary policy would fail to reduce interest rates. Thus, in the IS-LM model, firms would not increase investment following the expansionary monetary policy, nor would households increase consumption. Thus, in a liquidity trap, increases in the money supply fail to increase real GDP. People wind up just holding the dollars added to the money supply.

THE IS-LM MODEL, INCLUDING LIQUIDITY TRAPS

For readers unfamiliar, the IS-LM model finds an equilibrium point (where no one in the economy could gain by adjusting his or her behavior given what others in the economy are doing) where the equilibrium consists of an equilibrium level of real GDP and an equilibrium interest rate. At the equilibrium in the IS-LM model, both the goods market and the money market in the economy are in equilibrium. An economy achieves goods market equilibrium in the IS-LM model when firms' planned investments in inventory and other forms of physical capital equal the actual level of investment. At that equilibrium, sales are not greater than expected (so that actual inventory is less than firms want) or less than expected (so that actual inventory is greater than firms want). In the money market equilibrium, the quantity of money that people want to hold (versus storing the purchasing power in other forms) equals the quantity in circulation. Readers can refer to Chapters 10, 11, and 12 in Dornbusch, Fischer, and Startz (2008) for additional information about the IS-LM model.

Let's look more closely at the foundations of the IS-LM model. Economists often use a model of money supply and money demand to find equilibrium interest rates. Figure 4.1 below shows a downward-sloping money demand function. The thinking is that at a higher interest rate paid by assets such as bonds, people in the economy are willing to hold fewer dollars in the form of 'money,' which pay either no interest or a much lower interest rate than bonds. This leads to a decrease in the quantity of money demanded, as people want to place more buying power in the form of bonds to take advantage of the increase in their interest rates. On the other hand, when interest rates are lower, we expect an increase in the quantity of money demanded because people would be less willing to assume the risk of having an unplanned expense come up and being forced to sell the bonds before maturity, perhaps at a capital loss. People may also be less willing to place buying power in bonds at lower interest rates because most bonds have a risk that the bond issuer will default, and bond purchasers may feel that holding bonds is less worth the risks at a lower return. This analysis explains the downward-sloping money demand function.

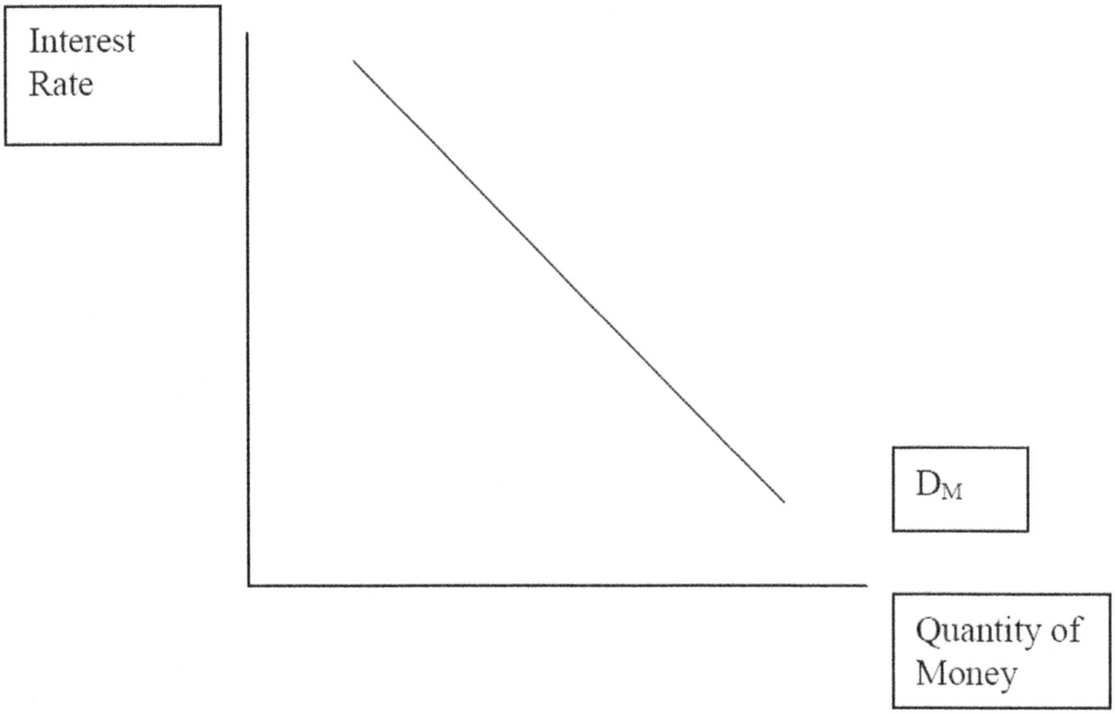

Figure 4.1 The Money Demand Function

While the money demand function is downward-sloping, the money supply function is vertical, as shown in Figure 4.2 below. The model assumes that the government can completely control the supply of money regardless of the interest rate, although information in Chapter 7 suggests otherwise.

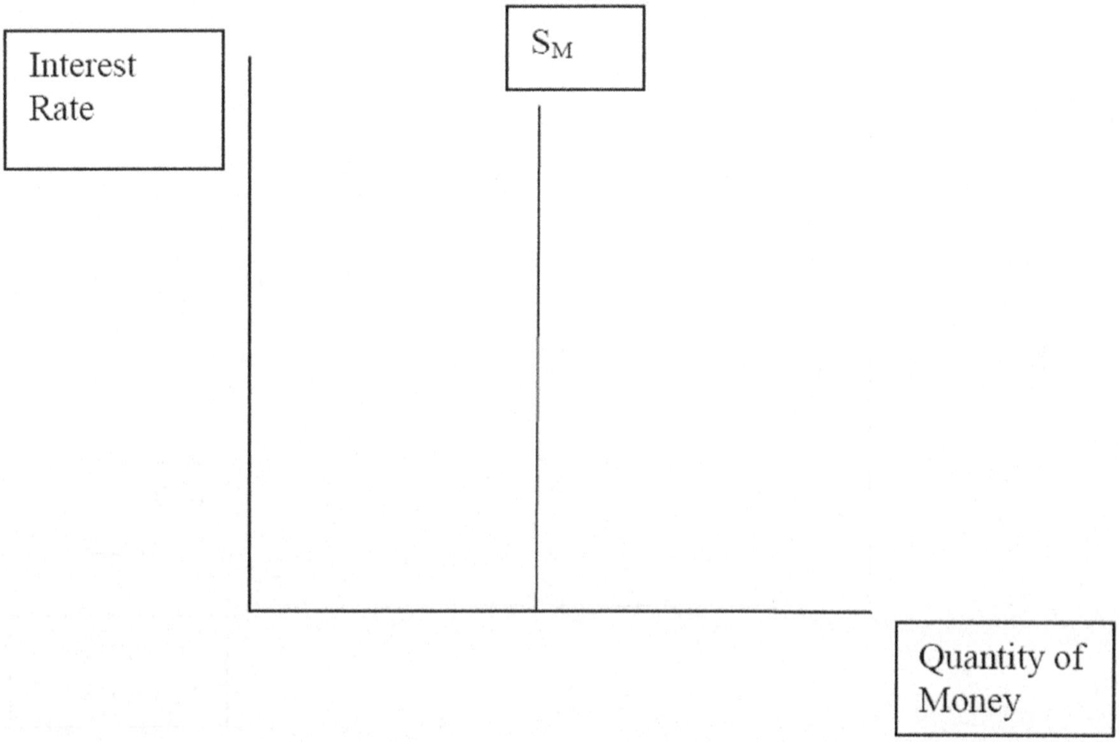

Figure 4.2 The Money Supply Function

Figure 4.3 below shows the equilibrium interest rate, R_1, at the intersection point between the downward-sloping money demand function and the vertical money supply function. All other things equal, an increase in the money supply would normally lead to a decrease in interest rates. This is shown in Figure 4.4, with the interest rate falling from R_1 to R_2. Likewise, Figure 4.4 implies that a decrease in the money supply would normally lead to an increase in interest rates, all other things equal. Figure 4.5 shows that an increase in money demand would, all other things equal, cause interest rates to rise (while it also implies a decrease in money demand would cause interest rates to fall, all other things constant). Readers can refer to Burton and Lombra (2006, Chapter 3, and pp. 116-125) or another suitable text for more about the model of money supply and money demand (and an alternate model of the supply of loanable funds and the demand for loanable funds that can be used to find equilibrium interest rates).

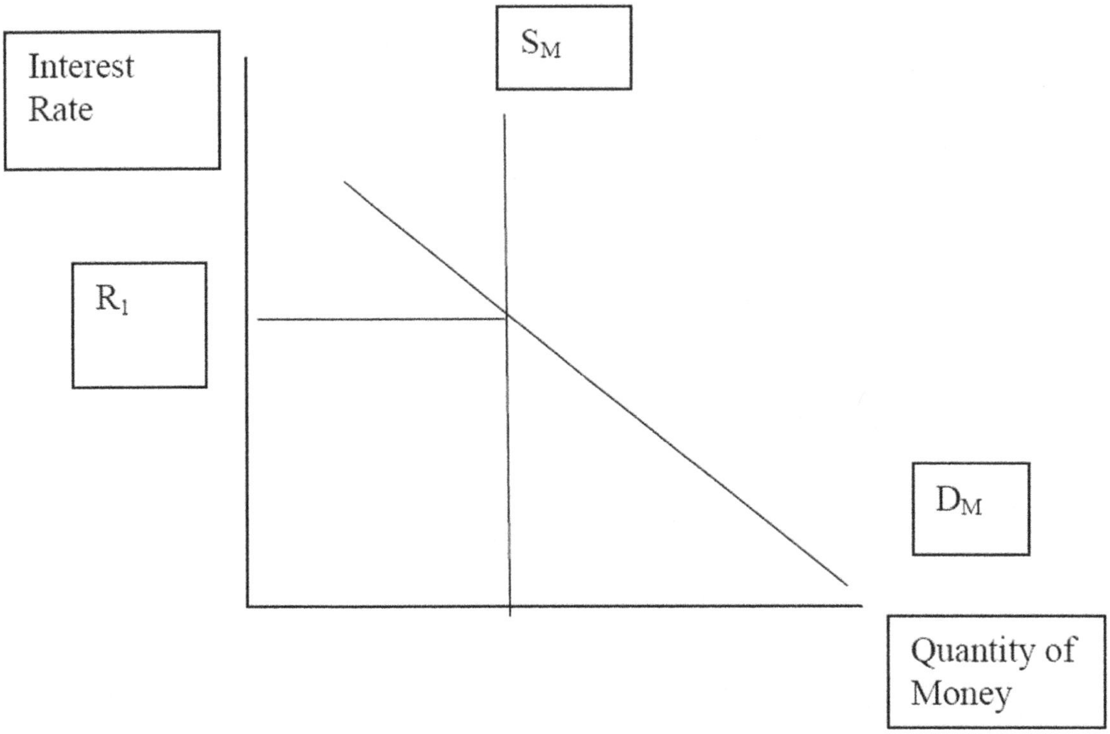

Figure 4.3 Equilibrium in the Money Supply-Money Demand Model

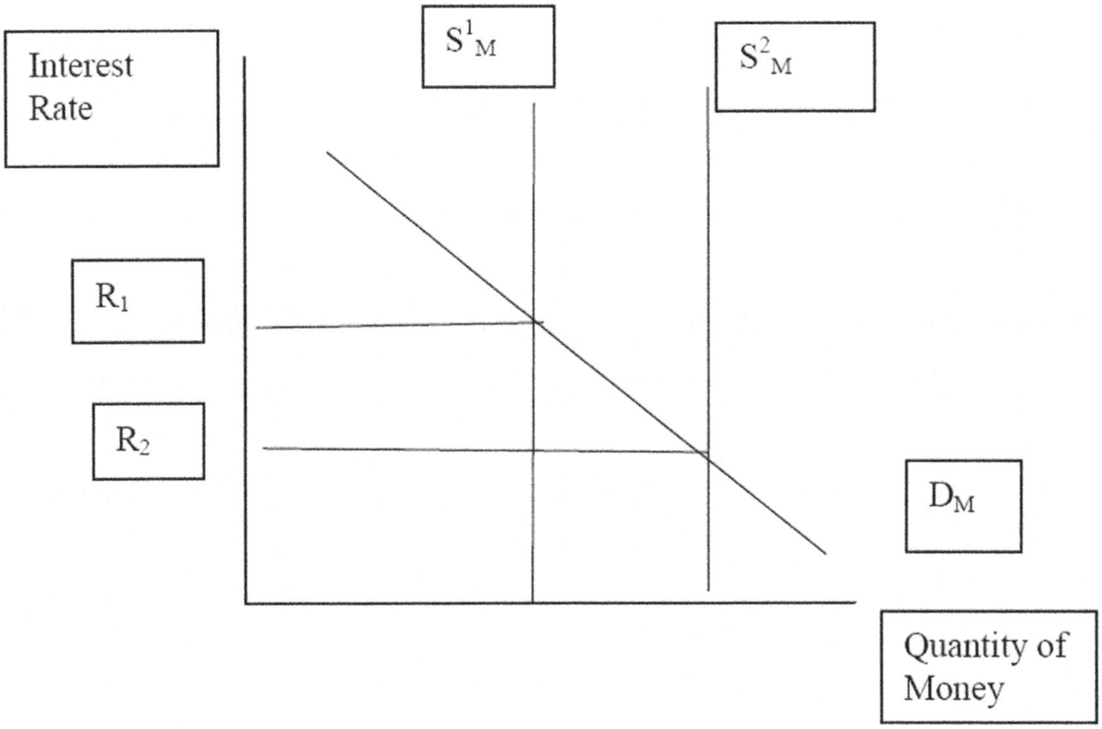

Figure 4.4 The Impact of an Increase in the Money Supply on Interest Rates

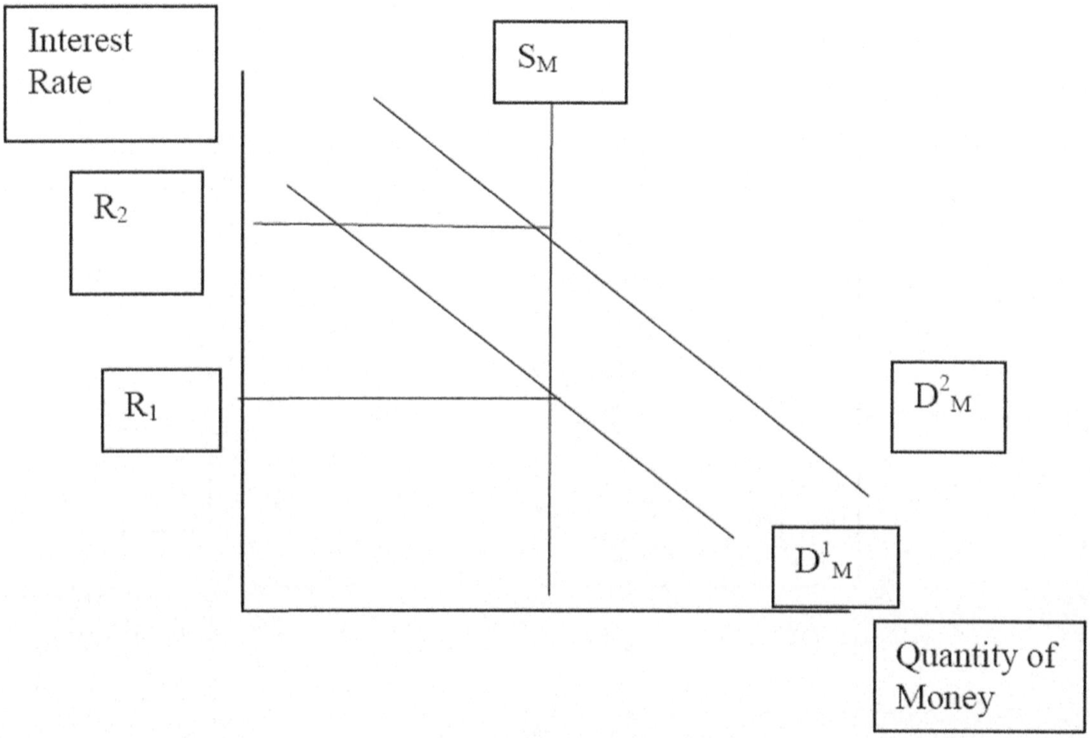

Figure 4.5 The Impact of an Increase in Money Demand on Interest Rates

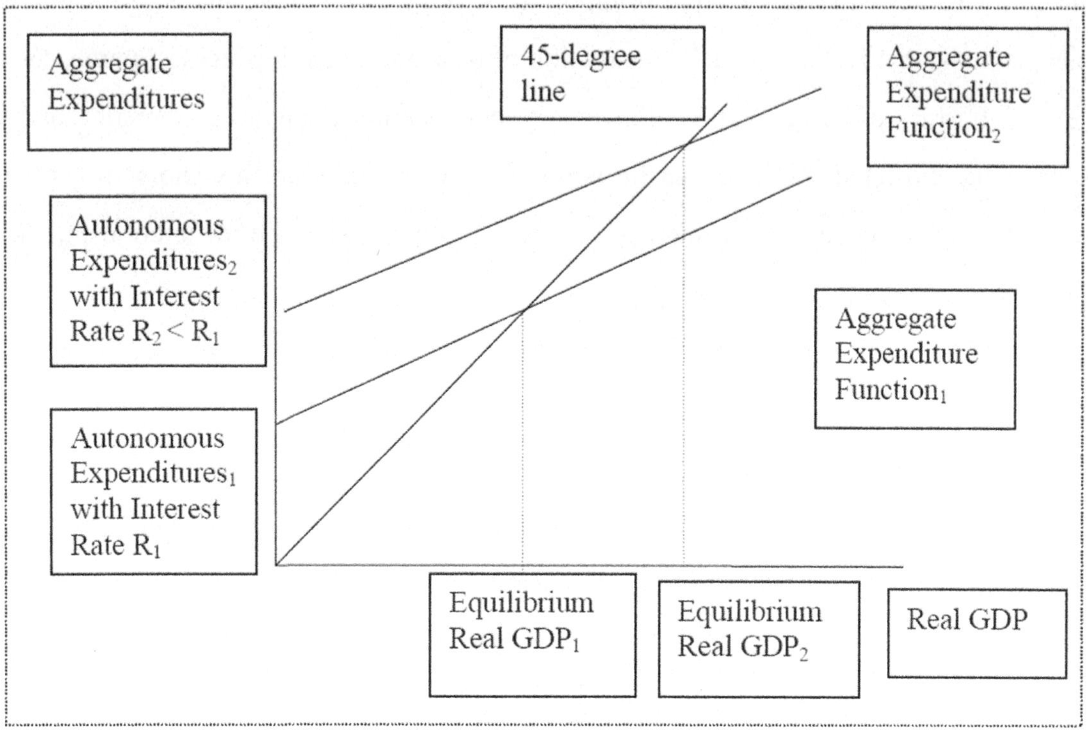

Figure 4.6 Impact of Lower Interest Rates, All Other Things Equal, on Equilibrium Real GDP

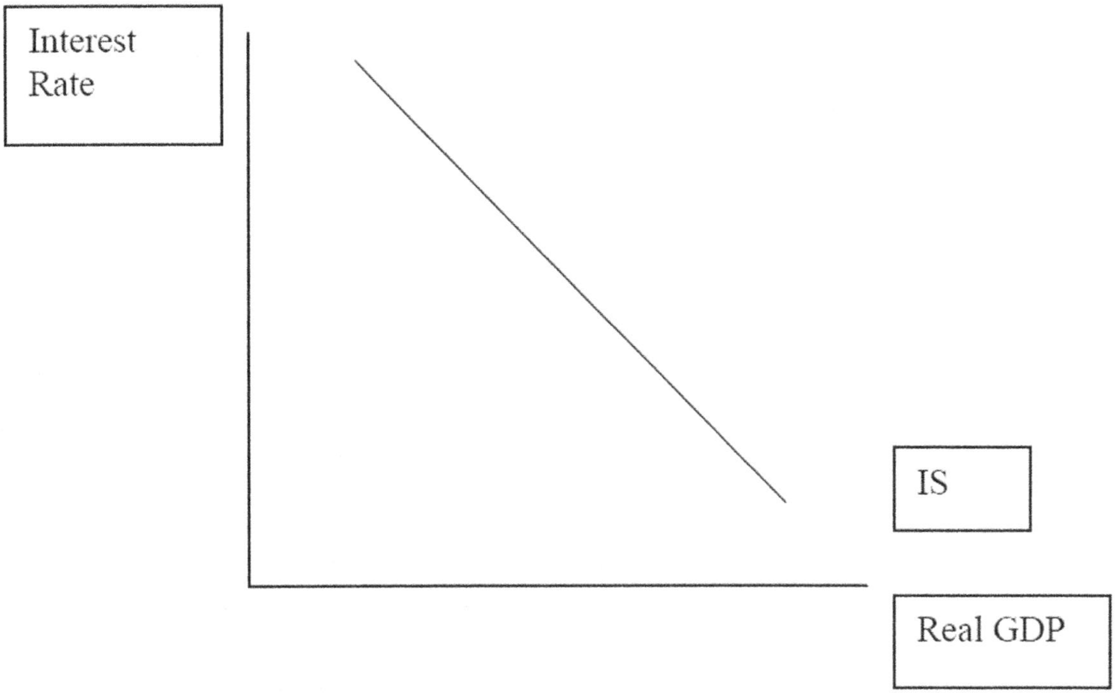

Figure 4.7 The IS Function

Recall from Chapter 1 that at the equilibrium in the income-expenditure model, firms' investment in physical capital (that is, businesses' construction of new buildings, businesses' purchases of new machines, and businesses' accumulation of inventory) equals firms' planned investment. This happens when sales equal expected sales, so that firms do not have either more inventory than planned or less inventory than planned. This occurs where the aggregate expenditure function intersects the 45-degree line.

Figure 4.6 above is very similar to Figure 1.14. Both figures show that an increase in autonomous expenditures leads to an increase in equilibrium real GDP. Figure 4.6, however, specifies that the increase in autonomous expenditures was due to a decrease in interest rates. (The lower interest rates probably would have increased firms' investment in physical capital and perhaps households' consumption expenditures.) This negative relationship between interest rates and equilibrium real GDP in the goods market gives rise to the downward-sloping IS function as shown above in Figure 4.7.

If real GDP rises, all other things constant, the demand for money in the money market increases. The thinking is that to pay for larger transactions that would be expected as the part of a growing economy, people would need to hold more dollars at each and every interest rate. This could have led to the increase in money demand illustrated in Figure 4.5 above. Note that the equilibrium interest rate rose as a result. Thus, while real GDP and interest rates are inversely related in the goods market, these two variables are positively related in the money market. The positive relationship between real GDP and interest rates in the money market gives rise to the upward-sloping LM function shown below in Figure 4.8.

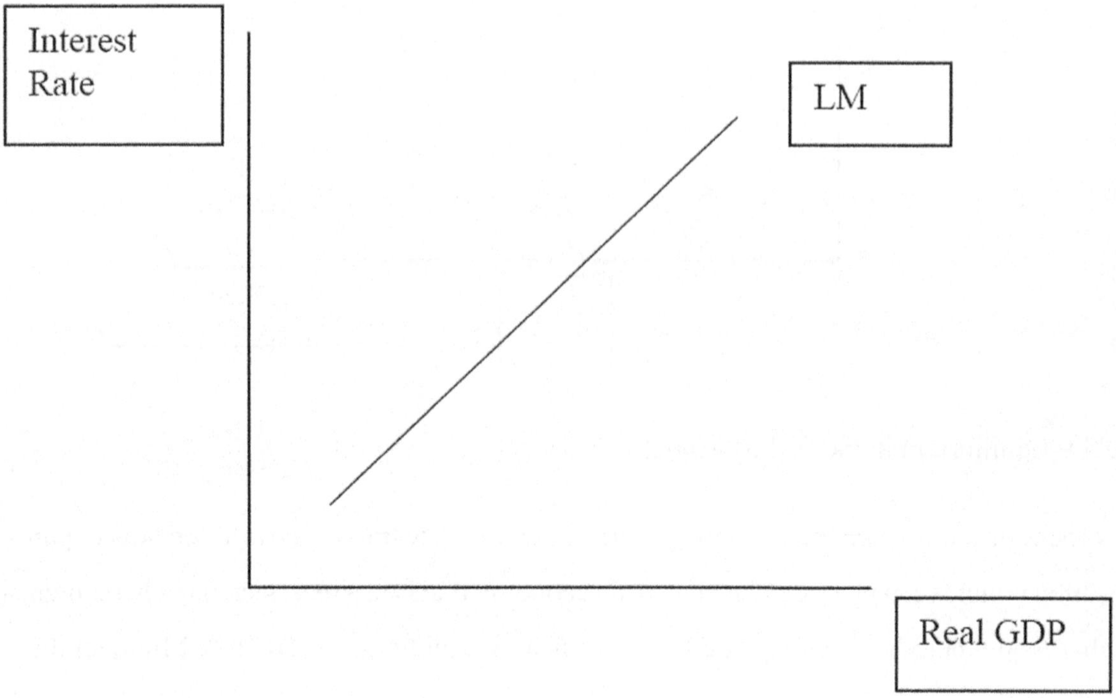

Figure 4.8 The LM Function

At the equilibrium point in the IS-LM model, both the goods market and the money market are simultaneously in equilibrium. Consider the intersection point between the downward-sloping IS function with goods-market equilibria and the upward-sloping LM function with money market equilibria in Figure 4.9 below. The intersection point with an interest rate equal to R_1 and a level of real GDP equal to Y_1 is the only combination of an interest rate and a level of real GDP where both the goods market and the money market are in equilibrium.

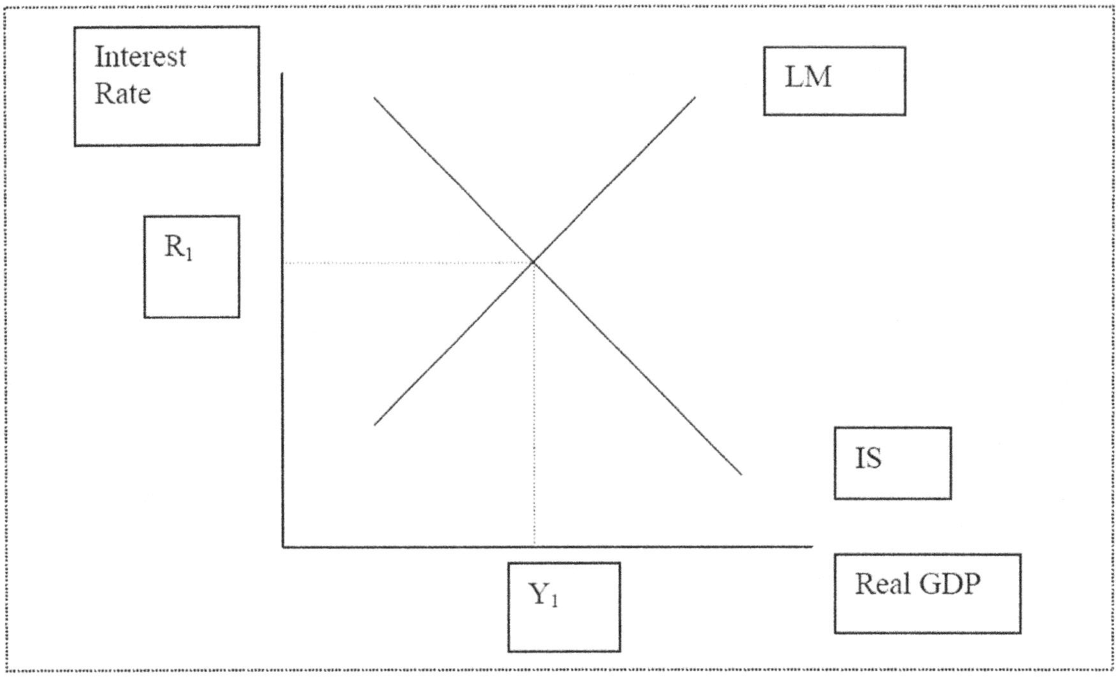

Figure 4.9 Equilibrium in the IS-LM Model

Let's focus on a closed economy neither in or near a liquidity trap for now to see how expansionary stabilization policies can increase real GDP in an economy that is in a recession but where interest rates are higher than when the economy is either in or near a liquidity trap. The IS-LM model discussion shows the difference between expansionary fiscal policy and expansionary monetary policy on interest rates.

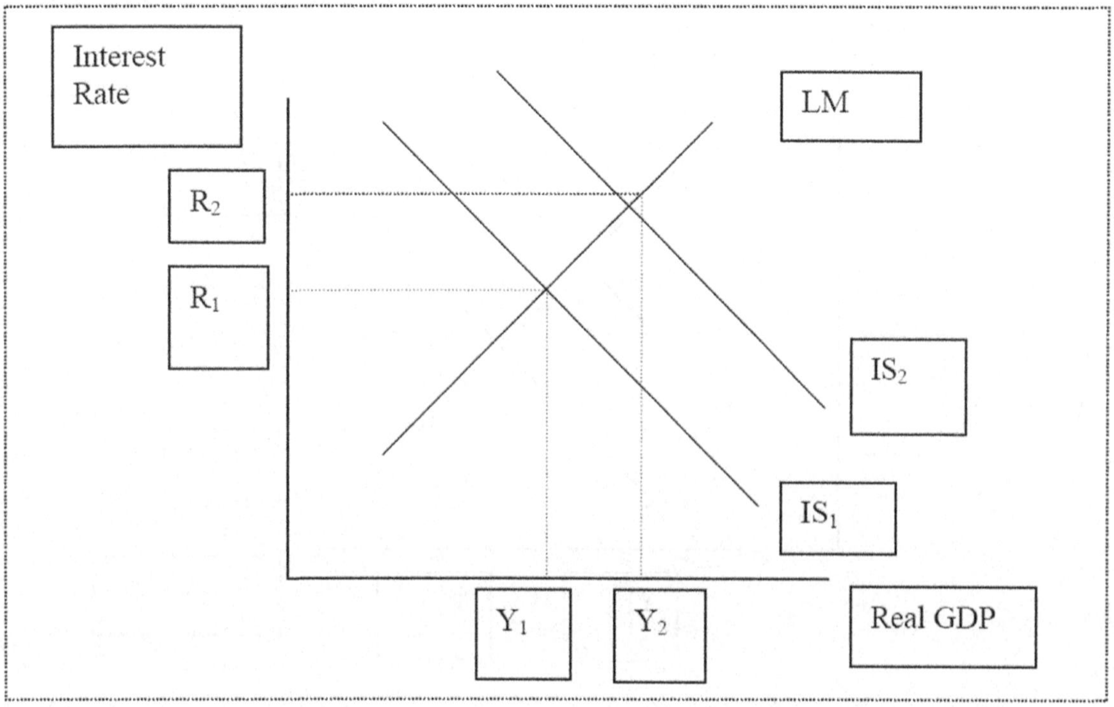

Figure 4.10 The Impact of Expansionary Fiscal Policy in the IS-LM Model

Expansionary fiscal policies, that is increases in government purchases and government transfer payments and reductions in taxes, shift the IS function to the right as shown in Figure 4.10 above. All other things equal, expansionary fiscal policies lead to larger budget deficits. When an economy is not near a liquidity trap or in a liquidity trap, the increased budget deficits result in higher interest rates as the government must in effect bid up interest rates to be able to borrow. This helps to explain the increase in interest rates from R_1 to R_2 shown in Figure 4.10. Real GDP also rises from Y_1 to Y_2 in the figure. Note however that the increase in real GDP would have been even larger if the interest rate would have remained at R_1.

Expansionary monetary policy also increases real GDP as shown in Figure 4.11. However, with more money in circulation, interest rates fall as a result, as shown in Figure 4.11 rather than rising following expansionary fiscal policy.

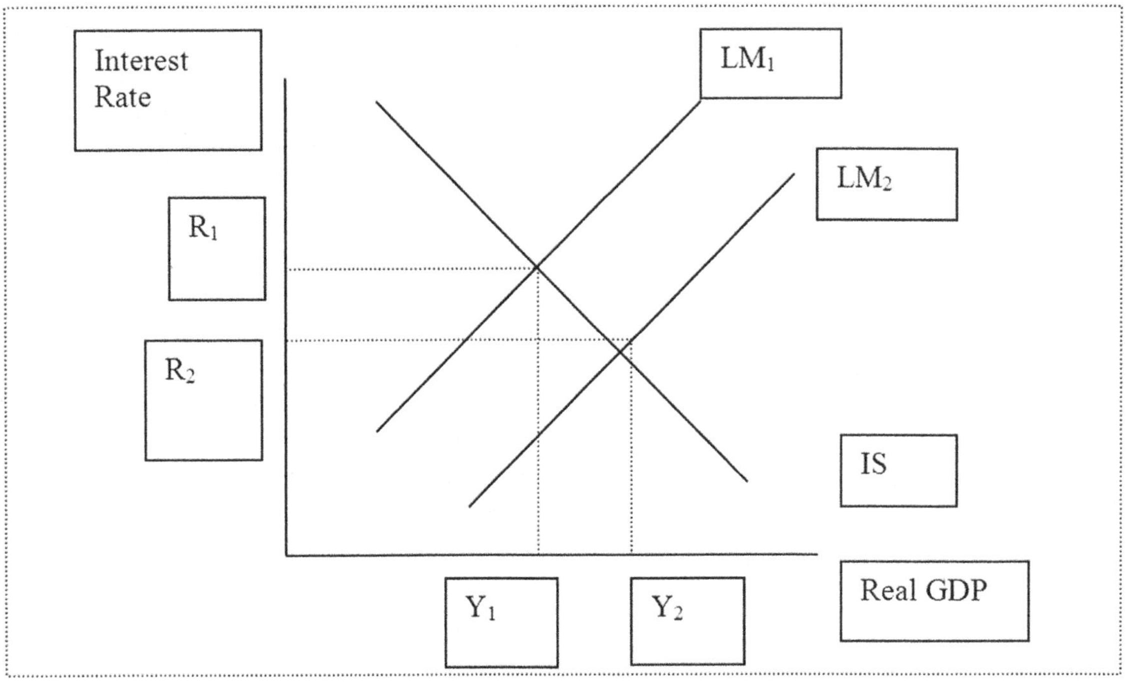

Figure 4.11 The Impact of Expansionary Monetary Policy in the IS-LM Model

How is the analysis different in a closed economy that is in a liquidity trap? At some very low interest rate but perhaps greater than zero, many assume that the money demand function becomes a horizontal line in order that an increase in the money supply does not drive the interest rate below zero. (Not necessarily all agree that the money demand function becomes perfectly horizontal at some low interest rate. Refer to Laidler (1993, pp. 150-152) for additional information.) In this situation, the model assumes that people in the economy are willing to hold any dollars supplied. The money demand function becoming horizontal also has an impact on the LM function, so that the LM function is also horizontal over some ranges of real GDP. The minimum interest rate, Rmin, is shown in Figure 4.12 at which the money demand function becomes a horizontal line. Note that the LM function is also horizontal at interest rate Rmin at lower levels of real GDP.

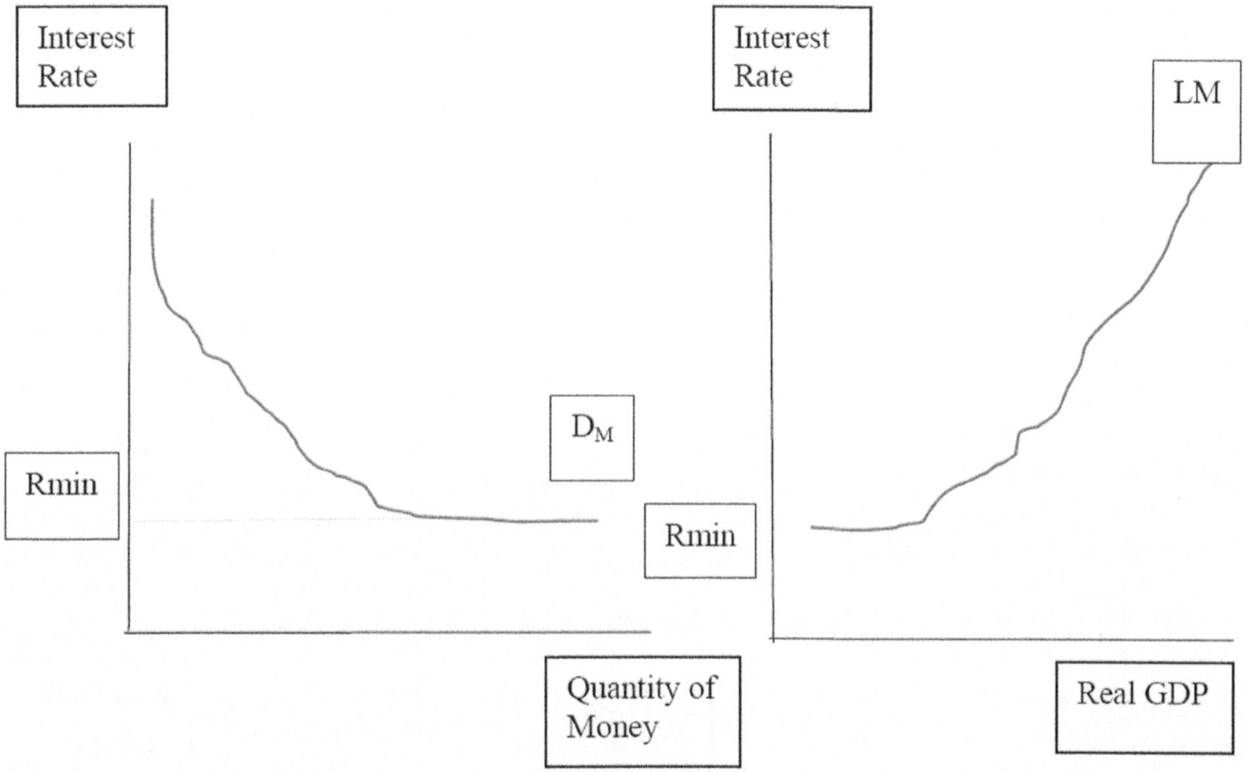

Figure 4.12 Money Demand and the LM Function when Interest Rates are Very Low

In a liquidity trap, the IS function intersects the LM function along its horizontal portion as shown in Figure 4.13 below. Expansionary monetary policy, increasing the money supply from M to M', cannot lower interest rates below Rmin if the money demand function is horizontal. Thus, the expansionary monetary policy cannot spur additional spending. Given the assumptions of the model, with the increase in the money supply failing either to reduce interest rates further or increase GDP spending, the LM function simply rotates from LM to LM' but does not change the equilibrium.

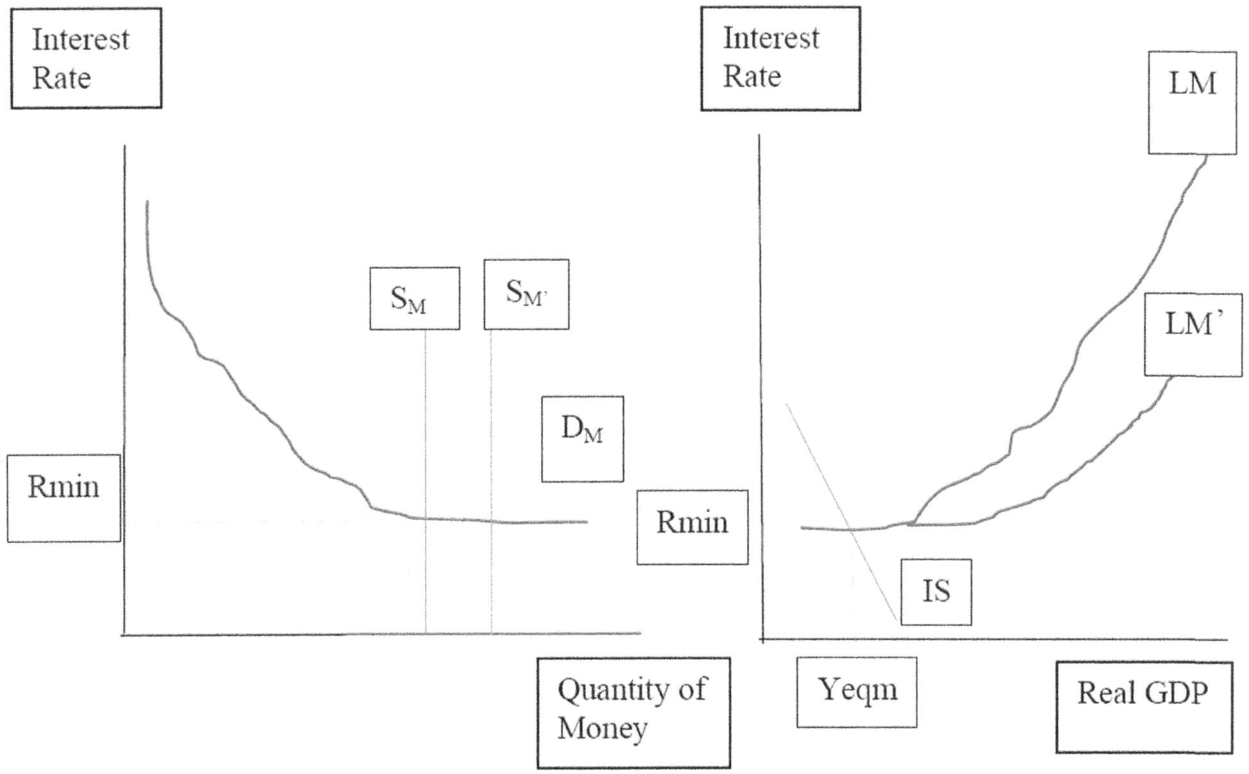

Figure 4.13 Expansionary Monetary Policy in a Liquidity Trap; Interest rates remain unchanged despite the increase in the money supply. The LM function rotates, and real GDP does not increase.

On the other hand, expansionary fiscal policy has its greatest impact compared with expansionary monetary policy when the economy is in a liquidity trap. Imagine what would have happened in Figure 4.10 had the LM function been a horizontal line so that the interest rate would have remained at R_1 despite the expansionary fiscal policy. The increase in real GDP would have been larger. Thus, the higher interest rates crowd out investment in physical capital and perhaps also consumption in Figure 4.10. This does not happen when the economy is in a liquidity trap. If an economy is near a liquidity trap but not in a liquidity trap, then interest rates would rise very slightly following expansionary fiscal policy. Thus, the degree of crowding out would be negligible.

Some (for example, Paul Krugman (2013)) at least implicitly have called for combining expansionary monetary policy with expansionary fiscal policy (by giving households and firms more after-tax income by increasing government spending and cutting taxes) to try to increase the growth rate of real GDP in the U.S. As Dornbusch, Fischer, and Startz (2008, p. 263) note, expansionary monetary policy could stop interest rates from rising and thus prevent any crowding out that could arise from expansionary fiscal policy.

WHY CORPORATIONS MAY BE HOLDING LARGE M1 BALANCES: AN EXAMPLE

As noted before, a key feature of a liquidity trap is that increases in the money supply fail to spark increases in spending. Data from www.economagic.com show that the rapid increase in M1 starting in 2008 has brought large increases in bank deposit holdings, many of which may be owned by corporations.

Several, if not many, accounts (for example, Smith (2014)) note that corporations in the United States are holding a combined total of more than one trillion dollars worth of highly liquid assets (although at least some of the analysis in Smith (2014) may differ from what follows here). A simple example will help to illustrate a possible reason why corporations in the United States are holding large quantities of assets that count toward the M1 measure of the money supply (and perhaps why banks are holding large quantities of total reserves). Readers seeking additional introductory information about balance sheets may refer to Baumol and Blinder (2012, pp. 248-250) or another textbook.

A profit-seeking corporation or a non-profit entity has assets, or things of actual or potential value, that it can use in an effort to achieve its goals. For the profit-seeking corporation, one of the goals would obviously be to earn a profit. In accounting, an entity such as a corporation can raise its assets in one of two ways. First, the owners of the corporation can contribute funds either indirectly by not paying all of the profits to the owners or directly by putting up cash or cash equivalents or other items that would be categorized as assets. Funds that are either contributed by the owners or that would accrue to the owners in the event of a liquidation are counted as part of equity. The second way that an entity can raise its assets is by borrowing. Borrowed funds or amounts owed are called liabilities. Because there are only two ways of amassing funds, through borrowed liabilities and through owners' equity or shareholders' equity, the total of all assets must equal the sum of total liabilities and total equity for each corporation, or algebraically, $A = L + E$, where A represents total assets, L represents total liabilities, and E represents total equity.

A simplified balance sheet helps to show the relationship between assets, liabilities, and equity. The left side of the balance sheet lists the assets of an organization. Both liabilities and equity appear on the right side of the balance sheet. Because $A = L + E$, the sum of all things listed on the left side of the balance sheet (assets) must equal the sum of all things listed on the right side of the balance sheet (liabilities and equity). Thus, as the old saying goes, 'the balance sheet must balance.' A change in the sum of liabilities and equity forces a change in assets, and a change in assets forces a change in the sum of liabilities and equity.

Suppose that Company XYZ begins operations on January 1st with $1 million of cash. Of that $1 million, the owners contributed $200,000 and Company XYZ borrowed $800,000 by issuing corporate bonds. Under these assumptions, Company XYZ would have the balance sheet below.

Balance Sheet for Company XYZ as of January 1st

Assets	Liabilities and Equity
1,000,000 Cash	800,000 Corporate Bonds
	200,000 Owners' Equity

Table 4.1 Initial Balance Sheet for Company XYZ as of January 1st

Suppose further that Company XYZ purchases a building on January 2nd to serve as the headquarters of its operations. The building costs $700,000. The purchase of the building would impact the balance sheet of Company XYZ because the company would no longer be holding $1,000,000 of cash as an asset. The company trades $700,000 of cash for another asset, a building. Thus, a revised simplified balance sheet listed below for Company XYZ would reflect this.

Balance Sheet for Company XYZ as of January 2nd

Assets	Liabilities and Equity
300,000 Cash	800,000 Corporate Bonds
700,000 Building	200,000 Owners' Equity

Table 4.2 Balance Sheet for Company XYZ as of January 2nd showing the impact of the purchase of a building

The reader should remember that one of the goals of Company XYZ is to turn a profit. Suppose for now that Company XYZ is a financial organization, so that one of the ways that Company XYZ can earn a profit is by lending funds and hopefully getting repaid with interest. Consider what would happen to the balance sheet of Company XYZ on January 3rd if the company would try to earn the greatest profits possible at the time by lending out all of its cash.

Balance Sheet for Company XYZ as of January 3rd

Assets	Liabilities and Equity
300,000 Loans	800,000 Corporate Bonds
700,000 Building	200,000 Owners' Equity

Table 4.3 Balance Sheet for Company XYZ as of January 3rd showing the initial impact of lending cash

One of the problems leading to the recent financial crisis in the United States is that a surge in defaults on loans and derivatives contracts occurred. Some home mortgage borrowers failed to make timely loan repayments, and some financial organizations failed to honor their commitments to make payments to other parties. A surge in defaults could reduce the value of these financial assets, whether they are loans, derivatives, or other types of assets, because the productive value of these assets for the owners could decrease as the likelihood of being paid or repaid decreases.

What would be the impact of a surge in loan defaults on June 15th on the balance sheet of Company XYZ? Suppose that the value of the asset 'Loans' on the left side of the balance sheet decreases. If so, then the total value of owners' equity on the right side of the balance sheet would also have to decrease for the balance sheet to remain in balance.

If the value of the loans made by Company XYZ would decrease from $300,000 to $250,000, then the total value of all assets on the left side of the balance sheet would be $950,000 ($250,000 of loans plus $700,000 for the building, assuming that the defaults have not impacted the value of the building). Again, the balance sheet must balance. Thus, the total of all liabilities and all owners' equity must equal $950,000. Because Company XYZ still owes $800,000 in corporate bonds, the total of owners' equity must decrease by $50,000 from $200,000 to $150,000. The revised balance sheet for Company XYZ as of June 15th is below.

Balance Sheet for Company XYZ as of June 15th

Assets	Liabilities and Equity
250,000 Loans	800,000 Corporate Bonds
700,000 Building	150,000 Owners' Equity

Table 4.4 Balance Sheet for Company XYZ as of June 15th showing the impact of a decrease in the value of loans that it granted

Now, suppose that many more defaults occur for Company XYZ. In this case, suppose that so many defaults on loans made by Company XYZ occur that the value of its loans decreases to just $75,000 by November 20th. What impact would that have on the balance sheet of Company XYZ? The total value of assets, the loans plus the building, (again, assuming that the building's value has not been impacted) would be $775,000. The total of liabilities and owners' equity would also have to add up to $775,000. But, because Company XYZ still owes $800,000 in corporate bonds, the depreciation in the value of loans from $250,000 to $75,000, a decrease of $175,000, must come out of owners' equity and drive the company into insolvency! The value of owners' equity is now less than zero in order for the balance sheet to balance. Company XYZ may be forced out of business because it owes more in bonds than the total value of its assets. The revised balance sheet is below.

Balance Sheet for Company XYZ as of November 20th

Assets	Liabilities and Equity
75,000 Loans	800,000 Corporate Bonds
700,000 Building	-25,000 Owners' Equity

Table 4.5 Balance Sheet for Company XYZ as of November 20th showing the impact (insolvency) of a further decrease in the value of loans that it granted

Had Company XYZ held $300,000 in cash rather than using it to grant loans, the balance sheet for Company XYZ would have remained the January 2nd balance sheet (the second balance sheet in this simple example) until something else would have changed. Although if the cash was literally in the form of currency and coins, so that the cash would not have grown in nominal value (and would have lost real value, on average, if the inflation rate was positive), then Company XYZ could have avoided the unfortunate scenario depicted in the November 20th balance sheet above.

During the Great Recession and perhaps heading into the year 2014 (and maybe beyond) in the U.S. economy, companies could have been trying to guard against situations like the one above where owners' equity would decrease below zero. This could help to explain why corporations may be holding such large volumes of highly liquid assets. Although the assets that are part of M1 either pay no nominal interest rate (in the case of cash) or possibly extremely low interest rates (in the case of *some* checking accounts that are part of M1) so that companies cannot receive much in interest by holding cash and cash equivalents, holding M1 assets on balance sheets can offset against actual and potential decreases in the value of loans, the value of stocks, the value of other financial assets, and the value of real estate holdings.

Suppose that the owners of Company XYZ contribute $100,000 of cash to the company on December 1. Assuming no other changes, this would restore solvency as shown below. Notice that the total of assets equals the total of liabilities plus equity.

Balance Sheet for Company XYZ as of December 1st

Assets	Liabilities and Equity
100,000 Cash	800,000 Corporate Bonds
75,000 Loans	75,000 Owners' Equity
700,000 Building	

Table 4.6 Balance Sheet for Company XYZ as of December 1st showing the impact of an influx of cash following the decreases in the value of the loans that it granted

The present section focuses primarily on choices made by businesses rather than households. However, businesses and households should realize that risks exist if they store buying power or wealth in less liquid forms. Obviously, most loans (including bonds) subject the lender to default risk, and other less liquid stores of buying power such as equity shares and real estate can decrease in value. Further, less liquid stores of wealth tend to impose a loss of liquidity on the holders so that they may not be able to convert wealth to money quickly without at least a small loss in purchasing power. These risks help explain why less liquid stores of purchasing power pay a higher expected return than do cash and checking account deposits, which pay a nominal interest rate equal to zero (for cash and some checking account deposits) or close to zero (for other checking deposits). A rate of inflation greater than zero means that cash and at least some checking accounts pay real returns *less* than zero. In a normal economy, most companies and households do not want to hold a large percentage of their buying power as cash (and either zero-interest-rate or low-interest-rate bank accounts) so that they can receive more income via less liquid stores of buying power.

However, in the Great Recession and the Not-So-Great Recovery, many companies (and perhaps many households) may have a much stronger desire for M1-assets, particularly low-interest bank account deposits. They may prefer the security of deposit-insured 'money in the bank' rather than other assets that may decrease in value. They may also be less willing to incur the liquidity risk of wanting or needing to spend more than initially planned and having to liquidate assets at a loss. Perhaps companies (and households) may feel that the relatively low interest rates offered by many lending opportunities today do not justify the liquidity risk and default risk that they would need to incur by granting the loans. Further, with inflation rates rather low, companies (and perhaps households) lose relatively little in real terms by holding either cash or zero-interest-rate or low-interest-rate bank accounts. This could help explain the rapid increase in M1 in the U.S. that began in 2008. But think of all of the jobs that could be created and all of the goods that could be produced (and perhaps additional wealth that could be created) if more of these dollars were trading more frequently! Are the dollars newly added to the U.S. economy being used to their greatest productive potential?

We will return to further discussions of balance sheets in Chapter 7. The balance sheets in that chapter will help to illustrate a concept known in economics as the simple money multiplier. For now, though, in the next chapter attention turns to financial crises, which seem to be associated with decreases in the velocity of money.

CHAPTER FOUR REFERENCES

Baumol, W. J. and Blinder, A. S. (2012) *Macroeconomics: Principles and Policy*, twelfth edition. South-Western Cengage Learning, Mason, Ohio.

Burton, M. and Lombra, R. (2006) *The Financial System and the Economy: Principles of Money and Banking*, fourth edition. Thomson South-Western, Mason, Ohio.

Dornbusch, R., Fischer, S., and Startz, R. (2008) *Macroeconomics*, tenth edition. McGraw-Hill Irwin, Boston, Massachusetts.

Hicks, J. R. (1937) "Mr. Keynes and the Classics: A Suggested Interpretation." *Econometrica*, vol. 5, April, pp. 147-159.

Keynes, J. M. (1936) *The General Theory of Employment, Interest, and Money*. Macmillan, New York, New York.

Krugman, P. (2013) "The Urge to Purge." April 4, 2013, accessed April 11, 2013; available online at: www.nytimes.com/2013/04/05/opinion/Krugman-The-Urge-To-Purge.html

Krugman, P. and Wells, R. (2009) *Macroeconomics*, second edition. Worth Publishers, New York, New York.

Laidler, D. E. W. (1993) *The Demand for Money: Theories, Evidence, and Problems*, fourth edition. Harper Collins College Publishers, New York, New York.

Smith, R. (2014) "Why are U.S. Corporations Still Hoarding $1.5 Trillion in Cash?" January 16, 2014, accessed October 4, 2014; available online at: www.dailyfinance.com/on/corporations-cash-hoard-trillion-profits/

www.economagic.com

CHAPTER 5

DO FINANCIAL CRISES, INNOVATION, STABILIZATION POLICY, AND REGULATION IMPACT THE VELOCITY OF MONEY?

A BRIEF INTRODUCTION TO FINANCIAL CRISES

Readers should realize that not all declines in velocity in the United States have come during times of the greatest financial distress. Some examples would be the declines in velocity in the U.S. from 1943 through 1946 and from the first quarter of 1985 through the second quarter of 1987. However, financial crises, or at least their aftermaths, have been associated with decreases in the velocity of money (likely in part due to the crises giving rise to recessions) not only in the Great Recession era but also in the Great Depression era of the 1930s, the Savings and Loans Crisis in the 1980s and the 1990s, and the bursting of the dot-com bubble in the 2000s. Thus, a discussion of financial crises should improve our understanding of why the velocity of money plummeted during the most recent U.S. financial crisis and its aftermath. To that end, some of the main factors that likely contributed to the recent financial crisis are also considered.

A thoroughly detailed study of the factors that led to the most recent financial crisis in the United States or the factors that could have led to any of the financial crises in the United States is beyond the scope of this book. Furthermore, if interested, the reader can consult works such as *The Financial System and the Economy: Principles of Money and Banking* by Maureen Burton and Raymond Lombra (2006, fourth edition, especially pp. 231, 246-247, and Chapter 13) and Mishkin's (2004, seventh edition, especially pp. 32-33, 189-199, and 273-285) book *The Economics of Money, Banking, and Financial Markets* for textbook-style explanations of many of the factors that can develop into financial crises. Further, the reader can refer to the *60 Minutes* (2008) web page and other sources for more on the specifics that many believe led to the most recent U.S. financial crisis.

However, the current book would be remiss if it did not present some of the factors that are potentially the most important in leading to financial crises, since financial crises as noted above seem to be associated with decreases in the velocity of money. A decrease in money velocity, however, does not imply that a financial crisis has occurred.

Financial crises in the United States are certainly not a new phenomenon. Burton and Lombra (2006, p. 56) discuss the Wildcat Banking Era, a period beginning in the 1830s and running into the 1860s. Banks in the United States used to issue private bank notes that traded as currency, where the notes could be redeemed for gold (and perhaps silver). Perhaps partly because of the multiple expansion of credit stemming from a fractional reserve system (where banks kept less than one hundred per cent of deposits in the form of gold), banks issued a greater quantity of these notes that can be considered as claims for gold than the quantity of gold that banks held in reserve, as per Burton and Lombra (2006, pp. 56, 478). From time to time, people would hurry to banks in 'bank runs' to make sure that they could withdraw their gold deposits. (Recall that this was before the days of deposit insurance.) Under this system, Burton and Lombra (2006, p. 56) point out that at least some states wound up forcing banks to put up collateral in the form of government bonds to be liquidated in the event that a bank could not trade its notes for gold. The name 'Wildcat Banking Era' probably arose at that time from the practice of some banks that relocated redemption centers to wilderness areas to make it harder for depositors to convert notes to gold (due to the travel required).

While a lot has changed since then, some of the basics behind a potential financial crisis still hold true. Depository institutions in normal times usually lend a large percentage of deposits, and many of the loans that depository institutions make may be relatively illiquid. Thus, if many depositors abruptly and unexpectedly decide to withdraw funds from a depository institution, the institution may have difficulty. (An alternate system, where banks would keep 100 per cent of their deposits as reserves, may prevent bank runs because people would not need to hurry to withdraw funds before others due to a potential insolvency. However, banks probably would need to charge much higher fees than they do presently in order to pay for operating expenses and hopefully earn profits. Under a 100 per cent reserve system, it is unlikely that banks would pay depositors an interest rate that was positive net of fees to store their funds.)

One factor helping to lead to financial crises is asymmetric information, which notes that borrowers (often) have more information than potential lenders regarding risks. Two forms of asymmetric information are adverse selection and moral hazard. Adverse selection observes that those with the greatest probability of defaulting may work the hardest to secure loans. Moral hazard occurs when borrowers use loan proceeds for riskier projects than announced. Readers can refer to Mishkin (2004, pp. 32-33), Burton and Lombra (2006, pp. 246-247), or another text for further information.

CREATION OF THE FEDERAL RESERVE

Bank runs or bank panics continued occasionally in the United States after the Wildcat Banking Era. Burton and Lombra (2006, p. 78) attribute the banking crises of 1873, 1884, 1893, and 1907 to shortages of currency. Despite the fact that the National Banking Acts of 1863 and 1864 (or more specifically the National Currency Act of 1863 and the National Banking Act of 1864) created nationally charted banks and currency that was uniform in the United States, and established a tax equal to ten per cent on notes originating at state banks, Burton and Lombra (2006, p. 56, 78, 232) question whether adequate control of currency in the U.S. was possible in the absence of a central bank. (The goal of the ten per cent tax was to force all state banks to close, but the advent of demand deposit accounts, as Burton and Lombra (2006, p. 232) observe, enabled state banks to continue to operate even though it was no longer practical for them to issue their own currency.) According to Burton and Lombra (2006, p. 64), Congress responded to the banking crisis of 1907 (and other crises) with the Federal Reserve Act of 1913, which created the Federal Reserve Bank as an entity to consider lending to financially distressed banks. This function of the Federal Reserve is often called 'the lender of last resort' function and was the leading purpose of the Federal Reserve Act.

Efforts in the U.S. to create a central bank predate the Federal Reserve Act of 1913 by more than 100 years. The Bank of the United States, which had functions of both a central bank and a commercial bank, was created in 1791. A tug-of-war may have existed between those in favor of a central bank in the U.S. and those against a central bank. Burton and Lombra (2006, p. 78) list perceptions of both the concentration of power and the operation for the well-being of the affluent as among the criticisms made by opponents of the Bank of the United States. Perhaps these arguments, now approximately 200 years old, would resonate with some members of both the Tea Party and the Occupy Movement in modern times. After what was evidently considerable opposition to the Bank of the United States, the initial twenty-year charter expired without renewal.

However, Congress established the Second Bank of the United States in 1816, at least in part to fund the War of 1812. But, Burton and Lombra (2006, p. 78) indicate that the aforementioned tug-of-war continued, with the two sides being Federalists in favor of a more centralized system and Anti-Federalists who favored less centralization. President Andrew Jackson, who would probably be characterized as an Anti-Federalist, opposed renewal of the charter of the Second Bank of the United States, and thus the Second Bank of the United States ceased existence in 1836. Much of the information in this paragraph and the one above is also in Mishkin (2004, pp. 229-231).

BANK FAILURES AND THE GREAT DEPRESSION

The repeated occurrence of banking crises from 1873 through the early 1900s probably led to Congress creating the Federal Reserve Bank. With the substantial benefit of hindsight, the functioning of the Federal Reserve essentially as just a lender of last resort may have been insufficient to stave off future bank runs. In fact, Burton and Lombra (2006, p. 234) estimate the number of bank failures in the U.S. between 1929 and 1933 to be greater than 8,000.

Consensus does not exist among economists as to the most important factor leading to such a large number of bank failures in such a short period of time. Some point out that crop failures possibly caused by severe drought led to large numbers of farmers defaulting on loans from banks. (For example, information in Baumol and Blinder (2012, pp. 73-74) may imply that many farmers defaulted on loans early in the Great Depression, although these two authors may not believe that these defaults caused either the Great Depression or the wave of bank failures early in the Depression.) Others list the stock market crash of 1929 and further declines in the values of many equity shares through 1932 as an important factor behind the massive wave of bank failures. The thinking of many, at least at the time, was that because commercial banks had been allowed to deal stocks and had been allowed to grant loans to stock market speculators (where the speculators needed to put up only ten per cent of the stock purchase price), the severe downturn in the stock market likely caused large numbers of stock market speculators to default on bank loans and reduced the asset value of most equity holdings that banks may have had on their balance sheets. (Some of the above analysis related to the possible impact of stock market speculation on bank failures is in Burton and Lombra (2006, p. 231), although the authors may or may not agree with this analysis).

However, from the perspective of the general public, panic could have resulted from concern about the liquidity and solvency of banks regarding whether depositors' banks made any loans either to stock market speculators or to farmers likely to go into default, perhaps even in cases where no such loans were granted. In short, in the absence of deposit insurance, perception may have been reality. As Burton and Lombra (2006, p. 234) observe, in the Great Depression era in the U.S., depositors could have hurried to pull money out of banks due to concern about the contagion of problems, and that in turn could have created problems for banks that would have been fine otherwise.

Still others, rather than focusing on crop failures or problems in equity markets, may point to what may be described as a relatively passive response of the Federal Reserve allowing such a large number of banks to fail and thereby allowing the money supply to decrease rapidly. Perhaps the acquiescence of the Fed was the main reason for so many bank failures early in the Great Depression. This seems to be consistent with analysis that Dornbusch, Fischer, and Startz (2008, pp. 468-469) attribute to Friedman and Schwartz (1963) in *A Monetary History Of The United States, 1867-1960.* Real interest rates at times during the Great Depression in the U.S. were quite high. This was likely the result of falling money supply which probably in turn contributed to falling price levels, if it was not the sole cause. Recall that during the early part of the Great Depression, the velocity of money in the United States fell. Although the recent past in the United States has been a time of rapid money supply growth, particularly M1 growth, and a sharp decline in the velocity of money, particularly the velocity of M1, the early part of the Great Depression in the U.S. was a time when both money supply and the velocity of money fell, rather than moving in opposite directions.

THE GLASS-STEAGALL ACT

Whether any of the factors discussed above is the most important factor leading to the surge in U.S. bank failures during the years 1929 through 1933 or whether another factor not discussed was the most important factor, the thinking of the time (whether correct or incorrect) helps to explain the legislative response by Congress. The Glass-Steagall Act introduced the Federal Deposit Insurance Corporation, divided investment banking and commercial banking, and initiated interest rate ceilings. (Burton and Lombra, 2006, p. 231)

In the view of Burton and Lombra (2006, p. 234) deposit insurance was a great accomplishment for Congress. To my knowledge, no surge in the number of depository institution failures comparable to the explosion of failures just prior to the passage of the Glass-Steagall Act has occurred in the U.S. since the advent of deposit insurance. The average number of bank failures per year from 1987 through 1990 was 189, much higher than an average of roughly 5 per year from 1955 through 1981 and 1995 through the middle of 2004, according to Burton and Lombra (2006, p. 235). Even in the Savings and Loans (S&L) Crisis of the late 1980s and early 1990s, Burton and Lombra (2006, p. 292) note that more than 1,500 S&Ls terminated operations. Combining the number of S&L failures with the number of commercial bank failures in the late 1980s and early 1990s would still amount to a number well short of the more than 8,000 failures early in the Great Depression. (As an aside, a failure of an insured savings and loans institution would not have led to a payout by the FDIC but rather the Federal Savings and Loans Insurance Corporation (FSLIC), later replaced by the Savings Association Insurance Fund (SAIF). (Burton and Lombra, 2006, pp. 286, 315)) Although deposit insurance could have led to greater risk-taking (and some might say too much risk-taking) by depository institutions, the United States has avoided large-scale bank runs the size of those early in the Great Depression since that time, likely in part due to the establishment of deposit insurance.

While deposit insurance still exists today, the other components of the Glass-Steagall Act are no longer in effect. Among other provisions, according to Burton and Lombra (2006, p. 320), the Depository Institutions Deregulation and Monetary Control Act of 1980 took steps to eliminate interest rate ceilings. Burton and Lombra (2006, p. 231) explain that in the 1930s, the thinking (whether correct or incorrect) was that banks competed too much for deposits and kept offering higher interest rates to attract more deposits. (In the absence of significant fees charged to depositors, banks must receive a higher interest rate on the loans that they grant than the interest rate that they pay to depositors to keep their deposits in order to have a chance to earn a profit.) The analysis in the mid-1930s maintained that commercial banks were forced to grant loans to borrowers with a higher default risk (for example, stock market speculators) because these borrowers would be willing to pay a higher interest rate to secure a loan. Congress created interest rate ceilings to prevent upward pressure on interest rates paid on deposits and the perceived search for borrowers willing to pay a higher risk premium. (Burton and Lombra, 2006, p. 231) But, Burton and Lombra (2006, p. 253) point out that institutions that offered the greatest interest rates were not necessarily statistically the most likely to become bankrupt.

Under the belief that commercial banks' participation in the stock market (at least indirectly) was a contributing factor in the wave of bank failures in the U.S. from 1929 through 1933, the Glass-

Steagall Act divided investment banking activities (such as new issues of stocks and bonds in the primary market) and commercial banking activities (such as granting business loans and issuing checkable deposit accounts). The Gramm-Leach-Bliley Act of 1999 (or the Gramm-Leach-Bliley Financial Services Modernization Act, as listed in Mishkin (2004, p. 251)), once again allowed a co-mingling of commercial banking and investment banking and also allowed at least some such firms to offer other financial services such as insurance (Burton and Lombra, 2006, pp. 222, 319). However, in the view of Burton and Lombra (2006, p. 323), the legislation may have been somewhat of a formality as the regulatory system previously had started to allow some mixture of commercial and investment banking.

INTEREST RATES AND INFLATION RATES

Interest rate ceilings, often called Regulation Q, imposed by the Glass-Steagall Act created problems that were likely not anticipated by the legislators of the 1930s. During the 1970s, market-determined interest rates often rose well above the rates that depository institutions were allowed to pay under Regulation Q, according to Burton and Lombra (2006, p. 262). This seems to have been largely the result of increasing inflation, with tighter monetary policy implemented by late 1979 to curb inflation. For those not familiar, Irving Fisher wrote that lenders add their forecasted inflation rate to a desired constant real return when they agree to grant loans at a specific nominal interest rate, as noted by Burton and Lombra (2006, p. 123) and many others. In turn, when lenders expect higher inflation, they require a higher nominal interest rate for the funds that they loan. (If borrowers too expect a higher inflation rate in the future, they are more willing to pay a higher nominal interest rate, all other things equal.)

Deflator data from www.economagic.com as of July 20, 2013 and the author's calculations show that in the 1960s, inflation calculated as the percentage change in the deflator from four quarters ago varied from between 0.90 per cent and 5.3 per cent. In the 1970s, by contrast, the lowest inflation rate calculated was just below four per cent, and that was in only one quarter. For three consecutive quarters, the fourth quarter of 1974 and the first two quarters of 1975, the inflation rate was greater than ten per cent, with inflation slightly greater than eleven per cent in the first quarter of 1975. After trending downward and reaching a local minimum of less than 5.4 per cent in the third quarter of 1976, inflation then trended back upward. The calculated inflation rates were between seven per cent and eight per cent in the third and fourth quarters of 1978 and the first quarter of 1979. Calculated inflation rates for the second, third, and fourth quarters of 1979 varied between eight and nine per cent before eventually reaching a local maximum of roughly 10.2 per cent in the first quarter of 1981.

Two likely factors leading to higher expected inflation and higher actual inflation rates in the 1970s would be (1) faster money supply growth and (2) the two energy crises when oil prices spiked. Data from www.economagic.com and the author's calculations show that in the 1960s, the quarter-to-quarter growth rate (not annualized) of M1 exceeded two per cent in only two quarters and averaged about 0.90 per cent per quarter. In the 1970s, the quarter-to-quarter growth rate (not annualized) of M1 exceeded two per cent in eight quarters and averaged around 1.6 per cent per quarter. Regarding the energy crises, note that inflation rates increased around the time of the energy shocks or soon thereafter.

Savers lacking high balances but who sought market returns while staying safe and rather liquid had relatively few options. U.S. Treasury bills (T-bills) paid a market-determined interest rate and were both quite liquid and safe. However, the smallest denomination for a T-bill was $10,000. Thus, those with less than $10,000 available but who wanted safety and liquidity may have been forced to take the returns offered by commercial banks and thrifts, all subject to Regulation Q interest rate ceilings. (Burton and Lombra, 2006, p. 258)

However, the advent of money market mutual funds gave these savers an option where they could get a liquid, relatively safe market interest rate, and it did not take $10,000 to 'get in the game.' Burton and Lombra (2006, p. 258) attribute at least part of the outflow of funds from depository institutions that could not raise interest rates in part to the creation of money market mutual funds, with some of the funds going to commercial paper, government debt, and perhaps corporate bonds. Data from www.economagic.com (accessed July 31, 2013) show that growth in money market mutual funds started accelerating in late 1978. Around that time, the federal funds rate was increasing, and the ten-year U.S. Treasury rate was also increasing, as per data from www.economagic.com accessed July 20, 2013. According to Burton and Lombra (2006, p. 259), depository institutions responded to incentives to stop funds from flowing out of depository institutions by finding ways around interest rate ceilings. One strategy was reclassifying deposit liabilities covered by Regulation Q as other types of instruments not under Regulation Q interest rate ceilings.

DEREGULATION IN THE 1980s

The Depository Institutions Deregulation and Monetary Control Act (DIDMCA) of 1980 brought other changes besides taking steps to remove interest rate ceilings and may have signaled a pendulum swinging toward deregulation. Two of the other features of DIDMCA were (1) the allowance of all depository institutions in the U. S. to grant Negotiable Orders of Withdrawal (NOW accounts) that paid interest and allowed account owners to withdraw funds by writing checks, and (2) granting savings banks and savings and loans associations the ability to make business loans. (Burton and Lombra, 2006, p. 311) Burton and Lombra (2006, p. 213) note that savings banks and savings associations were originally created to encourage the building and sales of new houses.

The Garn-St. Germain Depository Institutions Act of 1982 brought further deregulation to the financial services industry. Among several provisions, this act allowed Super NOW accounts and enabled savings and loans associations to hold junk bonds. (Burton and Lombra, 2006, pp. 311, 316) (Although I am not certain, the difference between NOW accounts and Super NOW accounts could have been that Super NOW accounts were not subject to interest rate ceilings, but NOW accounts may have been subject to interest rate ceilings, at least initially, as the DIDMCA gradually removed interest rate ceilings. Deposits in either NOW accounts or Super NOW accounts could have been withdrawn by writing a check. Perhaps instead the difference between the two was that limits on the number of checks that could be written each month existed on NOW accounts, at least initially, but not Super NOW accounts. Again, I am not certain.)

How do the changes in regulation discussed thus far relate to the velocity of money? While I am not certain, the timing of the first change point in the post-1958 sample period from a time of generally increasing velocity of the M1 money supply to a time (albeit a relatively short time) of generally decreasing velocity of M1 apparently falls in between the passage of the DIDMCA of 1980 and the Garn-St. Germain Act of 1982 (although this may be a coincidence). Moreover, a diagram in Baumol and Blinder (2012, p. 298) showing the velocity of M1 over time leads me to believe that the velocity of M1 grew steadily and at least somewhat predictably if not very predictably for decades, until the early 1980s. Could it be that financial innovation and deregulation resulted in changes in the payments system that were so fundamental that the predictability in the average number of times that a dollar traded in a Gross Domestic Product transaction largely evaporated in the early 1980s?

At least part of the decline in the velocity of M1 that began in the fourth quarter of 1981 could be attributed to the severe recession that began around that time. However, further examination of the diagram in Baumol and Blinder (2012, p. 298) reveals that the relatively close adherence of the velocity of M1 to following an upward-sloping line or an upward-sloping curve *for decades at a time* ended in the early 1980s. True, there have been periods since then when the velocity of M1 has fluctuated around a smooth curve or a line, but these lasted only years, not decades. A review of the graph in Baumol and Blinder (2012, p. 298) suggests that M1 velocity followed a line or a curve fairly closely since the minimum in the mid-1940s near the end of World War II until about 1980.

MARKET STRUCTURE: REGULATION AND DEREGULATION

The Interstate Banking and Branching Efficiency Act (IBBEA) of 1994 may have brought important changes to commercial banking. By removing nearly all of the restrictions on operating branches in other states (as noted by Burton and Lombra (2006, p. 319)), the IBBEA of 1994 may have increased the rewards for coming up with successful new financial innovations. A similar point about the reward for innovation in the face of competition was made by Burton and Lombra (2006, p. 259).

Legislators in the 1920s had opted to strive for a market structure in banking with many small banks rather than fewer but larger banks. Thus, the McFadden Act of 1927 prohibited banks (in most cases as per Burton and Lombra (2006, pp. 235-237)) from operating branches in multiple states to prevent banks from growing 'too large' from the perspective of legislators as larger banks may buy out smaller banks (or perhaps use cost economies to force them out of business). My reading of Burton and Lombra (2006, pp. 235-237) tells me that one of the reasons for trying to have many small banks was the belief that with more banks (with less market power), competition would lead to lower interest rates and lower fees charged by depository institutions for loans and services (and perhaps also higher interest rates paid to depositors). (Recall that the McFadden Act was passed before the Regulation Q interest rate ceilings that were created by the Glass-Steagall Act of 1933.) The disadvantage of a market structure with many small banks was that the probability of any one bank failing would increase if the interest rate spread, which is the difference between the interest rate that a bank receives from the loans that it makes minus the interest rate that it pays depositors, falls due to competition among banks, all other things equal. The perceived advantage of a smaller number of banks that are larger in size, on average, was that if the interest rate spread grew, the probability of one bank failing, all other things equal, would decrease. However, another advantage of a market structure of many small banks is that when one bank fails, there is less damage to the system.

Fitting a trend toward deregulation, Burton and Lombra (2006, p. 237) point out that a Supreme Court decision in 1985 allowed banks to create regional banking pacts operating across state lines. Further, bank holding companies may have provided a way for depository institutions to circumnavigate the rules prohibiting operations across state lines, as per Burton and Lombra (2006, p. 238-239). For example, a parent company could own two or more subsidiaries. One of the subsidiaries could be a commercial bank operating in one state. Another subsidiary of the parent company could be a commercial bank operating in a different state. Therefore, while the IBBEA of 1994 repealed the McFadden Act of 1927, it may not have brought as many changes to the banking market structure as one may have expected.

Nonetheless, the IBBEA of 1994 paved the way for potentially huge profits accruing to those depository institutions that could successfully develop and implement financial innovations nationwide by removing most of the remaining restrictions against operating branches in more than one state. Readers interested in more about market structure, the McFadden Act of 1927, the IBBEA of 1994, and interest rate spreads may see Burton and Lombra (2006, pp. 235-239, 247). Does market structure in commercial banking have an impact on the velocity of money?

TECHNOLOGY AND THE PAYMENTS SYSTEM: DO INNOVATIONS IMPACT VELOCITY?

Burton and Lombra (2006, pp. 33-37, 257) and others note that changes in technology have made an impact on how people pay for the goods and services that they buy. The creation of the credit card combined technology (by sending information over telephone lines and now perhaps the internet) with financial innovation (by developing a new way to lend money). In so doing, the growing use of credit cards has reduced the need for people to carry currency, and it may have also reduced the number of checks that people in the economy write each year. Could this have caused a change in the velocity of money? Mishkin (2004, pp. 518-519) notes that Irving Fisher discussed technological improvements applied to the payments system as having an impact on velocity.

Further, the advent of the ATM card and debit cards could have reduced the need for the public to hold currency. Also, as technology has improved, and as some of the technological improvements have been applied to the payments system and the financial system, the general public may have made some changes. For example, the ease of transferring funds from savings deposits, money market deposit accounts, and money market mutual funds that are part of M2 but not part of M1 to components that are part of both M1 and M2 has likely increased over the years. As a result, are people leaving more funds deposited in non-M1 components of M2 longer and not withdrawing such funds until right before the time that the funds are spent? Does that help in understanding why M2 has grown *at times* at a faster rate overall than M1 (although often not the case on a quarter-to-quarter basis in the U.S. after the fourth quarter of 2007)? Have these changes led to a change in the velocity of money? Also, with the increased usage of the internet, the opportunities to buy and sell stocks (and also bonds) for a relatively small broker's fee have grown. Has this led to a change in portfolio management by the general public and a change in the payments system resulting in a change in the velocity of money?

FOCUS ON THE MOST RECENT U.S. FINANCIAL CRISIS

A BRIEF INTRODUCTION TO FUTURES

Futures contracts are an example of a financial innovation that can be used to reduce risk. One source of additional information about futures is Burton and Lombra (2006, pp. 416-435). The use of the terms 'futures' and 'futures contracts' in my book may include items that some call 'forward contracts' and 'options.'

A frequently given example of how futures contracts can reduce risk is that of a farmer who wants to guard against a decrease in the price of a crop produced and sold by the farmer. In this case, the farmer can agree to a futures contract where someone on the side of the futures contract opposite the farmer agrees to buy a certain quantity of the farmer's produce at a pre-determined price and an expiration date. Perhaps the party opposite the farmer is a manufacturer who normally buys as an input the good that the farmer produces. Note that if the futures contract is structured in such a way that the farmer is obligated to sell in the future at a pre-determined price and if the market price of the item goes up rather than down, then the farmer probably would have been better off by not having signed the futures contract because the farmer could have made more money by selling in the spot market (where prices are not agreed upon in advance) rather than the futures market. The farmer may still believe that it would be worth taking the risk of the price rising (and thereby making less money) rather than risk the price falling and potentially suffering losses after considering costs. Also note that futures contracts are such that one party must deliver a certain quantity at a predetermined price, and another party must accept the delivery at that price, and that other conditions may also apply.

While hedgers use futures contracts to reduce risk, speculators use futures contracts to assume risks that they did not have before entering the futures market with the goal of gaining a profit. Therefore, if the speculator expects that the price of a commodity will rise above the strike price for that commodity either on or before the expiration date on a futures contract, the speculator can buy that contract (go long). If the spot price does rise above the strike price, the speculator can then sell the contract (cover the speculator's open position) in the futures market and thereby eliminate the risk assumed by the speculator and receive the difference between the spot price at the time the speculator sells the contract and the strike price of that contract.

While futures contracts like the agricultural example above exist, the commodities involved in futures contracts are certainly not restricted to crops. Financial organizations often seek to reduce different types of risk, for example, the risk that an increase in interest rates, all other things equal, will reduce the value of assets on their balance sheets. Higher interest rates could also create other problems for depository institutions. For example, an increase in interest rates could mean that the depository institution has to pay depositors more to keep their funds, while it cannot increase the rates on loans that it already made unless the loans are adjustable rate loans.

To reduce this risk, a depository institution could enter a futures contract where the institution agrees to sell in the future a certain quantity of an asset, such as T-bills, at a predetermined price. If the depository institution's concern about interest rates rising comes true, the institution sells the T-bills as per the futures contract at the higher price and can re-purchase T-bills at the lower price in the spot market. The gains received by the financial institution can be used to offset losses that it may incur as interest rates rise. Also, as was the case with the agricultural example, some may use futures contracts dealing with stocks, bonds, and other financial instruments as a way to reduce risk by hedging, while others may use futures contracts to take risks by speculating. The next section on credit default swaps briefly discusses how one particular type of futures contract helped to amplify a surge in loan defaults into the largest financial crisis in the United States since the Great Depression.

CREDIT DEFAULT SWAPS

At the turn of the millennium, the pendulum seemed to be swinging in the favor of deregulation again, after perhaps a brief period of re-regulation following the Savings and Loans Crisis. One year after the Financial Modernization Act of 1999 which, among other features, repealed the barrier between investment banking and commercial banking, as noted above, Congress passed the Commodity Futures Modernization Act of 2000, which nullified any state laws regulating futures contracts. After watching a segment on *60 Minutes* (2008) and reading some of the transcript from the segment on the internet, I notice a similarity between the bucket shops of the past and the unbridled activity that unfolded in financial markets in later years. Perhaps that was one of the main themes of the *60 Minutes* (2008) segment.

In the early 1900s, bucket shops were places where people could place bets on equities (without purchasing equity shares). When most stock prices were likely rising, gains could have exceeded losses and could have resulted in net wealth creation from a macroeconomic perspective. However, when many stock prices fell, the macroeconomic impact was likely amplified as people who did not own stocks could have been affected by decreases in equity values. After a stock market crash in the early 1900s, the *60 Minutes* piece (2008) noted that bucket shops were outlawed.

However, terminating bucket shops failed to stop speculation because buyers were required to pay only ten per cent of stock purchase prices up front for the stocks they bought. The stock market collapsed, with the Dow Jones Industrial Average falling from 381 to 41 between September 1929 and July 1932. (Burton and Lombra, 2006, p. 231) In response, legislation discussed earlier in this chapter prohibited the co-mingling of investment banking and commercial banking in the U.S. for decades.

Moving ahead in analysis to much more recent times, information in Burton and Lombra (2006, p. 294) and Mishkin (2004, p. 309) suggests that futures contracts in financial markets are a form of derivatives. (Some, however, may focus primarily if not exclusively on using the term 'derivatives' to refer to options contracts related to financial futures contracts. Options contracts afford buyers of such contracts the opportunity to buy or sell financial assets at a predetermined price on or before an expiration date, as per Mishkin (2004, p. 320).) The proliferation of derivatives has been nothing short of stunning. As a result of the Commodity Futures Modernization Act of 2000, virtually no regulation of derivatives existed, at least prior to the most recent U.S. financial crisis.

One type of derivative became famous (or infamous, in the view of at least some) as a result of the near financial meltdown – the credit default swap. The premise of a credit default swap, from the perspective of a hedger, is rather similar to that of a futures contract from the perspective of a bank guarding against an increase in interest rates that would reduce asset values. The issuer or purchaser of a home mortgage (where the purchaser receives the interest and principal repayments that would have been received by the issuer who originally granted the loan) may want to guard against the borrower defaulting on the loan. A risk-averse mortgage loan issuer (or a third party) can purchase a credit default swap (assuming that another party is willing to sell one) where, in the event of a default, the seller is obligated to compensate the buyer for the agreed upon amount. While some may use credit default swaps to hedge against risks, others can use credit default swaps to speculate. My understanding is that each credit default swap covered not just one individual mortgage, but rather was an income stream guarantee covering multiple mortgages part of a mortgage-backed security.

According to *60 Minutes* (2008), American International Group (AIG), Lehman Brothers, and Bear Stearns sold large quantities of credit default swaps in the 2000s. But at least one person, Eric Dinallo, interviewed in the *60 Minutes* (2008) segment stated that these financial organizations held either little or none of the funds paid to them for the credit default swaps in an extremely liquid form in the event that defaults would cause buyers of the credit default swaps to seek payment from these financial organizations. The surge in home mortgage defaults wound up forcing these financial organizations either into bankruptcy or nearly into bankruptcy, as these financial organizations were legally obligated to pay the owners of the credit default swaps in cases where the borrowers defaulted and those who bought the credit default swaps from these financial organizations made claims. According to Eric Dinallo in the *60 Minutes* (2008) segment, however, the main reason for the financial difficulties of these financial organizations is that they did not have enough liquid assets to pay the claims. Without a substantial bailout from the federal government, it is nearly certain that AIG would have ceased operations.

RESPONSES BY THE FEDERAL RESERVE BANK, THE U.S. TREASURY, AND CONGRESS

Troubled Assets Relief Program (TARP)

An unprecedented policy response in the United States was the Troubled Assets Relief Program, or TARP. Baumol and Blinder (2012, p. 285, 290) state that the number of trades of mortgage-backed securities, or bundled mortgages where the holder of one such security received income streams from multiple mortgages, dropped to such low numbers that financial market participants could not determine their market value. Given rather widespread holdings of mortgage-backed securities (despite plummeting numbers of trades of these securities), Baumol and Blinder (2012, p. 290) discuss how people in the economy grew leery of lending to financial organizations that could be experiencing financial difficulties, at least in part due to potential losses from mortgage-backed securities. After all, how much would you have been willing to pay for an asset whose cash payments to the holder depended on mortgage payments when a surge in defaults was occurring? Further, how much would you have been willing to deposit (particularly if the deposit was not insured) with or lend to a financial organization that could potentially have gone bankrupt due to losses from defaults or a general decline in the value of its assets?

Baumol and Blinder (2012, pp. 290-291) note that, at first, the $700 billion of Troubled Assets Relief Program funds approved by Congress in October 2008 were to be spent by the Treasury to purchase mortgage-backed securities to help stabilize the financial system with the securities to be liquidated later, but the funds wound up purchasing equity in some banks so that the federal government had partial ownership of those banks for a time. Later, Baumol and Blinder (2012, p. 291) note that the federal government wound up earning a profit from TARP as banks returned the TARP funds.

In addition to the increase in equity, Baumol and Blinder (2012, p. 291) observe that TARP funds led to increases in reserves for financial organizations, which, all other things equal, would increase their ability to lend. However, at least some question the degree to which financial organizations increased their lending after at least some of the rounds of quantitative easing (a form of monetary policy discussed later in this chapter) and TARP. A blog written by Brad Plumer (2012) is an example of a piece that notes that banks may have been hesitant to lend funds after problems occurred in the housing market.

Without further expansionary fiscal policy, the United States may be relying primarily on expansionary monetary policy to try to complete the recovery from the Great Recession. In my view, this reliance may be slowing down the recovery, and the decline in the velocity of money could be a key indicator. Without more spending (and perhaps also more lending), it will take longer for real output to return to its trend and for the unemployment rate to return to its natural rate.

Fiscal Stimuli

One of the advantages of fiscal policy over monetary policy when an economy is either in a liquidity trap or near a liquidity trap is that expansionary fiscal policy will more likely result in additional spending. In fact, a government purchase by definition implies that spending by the government sector on the production of a good or a service has occurred. As of this writing, unemployment rates remain relatively high, and growth in real GDP is slower than during many other recoveries. Expansionary fiscal policy can help to increase velocity (or at least keep velocity unchanged or prevent velocity from declining as much) in economies that seem to be suffering from insufficient spending.

To the extent that expansionary fiscal policy prevents other economic activity from occurring, the ability of expansionary fiscal policy to stimulate economic growth is either reduced or eliminated. However, when unemployment rates are high and interest rates are low, it is difficult to identify private sector economic activity that is being curbed by the expansionary fiscal policy as noted in Chapter 2 and the works of others.

To the extent that the theory holds regarding the stimulatory effects of fiscal policy versus monetary policy when interest rates are quite low, one might have expected more from the stimulus measures. The inability of both the first stimulus measure (officially named the Recovery Rebate and Stimulus for the American People Act) approved in early 2008 according to Krugman and Wells (2009, p. 351) and the second stimulus (officially named the American Recovery and Reinvestment Act according to Posner (2009, p. 164)) approved in 2009 according to Baumol and Blinder (2012, p. 215, 292) to stimulate more growth would be because, in my view, these two measures were not large enough and were probably not optimally targeted. For example, more infrastructure projects and more spending in ways likely to generate additional production and additional spending could have been beneficial.

Bailouts and the Fed's Balance Sheet

Krugman and Wells (2009, p. 401) note that problems in the U.S. housing market surfaced in 2006. After housing market problems became evident, Bear Stearns (a highly leveraged firm) failed to make required payments that were necessitated by its leveraged operations, and according to Krugman and Wells (2009, p. 402), faith in Bear Stearns disappeared in 2008. Lehman Brothers was another financial organization that, like Bear Stearns, was not a depository institution. When Lehman Brothers encountered difficulty, it was allowed to fail, unlike Bear Stearns and AIG, which were judged too important to be allowed to cease operations, as per Krugman and Wells (2009, p. 408).

Concerned that the financial system and the entire U.S. macroeconomy were probably on the brink of a catastrophe similar to the Great Depression, the Federal Reserve and the U.S. Treasury took steps in response, some of which are discussed by Krugman and Wells (2009, pp. 408-409). Given the anticipation of 'once in a lifetime'-sized huge problems and economic collapse, the responses may seem more understandable to those skeptical about the merit of such preventative measures. The old adage is, 'better safe than sorry.'

Reacting to the financial crisis of 2008 (and the subsequent recession), the Federal Reserve greatly expanded its balance sheet holdings, both in terms of the total value of assets that the Fed held and also in terms of the types of assets that it held. Krugman and Wells (2009, pp. 408-409) note that usually, the Fed keeps most of its assets in the form of highly liquid government debt – U.S. Treasury bills (T-bills) to be more specific. But in response to the financial crisis, Krugman and Wells (2009, pp. 408-409) point out that the Fed decreased the quantity of T-bills that it owned and established entities to increase lending to provide liquidity to non-depository institutions having financial difficulties. A diagram in Krugman and Wells (2009, p. 409) shows that the assets of the Fed approximately doubled in 2008, from less than $1 trillion in January 2008 to roughly $2 trillion by the end of 2008. The categories of assets in the diagram on page 409 of Krugman and Wells (2009) that seem to have the greatest increases (in dollar amounts) were 'other assets' and 'other loans.'

Targeted Federal Funds Rate and M1 Velocity

Related to the expansion of the Fed's balance sheet were the reduced targets for the federal funds rate. The Federal Open Market Committee (FOMC) of the Federal Reserve Bank changes its target for the federal funds rate or leaves the target unchanged based on economic conditions. For example, the FOMC could instruct the New York branch of the Federal Reserve to buy U.S. government debt (normally T-bills) to reduce interest rates. The T-bills that the Fed would acquire as a result would be counted as assets on its balance sheet.

In instances of rate changes, the FOMC usually decides upon relatively small changes in the target interest rate of one quarter of one percentage point or one half of one percentage point at a time. A benefit of this strategy of small changes when the FOMC feels a change is in order is that the FOMC can more easily avoid overacting to disturbances that prove to be minor and very temporary. A disadvantage of the cautious 'wait and see' approach of the FOMC is that if larger changes in interest rates are necessary to solve a problem, it will take longer to solve that problem. Similar information about stabilization policy in general is in Dornbusch, Fischer, and Startz (2008, p. 423).

Given the relationship between (1) the federal funds rate and other interest rates, and (2) interest rates and liquidity traps and the implication for the velocity of money during monetary expansions in liquidity traps and near liquidity traps, an overview of the federal funds rate targets beginning with the year 2000 would be useful in better understanding current economic conditions. Data from the Saint Louis Federal Reserve web page show that the FOMC's seven-day targeted federal funds rate (not seasonally adjusted) was 6.5 per cent from May 16, 2000 through January 2, 2001. (research.stlouisfed.org/fred2/data/DFEDTAR.txt, accessed February 14, 2013) The target rate had been 5.5 per cent for more than a month before January 1, 2000 through February 1, 2000; 5.75 per cent from February 2, 2000 through March 20, 2000, and six per cent from March 21, 2000 through May 15, 2000. The rate increases were probably implemented to curb perceived inflation pressure. Concern over the possibility of a recession materializing followed by a desire to increase economic growth when a recession occurred (after the bursting of the dot-com bubble) would explain a series of reductions for the targeted federal funds rate falling initially to six per cent and eventually to one per cent after twelve more steps by late June 2003. The targeted federal funds rate remained at one per cent for approximately one year. Krugman and Wells (2009, p. 488) note that this targeted interest rate was approaching a liquidity trap. The increases in the money supply associated with the decline in the federal funds rate from 2001 through late June of 2003 almost certainly helped to reduce the velocity of M1 during that period.

Data from research.stlouisfed.org/fred2/data/DFEDTAR.txt accessed February 14, 2013 show that in late June 2004, the FOMC began a series of increases in the targeted federal funds rate, eventually reaching 5.25 per cent by late June 2006 and remaining there for more than a year. The goal of increasing the federal funds rate target was probably preventing inflation. However, before the end of the decade, other concerns besides inflation became more pressing for the FOMC. The seeds of the financial crisis and the Great Recession in the U.S. may have been planted no later than 2003. Many have argued that keeping the targeted federal funds rate at a relatively low rate (i.e. at one per cent from late June 2003 through late June 2004) led to other interest rates in the economy being artificially low so that excessive speculation in housing resulted in a bubble. My reading of Krugman and Wells (2009, p. 488) is that the authors mention this view (although the extent of their agreement is unclear) within the context of a debate on whether Fed policy should be sensitive to asset prices. Others have argued that the bubble may have been the result of a lax, permissive regulatory environment, as noted by Baumol and Blinder (2012, pp.292-293) (but again, the extent of these authors' agreement is not completely clear).

Regardless of which of the previous two arguments is more correct or if they are both equally correct (or equally incorrect), when a higher percentage of both sub-prime loans and other types of loans went into default, problems resulted and then spread and amplified. Many who sought compensation from credit default swap issuers upon the defaults of mortgage loans covered by swaps could not be compensated as stated in the swaps because the counterparties had insufficient funds. Moreover, the resulting financial difficulties for at least some financial organizations that granted loans or credit default swaps that went into default caused these financial organizations in turn to default on payments that they were supposed to make to counterparties, creating problems for other parties in the economy, and so on. Such is the nature of the financial system. Still further, financial organizations taking control of foreclosed properties often absorbed sizable losses despite taking ownership of the properties as the surge in available housing pushed re-sale prices down.

Thus, in September 2007 (before the worst of the most recent U.S. financial crisis), having grown concerned about the economy as problems in the housing market may have surfaced, the FOMC lowered the target federal funds rate from 5.25 per cent to 4.75 per cent, according to data from research.stlouisfed.org/fred2/data/DFEDTAR.txt (accessed February 14, 2013). After eight more reductions in the target federal funds rate, the target rate stood at 1.00 per cent on October 29, 2008 (having been reduced from 1.50 per cent). In December 2008, the FOMC began to announce a target range for the federal funds rate rather than just one target interest rate. The use of a target range by the Fed was verified in a speech by then FOMC chair Bernanke (2010). The target rate range announced was from 0.00 per cent to 0.25 per cent on December 16, 2008, and has been at that range for more than five years, at least through early October 2014, according to the Saint Louis Federal Reserve

Bank web page. (research.stlouisfed.org/fred2/data/DFEDTARU.txt, accessed online October 13, 2014) Thus, the U.S. economy is either near a liquidity trap or in a liquidity trap and has been at least close to a liquidity trap since December 2008 at the latest.

As noted before, the implication for velocity is that an increase in the money supply during a liquidity trap will reduce the velocity of money because money supply growth and spending capacity growth exceed growth in aggregate demand as measured by nominal GDP. The money supply growth in effect drives velocity down. (This suggests that, at least in complete liquidity traps, a NDVMSL exists, and a NDVMSL is likely to exist when an economy is near a liquidity trap.) Much overlap exists between the time when M1 velocity rose from the third quarter of 2003 through 2007 and the time when the quarterly average federal funds rate was usually rising (from the first quarter of 2004 through the first quarter of 2007). When the quarterly average federal funds rate started falling rapidly in early 2008, the velocity of M1 around that time started decreasing in most quarters as shown by data from www.economagic.com accessed July 20, 2013, and the trend of falling velocity has continued as interest rates remain rather low in the U.S. as of this writing.

Quantitative Easing

When the FOMC started to reduce its target for the federal funds rate in 2007, although the committee may not have realized it at the time, the committee was putting the economy on a path toward either a liquidity trap or a situation close to a liquidity trap, with interest rates near zero and a diminished ability of additional expansionary monetary policy, at least conventional expansionary monetary policy, to spur economic growth. This view helps explain the Federal Reserve's quantitative easing programs. As Baumol and Blinder (2012, p. 271) note, in the case of the United States, quantitative easing consists of the Federal Reserve buying assets that are not T-bills. For example, the Fed could buy Treasury notes or Treasury bonds with longer terms to maturity, but the assets bought by the Fed need not be Treasury debt instruments. Information in Baumol and Blinder (2012, p. 271) and Plumer (2012) implies that the Fed's quantitative easing in the United States started in 2008 when the Fed bought non-Treasury assets to help the market for mortgages.

According to the speech given by Bernanke (2010), quantitative easing has been used very infrequently, if ever, by central banks (except for Japan) prior to the most recent financial crisis. Baumol and Blinder (2012, p. 270-271) note that unconventional monetary policies include not only quantitative easing but also could include much larger loans and atypical loans made by the central bank. Examples of the latter would be loans made by the Federal Reserve to non-depository institutions early in the recent financial crisis.

In his speech, Bernanke (2010) also noted that quantitative easing results in an increase in the monetary base. According to Baumol and Blinder (2012, p. 271), one of the goals of quantitative easing would be a reduction in interest rates. All other things equal, conventional expansionary monetary policy leads to similar results and to a predicted increase in real GDP, at least in the short run, if the economy is not in a liquidity trap. In principle, the zero interest rate bound and the liquidity trap possibility would likely also apply to quantitative easing as well as conventional open market purchases of Treasury debt instruments with short terms to maturity. In fact, in the case of the United States, if the 'target' interest rate is not the federal funds rate but rather the interest rate on Treasury debt with a longer term to maturity, the level below which the interest rate cannot realistically go may be noticeably higher than it is for the federal funds rate (although as of this writing in July 2014 the federal funds rate may be closer to its limit than the ten-year rate).

For example, the interest rate on ten-year U.S. Treasury debt reached around 1.5 per cent during July 2012, according to www.economagic.com accessed July 20, 2013. Would a saver be willing to lend money to the U.S. government or any borrower at a much lower rate for ten years? Inflation is likely to be higher than 1.5 per cent per year for much of the loan, implying that (after subtracting the inflation rate from the nominal interest rate) the saver would be getting a real return less than zero during years when the nominal interest rate is less than the inflation rate. If the saver decides to sell the debt, the saver would incur a capital loss if interest rates rise in the future, thus driving down the resale price of the debt that initially had ten years to maturity. Thus, considering these risks, it appears not very likely that the ten year rate on U.S. Treasury debt would reach, say, 0.5 per cent and perhaps maybe not even one per cent. But, if that is correct, then the *ten year* rate could not have fallen much farther than it had by July 2012 barring unforeseen circumstances.

Unconventional monetary policy has probably helped prevent an economic disaster much worse than the unfortunate most recent financial crisis, recession, and sluggish recovery from occurring in the United States. It has probably also provided some benefit in stimulating spending, helping to increase real GDP somewhat. However, the expansionary effects may also be diminished, just like conventional monetary policy. Quantitative easing may have also approached the limit of its ability to stimulate increases in real GDP in July 2012 with the ten-year Treasury rate so low, and the effectiveness of quantitative easing in early 2014 may still be diminished. If unconventional expansionary monetary policy was having 'rip-roaring' success at stimulating spending, why is the velocity of money continuing to decline, falling nearly every quarter since the fourth quarter of 2007, while nominal GDP is increasing at a much slower rate than the M1 money supply? As longer-term interest rates have fallen sharply, have further increases in the monetary base (equal to total reserves plus currency, as per Mishkin (2004, p. 359) and many others) and the money supply tended to lead to additional dollars and reserves newly part of the money supply and the monetary base being held rather than being spent?

According to Brad Plumer (2012), the Federal Reserve began to purchase mortgage- backed securities as part of what would be the first phase of quantitative easing in November 2008. Information in Plumer's (2012) blog implies that the Fed purchased more than $2 trillion of securities by June 2010, when the first phase of quantitative easing ended. The blog of Plumer (2012) also points out that a second phase of quantitative easing began a few months later in August 2010.

A blog written by Dylan Matthews (2012) notes that the Federal Reserve announced a third quantitative easing program on September 13, 2012. Matthews' (2012) blog describes the main difference between the first two quantitative easing programs (QE 1 and QE2) and the third quantitative easing program (QE3) as being that with QE1 and QE2, the Fed announced certain total quantities of purchases (in dollar amounts) of longer-term securities, while with QE3, the Fed will keep buying securities with longer terms to maturity until the economic recovery is either complete or closer to completion. According to Matthews' (2012) blog, the Fed was planning on buying $85 billion of additional securities (probably) per month through the end of 2012 and beyond. At least some of the information in the Matthews (2012) blog is also in the Plumer (2012) blog.

MORE ABOUT LIMITS OF MONETARY POLICY

With a target range for the federal funds rate currently standing between 0 per cent and 0.25 per cent, many have noted that the low end of the target cannot go lower, assuming a zero interest rate boundary. In that vein, Paul Krugman (2008 and 2011) has repeatedly characterized the United States economy as being in a liquidity trap. Further, Krugman and Wells (2009, p. 488) cautioned that when the federal funds rate target was at 1.0 per cent in the early 2000s, the U.S. economy was approaching a liquidity trap.

Recall that if a liquidity trap in its extreme form exists (not merely a situation near a liquidity trap), then the general public elastically absorbs all dollars added to the money supply but does not spend the dollars on items counted as part of GDP. Many economists today assume that at some very low interest rate, a liquidity trap scenario unfolds as further expansionary monetary policy is unable to drive interest rates any lower. In "The Effectiveness of Fiscal Policy in (Near) Liquidity Traps," Hartman (2010) suggests that the United States economy could have been in a situation close to a liquidity trap, where further increases in the money supply could still lead to economic growth, but with much less effectiveness than in an economy with higher interest rates.

Whether the U.S. economy is actually in a liquidity trap or in a situation close to a liquidity trap but not in a complete liquidity trap, the ability to increase real GDP by increasing the money supply and reducing interest rates presently seems greatly diminished compared with the use of expansionary monetary policy following many previous economic downturns. While Krugman and Wells (2009, p. 488) note the proximity of the U.S. to a liquidity trap in the early 2000s and note that the recovery was relatively sluggish, the reader may want to note that the expansionary monetary policy implemented around that time was probably at least partially responsible for helping to turn economic contraction to growth and helping to prevent unemployment rates from rising nearly as much as they would have without the expansionary monetary policy.

In my opinion, the expansionary monetary policy implemented in the United States in recent years deserves credit for a few reasons. The expansionary monetary policy in my view helped to preclude a much more severe economic downturn from occurring by providing liquidity to reduce borrowing costs (although it may not be possible to reduce interest rates further if the economy is in a liquidity trap) and promoting solvency of financial organizations and access to credit, and it may have increased asset values. Further, to the extent that the U.S. economy was not in a complete liquidity trap, I believe that the higher money supply likely led to gains in real GDP but by a relatively small percentage compared to the percentage increase in the money supply. Moreover, the expansionary policy has reduced the interest cost of federal deficits and helped to reduce, if not eliminate, the deficits' potential for crowding out private sector activities. However, expansionary conventional monetary policies and perhaps unconventional monetary policies (in the absence of expansionary fiscal policy) may have reached their limits or may be about to reach their limits.

An analogy may help illustrate the situation of the Federal Open Market Committee in July 2012 if not at the present time. Think about a sports team practicing for a game. Although a lot of factors impact how well the team will play, how much time the team practices for the game is likely to be an important factor. Most teams spend time practicing before the season begins. Teams usually also practice in between games during the season. When the team first starts practice, additional time spent practicing for any particular game is probably most beneficial to improving performance. But, the more time the team spends practicing for that game, additional time spent practicing becomes less beneficial, at least at some point. In the extreme case where the team spends 24 hours a day (minus the time that games take up) practicing, the team may actually benefit from *less* time spent practicing as fatigue can become a large problem. The key thing to notice is that with a finite amount of time to prepare for any game, a limit exists to how much a team can improve for any one game by increasing the time spent practicing for the game.

Also, for another analogy, consider the example of a student preparing for an exam. Initial time devoted to studying could be the most helpful in preparing the student. But, just like with the sports team, with a finite amount of time, a limit may exist to how much better a student will master the material and perform on the exam based on additional time spent studying. Just like the sports team, a student who spends 24 hours a day preparing for the exam may become fatigued and not perform as well on the exam. Similarly, a music group practicing for a concert may find that the initial time spent practicing may be the most helpful, but spending 24 hours a day practicing could be tiring and counterproductive.

Like the student studying for the exam or the team practicing for a game or the music group preparing for a concert, the FOMC faces a limit in terms of how much the committee can stimulate the economy. If interest rates in the economy are initially considerably higher than zero, initial reductions in interest rates and increases in the money supply frequently if not usually can help to spur the economy. But, when interest rates approach zero per cent after the FOMC has already reduced its target for the federal funds rate, further expansionary monetary policy is likely to have diminished effectiveness. The text of a speech on central bank independence made by FOMC chairman Ben Bernanke (2010) at the Bank of Japan seemed to acknowledge that non-quantitative easing monetary policy in essence did all that it could in more than one country during the recent financial crisis. If longer-term interest rates cannot go much lower, then unconventional expansionary monetary policies alone (without expansionary fiscal policies) may also approach a limit by failing to spark much of an increase in either consumption or investment in physical capital. However, I want to emphasize that unlike a possibility in the examples with the sports team, the student, and the music group practicing 24 hours a day, I am *not* suggesting that monetary policy has been counterproductive in combatting the financial crisis and the Great Recession.

POTENTIAL IMPACT ON VELOCITY

What was the impact of these developments on the velocity of money? Remember that the velocity of M1 peaked in the fourth quarter of 2007. This was less than one year before the collapse of Bear Stearns and the failure of Lehman Brothers.

The short, simple answer to the question (as noted above) is that it appears that the velocity of M1 fell as a result of many, but not all, of the events and measures taken discussed above. The Fed's purchases of T-bills and other assets combined with loans made by the Fed led to a dramatic increase in the M1 money supply. As noted above, data from www.economagic.com and the author's calculations show that the M1 money supply increased by more than 70 per cent in the five years after the peak of M1 velocity.

Recall from the equation of exchange that the velocity of M1 equals nominal GDP divided by M1. Thus, all other things equal, an increase in M1 leads to a decrease in the velocity of M1. Clearly, not all other things have been equal since the fourth quarter of 2007, but as noted above, the growth in nominal GDP since the fourth quarter of 2007 has been quite modest when compared with the rapid acceleration in M1. Thus, the velocity of M1 fell as a consequence of a rapid increase in M1 combined with a relatively sluggish response in total GDP spending. Of course, the recent rapid increase in M1 and the downward trend in both interest rates and velocity seem to be linked to the most recent financial crisis, recession, and sub-par recovery in the United States.

At first, the recent decline in the velocity of M1 in the U.S. was fairly slow. Data from www.economagic.com show that M1 velocity fell initially from approximately 10.37 times per year in the fourth quarter of 2007 to approximately 10.32 times per year in the first quarter of 2008, representing a decrease of only approximately 0.05 times per year. In the following quarter, the second quarter of 2008, the velocity of M1 increased slightly to roughly 10.33 times per year.

Data from www.economagic.com show that a faster decline (than from the fourth quarter of 2007 to the first quarter of 2008) in the velocity of M1 began in the third quarter of 2008, as M1 velocity decreased to about 10.08 times per year, followed by a drop to roughly 9.20 times per year in the fourth quarter of 2008. The latter decline in the velocity of M1 was nearly one full time per year (on an annualized basis). The reader may notice that these sharper declines in M1 velocity began approximately at the time when large financial organizations encountered substantial difficulty.

Careful analysis of monthly M1 data from www.economagic.com shows that despite some months of declining values for M1, overall M1 growth accelerated starting in or around July 2008 (despite a decline in M1 in August of 2008) with even faster growth in September 2008. July 2008 is of course the first month of the third quarter of 2008. This is also when the more rapid decreases in the velocity of M1 began. (As noted, the percentage growth rate of M1 was even higher in September 2008. In the quarterly data sample period from the first quarter of 1959 through the first quarter of 2013, the monthly growth rate from September 2008 was topped only by the growth rates from December 2008, August 2011, and September 2001, with the highest growth rate in December 2008.)

The reader may wish to note that increases in real GDP and the implicit deflator in the second quarter of 2008 were responsible for the slight 'up tick' in M1 velocity that quarter. Moreover, the percentage decreases in real GDP in the third quarter and the fourth quarter of 2008 and the first quarter of 2009 were at a faster rate than the decline in real GDP in the first quarter of 2008, thus helping to explain the more rapid decrease in the velocity of M1. But, as noted before, it seems that the decline in real GDP and perhaps the rapid increase in M1 were linked to the financial crisis. So, does the rapid decrease in the velocity of M1 all come back, at least in a sense, to the financial crisis? The financial crisis certainly could have led to a decrease in the desire to spend, which would have resulted in a decrease in velocity, all other things equal.

Although the decline in the velocity of M1 slowed down in the first quarter of 2009 compared with the sharp decline in the fourth quarter of 2008, the velocity of M1 continued to decrease nearly every quarter since then. The timing of the smaller decreases in the velocity of M1 began perhaps soon after financial markets regained some stability and soon before real GDP started increasing again. Still, it may be too early to conclude that the financial crisis alone explains the decrease in the velocity of

M1. Although slower in most subsequent quarters than in the fourth quarter of 2008, quarterly M1 growth (on a percentage basis) continued at a pace usually faster than the growth rate of nominal GDP through the first quarter of 2013 (and beyond). Thus, the velocity of M1 continued to trend downward despite the fact that the worst of the most recent U.S. financial crisis had ended more than four years earlier.

Whether plummeting M1 velocity in the U.S. was only due to the most recent U.S. financial crisis could possibly be essentially a matter of semantics given what could be a very close relationship between (1) the most recent financial crisis in the U.S., (2) the decline in nominal GDP followed by slow growth in nominal GDP, and (3) the Fed's expansionary monetary policy implemented to offset the financial crisis, the Great Recession, and the Not-So-Great Recovery.

Whether one takes the view that the Fed initiated an increase in the money supply in an effort to reduce interest rates and increase growth in real output, or one instead takes the view that the Fed reacted to a large increase in money demand by supplying more dollars to those who wanted to hold them, the fact remains that after the fourth quarter of 2007, nominal GDP growth has been slower than the growth in the quarterly average money supply in most quarters in the U.S., thus accounting for the decrease in velocity. The second explanation with the Fed reacting rather than initiating could be important given that the percentage growth in M1 has been faster than the percentage growth in M2 recently. Even so, the Fed may not have wanted interest rates to remain around their previous levels or to rise following what could have been a surge in money demand during the most recent financial crisis, recession, and sluggish recovery.

What is behind what was initially a decrease in aggregate demand followed by a return to growth in aggregate demand but at a slower rate (or at least what feels like a slower rate) than before the financial crisis? One of the results of the financial crisis is a process of deleveraging, or the cancellation of debt. Obviously, when debt is repaid, the amount that was owed is cancelled upon repayment. However, repayment of debt forces borrowers to use funds that could have been used toward GDP spending to repay loans, where the loan repayments do not count toward GDP (although the interest payments probably do). Deleveraging could also include debts written off due to default. In this case, lenders may wind up reducing their demand for GDP spending due to a smaller income stream from loans. Whether due to defaults or paying down debt or a combination of both, aggregate demand would decrease, all other things equal, which in turn would reduce velocity.

Could distributional factors be at work as well? My reading of Mankiw (2007, p. 435) is that those with the greatest incomes spend a smaller percentage of their incomes, on average, than those with less income. Combining this with the observation made by Morici (2013) and Krugman (2013) and many others that an overwhelming majority of the recent increases in income in the U.S. economy have gone to a small group may raise the question, 'Has velocity in the U.S. plummeted because more dollars in the U.S. are in the hands of those less likely to spend them than before?' Are there other explanations?

BRIEF COMMENTS ON THE U.S. ECONOMY IN 2013 AND 2014

The sharp decline in the velocity of M1 in the United States following the fourth quarter of 2007 is certainly consistent with the U.S. economy either being in a liquidity trap or being near a liquidity trap. In theory, however, the velocity of money can decline without the economy being in a situation of extremely low interest rates. (Periods of very low interest rates, in turn, may bring to mind either contraction in real output, stagnant real output, or sluggish growth in real output. However, the World War II years in the United States are probably a counterexample.)

The sub-sample period following the fourth quarter of 1984 through the second quarter of 1987 was a period further discussed in Chapters 3 and 4 when the velocity of M1 fell from approximately 7.4 times per year (on an annualized basis) in the fourth quarter of 1984 to approximately 6.3 times per year in the second quarter of 1987, while the quarterly average for the federal funds rate was greater than six per cent each quarter and the quarterly average ten-year Treasury rate during that period exceeded seven per cent each quarter during that time. In fact, the quarterly average federal funds rate was between 7.8 per cent and 8.5 per cent for five quarters from the first quarter of 1985 through the first quarter of 1986, with the quarterly average ten-year rate between 8.5 per cent and 11.6 per cent during those quarters. Starting with the first quarter of 1985 and running through the second quarter of 1987, real GDP grew at a quarterly average rate (ignoring compounding) of nearly 0.9 per cent or roughly 3.5 per cent per year, based on data from www.economagic.com and the author's calculations. These are hardly statistics that would bring up thoughts of liquidity traps among economists, and yet the velocity of money fell noticeably during this period.

Clearly, the data on interest rates and real GDP growth in the U.S. economy in late 2012, 2013, and into early 2014 are quite different, with much lower interest rates and much lower real GDP growth, the latter at least on average. The combination of extremely low interest rates, below-average growth in real GDP (if not a return to contracting real GDP), and falling velocity of M1 combined with relatively rapid growth in the M1 money supply suggest that the U.S. economy either is approaching a liquidity trap or was already in a liquidity trap. If an economy is in a complete liquidity trap, then additional dollars added to the money supply will be held rather than being spent, resulting in a decrease in the velocity of money as nominal GDP will not change despite the increase in the money supply. If an economy is closing in on a liquidity trap but is not yet completely in such a trap, then some of the dollars newly added to the money supply will be spent but total spending on the goods part of nominal GDP increases at a rate much less than the rate of increase in the money supply, resulting in a decrease in the velocity of money.

Given a diagnosis that the U.S. economy is either near a liquidity trap or in a liquidity trap, I find it at best debatable as to whether quantitative easing alone will be able to generate enough spending increases to return real GDP in the U.S. back to its potential or trend level and return the unemployment rate to its natural rate (with full-time employment rather than either no job or only part-time work for more job seekers who seek full-time jobs), and at middle-class-maintaining (if not higher) wages and salaries in the near future. The reason why, in short, is that financial organizations and others in the economy seem to be holding the vast majority of the dollars newly added to the money supply rather than spending the dollars. Given the phasing out of quantitative easing discussed by Crutsinger (2014) and many others, the effectiveness of monetary policy going forward will be diminished even further in the short term barring a reversal.

Although the worst of the most recent U.S. financial crisis may be over, the after effects may still be holding the economy back. Regarding monetary policy, Crutsinger (2014) and others have noted that the FOMC started to reduce its monthly quantitative easing purchases by $10 billion in or around January 2014. This 'tapering' as it is often called could be premature if as a result interest rates rise substantially (which could increase the likelihood of crowding out) and/or if economic growth slows down. Phasing out quantitative easing could be comparable to a driver taking her or his foot off of the gas pedal (if not hitting the break) too soon before the journey is over. Although continuing QE alone may not provide substantial help in stimulating growth in employment and real output, phasing it out too early may possibly be harmful.

In my view, the U.S. economy has plenty of dollars. Now it is time (and actually it may have been time a while ago) to get the dollars moving again more rapidly as part of trades for economic production. Regarding stabilization policy measures, combining expansionary fiscal policy in the lead role with expansionary monetary policy in a support role, in my view, gives the best chance of increasing growth quickly.

Paradoxically, the United States may have implemented contractionary fiscal policy in the year 2013. The payroll tax holiday has expired as pointed out by Schwartz (2013) and others. This implies an increase in taxes collected. Additionally, Malewitz (2013) and others have pointed out that sequestration has occurred. This is one of the causes of *de*creases in government spending. The normal fiscal policy prescription for trying to stimulate growth in an economy like the U.S. economy in 2013 is to *in*crease government spending and reduce taxes (and thus increase the federal budget deficit). The estimated *de*crease in quarterly real GDP (on a seasonally adjusted, annualized basis) for the first quarter of 2014 was more than two per cent, based on data from www.economagic.com accessed September 28, 2014 and the author's calculations. While weather and other factors contributed to this decline and although the decline was temporary, could the contractionary fiscal policy measures noted above have played a role?

Readers may wonder if we as an economy chose the best possible policy responses to the Great Recession and the Not-So-Great Recovery. If the responses were less than optimal, how many more jobs could the economy have created, how many more goods and services could have been produced and consumed, how many failed ventures could have been saved, and how much less hardship and suffering would have been imposed? Quantitative easing can help to reduce crowding out, the interest burden of the national debt, and longer-term interest rates (further), while increasing reserves and the money supply; but it cannot guarantee increases in real GDP and decreases in unemployment rates equal to the sizes that seem to be desired by many policymakers and many members of the general public. The reason why is that QE cannot guarantee that the newly added dollars will be spent frequently enough to achieve the goals. Regarding the effectiveness of monetary policy, conventional or otherwise, in an economy that is either in a liquidity trap or close to a liquidity trap, readers may remember the old cliché which begins, 'You can lead a horse to water…' Although perhaps in a somewhat different context, Posner (2009, p. 211) makes a similar point.

Because the money supply itself may have an important impact on velocity, the next chapter estimates velocity functions as an initial step in quantifying the effect. To conclude this chapter, Table 5.1 presents a brief summary of some of the most important factors that possibly led up to the U.S. Financial Crisis of 2007 and 2008. It also summarizes some of the main bankruptcies and policies implemented to try to stimulate economic recovery and perhaps the phasing out of some of these policies.

LIST OF EVENTS (continued on next page)

Gramm-Leach-Bliley Financial Services Modernization Act of 1999
Among other features, repealed Glass-Steagall barrier that divided commercial banking and investment banking

Commodity Futures Modernization Act of 2000
Prohibited states from having regulations of financial futures

Target Federal Funds Rate at 1.0 per cent from late June 2003 through late June 2004
According to some, fueled excessive speculation in housing market

Target Federal Funds Rate back to 5.25 per cent late June 2006
Did higher interest rates lead to an increase in mortgage-loan defaults when interest rates on adjustable-rate-mortgages rose?

FOMC begins to lower targets for Federal Funds Rate mid-September 2007

First Stimulus Passed February 2008
Short-term increase in growth rate of real GDP following a one-time tax rebate, unable to stave off the Great Recession

Lehman Brothers fails in September 2008 despite government bailouts for AIG and Bear Stearns
Bailouts and non-bailouts that end in bankruptcy can shake confidence in the economy and potentially lead to a decrease in the velocity of money

Troubled Assets Relief Program (TARP) Passed October 2008
U.S. Treasury wound up with partial ownership of some banks for a time; the government eventually earned a profit

Target Range for Federal Funds Rate reduced to between 0.00 and 0.25 per cent December 2008
Close to a liquidity trap, if not a liquidity trap; to the extent that velocity is positively correlated with the federal funds rate and other interest rates (assuming causality) that fell, the decrease in rates helped cause the fall in the velocity of M1

Quantitative Easing Commenced November 2008, with two additional programs introduced later
The Fed began unconventional monetary policies such as buying non T-bill assets; partially responsible for more rapid money supply growth and the decrease in the velocity of M1 (to the extent that the decrease in velocity was caused by the rapid growth in the money supply (combined with sluggish growth in nominal GDP))

Table 5.1 (Part One) Overview of Some of the Main Events Related to the U.S. Financial Crisis of 2007 and 2008, the Great Recession, Sluggish Recovery, Efforts to Combat the Recession, and the Decrease in the Velocity of Money

LIST OF EVENTS (continued from previous page)

Second Stimulus Passed 2009
May have prevented the Great Recession from becoming much worse; however unable to keep unemployment rates from soaring and subsequently slowing falling

Payroll tax holiday expiration

Sequestration

Tapering of Quantitative Easing

Real GDP contraction by more than two per cent in the first quarter of 2014

Table 5.1 (Part Two) Overview of Some of the Main Events Related to the U.S. Financial Crisis of 2007 and 2008, the Great Recession, Sluggish Recovery, Efforts to Combat the Recession, and the Decrease in the Velocity of Money

Sources: Burton and Lombra (2006), Mishkin (2004), *60 Minutes*, Saint Louis Federal Reserve Bank web page, Krugman and Wells (2009), Baumol and Blinder (2012), Posner (2009), Plumer (2012), Matthews (2012), Schwartz (2013), Malewitz (2013), Crutsinger (2014), www.economagic.com

CHAPTER FIVE REFERENCES

Baumol, W. J. and Blinder, A. S. (2012) *Macroeconomics: Principles and Policy*, twelfth edition. South-Western Cengage Learning, Mason, Ohio.

Bernanke, B. (2010) "Central Bank Independence, Transparency, and Accountability." May 25, 2010, accessed February 11, 2013; available online at: www.federalreserve.gov/newsevents/speech/bernanke20100525a.htm

Burton, M. and Lombra, R. (2006) *The Financial System and the Economy: Principles of Money and Banking*, fourth edition. Thomson South-Western, Mason, Ohio.

Crutsinger, M. (2014) "Fed Minutes: Pare Stimulus." *Atlanta Journal-Constitution*, February 20, 2014, p. A13.

Dornbusch, R., Fischer, S., and Startz, R. (2008) *Macroeconomics*, tenth edition. McGraw-Hill Irwin, Boston, Massachusetts.

Hartman, H. C. (2010) "The Effectiveness of Fiscal Policy in (Near) Liquidity Traps." *International Journal of Accounting Information Science and Leadership,* vol. 3, iss. 7, pp. 1-10.

Friedman, M. and Schwartz, A. (1963) *A Monetary History of the United States, 1867-1960.* Princeton University Press, Princeton, New Jersey.

Krugman, P. (2008) "Macro Policy in a Liquidity Trap (Wonkish)." November 15, 2008, accessed February 19, 2014; available online at: krugman.blogs.nytimes.com/2008/11/15/macro-policy-in-a-liquidity-trap-wonkish

Krugman, P. (2011) "Yes, We're in a Liquidity Trap." March 16, 2011, accessed February 19, 2014; available online at: krugman.blogs.nytimes.com/2011/03/16/yes-were-in-a-liquidity-trap

Krugman, P. (2013) "Plutocrats Feeling Persecuted." September 26, 2013, accessed October 9, 2013; available online at: www.nytimes.com/2013/09/27/opinion/krugman-plutocrats-feeling-persecuted.html?_r=0

Krugman, P. and Wells, R. (2009) *Macroeconomics*, second edition. Worth Publishers, New York, New York.

Malewitz, J. (2013) "Universities Scale Back Research." *Atlanta Journal-Constitution*, April 14, 2013, p. A16.

Mankiw, N. G. (2007) *Brief Principles of Macroeconomics*, fourth edition. Thomson South-Western, Mason, Ohio.

Matthews, D. (2012) "QE 3 Is On! Fed to Buy $85b through December, and Then Keep Going." September 13, 2012, accessed February 12, 2013; available online at: www.washingtonpost.com/blogs/wonkblog/wp/2012/09/13/qe3-is-on

Mishkin, F. S. (2004) *The Economics of Money, Banking, and Financial Markets*, seventh edition. Pearson Addison Wesley, Boston, Massachusetts.

Morici, P. (2013) "Obama Policies Increasing Inequality." September 16, 2013, accessed October 9, 2013; available online at: www.breitbart.com/Big-Government/2013/09/16/Obama-Policies-Make-Inequality-a-lot-Worse

Plumer, B. (2012) "QE3: What Is Quantitative Easing? And Will It Help the Economy?" September 13, 2012, accessed February 12, 2013; available online at: www.washingtonpost.com/blogs/wonkblog/wp/2012/09/13/qe3-what-is-quantitative-easing-and-will-it-help-the-economy

Posner, R. A. (2009) *A Failure of Capitalism*. Harvard University Press, Cambridge, Massachusetts.

research.stlouisfed.org/fred2/data/DFEDTAR.txt

research.stlouisfed.org/fred2/data/DFEDTARU.txt

Schwartz, N. D. (2013) "Higher Payroll Tax Saps Buying Power." *Atlanta Journal-Constitution*, February 10, 2013, p. A2.

60 Minutes. (2008) Steve Kroft, reporter. First broadcast October 26, 2008, accessed online May 6, 2014 at www.cbsnews.com/news/the-bet-that-blew-up-wall-street

www.economagic.com

CHAPTER 6

THE VELOCITY OF MONEY AS A FUNCTION OF M1 OR OTHER VARIABLES

SOME OF THE VARIABLES THAT IMPACT VELOCITY

After the Preface and the first five chapters, the importance of the velocity of money should be clear. What causes the velocity of money, particularly the velocity of M1, to change? More specifically, are some variables more important for determining velocity than others? What is the relationship between these variables and velocity? And, could these relationships change over time? This chapter *begins* to address these four questions. Of course, by the algebraic definition of the velocity of money, any change in velocity must be caused by one or more of the following: a change in real GDP, a change in the price level (measured by the implicit deflator), or a change in the nominal money supply. However, changes in these variables do not preclude the possibility that other factors caused changes in real GDP, the price level, or the nominal money supply.

Interest rates provide examples of variables that could be intertwined with real GDP, the implicit deflator, the nominal money supply, and velocity. More specifically, changes in real GDP, the deflator, and the nominal money supply could cause changes in interest rates, while changes in interest rates could lead to changes in real GDP, the deflator, and the nominal quantity of money demanded. If changes in interest rates do cause changes in real GDP, the deflator, and the nominal money supply, then all other things equal changes in interest rates would cause changes in velocity unless the percentage changes in nominal GDP resulting from changes in interest rates are exactly equal to the percentage changes in the nominal money stock due to the changes in interest rates, thus keeping velocity unchanged.

While acknowledging that changes in interest rates and other factors can impact velocity by impacting the component parts of velocity, the following analysis of various sub-sample periods will focus more on the impact of real GDP, price levels, the nominal money supply, the real money supply, and nominal GDP on velocity. However, some discussion of interest rates will be presented. For example, the next section under the heading beginning with "A Note on the Real Money Supply…" explains the inclusion of the 'combined variables' real money supply and nominal GDP in the analysis. Less emphasis on the two interest rate variables, the federal funds rate and the ten-year U.S. Treasury rate, is in part due to at least two of the other variables considered (including the 'combined variables' nominal GDP and real money supply) performing better in each sub-sample period. Particular emphasis will be placed on both the nominal M1 money supply and the real M1 money supply. The finding of a negative relationship between either one of these two money supply measures and the velocity of money supports *but does not prove* the existence of a non-decreasing-velocity money supply level (NDVMSL). For example, perhaps it is a coincidence that nominal M1 and its velocity seem to move in opposite directions in most quarters in some sub-sample periods but not in other sub-sample periods.

To help in the study of velocity, let's consider regressions during each of the quarterly data sub-sample periods identified in Chapter 3 of this book. The velocity of M1 serves as the dependent variable on the left side of each regression equation. The lone independent variable on the right side of each equation is either (1) one of the three variables from the ratio used to calculate velocity (real GDP, the implicit deflator, and the quarterly average of nominal M1, each of which could be described as a 'non-combined variable'), or (2) an interest rate measure (either the federal funds rate or the ten-year U.S. Treasury rate), or (3) one of the 'combined' variables, either nominal GDP or the real money supply. The regression equations also include a constant term (not considered a variable) on the right side.

The reader can think about the parts of the regression results presented below as finding both the slope and the intercept-term for the 'best-fit' lines using ordinary least squares for scatter graph plots of data. (For those not familiar, the value of the intercept is the point on the vertical axis where the best-fit line intersects the vertical axis.) Each best-fit line has velocity as the dependent variable on the left side of each equation and on the vertical axis of each diagram. One of the seven other variables mentioned in the previous paragraph, for example, M1 or real GDP; serves as the independent variable on the right side of each equation and on the horizontal axis of each diagram. By estimating each best-fit line, this study aims to estimate a linear function for the velocity of money as a function of *one* of the other variables mentioned in the previous paragraph.

A NOTE ON REAL MONEY SUPPLY, NOMINAL GDP, AND DIVIDING THE FIRST SUB-SAMPLE PERIOD

Given that velocity can be decomposed into two main components as noted by Mishkin (2004, p.523) and likely others, namely, real GDP and real money supply or real money demand, then it may be useful to look at a graph showing velocity and real money supply from the first quarter of 1959 through the first quarter of 2013. From the equation of exchange, any change in velocity not attributable to the real money supply (or real money demand) must be attributable to changes in real GDP. Figure 6.1 below shows the velocity of M1 and the real money supply calculated by the author as quarterly average M1 multiplied by 100 and divided by the GDP deflator based on data from www.economagic.com as of July 20, 2013. This procedure produces an estimate of the quarterly-average real money supply measured in billions of constant-buying-power dollars, with the buying power of each of these dollars approximately equal to the buying power of one U.S. dollar in the year 2005 (or the buying power of one billion of these constant-buying-power dollars having the buying power of one billion dollars in the year 2005). The general pattern of the points in Figure 6.1 is somewhat similar to the pattern in Figure 2.1 in Chapter 2, but with some potentially important exceptions.

Similarly, velocity could also be broken into nominal GDP and nominal M1, where nominal GDP is simply real GDP times the deflator divided by 100. Thus, a scatter graph diagram somewhat similar to Figure 6.1 could be constructed for the full sample period from 1959q1 through 2013q1 showing the velocity of M1 on the vertical axis and nominal GDP on the horizontal axis rather than the real money supply. From the algebraic definition of velocity, any change in velocity not attributable to a change in nominal GDP must be attributable to a change in the money supply. The importance of real M1 at least at times in determining the velocity of M1 and the importance at least at times of nominal GDP impacting the velocity of M1 lead to the inclusion of these two variables in regression analysis in this chapter.

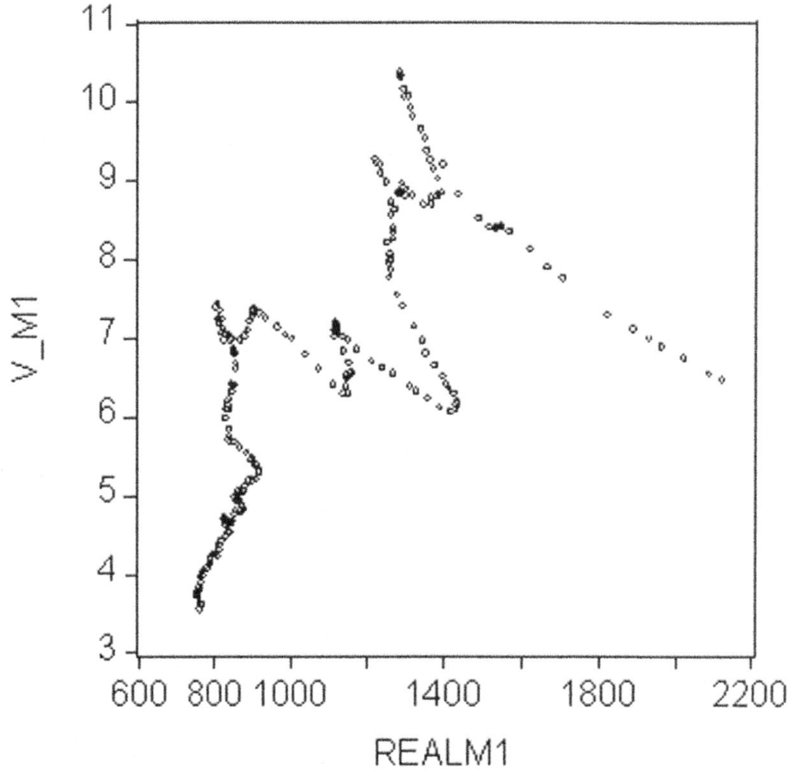

Figure 6.1 The Velocity of (Nominal) M1 and Real M1 in billions of 2005 dollars
1959q1 through 2013q1
Source: www.economagic.com and the author's calculations

Figure 6.1 suggests that changes in real M1 could be important for explaining the velocity of M1. In three of the ten sub-sample periods, the use of real M1 as the only independent variable in regressions minimizes the sum of squared residuals and maximizes the adjusted R-squared statistic. Thus, attention will be paid not only to nominal M1 but also to real M1 in the analysis to follow. In two sub-sample periods, nominal GDP produces the smallest sum of squared residuals and the largest adjusted R-squared statistic of the variables considered, further explaining its inclusion.

Initially during the first sub-sample period (which ran from the first quarter of 1959 through the third quarter of 1981), not only was nominal M1 trending upward, but real M1 also was trending upward most quarters. However, in the first quarter of 1973, real M1 reached a local maximum. Starting in the second quarter of 1973, real M1 began to trend downward most quarters through the fourth quarter of 1975, likely due largely to rising inflation. Although real M1 then increased most quarters through the third quarter of 1978, real M1 failed to reach its level of the first quarter of 1973 or its level in the four quarters of the years 1971 and 1972 and in some quarters prior to the year 1971. Beginning again with the fourth quarter of 1978, real M1 decreased most quarters until reaching a local minimum in the fourth quarter of 1981, one quarter after the end of the first sub-sample period. At that point, real M1 was below its local minimum from the fourth quarter of 1975.

In light of (1) the change starting around the second quarter of 1973 from generally increasing real money supply to generally decreasing real money supply and then going through a partial recovery followed by another period of generally decreasing real money supply through the year 1981, and perhaps more importantly, (2) rising inflation starting around the second quarter of 1973; the first sub-sample period of quarterly data has been further divided in the descriptive analysis to follow. The first part runs from the first quarter of 1959, the beginning of the quarterly data sample period, through the first quarter of 1973. The second part spans from the second quarter of 1973 through the third quarter of 1981, the end of the first sub-sample period. Further dividing the first sub-sample period in this way may also help to break up the analysis of a sub-sample period that is relatively long compared with the other sub-sample periods.

COMMENTS ABOUT METHODOLOGY AND CAVEATS

Much of the methodology in this chapter consists of specifying regressions in each sub-sample period with the velocity of the M1 money supply as a function of a constant and one of the following variables: either nominal M1, real GDP, the implicit deflator, the federal funds rate, the ten-year rate, nominal GDP, or the real money supply. The data were from www.economagic.com as of July 20, 2013. Comparisons between the sums of squared residuals for the different regressions from EViews 5.1 software in each sub-sample period and between the adjusted R-squared statistics in each sub-sample period show that the use of nominal M1 as the sole right-hand-side variable in many sub-sample periods provides either the best fit or the second best fit of the seven variables that serve as the sole variable on the right side of each equation (not counting the estimated constant terms or the error terms as variables). I interpret this as showing that at times the M1 money supply has a very important impact on the velocity of money or at least that compared with the other variables considered, changes in nominal M1 seem to be fairly closely associated with changes in velocity at times.

The reader should first note that the regressions are illustrative for a general audience and are *not* intended as a formal, rigorous proof of a hypothesis. The purpose of the regressions is to show that, *at times*, a simple function with the velocity of M1 as a function of the level of nominal M1 appears to explain a great deal of the variation in the velocity of M1 and *at times* appears better at explaining the variation than any of the other 'non-combined variables' considered, or at least that compared with the other variables considered, it appears that there is a close relationship at times between nominal M1 and its velocity. As a reminder, this would be consistent with the non-decreasing velocity money supply level (NDVMSL) theory, but it is *not* proof of the NDVMSL theory. Sometimes, nominal M1 performs better than either of the two 'combined variables.'

For completeness and for those who prefer it, the Appendix to Chapter Six also contains correlations between the velocity of M1 and each of the seven explanatory variables. However, the relative rankings of the absolute values of the correlations between each variable and the velocity of M1 from greatest to smallest in each sub-sample period match the relative rankings for each variable in minimizing the sum of squared residuals in a regression for velocity from smallest to largest in each of the ten sub-sample periods.

I acknowledge that many areas for improving the econometric analysis presented in this chapter may exist. For example, the points made by Laidler (1993, pp. 112-118) and others regarding identification problems (which in the context of Chapter 6 could include potential difficulty distinguishing movements along versus shifts in the velocity functions) and simultaneity problems (because the error term in each period from each regression equation may be correlated with the variable value on the right side of that equation) may merit additional attention. Further, I would expect that the error terms from many, if not all, of the regressions would exhibit serial correlation, where knowing the value of an error term from one period provides useful knowledge for predicting the error term from another period. Readers interested in learning more about serial correlation may consult Hamilton (1994, pp. 225-227) or other sources for further information.

Additionally, in the following regression equations for velocity, each regression has omitted variables that could help in explaining the variation of velocity. (EViews 5.1 software offers a test for omitted variables, indicating that this could be a general econometric problem.) Given analysis in Dougherty (2007, pp. 61-63, 150-151) and likely elsewhere about factors such as (1) whether a variable not included in a regression is actually responsible for any regression relationships found and (2) less reliance over time on the R-squared and adjusted R-squared statistics, readers should interpret the results in this chapter accordingly. Moreover, the variables in the regression may be unit root processes and are thus not stationary. Still further, the statistical results to follow do not adequately address the interrelationship between M1, real GDP, the deflator, and interest rates that many believe exists.

According to Hamilton (1994, p. 561), one method for preventing spurious regressions when using nonstationary variables is to use past values of both the dependent variable and the independent variable (and the current value of the independent variable) all on the right side of the regression equation. If my understanding of Hamilton (1994, p. 226) is correct, the presence of lagged independent and dependent variables could also reduce, if not eliminate, problems associated with serial correlation. Hamilton (1994, p. 562) also discusses other methods for preventing spurious regressions including the use of differenced data and notes that many use this method.

Further, Hamilton (1994, p. 652-653) discusses a method with several phases given what he seems to indicate was (and may still be) a lack of consensus. The first phase is to specify a vector autoregression (VAR) with the data in levels. The second phase is to identify any variables in the analysis that are not stationary (for example, those with unit roots). If one or more of the variables are not stationary, then a VAR model with any nonstationary variables on the left sides of the equations in differenced form to achieve stationarity could be estimated. If two or more of the variables are cointegrated, the VAR model with data in differenced form should be a vector error correction (VEC) model which incorporates the cointegrating relationship. Results from the VAR model with no differenced variables can be compared with results from the model with at least some of the variables in differenced form. Future work could utilize this method.

(For those not familiar, a VAR model has two or more variables with each variable in the model a function of one or more lagged values of both that variable and all of the other variables in the model plus an error term and perhaps other terms. Frequently, VAR models impose a form such that at least one variable in the model may be impacted by a contemporaneous error term from another variable in the model within the same period, but at least one other variable may be such that the error term from one or more of the other variables impacts that other variable only after the delay of one period.

Briefly, two or more nonstationary variables are cointegrated if each of the variables individually is not stationary but a linear combination of these variables produces a new variable that is stationary. If cointegration is present, a VEC model which includes the cointegrating relationship is appropriate.

For more about VAR models, cointegration, and VEC models, readers may consult Hamilton (1994, pp. 257-268, 571-618) or other sources.)

Given the areas noted above, readers should interpret the results to follow with appropriate caution. However, despite this disclaimer, readers may benefit nonetheless from reviewing the regression results. Further, regarding serial correlation and unit roots (where the presence of either or both could call into question the ability of regression analysis to 'prove' causality), this study does not need to try to prove *statistically* that real GDP, the deflator, and the level of nominal M1 have an impact on the velocity of M1 *because all three of those variables are in the algebraic definition of the velocity of M1*. To help see this, recall that, from the equation of exchange, $V = (P*Y)/M$. In the special case where two of the three variables in the algebraic definition of velocity (the deflator, real GDP, and money supply) are constant, a change in the third variable *must* be associated with a change in velocity in order to preserve the equality. Further, considerable discussion in the text has addressed the relationship between these three variables and the velocity of M1.

Regarding interest rates, Hartman (2011 and 2013) finds that interest rates (or changes in interest rates in some cases in Hartman (2013)) can impact the velocity of money. At least some other studies have similar findings. According to Laidler (1993, p. 144), findings of Brunner and Meltzer (1963) include that interest rates impacted velocity in the U.S.

The estimates of the *magnitude* of the impact of each variable considered in this chapter on velocity, however, could be subject to considerable debate. To the extent that the above points or others detract from the econometric analysis to be presented, future work could make appropriate adjustments, corrections, and improvements. For example, the velocity of money and other variables could be expressed in first difference form, where appropriate. Also, steps could be taken, if necessary, to correct for serial correlation. In this regard, the results in this chapter could be thought of as an early step, if not a preliminary step, in the analysis. In the interest of documenting and disseminating findings, let's proceed with the caveats in mind.

INTRODUCTORY REMARKS ABOUT THE RESULTS

Again, readers may consider parts of the regression results as giving the slopes and intercepts of the best-fit lines for graphs of data with the velocity of money on the vertical axis and one of the other variables on the horizontal axis. This is, by analogy, similar to estimating a linear demand function for a good. For example, given data on the price per gallon of lemonade (the independent variable on the vertical axis rather than the dependent variable, as in our case) and the quantity of lemonade that U.S. consumers bought each week at different prices over different time periods, we could estimate a linear relationship between the two variables if other factors were nearly constant. This is often called a demand function or a demand curve, even if the function is linear. (In reality, demand functions may be more likely curved rather than linear.)

Other factors likely influence the number of gallons of lemonade each week that U.S. consumers want to buy at different prices per gallon. One example would be the prices of milk, colas, juices, and other soft drinks. Another would be consumers' incomes. Yet another would be the number of consumers. These other factors are often thought of as shifters of the demand function. By analogy, if we think about the velocity of money as a function of just one other variable (for example, the M1 money supply), we could consider the other variables (real GDP and the implicit deflator) as shifters of the function.

These other factors not directly included in the regression explain (or at least help to explain) why the observed data points are not exactly on the best-fit line. One reason for including only one independent variable on the right side of the equation is simplicity. Another reason is that this implicitly assumes that either other variables are unchanged or that changes in other variables are unimportant. The study then compares results from regressions, primarily the sums of squared residuals and adjusted R-squared statistics, within the same sub-sample period to determine which variable or variables in each sub-sample period seem most capable of explaining changes in velocity, with a smaller sum of squared residuals produced by one variable rather than another implying a better fit for the regression with the smaller sum. Comparison of estimated velocity functions between sample periods may help to illustrate changes in the relationships between variables. Again, readers can consider the estimation of the following velocity functions an early, if not preliminary, step.

In the regression results with only one independent variable to follow, the dependent variable in all of the regressions below is the velocity of M1. The period for each regression covers one of the sub-sample periods identified in the study (where quarterly data were readily available) based primarily on whether the velocity of M1 appears to be trending upward or trending downward. Each sub-sample period is identified above each table. The first two columns of estimates in each table have the estimated coefficient for the one variable on the right side of each equation and the estimated constant term in each equation. These two estimates could be substituted into the algebraic equation from each figure below. The general formula for the best fit lines is below in equation (6.1).

(6.1) VELOCITY = ESTIMATED COEFFICIENT*VARIABLE + ESTIMATED CONSTANT + ERROR.

The next two columns of numbers are the R-squared and the adjusted R-squared estimates from each regression. These estimates, with a maximum possible value of +1.0, deal with how much of the variation in velocity is attributable to or is explained by the changes in the values of the dependent variable on the right side of the equation. The adjusted R-squared assesses a penalty for inclusion of additional variables that add little to explaining the variation of the dependent variable.

The final column of numbers shows the sum of squared residuals from each regression. The sum of squared residuals seems to provide a measure of how well the regression line fits that scatter-graph plot of data. A smaller sum of squared residuals for a variable is associated with greater R-squared and adjusted R-squared statistics based on the formulas for calculating the R-squared and the adjusted R-squared statistics. Readers may refer to sources such as Dougherty (2007, pp. 61-64, 150-151) for more information about the sum of squared residuals and the R-squared and adjusted R-squared statistics.

Regression results for the five 'non-combined' variables precede the results for the two 'combined variables,' nominal GDP and the real M1 money supply. A blank row separates the two sets of variables. The first row of results labeled 'M1' has the regression results for nominal M1. The second row labeled 'GDP' has the regression results for real GDP. The remaining variables appear below 'GDP' in the following order: the implicit deflator labeled 'Defl,' the federal funds rate labeled 'FFR,' the ten-year U.S. Treasury rate labeled "10YR,' nominal GDP labeled 'NomY' (for nominal income from production, which is nominal GDP), and the real M1 money supply labeled 'RealM.'

What patterns emerge from looking at results of regressions for the velocity of M1 on a constant and either the level of M1, real GDP, the deflator, the federal funds rate, the ten-year U.S. Treasury rate, nominal GDP, or real M1 from the ten sub-sample periods (for a total of seventy regressions)? In three of the ten sub-sample periods, the regression with nominal M1 as the dependent variable on the right side of the equation has the smallest sum of squared residuals and also the greatest adjusted R-squared of the variables considered. In three other sub-sample periods, the performance of *nominal* M1 is topped only by the performance of *real* M1. Thus, one pattern is that for six of the ten sub-sample periods, the use of nominal M1 was either the best or second best for producing the smallest sum of squared residuals and the largest adjusted R-squared statistic. Does this indicate that changes in the M1 money supply are very important in determining changes in the velocity of M1 during those sub-sample periods? Could this indicate that changes in nominal M1 help substantially *at times* in forecasting changes in velocity?

Based in part on results from the quarterly-data sample period (beginning with the first quarter of 1959), when focusing on the 'non-combined' variables (thus ignoring nominal GDP and real money supply), in *some* sub-sample periods, the nominal M1 money supply seems to dominate the impact of real GDP, the implicit deflator, the federal funds rate, and the ten-year U.S. Treasury interest rate on the velocity of M1. However, it looks like the relationships between velocity, its algebraic determinants, and interest rates change over time. In the four sub-sample periods when the quarterly average growth rate (neither annualized nor compounded, with the calculations described further in the next paragraph) of nominal M1 exceeded or equaled 2.4 per cent in a sub-sample period, the velocity of M1 decreased either most quarters or all quarters in each of the four sub-sample periods. On the other hand, in all but one of the sub-sample periods when the quarterly average growth rate of nominal M1 was less than 2.4 per cent, the general direction of the velocity of M1 was upward.

The reader should note that quarterly growth rates in the analysis to follow that are calculated for sub-sample periods do not reflect compounding. The reader should also note that for many comparisons to follow such as changes in variable values between sub-sample periods and growth rates in variable values over a sub-sample period, the study often uses the quarterly value for a variable from the last quarter of the previous sub-sample period as the beginning variable value (with an exception being the first sub-sample period, where the beginning variable value is the value from the first quarter of 1959 given that I do not have data from the fourth quarter of 1958) and the quarterly variable value from the last quarter within the sub-sample period as the ending value. Average percentage growth rate calculations for a sub-sample period divide the growth rate calculated by the number of quarters in the sub-sample period (or, in the case of the first sub-sample period, the number of quarters minus one).

The format for analyzing sub-sample periods is as follows. A table summarizing the regression results appears below the heading listing the sub-sample period. Next, scatter graph plots and analysis of the regression results appear. Afterward, discussion of the data within each sub-sample period concludes the extensive focus on the particular sub-sample period being analyzed. This chapter tends to deemphasize, except for being either positive or negative, comparisons of the coefficients estimated for each of the velocity functions given that (1) the units of measurement for the variables on the right sides of the equations can be dramatically different (i.e. billions of constant-buying-power dollars versus percentage points), and that can impact the sizes of the coefficients estimated, and (2) the coefficients estimated are not necessarily accurate given the econometric questions raised. The 'In-Chapter Appendix' in Chapter Eight focuses more on comparisons of estimated coefficients in a different context.

The first sub-sample period has a lengthier discussion of the regression results than most, if not all of the other sub-sample periods to try to explain two positive estimated coefficients that would have been expected to be negative. The description of the data for the first sub-sample period is divided into an earlier period through the first quarter of 1973 when the real money supply was generally increasing and a later period when the real money supply decreased overall compared with its level in the first quarter of 1973. The Appendix to this chapter also has regression results, figures, and further analysis of the divided first sub-sample period from 1959q1 through 1973q1 and from 1973q2 through 1981q3.

FIRST SUB-SAMPLE PERIOD: 1959Q1 THROUGH 1981Q3

	Coeffi.	Const.	R-Squ.	Adj. R-Squ.	Sum Squ. Res.
M1	0.012566	2.227468	0.977045	0.976787	2.412323
GDP	0.001057	0.593581	0.968687	0.968335	3.290708
Defl	0.107516	2.165219	0.949592	0.949025	5.297377
FFR	0.234705	3.689202	0.630640	0.626490	38.81589
10YR	0.413441	2.471442	0.858418	0.856827	14.87882
NomY	0.001419	3.323898	0.965116	0.964724	3.665915
RealM	0.012331	-5.109390	0.251136	0.242722	78.69781

Table 6.1 Regression Results from Equations for Velocity as a Function of One Other Variable (listed at the beginning of each row of numbers) and a Constant
First Sub-Sample Period (1959q1-1981q3)
Source: www.economagic.com and the author's calculations

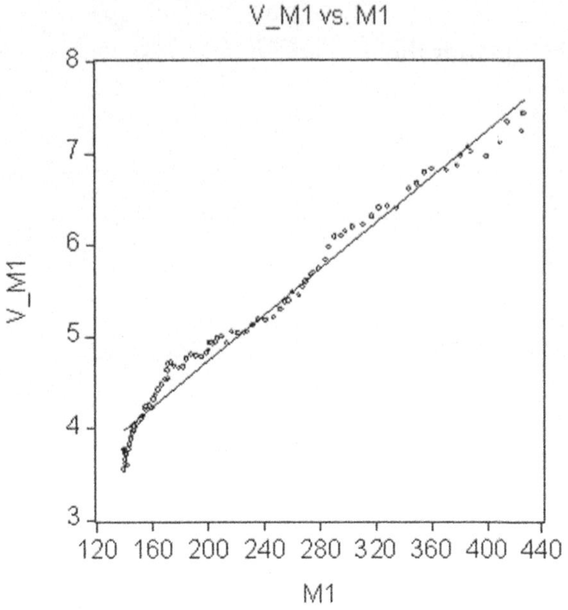

Figure 6.2 Scatter-Graph Plot of the Velocity of M1 (on the Vertical Axis) and Quarterly Average M1 (Nominal)
Regression Line Included
1959 quarter one through 1981 quarter three
Source: www.economagic.com and the author's calculations

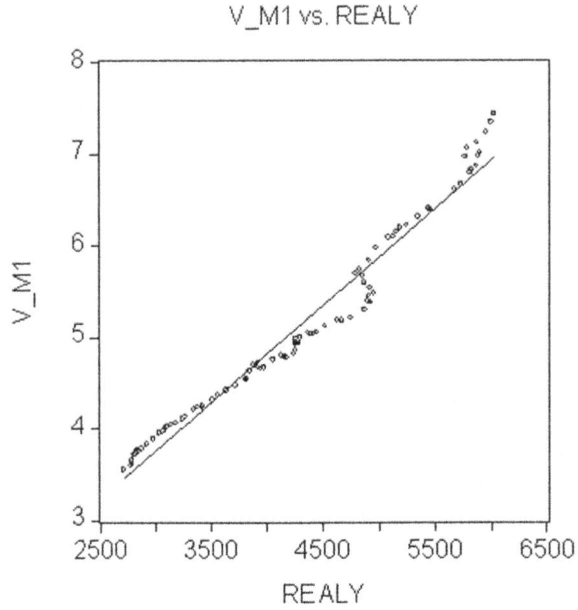

Figure 6.3 Scatter-Graph Plot of the Velocity of M1 (on the Vertical Axis) and Real GDP
Regression Line Included
1959 quarter one through 1981 quarter three
Source: www.economagic.com

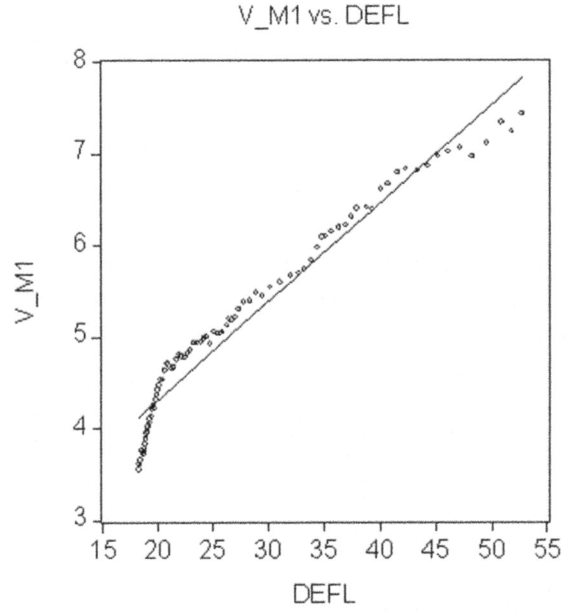

Figure 6.4 Scatter-Graph Plot of the Velocity of M1 (on the Vertical Axis) and the Deflator
Regression Line Included
1959 quarter one through 1981 quarter three
Source: www.economagic.com

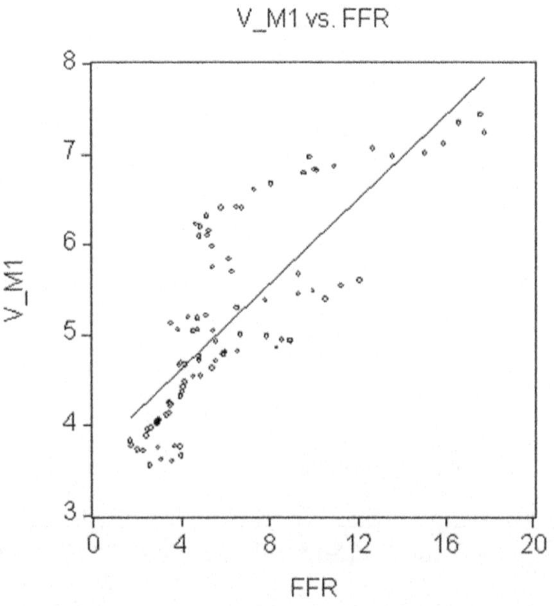

Figure 6.5 Scatter-Graph Plot of the Velocity of M1 (on the Vertical Axis) and the Quarterly Average Federal Funds Rate
Regression Line Included
1959 quarter one through 1981 quarter three
Source: www.economagic.com and the author's calculations

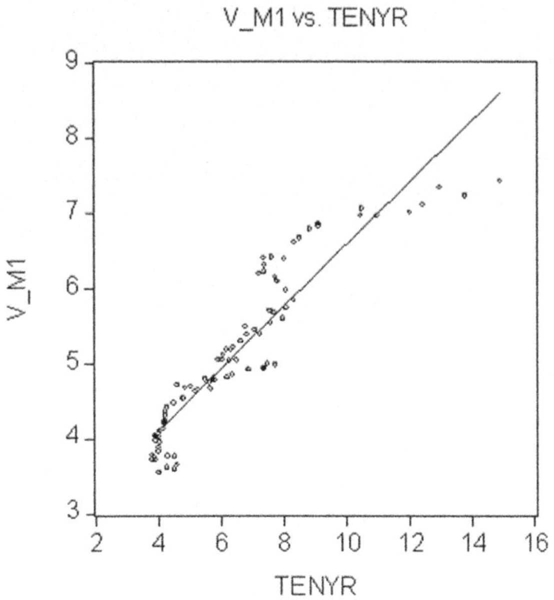

Figure 6.6 Scatter-Graph Plot of the Velocity of M1 (on the Vertical Axis) and the Quarterly Average Ten-Year Treasury Interest Rate
Regression Line Included
1959 quarter one through 1981 quarter three
Source: www.economagic.com and the author's calculations

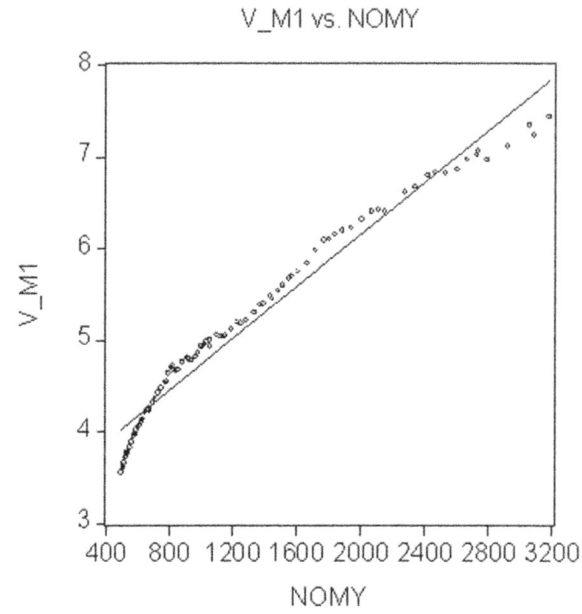

Figure 6.7 Scatter-Graph Plot of the Velocity of M1 (on the Vertical Axis) and Nominal GDP
Regression Line Included
1959 quarter one through 1981 quarter three
Source: www.economagic.com

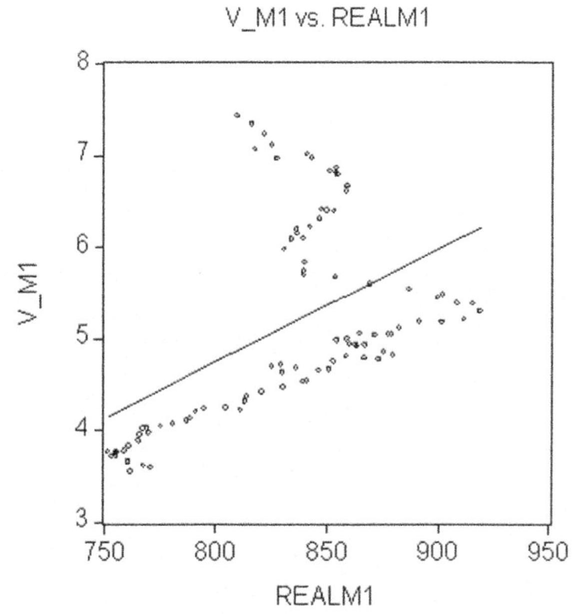

Figure 6.8 Scatter-Graph Plot of the Velocity of M1 (on the Vertical Axis) and Quarterly Average Real M1
Regression Line Included
1959 quarter one through 1981 quarter three
Source: www.economagic.com and the author's calculations

REGRESSION DISCUSSION: 1959q1-1981q3

In equations for the velocity of M1 in this sub-sample period with only a constant and one independent variable on the right side of each regression equation, the use of nominal M1 as the sole independent variable produces the smallest sum of squared residuals and the largest adjusted R-squared statistic of the variables considered, while the use of real M1 produces the largest sum of squared residuals and the smallest adjusted R-squared statistic. One possible explanation is that of the variables considered, nominal M1 best explains the variation in the velocity of M1, while real M1 least explains the variation. Regardless of whether using nominal M1 or real M1, the estimated coefficients are positive. Further discussion of this unexpected result begins in the next paragraph. The use of real GDP is second best at minimizing the sum of squared residuals and maximizing the adjusted R-squared statistic, while nominal GDP is third best, and the implicit deflator is fourth best. The ten-year rate and the federal funds rate are fifth best and sixth best, performing better than only real M1 of the variables considered.

Recall that the results are not intended as proof of a hypothesis, given concerns about identification problems, serial correlation and other factors. Thus, the reader should view the results with appropriate skepticism. The first sub-sample period, the first quarter of 1959 through the third quarter of 1981, is one of the six sub-sample periods where the level of nominal M1 seems to perform well (best or second best) relative to the other variables considered in terms of minimizing the sum of squared residuals and maximizing the adjusted R-squared statistic. In fact, with data from the first sub-sample period, the use of nominal M1 as the sole independent variable produces the smallest sum of squared residuals and the largest adjusted R-squared statistic of the variables considered.

However, the estimated coefficient for the level of M1 in the velocity equation is positive for the sub-sample period 1959q1-1981q3, as shown in the table above. But, from the algebraic definition of velocity ($V = [P^* Y]/M$) where M = nominal M1), an increase in nominal M1 would, all other things equal, lead to a decrease in the velocity of M1. Thus, the expected coefficient would be negative rather than positive. The estimated coefficient for each of the other variables is also positive, including real M1, which like nominal M1 would have an expected negative coefficient. This could be due to all of the variables, including the velocity of M1, overall trending upward during this period, although real M1 was clearly at its in-sub-sample peak in the first quarter of 1973.

Returning to the estimated positive coefficient for nominal M1, increases in the money supply could have led to increases in real GDP (at least in the short term) and the deflator, so that nominal GDP increased during the first sub-sample period by a greater percentage than nominal M1 because of both the increase in nominal M1 and other factors, thus increasing velocity. (Some discussion relevant to this appears in the 'In-Chapter Appendix' in Chapter Eight.) Additionally, other factors unrelated to nominal M1 could have caused nominal GDP to rise while nominal M1 was also rising. All other things equal, an increase in nominal GDP or its components would lead to an increase in velocity. With the methodology of including only one independent variable (not counting the constant term) on the right side of each equation, could the estimated positive effect of the impact of an increase in nominal M1 on the velocity of M1 be capturing the positive effects of the nominal money supply on both real GDP (at least in the short term) and the deflator plus the effect of other factors causing nominal GDP to increase most quarters while M1 was also usually increasing as well as the negative effect of the money supply on velocity, but with the positive indirect effects of nominal M1 growth on nominal GDP plus the impact of other factors on nominal GDP clearly dominating?

Matters of causality also deserve discussion. Does an increase in nominal M1 cause an increase in nominal GDP, or does an increase in nominal GDP cause an increase in nominal M1? Regarding the latter, as nominal GDP grew in the first sub-sample period, people in the economy demanded more dollars to finance greater expenditures. The Federal Reserve could have responded by increasing the nominal money supply to prevent interest rates from rising as much as they otherwise would have following an increase in money demand in a growing economy. The increases in the deflator and real GDP could have been largely responsible for the increases in both velocity and nominal M1, but the regression in the table above could lead us to believe incorrectly that the increase in nominal M1 'caused' the increase in the velocity of M1 in the first sub-sample period. In reality, nominal M1 may have an effect on nominal GDP, and nominal GDP may have an effect on nominal M1.

In the short term, increases in the money supply could have led to decreases in the federal funds rate and other interest rates. Mishkin (2004, p. 523-524) and others observe that higher interest rates could lead to an increase in the velocity of money, all other things equal, via a real money demand equation (a function of interest rates and real income) which can be substituted for the reciprocal of the real money supply (P/M) in the algebraic definition of the velocity of money ($V = (P*Y)/\mathrm{M}$ or $V = (P/M) * Y$). From the first quarter of 1959 through the third quarter of 1981, the sums of squared residuals

(SSR) for both of the interest rate variables are much greater than the sums for nominal M1, real GDP, the implicit deflator, and nominal GDP but less than the SSR for real M1.

For the other sub-sample periods considered, the interest rate variables have larger sums of squared residuals than at least one of the other 'non-combined' variables (real GDP, the implicit deflator, and nominal M1). Perhaps this is to be expected because real GDP, the deflator, and M1 all impact velocity directly in the algebraic definition, while interest rates may have more of an indirect effect on velocity through the money supply (and perhaps nominal GDP). In most sub-sample periods, regressions for each of the two interest rate variables also have a higher sum of squared residuals than at least one of the 'combined variables,' nominal GDP and real M1, and in some cases higher than both nominal GDP and real M1. An exception is in the second sub-sample period, from the fourth quarter of 1981 through the second quarter of 1983, when the use of the ten-year rate as the independent variable produces a slightly lower sum of squared residuals and a slightly higher adjusted R-squared than the real money supply and clearly a lower sum of squared residuals and a higher adjusted R-squared than the use of nominal GDP.

DATA DESCRIPTION

Part One of First Sub-Sample Period: 1959q1 through 1973q1

From the first quarter of 1959 through the first quarter of 1973, both the real money supply and velocity were usually trending upward, with the real money supply increasing from approximately 762 billion 2005-constant-buying-power dollars to approximately 919 billion 2005-constant-buying-power dollars (an increase of about 20.7 per cent), and with M1 velocity increasing from roughly 3.56 times per year to roughly 5.30 times per year (an increase of roughly forty-nine per cent). The GDP deflator increased by roughly fifty per cent during this period, from about 18.3 to about 27.4. Meanwhile, quarterly average M1 in nominal terms grew by roughly 81 per cent, from roughly 139.333 billion dollars to 251.8 billion dollars. Real GDP growth over this period was robust, increasing by nearly eighty per cent, from around 2.71 trillion constant-buying-power dollars to 4.87 trillion constant-buying-power dollars. This amounts to quarterly growth of approximately 1.43 per cent per quarter (neither compounded nor annualized) over fifty-six quarters.

One interpretation of these findings would be that the main driver for the increase in the velocity of M1 through the first quarter of 1973 was the implicit GDP deflator, as both velocity and the deflator increased by about fifty per cent, while the ratio of real GDP to nominal money supply in the first quarter of 1973 was roughly equal to its value in the first quarter of 1959. Another way to interpret the data begins with the realization that the real money supply grew a little bit more than twenty per cent over this period, and that all other things equal (read: no change in real GDP), the velocity of money would have to fall. But, the velocity of money increased by roughly forty-nine per cent over this period because the impact of real GDP increasing by nearly eighty per cent dominated the impact of the increase in the real money supply on the velocity of money. Either way, does it appear that nominal GDP was the main driver of the velocity of M1 from the first quarter of 1959 through the first quarter of 1973? Nominal GDP (in the numerator of the velocity of M1) increased by roughly 170 per cent from the first quarter of 1959 through the first quarter of 1973, while quarterly-average nominal M1 (in the denominator of the algebraic definition for the velocity of M1) increased by roughly eighty per cent, thus leading to an increase in the velocity of M1 of nearly fifty per cent.

Part Two of First Sub-Sample Period: 1973q2 through 1981q3

The impact of the first of two energy crises may have begun to affect the real money supply data in 1973, as the GDP deflator began to increase at a faster quarter-to-quarter rate in the second quarter of 1973 than in any other earlier quarter in the sample period and at an even faster rate in the third quarter of 1973. Evidently, the growth rate of the implicit GDP deflator increased for a while at a faster rate than the nominal money supply, causing the real money supply to fall. The reader should realize that quarterly growth in the deflator was generally increasing even before 1973, perhaps due to faster nominal money supply growth. The velocity of M1 continued to rise most quarters through the third quarter of 1981.

Regarding the numbers, in the second quarter of 1973, quarter-to-quarter inflation (not annualized) was approximately 1.551 per cent, while in the next quarter it was roughly 1.948 per cent. During only two other quarters between first quarter of 1959 and the first quarter of 1973 (the first quarter of 1971 and the first quarter of 1972) was the quarter-to-quarter inflation rate calculated from the implicit GDP deflator greater than 1.50 per cent, and as implied above the rates in those two quarters were below the rate of the second quarter of 1973. Starting with the fourth quarter of 1972, quarterly inflation exceeded one per cent each quarter, at least through the third quarter of 1981 and for many quarters in the next sub-sample period. In many quarters prior to the fourth quarter of 1972 including each quarter prior to the third quarter of 1966, the quarter-to-quarter inflation rate was below one per cent.

An overall increase in the money supply growth rate was likely a factor, but the energy crises could also have been a factor, as quarterly inflation not annualized first exceeded two per cent in the quarterly data sample period in the second quarter of 1974 (soon after the first energy crisis in the 1970s) and exceeded the two per cent mark for three more quarters through the first quarter of 1975 (nearly reaching the three per cent mark in the third and fourth quarters of 1974). After falling below two per cent in most quarters, the quarter-to-quarter inflation rate returned to exceeding the two per cent mark for consecutive quarters beginning with the second and third quarters of 1979 (around the time of the second energy crisis of the 1970s). After the first quarter of 1975 but before the second quarter of 1979, quarterly inflation exceeded the two per cent mark in just two quarters, the fourth quarter of 1977 and the fourth quarter of 1978. However, starting with the second quarter of 1979, quarterly deflator inflation exceeded two per cent for eight consecutive quarters.

Real GDP grew at a slower rate from the second quarter of 1973 through the third quarter of 1981 than it had from the first quarter of 1959 through the first quarter of 1973. The quarterly growth rate of real GDP over this period at approximately 0.70 per cent per quarter over thirty-four quarters (or about 23.7 per cent) was only about half of the growth rate of roughly 1.4 per cent from the first quarter of 1959 through the first quarter of 1973. (Recall that the quarterly growth rates of roughly 0.70 per cent and about 1.4 per cent do not reflect compounding and are not annualized.) Some (for example Dornbusch, Fischer, and Startz (2008, p. 568-570)) note a slowdown in the growth rate of real GDP in the United States in 1973. This coincided at least approximately with the beginning of a decrease in the growth of labor productivity from 1973 through 1995 noted by Baumol and Blinder (2012, p. 140) and likely others. However, the two energy crises could have also contributed between 1973 and 1981.

From the local maximum of real GDP in the fourth quarter of 1973 to the local minimum in the first quarter of 1975, real GDP fell by roughly 3.2 per cent. From the first quarter of 1980 through the third quarter of 1980, real GDP fell by roughly 2.2 per cent. The greatest cumulative loss before the first quarter of 1973 (but after the first quarter of 1959) was from the first quarter of 1960 through the fourth quarter of 1960, when real GDP decreased by about 1.6 per cent. (Real GDP also had small declines in the second part of the first sub-sample period of about 0.53 per cent from the second quarter to the third quarter of 1973, 0.02 per cent from the third quarter to the fourth quarter of 1977, and about 0.80 per cent from the first quarter to the second quarter of 1981. The first and third of these declines could have contributed noticeably to the slower growth rate of the period after the first quarter of 1973. Other declines in real GDP in the first part of the first sub-sample period are approximately 0.12 per cent from the second quarter to the third quarter of 1959, about 0.63 per cent from the third quarter of 1969 through the first quarter of 1970, and roughly 1.06 per cent from the third quarter of 1970 through the fourth quarter of 1970.)

Overall slower growth in real GDP would imply slower growth in velocity, all other things equal. But while real GDP growth was slower from the second quarter of 1973 through the third quarter of 1981, the real money supply trended downward through 1981 (despite periods of growth) during that period. The downward trend in the real money supply (or the real quantity of money demanded) in a sense forced the velocity of money to grow at a faster rate than it would have under a constant real money stock in light of growth in real GDP, although real GDP grew at a slower rate on average in the second part of the first sub-sample period than in the first part of the first sub-sample period.

In fact, despite the slower growth in real output, velocity grew at a faster rate per quarter in the second part of the first sub-sample period (starting in the second quarter of 1973) than in the first, aided by the downward trend in real M1. From the first quarter of 1959 through the first quarter of 1973, the velocity of M1 increased by roughly forty-nine per cent, or roughly 0.88 per cent per quarter. From the first quarter of 1973 through the third quarter of 1981 (a shorter time span), the velocity of M1 increased by approximately forty per cent, or roughly 1.19 per cent per quarter. (Again, remember that the quarterly average growth rates of velocity (and other variables) reported in this chapter are not compounded and are not annualized unless otherwise noted.)

From the first quarter of 1973 through the third quarter of 1981, the *real* money supply fell by approximately 11.9 per cent. The *nominal* money supply over this interval increased by approximately 69.6 per cent, while the GDP deflator increased by about 92.4 per cent, accounting for the decrease in the real money supply of roughly 11.9 per cent over this period. The decrease in the real M1 money supply of approximately twelve per cent combined with an overall increase in real GDP of approximately twenty-four per cent explain the increase in M1 velocity of roughly forty per cent when comparing the variable values in the third quarter of 1981 with those from the first quarter of 1973.

In the third quarter of 1981, the real money supply, at roughly 809.7 billion 2005-constant-buying-power dollars, was still greater than it was in the first quarter of 1959, when it was approximately 761.5 billion 2005-constant-buying-power dollars. The real money supply first exceeded the 800 billion 2005-constant-buying-power-dollar mark in the third quarter of 1964 at around 804.6 billion. Although the real money supply was again between 804 billion and 810 billion 2005-constant-buying-power dollars in the third quarter of 1981, the fourth quarter of 1981, and the third quarter of 1982; the real money supply was greater than 800 billion (in 2005-buying-power dollars) each quarter from the third quarter of 1964 through the end of the sample period (the first quarter of 2013) and beyond. After the real money supply trended downward somewhat between the first quarter of 1973 and the third quarter of 1981, the real money supply in the third quarter of 1981 was about 6.3 per cent greater than it was in the first quarter of 1959 – a relatively small net increase over ninety quarters. However, faster growth in the real money supply was forthcoming.

SECOND SUB-SAMPLE PERIOD: 1981Q4 THROUGH 1983Q2

	Coeffi.	Const.	R-Squ.	Adj. R-Squ.	Sum Squ. Res.
M1	-0.006104	9.969859	0.887051	0.864461	0.016683
GDP	-0.000780	11.76961	0.151000	-0.018800	0.125397
Defl	-0.106882	13.10741	0.842065	0.810478	0.023327
FFR	0.049882	6.584978	0.696782	0.636138	0.044785
10YR	0.079852	6.160870	0.823976	0.788772	0.025999
NomY	-0.001250	11.27523	0.722234	0.666681	0.041026
RealM	-0.005745	11.90959	0.822557	0.787069	0.026208

Table 6.2 Regression Results from Equations for Velocity as a Function of One Other Variable (listed at the beginning of each row of numbers) and a Constant
Second Sub-Sample Period (1981q4-1983q2)
Source: www.economagic.com and the author's calculations

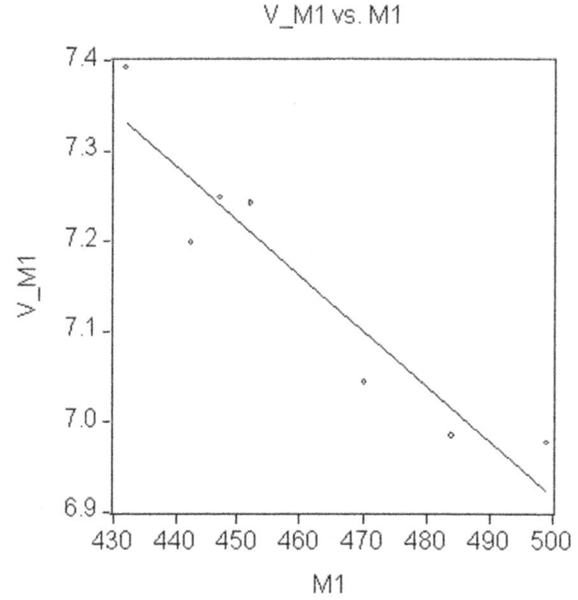

Figure 6.9 Scatter-Graph Plot of the Velocity of M1 (on the Vertical Axis) and Quarterly Average M1 (Nominal)
Regression Line Included
1981 quarter four through 1983 quarter two
Source: www.economagic.com and the author's calculations

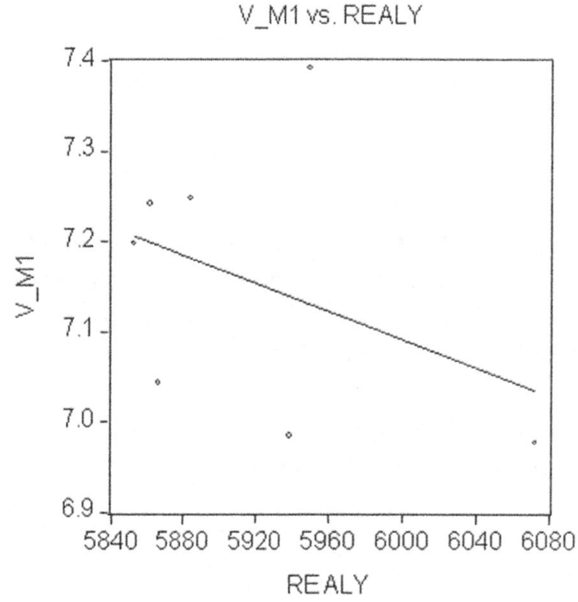

Figure 6.10 Scatter-Graph Plot of the Velocity of M1 (on the Vertical Axis) and Real GDP
Regression Line Included
1981 quarter four through 1983 quarter two
Source: www.economagic.com

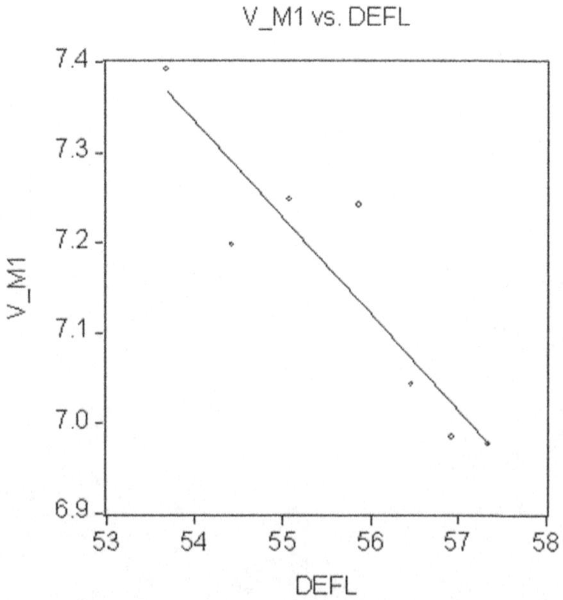

Figure 6.11 Scatter-Graph Plot of the Velocity of M1 (on the Vertical Axis) and the Deflator
Regression Line Included
1981 quarter four through 1983 quarter two
Source: www.economagic.com

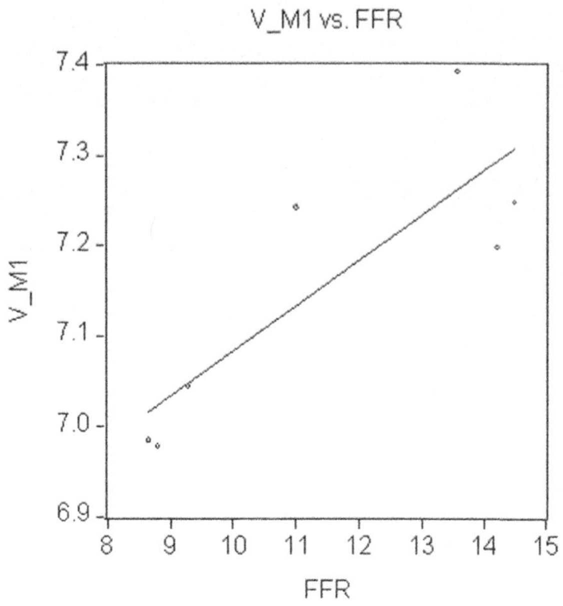

Figure 6.12 Scatter-Graph Plot of the Velocity of M1 (on the Vertical Axis) and the Quarterly Average Federal Funds Rate
Regression Line Included
1981 quarter four through 1983 quarter two
Source: www.economagic.com and the author's calculations

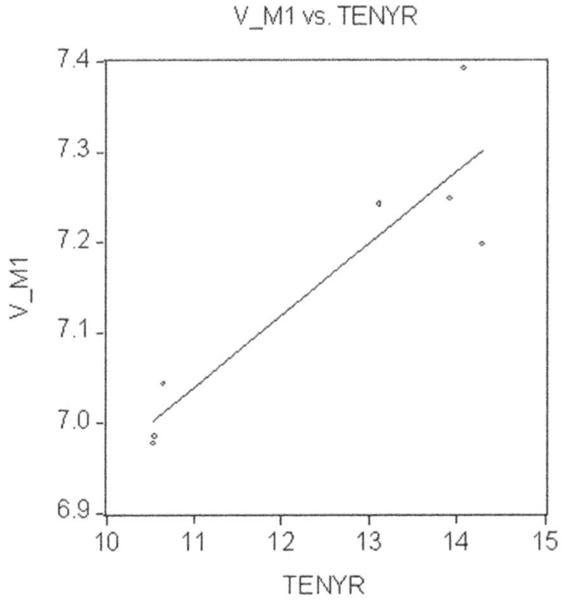

Figure 6.13 Scatter-Graph Plot of the Velocity of M1 (on the Vertical Axis) and the Quarterly Average Ten-Year Treasury Interest Rate
Regression Line Included
1981 quarter four through 1983 quarter two
Source: www.economagic.com and the author's calculations

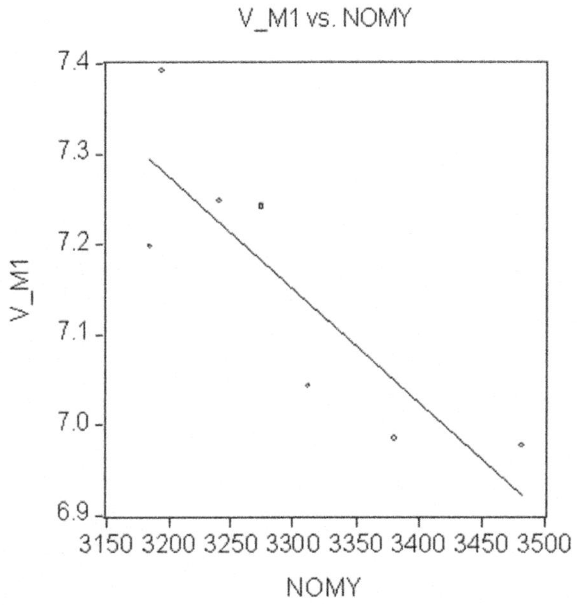

Figure 6.14 Scatter-Graph Plot of the Velocity of M1 (on the Vertical Axis) and Nominal GDP
Regression Line Included
1981 quarter four through 1983 quarter two
Source: www.economagic.com

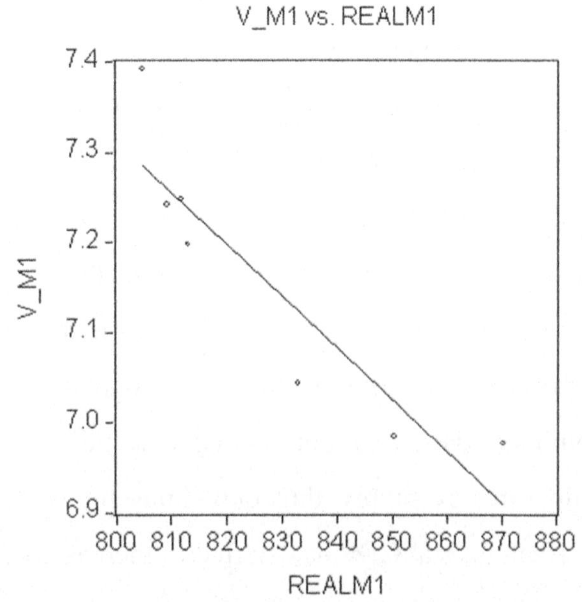

Figure 6.15 Scatter-Graph Plot of the Velocity of M1 (on the Vertical Axis) and Quarterly Average Real M1
Regression Line Included
1981 quarter four through 1983 quarter two
Source: www.economagic.com and the author's calculations

REGRESSION DISCUSSION: 1981q4-1983q2

For the second sub-sample period running from the fourth quarter of 1981 through the second quarter of 1983, the use of M1 as the sole independent variable again produces a smaller sum of squared residuals than the use of any other variable in the study. As noted earlier, this was also the case for the first sub-sample period from the first quarter of 1959 through the third quarter of 1981.

However, while the first sub-sample period was one of frequently increasing velocity and real GDP from one quarter to the next as both variables trended upward, the second sub-sample period brought on a time when velocity decreased in most quarters in the sub-sample period, and a severe recession forced real GDP below where it was in the third quarter of 1981 until the second quarter of 1983, the last quarter of the sub-sample period. The second sub-sample period which began in the fourth quarter of 1981 brought other important differences as well. The estimated coefficient for M1 is less than zero, as would be expected by looking at the algebraic definition of the velocity of M1. However, the estimated coefficients for real GDP and the deflator both individually and collectively through nominal GDP are also less than zero. This result could also arise from the recession and early recovery at that time, as explained in the paragraph below.

Using data from www.economagic.com, quarterly average nominal M1 started to grow more rapidly in the fourth quarter of 1982. In fact, in that quarter, M1 grew at a faster quarterly rate than in any other quarter to that point in the sample period which began in 1959. The FOMC of the Federal Reserve may have felt that inflation was under control by that point so that stimulating the economy and reducing unemployment rates may have become higher priorities than inflation control. The velocity of M1 continued to decline in the fourth quarter of 1982 and for two more quarters as real GDP started to increase from the local minimum. However, nominal GDP spending in the U.S. failed to increase at the same rate as the nominal money supply, thus explaining the decline in velocity through the second quarter of 1983. Nonetheless, real GDP had started to increase, and the deflator continued to increase, both while velocity was falling. This could help explain the negative coefficients estimated in the equations using real GDP, the deflator, and nominal GDP each as the lone dependent variable.

Use of the deflator has the second smallest sum of squared residuals, but the sign of the coefficient is less than zero, as noted above, while the algebraic definition of velocity implies a positive coefficient. The estimated coefficient for the real money supply is negative as would be expected from the algebraic definition of velocity. However, the sum of squared residuals from this regression is greater than the ones which use nominal M1, the deflator, and the ten-year rate. Of the variables considered, the three variables with the largest sums of squared residuals in descending order are real GDP, the federal funds rate, and nominal GDP.

DATA DESCRIPTION: 1981q4-1983q2

The velocity of M1 began to trend downward in the fourth quarter of 1981, falling from about 7.44 times per year in the third quarter of 1981 to about 7.39 times per year in the fourth quarter of 1981. In fact, the velocity of M1 decreased in six out of seven quarters starting with the fourth quarter of 1981 and running through the second quarter of 1983. The real money supply hit a local minimum of around 804.8 billion 2005-constant-buying-power dollars in the fourth quarter of 1981, just one quarter after the velocity of M1 reached its local maximum. Does this suggest that, at least at times, there is an inverse relationship between the real money supply and the velocity of money and that a major factor leading to money velocity temporarily peaking in the third quarter of 1981 was the beginning of a surge in the real money supply? The velocity of M1 reached a local minimum near 6.977 times per year in the second quarter of 1983, representing a decrease of roughly 6.2 per cent from the local maximum of M1 velocity of roughly 7.441 times per year in the third quarter of 1981.

The real money supply increased more rapidly between the third quarter of 1981 and the second quarter of 1983 than in either one of the two parts of the first sub-sample period discussed above. By the second quarter of 1983, the real money supply increased by about 7.49 per cent over its value in the third quarter of 1981 to approximately 870.3 billion dollars of 2005-buying power. This was an increase of about 1.07 per cent per quarter, much larger than +0.37 and -0.35 percentage growth rates per quarter from the first quarter of 1959 through the first quarter of 1973 and from the first quarter of 1973 through the third quarter of 1981, respectively. Could there be a stronger inverse relationship between real money supply and velocity when the real money supply grows at a more rapid rate? Is it that in a relatively low inflation economy like the United States, some periods of relatively rapid nominal money supply growth have also been periods of relatively rapid real money supply growth with the price level not initially rising by the same percentage as the money supply? Thus, does nominal money supply growth drive down the velocity of money?

Another factor behind M1 velocity beginning to decline in the fourth quarter of 1981 was the commencement of a severe recession, where real GDP declined for three out of four quarters starting in the fourth quarter of 1981 and running through the third quarter of 1982. The cumulative loss of real GDP from the third quarter of 1981 through the third quarter of 1982 was about 2.7 per cent. But, despite this decline, real output then rebounded so that by the second quarter of 1983, quarterly but annualized real GDP reached roughly 6,072.4 billion 2005-buying-power dollars, nearly 0.80 percentage points greater than in the third quarter of 1981 and higher than real GDP in any prior quarter in the U.S. This represents a relatively rapid recovery given that real GDP barely increased in the fourth quarter of 1982 compared with the third quarter of 1982, having increased by less than 0.08 per cent between those two quarters. Thus, most of the losses recouped from the downturn in late 1981 and 1982 were regained (plus some additional output) in just two quarters, the first two quarters of 1983.

Still, the velocity of M1 continued to fall due to relatively high real money supply growth. In fact, the real money supply in the third quarter of 1982, the trough of the recession, stood at about 809.3 billion 2005-constant-buying-power dollars, only slightly greater than the local minimum of around

804.8 billion 2005-constant-buying-power dollars in the fourth quarter of 1981 and actually just a bit less than the approximate 809.7 billion-dollar figure from the third quarter of 1981. (In the first two quarters of 1982, the real money supply was between 811 and 813 billion 2005-constant-buying-power dollars.) The real money supply grew by more than 23 billion 2005-constant-buying-power dollars in the fourth quarter of 1982 and by between 17 billion and 21 billion constant-buying-power dollars in the first two quarters of 1983, thus explaining the continued decrease in velocity despite a growing economy.

Rapid nominal money supply growth was clearly the driving force behind increasing real money supply. From the third quarter of 1981 through the second quarter of 1983, the quarterly average M1 money supply in nominal terms increased nearly 16.9 per cent, or about 2.4 per cent per quarter over seven quarters. This was roughly double the approximate 8.8 per cent growth in the deflator over the same period, or roughly 1.3 per cent per quarter. The fact that the growth rate of nominal M1 was roughly twice the growth rate of the deflator helps to explain the faster growth in the real money supply during this period when compared with growth rates between the first quarter of 1959 and the first quarter of 1973, and from then through the third quarter of 1981 (although the rapid growth was concentrated in the fourth quarter of 1982 and the first two quarters of 1983).

The decline in real GDP which began in the fourth quarter of 1981 where real GDP fell for three out of four consecutive quarters, decreasing by about 2.7 per cent, could have been due to rising interest rates toward the end of the previous sub-sample period. The quarterly average federal funds rate reached a maximum, at least within the sample from the first quarter of 1959 through the first quarter of 2013, in the second quarter of 1981 of 17.78 per cent and declined only slightly in the third quarter of 1981 to about 17.577 per cent. The ten-year rate reached a maximum of approximately 14.85 per cent in the third quarter of 1981. The higher federal funds rate was likely a goal of the FOMC to try to curb inflation. Both the quarterly average federal funds rate and the quarterly average ten-year rate trended downward during the second sub-sample period, with the quarterly average federal funds rate at approximately 8.80 per cent and the quarterly average ten-year rate at approximately 10.54 per cent in the second quarter of 1983. All other things equal, we would expect that lower interest rates would be associated with reductions in velocity.

THIRD SUB-SAMPLE PERIOD: 1983Q3 THROUGH 1984Q4

	Coeffi.	Const.	R-Squ.	Adj. R-Squ.	Sum Squ. Res.
M1	0.009366	2.249481	0.989604	0.987005	0.000924
GDP	0.000721	2.555809	0.994110	0.992638	0.000523
Defl	0.134681	-0.760444	0.992116	0.990145	0.000701
FFR	0.074640	6.476225	0.218622	0.023278	0.069435
10YR	0.101973	5.978208	0.270095	0.087619	0.064861
NomY	0.000772	4.259129	0.996043	0.995054	0.000352
RealM	0.014156	-5.456356	0.952983	0.941229	0.004178

Table 6.3 Regression Results from Equations for Velocity as a Function of One Other Variable (listed at the beginning of each row of numbers) and a Constant
Third Sub-Sample Period (1983q3-1984q4)
Source: www.economagic.com and the author's calculations

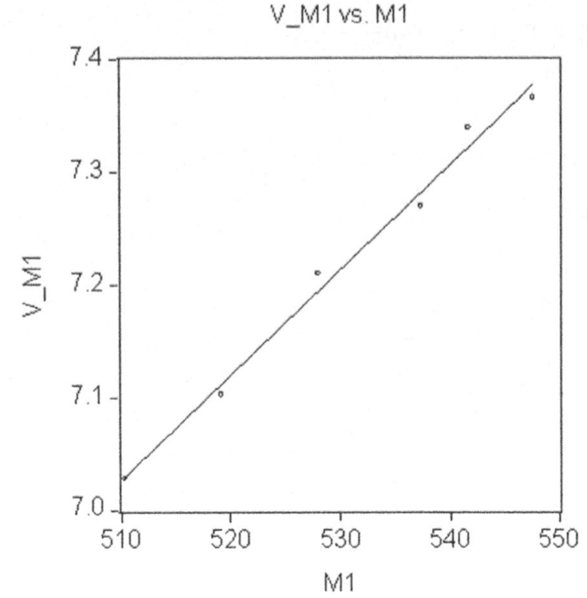

Figure 6.16 Scatter-Graph Plot of the Velocity of M1 (on the Vertical Axis) and Quarterly Average M1 (Nominal)
Regression Line Included
1983 quarter three through 1984 quarter four
Source: www.economagic.com and the author's calculations

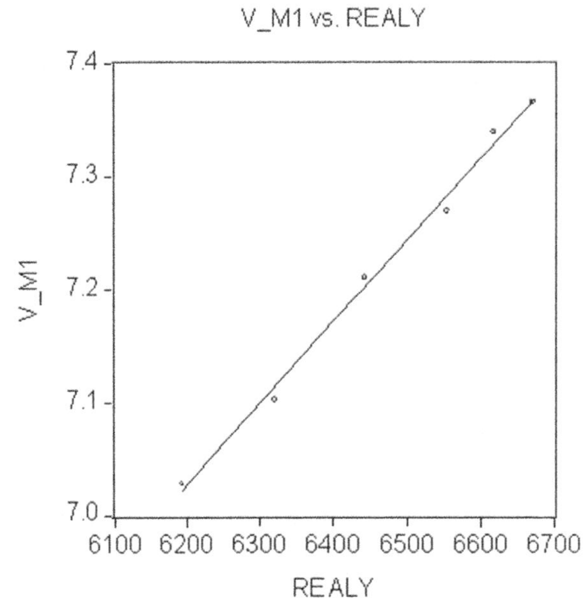

Figure 6.17 Scatter-Graph Plot of the Velocity of M1 (on the Vertical Axis) and Real GDP
Regression Line Included
1983 quarter three through 1984 quarter four
Source: www.economagic.com

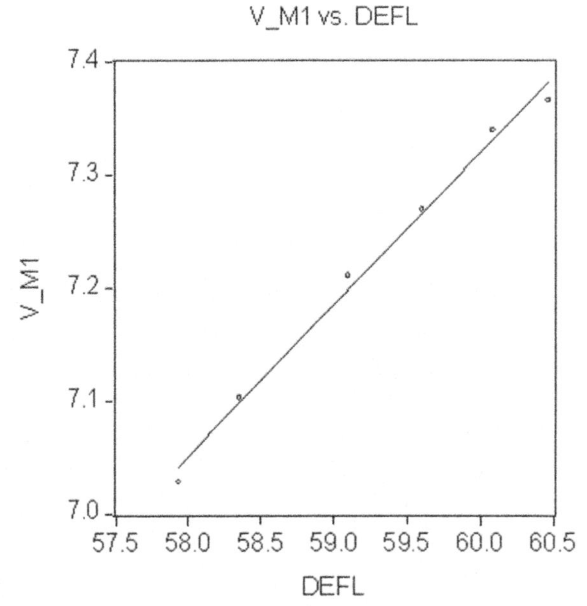

Figure 6.18 Scatter-Graph Plot of the Velocity of M1 (on the Vertical Axis) and the Deflator
Regression Line Included
1983 quarter three through 1984 quarter four
Source: www.economagic.com

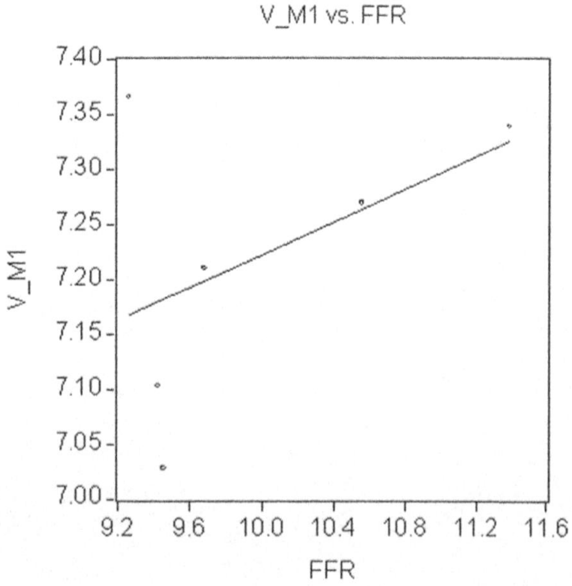

Figure 6.19 Scatter-Graph Plot of the Velocity of the M1 (on the Vertical Axis) and the Quarterly Average Federal Funds Rate
Regression Line Included
1983 quarter three through 1984 quarter four
Source: www.economagic.com and the author's calculations

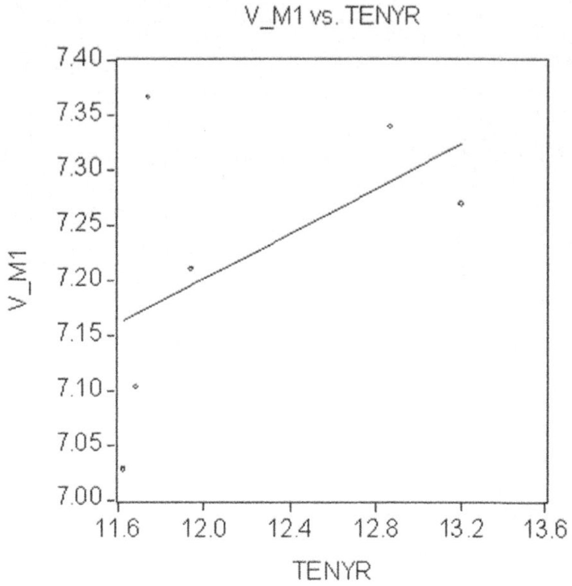

Figure 6.20 Scatter-Graph Plot of the Velocity of M1 (on the Vertical Axis) and the Quarterly Average Ten-Year Treasury Interest Rate
Regression Line Included
1983 quarter three through 1984 quarter four
Source: www.economagic.com and the author's calculations

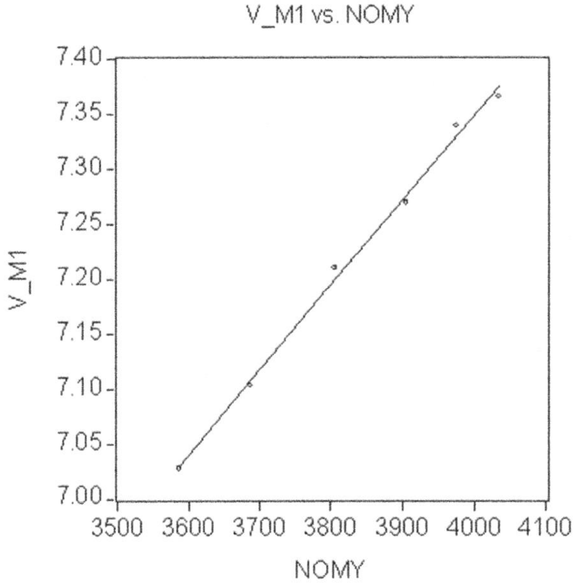

Figure 6.21 Scatter-Graph Plot of the Velocity of M1 (on the Vertical Axis) and Nominal GDP
Regression Line Included
1983 quarter three through 1984 quarter four
Source: www.economagic.com

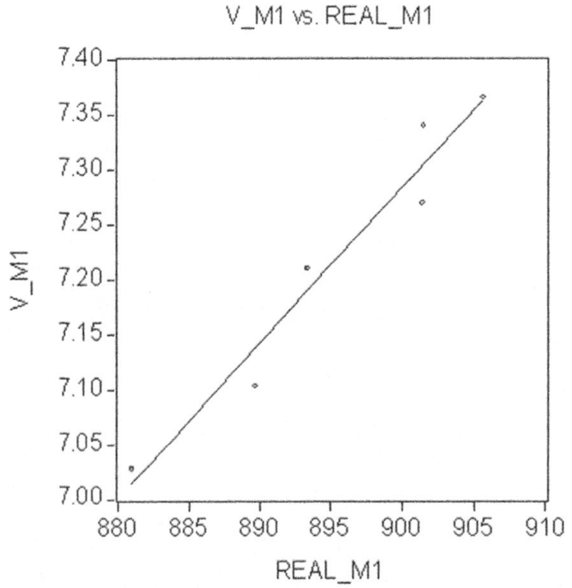

Figure 6.22 Scatter-Graph Plot of the Velocity of M1 (on the Vertical Axis) and Quarterly Average Real M1
Regression Line Included
1983 quarter three through 1984 quarter four
Source: www.economagic.com and the author's calculations

REGRESSION DISCUSSION: 1983q3-1984q4

During this period, using nominal GDP as the lone independent variable in regressions produces the smallest sum of squared residuals and the largest adjusted R-squared statistic of the variables considered in this study. Real GDP is 'second best,' followed by the implicit deflator. Nominal M1 is 'fourth best,' with real M1, the ten-year rate, and the federal funds rate generating higher sums of squared residuals in ascending order. As was the case with the first sample period, the estimated coefficients for nominal M1 and real M1 were positive, while the algebraic definition for velocity may lead us to expect a negative coefficient.

DATA DESCRIPTION: 1983q3-1984q4

Real money supply growth slowed down over the next year-and-a-half compared with the fourth quarter of 1982 and the first two quarters of 1983. Combining slower money supply growth with continued strong economic growth, particularly through the second quarter of 1984, helps to explain an increase in M1 velocity that started in the third quarter of 1983. The velocity of M1 increased from approximately 6.977 times per year in the second quarter of 1983 to roughly 7.367 times per year in the fourth quarter of 1984. This represents an increase in the velocity of M1 by nearly 5.6 per cent over six quarters, or about 0.93 per cent per quarter.

The percentage growth in M1 velocity over this time outpaced the percentage growth in the real money supply, which was roughly 4.1 per cent during this period, or approximately 0.68 per cent per quarter, with the real money supply having risen to about 905.6 billion 2005-constant-buying-power dollars in the fourth quarter of 1984 from 870.3 billion dollars in the second quarter of 1983. That represents an increase of roughly 35 billion 2005-constant-buying-power dollars. Much of this increase occurred relatively early within the sub-sample period, as the real money supply reached nearly 901.5 billion 2005-constant-buying-power dollars by the second quarter of 1984. The real money supply increased by less than 100 million 2005-buying-power dollars in the third quarter of 1984 and by about 4 billion 2005-buying-power dollars in the fourth quarter of 1984. The impact of growing real GDP dominated the impact of a growing real money supply on the velocity of money, as M1 velocity continued to rise through the fourth quarter of 1984.

Nominal M1 increased by about 9.7 per cent from the second quarter of 1983 through the fourth quarter of 1984, while the deflator increased by about 5.4 per cent over the same period. This explains the approximately 4.1 per cent increase in the real money supply over this period which lasted six quarters. Thus, the quarterly increase in the real money supply was about 0.68 per cent per quarter, clearly slower than the rate of around 1.07 per cent per quarter from the third quarter of 1981 through the second quarter of 1983.

FOURTH SUB-SAMPLE PERIOD: 1985Q1 THROUGH 1987Q2

	Coeffi.	Const.	R-Squ.	Adj. R-Squ.	Sum Squ. Res.
M1	-0.006003	10.71216	0.994124	0.993389	0.008032
GDP	-0.002189	22.17286	0.931736	0.923203	0.093314
Defl	-0.338096	28.02023	0.974124	0.970889	0.035372
FFR	0.408413	3.856395	0.857410	0.839586	0.194915
10YR	0.207515	4.975214	0.752851	0.721957	0.337844
NomY	-0.002046	15.82274	0.960227	0.955255	0.054368
RealM	-0.004614	11.58457	0.996461	0.996019	0.004837

Table 6.4 Regression Results from Equations for Velocity as a Function of One Other Variable (listed at the beginning of each row of numbers) and a Constant
Fourth Sub-Sample Period (1985q1-1987q2)
Source: www.economagic.com and the author's calculations

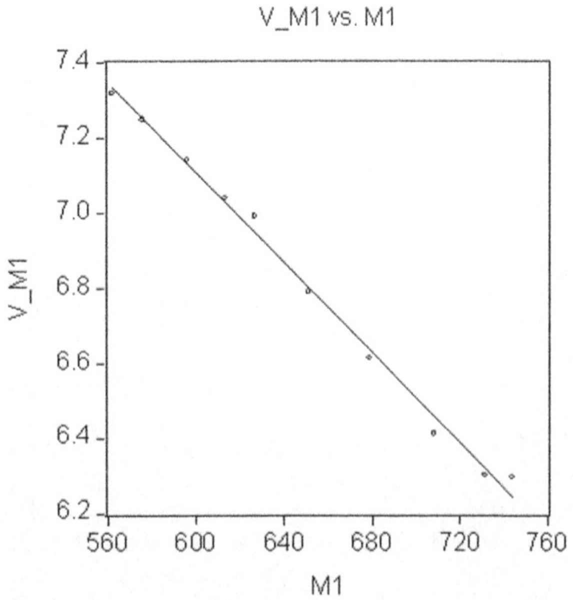

Figure 6.23 Scatter-Graph Plot of the Velocity of M1 (on the Vertical Axis) and Quarterly Average M1 (Nominal)
Regression Line Included
1985 quarter one through 1987 quarter two
Source: www.economagic.com and the author's calculations

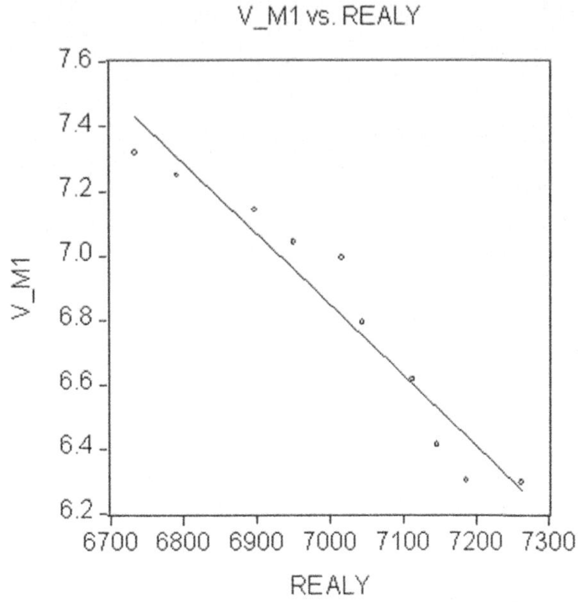

Figure 6.24 Scatter-Graph Plot of the Velocity of M1 (on the Vertical Axis) and Real GDP
Regression Line Included
1985 quarter one through 1987 quarter two
Source: www.economagic.com

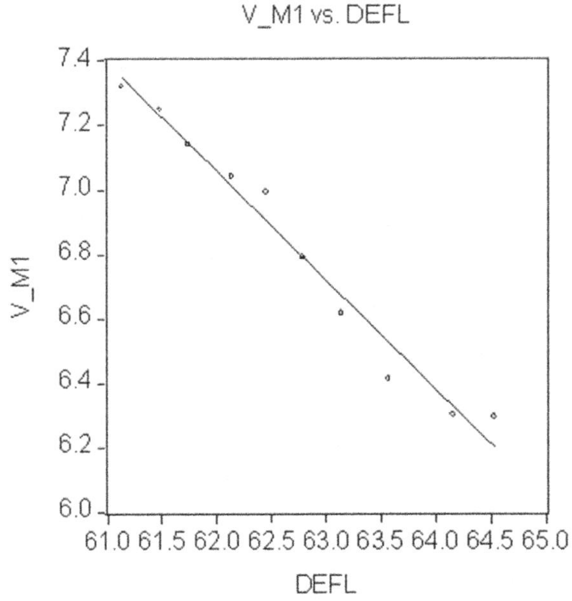

Figure 6.25 Scatter-Graph Plot of the Velocity of M1 (on the Vertical Axis) and the Deflator
Regression Line Included
1985 quarter one through 1987 quarter two
Source: www.economagic.com

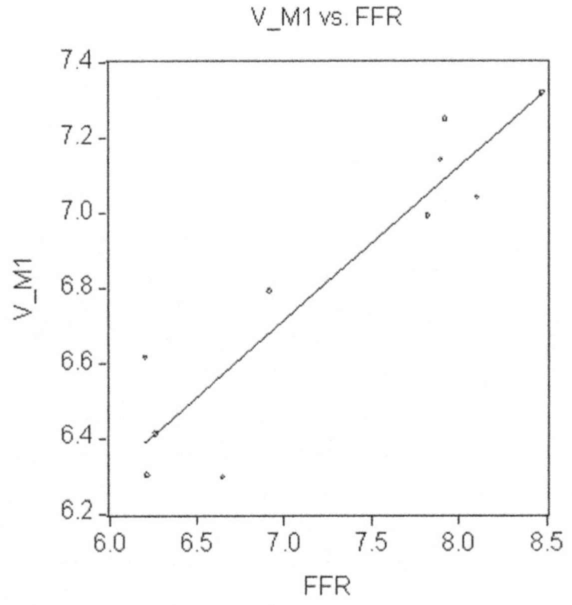

Figure 6.26 Scatter-Graph Plot of the Velocity of M1 (on the Vertical Axis) and the Quarterly Average Federal Funds Rate
Regression Line Included
1985 quarter one through 1987 quarter two
Source: www.economagic.com and the author's calculations

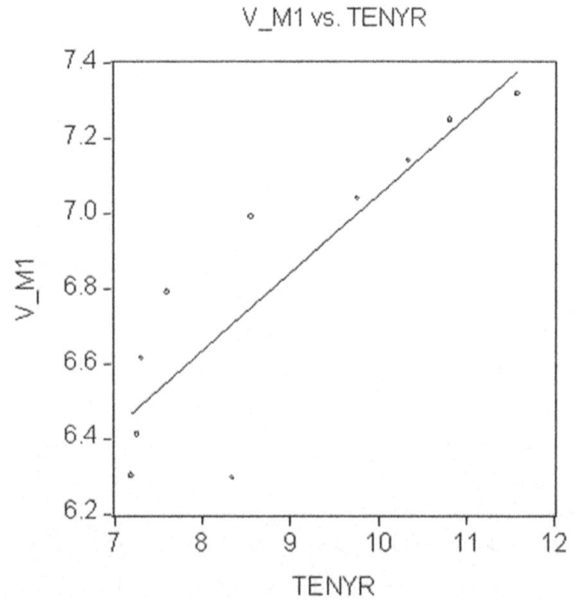

Figure 6.27 Scatter-Graph Plot of the Velocity of M1 (on the Vertical Axis) and the Quarterly Average Ten-Year Treasury Interest Rate
Regression Line Included
1985 quarter one through 1987 quarter two
Source: www.economagic.com and the author's calculations

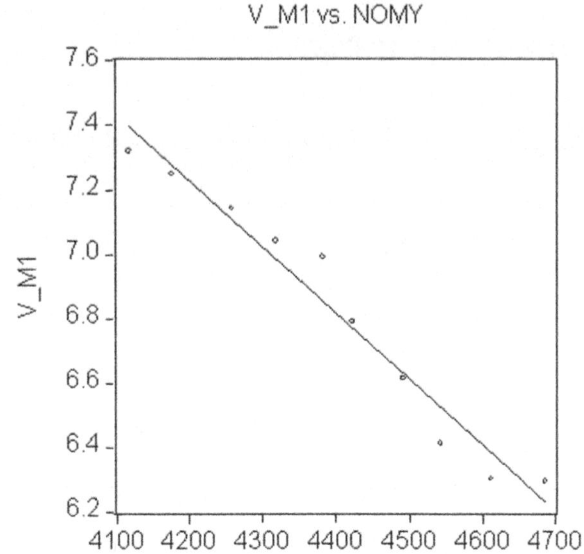

Figure 6.28 Scatter-Graph Plot of the Velocity of M1 (on the Vertical Axis) and Nominal GDP
Regression Line Included
1985 quarter one through 1987 quarter two
Source: www.economagic.com

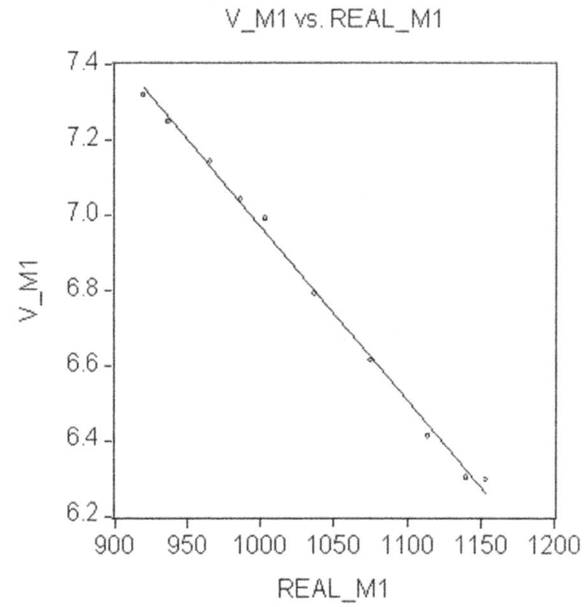

Figure 6.29 Scatter-Graph Plot of the Velocity of M1 (on the Vertical Axis) and Quarterly Average Real M1
Regression Line Included
1985 quarter one through 1987 quarter two
Source: www.economagic.com and the author's calculations

REGRESSION DISCUSSION: 1985q1-1987q2

In regressions from the first quarter of 1985 through the second quarter of 1987, the only variable that produced a smaller sum of squared residuals and a larger adjusted R-squared than the use of nominal M1 as the sole independent variable was the use of real M1. It may be worth noting that the adjusted R-squared statistic from the regression with real M1 as the sole independent variable is only slightly larger than the adjusted R-squared statistic for the regression with nominal M1 as the only independent variable. The deflator was 'third best,' followed by nominal GDP and then real GDP. The federal funds rate and the ten-year U.S. Treasury rate produced results with clearly the smallest adjusted R-squared values and the greatest sums of squared residuals.

As was the case with the second sub-sample period, the estimated coefficients for all of the variables (including nominal M1 and real M1) except the two interest rate measures were negative. Given that the algebraic definition of velocity suggests that all other things equal we would expect positive coefficients for the deflator, real GDP, and nominal GDP, the use of nominal M1 and real M1 may be even better at explaining the variation of velocity than the deflator, real GDP, and nominal GDP than the sum of squared residuals and adjusted R-squared results would indicate. In light of these results, when looking only at the 'non-combined' variables, it seems that nominal money supply growth may have driven down the velocity of M1.

DATA DESCRIPTION: 1985q1-1987q2

While nominal M1 money supply growth (quarter-to-quarter, not annualized) had slowed down toward the end of the previous sub-sample period (dropping from about 2.3 per cent in the third quarter of 1983 to around 0.81 per cent in the third quarter of 1984 and roughly 1.10 per cent in the fourth quarter of that year), nominal money supply growth increased sharply from the first quarter of 1985 through the second quarter of 1987. Quarterly money supply growth was around 2.70 per cent in the first quarter of 1985 and was greater than 2.0 per cent each quarter through the first quarter of 1987. In the second quarter of 1987, nominal M1 growth was slightly less than 1.75 per cent.

So rapid was the increase in the money supply compared with earlier quarters from 1959q1 through 1984q4 that in the third quarter of 1986, the quarterly money supply growth rate (around 4.24 per cent) exceeded 4.0 per cent for only the second time in the sample period, with the first time being the fourth quarter of 1982 (with a quarterly growth rate around 4.02 per cent). Just one quarter later, in the fourth quarter of 1986, the quarterly nominal M1 growth rate increased to around 4.35 per cent. Before that, in the second quarter of 1986, the quarterly growth rate of nominal M1 was around 3.91 per cent. The second quarter of 1986 had the second greatest percentage quarterly growth rate in nominal M1 up to that point in the quarterly data period, surpassed only by the growth rate in the fourth quarter of 1982 in terms of growth rates from earlier quarters. Between the fourth quarter of 1984 and the second quarter of 1987, nominal M1 increased by roughly 35.9 per cent (547.6 billion dollars to 744.3 billion dollars) over ten quarters, or averaging 3.59 per cent growth per quarter. This represents the second greatest quarterly nominal M1 growth for any sub-sample period considered in this study.

The GDP deflator continued to increase from the fourth quarter of 1984 through the second quarter of 1987, but only by about 6.72 per cent, from roughly 60.5 in the fourth quarter of 1984 to approximately 64.5 in the second quarter of 1987. Real GDP continued to increase over this period, but at a slower rate. For the second quarter of 1987, real GDP was about 8.9 per cent greater than it was for the fourth quarter of 1984, or averaging about 0.89 per cent growth per quarter. While many (including myself), if not most, would consider this growth rate to be consistent with a healthy economy, the growth rate is only a little more than half of the growth rate during the previous period (1983q3 through 1984q4, when the growth rate was about 1.6 per cent per quarter).

Why did the nominal money supply grow so rapidly after the fourth quarter of 1984 through the second quarter of 1987? With real GDP increasing very roughly by nine per cent and the deflator increasing less than seven per cent during this time, the increase in nominal GDP implied by these data would not be large enough for the general public to want to hold nearly thirty-six per cent more dollars solely for GDP spending, all other things equal.

Perhaps the explanation lies in what happened to interest rates in the last quarter of 1984, 1985, 1986, and the first quarter of 1987. From the third quarter of 1984 (part of the previous sub-sample period which ended at the end of the fourth quarter of 1984) through the first quarter of 1987, both the federal funds rate and the ten-year U.S. Treasury interest rate had a net decrease of more than five percentage points. With the belief that inflation rates were under control, the members of the Federal Open Market Committee (FOMC) likely decided to lower the targeted federal funds rate to reduce other interest rates in the economy, either in nominal terms or in real terms or in both, to continue to accommodate expansion, as not only nominal interest rates but also real interest rates in the U.S. were high at times in the 1980s. To lower interest rates, the FOMC would instruct the New York branch of the Federal Reserve to purchase U.S. government debt, thus injecting liquidity into the economy in exchange for the government debt. As banks wound up lending out a large percentage of newly found reserves, the money supply grew.

What happened to the velocity of money? As we will see again later, rapid money supply growth is correlated with a decline in the velocity of money. The velocity of M1 fell from about 7.367 times per year in the fourth quarter of 1984 to about 6.297 times per year in the second quarter of 1987, a decrease of more than 14.5 per cent over ten quarters.

FIFTH SUB-SAMPLE PERIOD: 1987Q3 THROUGH 1990Q2

	Coeffi.	Const.	R-Squ.	Adj. R-Squ.	Sum Squ. Res.
M1	0.013331	-3.566917	0.656332	0.621965	0.330759
GDP	0.001215	-2.597996	0.949650	0.944615	0.048459
Defl	0.127281	-1.900699	0.950682	0.945750	0.047466
FFR	0.209171	5.100959	0.536651	0.490316	0.445945
10YR	-0.407336	10.34505	0.324245	0.256669	0.650373
NomY	0.000860	2.246475	0.956054	0.951659	0.042295
RealM	-0.015307	24.21852	0.795392	0.774931	0.196923

Table 6.5 Regression Results from Equations for Velocity as a Function of One Other Variable (listed at the beginning of each row of numbers) and a Constant
Fifth Sub-Sample Period (1987q3-1990q2)
Source: www.economagic.com and the author's calculations

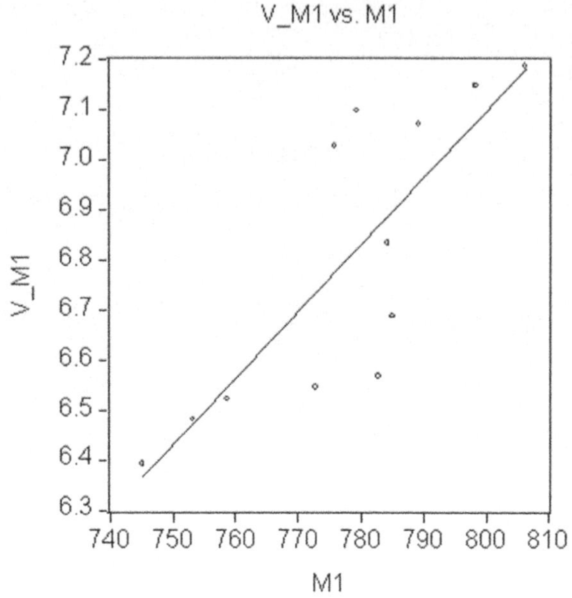

Figure 6.30 Scatter-Graph Plot of the Velocity of M1 (on the Vertical Axis) and Quarterly Average M1 (Nominal)
Regression Line Included
1987 quarter three through 1990 quarter two
Source: www.economagic.com and the author's calculations

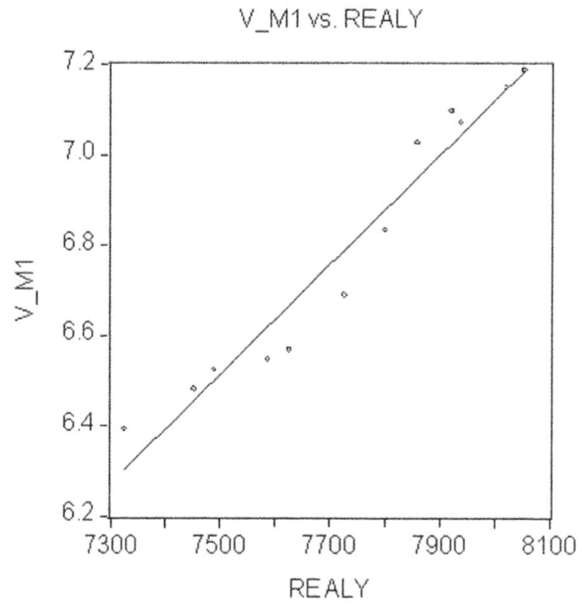

Figure 6.31 Scatter-Graph Plot of the Velocity of M1 (on the Vertical Axis) and Real GDP
Regression Line Included
1987 quarter three through 1990 quarter two
Source: www.economagic.com

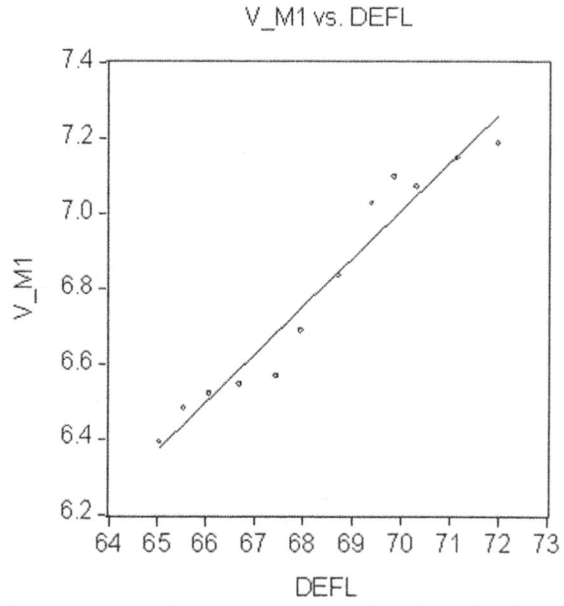

Figure 6.32 Scatter-Graph Plot of the Velocity of M1 (on the Vertical Axis) and the Deflator
Regression Line Included
1987 quarter three through 1990 quarter two
Source: www.economagic.com

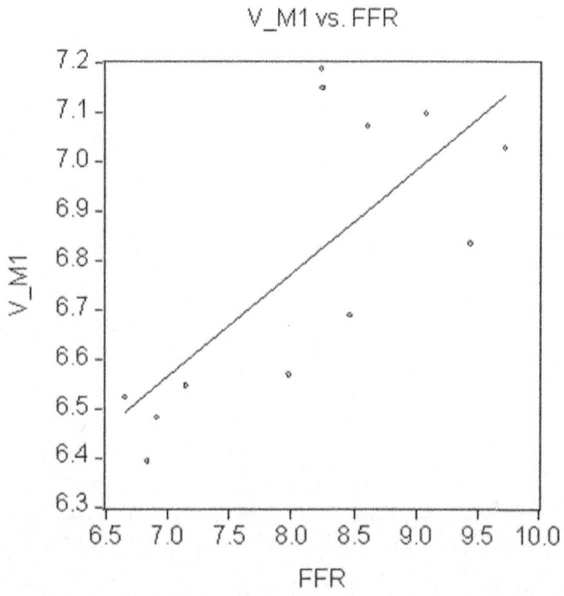

Figure 6.33 Scatter-Graph Plot of the Velocity of M1 (on the Vertical Axis) and the Quarterly Average Federal Funds Rate
Regression Line Included
1987 quarter three through 1990 quarter two
Source: www.economagic.com and the author's calculations

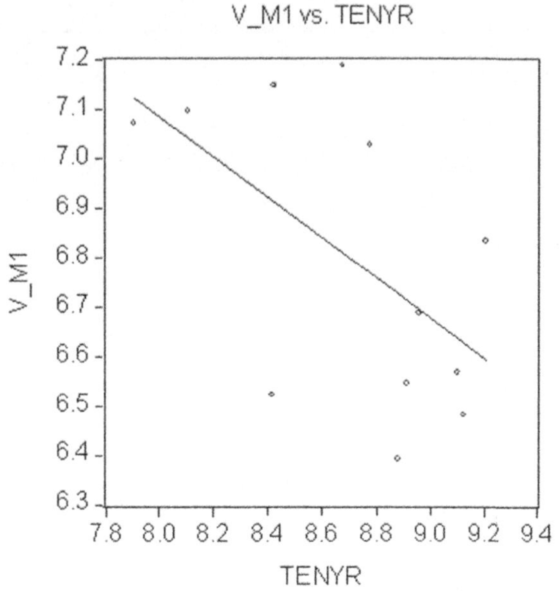

Figure 6.34 Scatter-Graph Plot of the Velocity of M1 (on the Vertical Axis) and the Quarterly Average Ten-Year Treasury Interest Rate
Regression Line Included
1987 quarter three through 1990 quarter two
Source: www.economagic.com and the author's calculations

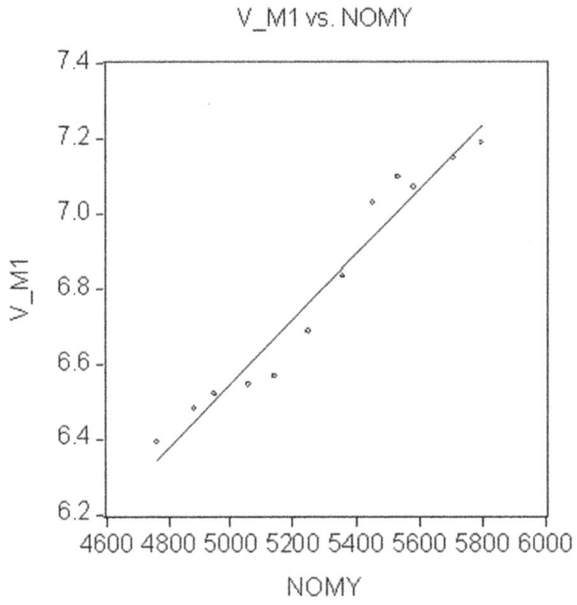

Figure 6.35 Scatter-Graph Plot of the Velocity of M1 (on the Vertical Axis) and Nominal GDP
Regression Line Included
1987 quarter three through 1990 quarter two
Source: www.economagic.com

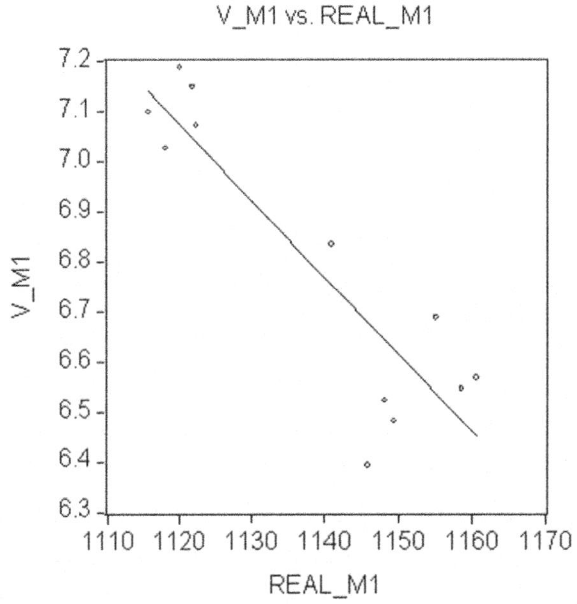

Figure 6.36 Scatter-Graph Plot of the Velocity of M1 (on the Vertical Axis) and Quarterly Average Real M1
Regression Line Included
1987 quarter three through 1990 quarter two
Source: www.economagic.com and the author's calculations

REGRESSION DISCUSSION: 1987q3-1990q2

While nominal M1 seemed to explain a great deal of the changes in velocity in the previous sub-sample period (1985q1 through 1987q2), nominal M1 seems to explain little of the variation in velocity, at least when compared with nominal GDP, the implicit deflator, real GDP, and the real money supply in the sub-sample period from the third quarter of 1987 through the second quarter of 1990 as the sum of squared residuals for nominal M1 is greater and the estimated coefficient is positive. The weaker performance of nominal M1 as the sole independent variable coincides with a decrease in the growth rate of nominal M1, as discussed below under 'Data Description: 1987q3-1990q2.'.

The regressions with the two interest rate variables are the only regressions from this sub-sample period with greater sums of squared residuals and lesser adjusted R-squared values than those from the regression with nominal M1 as the independent variable. The ten-year Treasury rate performs perhaps the worst of the seven variables in the sub-sample period. Not only is the sum of squared residuals the largest and the adjusted R-squared statistic the smallest for the ten-year rate, but the estimated coefficient is negative rather than positive.

DATA DESCRIPTION: 1987q3-1990q2

Nominal M1 growth nearly stalled in the third quarter of 1987. Average nominal M1 for the quarter was about 745.17 billion dollars, only a slight increase over 744.3 billion dollars for the second quarter of 1987. This is an increase of less than 0.12 per cent. The growth rate of nominal M1 was higher from the fourth quarter of 1987 through the fourth quarter of 1988, but the growth rate each quarter from the fourth quarter of 1987 through the fourth quarter of 1988 was slower than in most quarters from the first quarter of 1985 through the second quarter of 1987. Nominal M1 then declined for two consecutive quarters before returning to positive growth in the third quarter of 1989. But the quarterly growth rate of nominal M1 in the third and fourth quarters of 1989 and the first two quarters of 1990 was at least 0.49 percentage points less than in any quarter from the first quarter of 1985 through the second quarter of 1987, and at least one percentage point less than the growth rate from any quarter in the fourth sub-sample period except the first quarter of 1986 and the second quarter of 1987. By the second quarter of 1990, nominal M1 had grown about 8.3 per cent greater than it was in the second quarter of 1987, amounting to growth of about 0.69 per cent per quarter over twelve quarters, much slower quarterly growth than the approximate 3.6 per cent rate per quarter during the 1985q1-1987q2 period.

While nominal M1 grew during the 1987q3-1990q2 period, the real money supply actually decreased by nearly 2.9 per cent during this period, from about 1,153.5 billion (or about 1.1535 trillion) dollars having the constant buying power of a U.S. dollar in the year 2005 to around 1,120.1 billion (or around 1.1201 trillion) 2005-constant-buying-power dollars. Given that the nominal money supply continued trending upward but the real money supply had a net decrease between the second quarter of 1987 and the second quarter of 1990, the implicit deflator must have grown at a rate faster than nominal M1 to cause the real money supply to decrease. The deflator increased from 64.526 in the second quarter of 1987 to 71.993 in the second quarter of 1990, an increase of nearly 11.6 per cent over twelve quarters, or an increase of roughly 0.96 per cent per quarter. The fact that the implicit GDP deflator grew at a rate faster than the nominal money supply over this period explains why the real money supply decreased during this period.

Real GDP also continued growing from the second quarter of 1987 through the second quarter of 1990, increasing by about 10.9 per cent, or roughly 0.91 per cent per quarter from approximately 7.263 trillion constant-buying-power dollars to about 8.052 trillion constant-buying-power dollars. The percentage growth rate per quarter was roughly equal to the 0.89 percentage growth rate during the 1985q1-1987q2 period. With real GDP increasing each quarter but the real money supply decreasing most quarters from the third quarter of 1987 through the second quarter of 1990, velocity must have increased most, if not all quarters. M1 velocity rose to from 6.2968 times per year in the second quarter of 1987 to 7.1895 times per year in the second quarter of 1990.

Perhaps the slower nominal money supply growth was implemented to slow longer-term inflation pressures that the Federal Open Market Committee likely believed would have resulted from the rapid nominal money supply growth rate during the 1985q1-1987q2 period. The slower nominal money supply growth was likely associated with an increase in nominal interest rates. The quarterly-average federal funds rate rose nearly every quarter from the second quarter of 1987, when it was 6.65 per cent, through the second quarter of 1989, when it was approximately 9.73 per cent.

However, beginning with the third quarter of 1989, the quarterly-average federal funds rate began to decrease each quarter through the fourth quarter of 1992 (which is part of a later sub-sample period to be discussed in further detail later). Then in the year 1993, the quarterly average federal funds rate alternated between increasing by less than 0.10 percentage points in a quarter and decreasing by less than 0.10 percentage points in a quarter. (Larger increases in the federal funds rate began in first quarter of 1994, the beginning of a later sub-sample period.)

Although the quarterly average federal funds rate decreased each quarter from the third quarter of 1989 through the second quarter of 1990 (and beyond, as noted above), in the second quarter of 1990 (the last quarter in the sub-sample period), the quarterly average federal funds rate was around 8.24 per cent. This is still higher than it was in the second quarter of 1987, the last quarter of the previous sub-sample period. The quarterly average of the U.S. Treasury ten-year rate was also higher than in the second quarter of 1987 in every quarter from the third quarter of 1987 through the second quarter of 1990 except the third and fourth quarters of 1989. As may have been expected, given much slower nominal money supply growth, a net decrease in the real money supply, faster growth in the implicit deflator, continued growth in real GDP, and higher federal funds rates and ten-year rates; the velocity of M1 increased during this sub-sample period.

SIXTH SUB-SAMPLE PERIOD: 1990Q3 THROUGH 1993Q4

	Coeffi.	Const.	R-Squ.	Adj. R-Squ.	Sum Squ. Res.
M1	-0.003630	10.09386	0.996263	0.995951	0.007160
GDP	-0.001621	20.00641	0.955309	0.951585	0.085615
Defl	-0.192398	21.29028	0.960098	0.956773	0.076442
FFR	0.190441	5.776679	0.829896	0.815721	0.325871
10YR	0.367813	4.029572	0.967580	0.964878	0.062108
NomY	-0.001152	13.87713	0.991884	0.991208	0.015548
RealM	-0.003559	11.07915	0.991177	0.990442	0.016902

Table 6.6 Regression Results from Equations for Velocity as a Function of One Other Variable (listed at the beginning of each row of numbers) and a Constant
Sixth Sub-Sample Period (1990q3-1993q4)
Source: www.economagic.com and the author's calculations

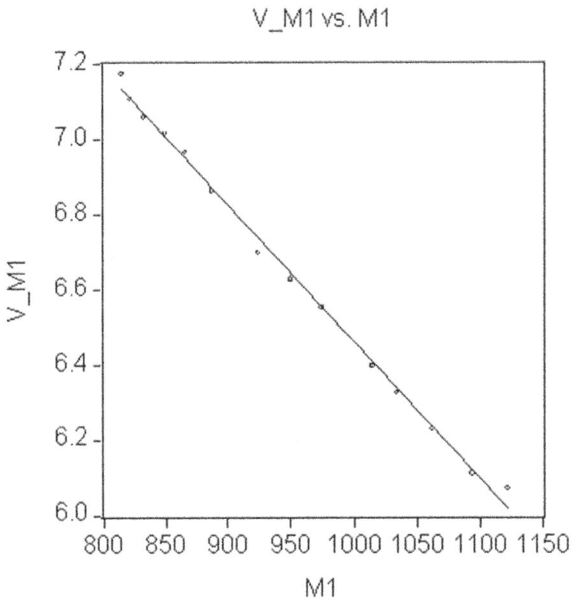

Figure 6.37 Scatter-Graph Plot of the Velocity of M1 (on the Vertical Axis) and Quarterly Average M1 (Nominal)
Regression Line Included
1990 quarter three through 1993 quarter four
Source: www.economagic.com and the author's calculations

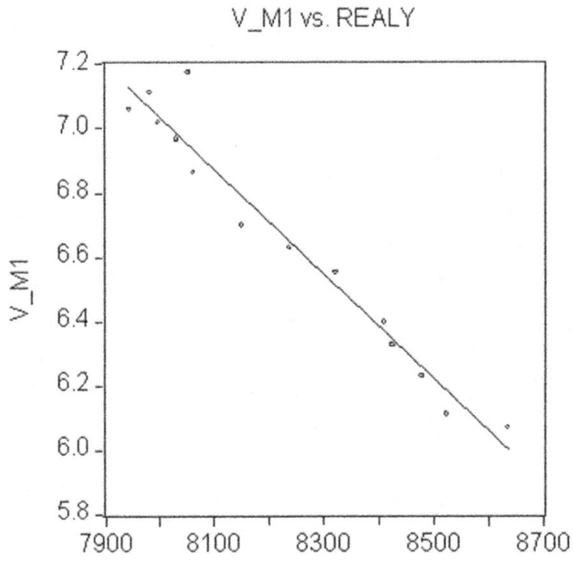

Figure 6.38 Scatter-Graph Plot of the Velocity of M1 (on the Vertical Axis) and Real GDP
Regression Line Included
1990 quarter three through 1993 quarter four
Source: www.economagic.com

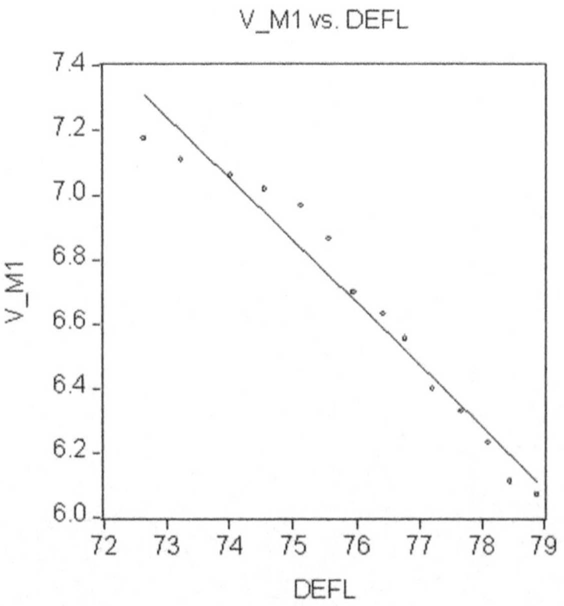

Figure 6.39 Scatter-Graph Plot of the Velocity of M1 (on the Vertical Axis) and the Deflator
Regression Line Included
1990 quarter three through 1993 quarter four
Source: www.economagic.com

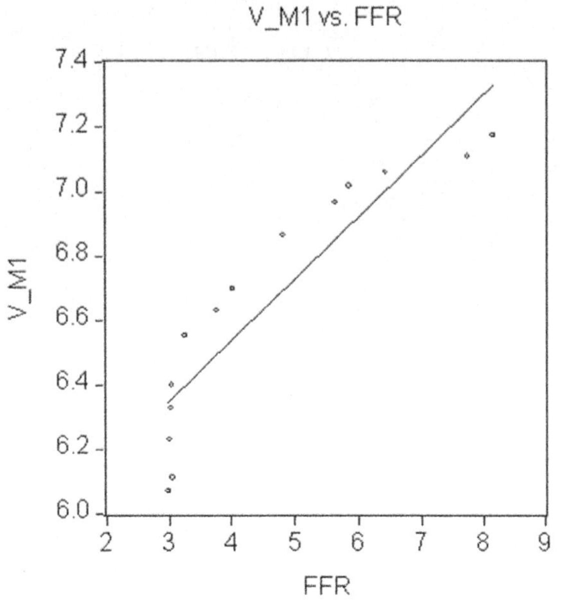

Figure 6.40 Scatter-Graph Plot of the Velocity of M1 (on the Vertical Axis) and the Quarterly Average Federal Funds Rate
Regression Line Included
1990 quarter three through 1993 quarter four
Source: www.economagic.com and the author's calculations

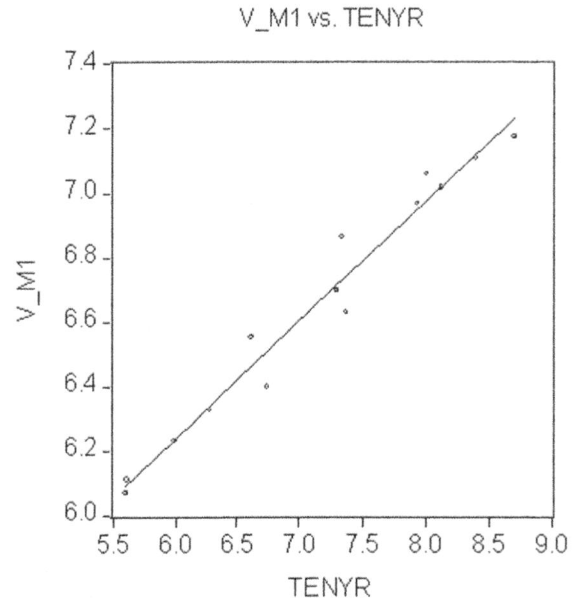

Figure 6.41 Scatter-Graph Plot of the Velocity of M1 (on the Vertical Axis) and the Quarterly Average Ten-Year Treasury Interest Rate
Regression Line Included
1990 quarter three through 1993 quarter four
Source: www.economagic.com and the author's calculations

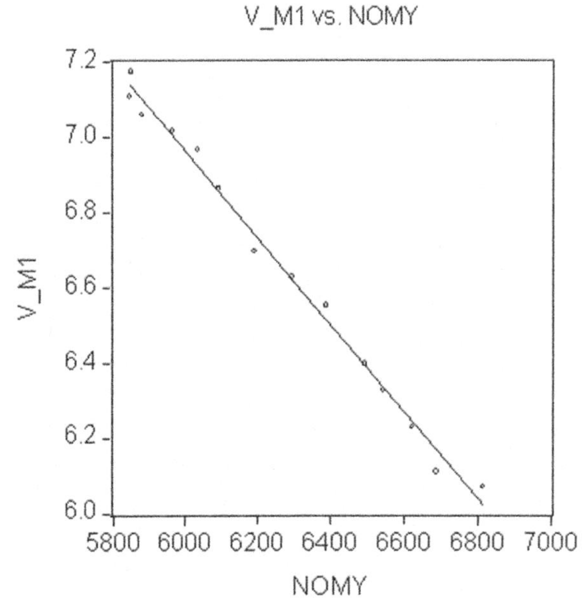

Figure 6.42 Scatter-Graph Plot of the Velocity of M1 (on the Vertical Axis) and Nominal GDP
Regression Line Included
1990 quarter three through 1993 quarter four
Source: www.economagic.com

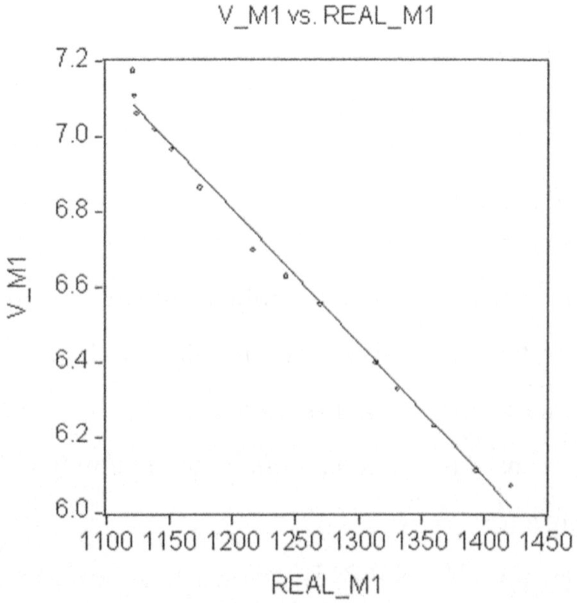

Figure 6.43 Scatter-Graph Plot of the Velocity of M1 (on the Vertical Axis) and Quarterly Average Real M1
Regression Line Included
1990 quarter three through 1993 quarter four
Source: www.economagic.com and the author's calculations

REGRESSION DISCUSSION: 1990q3-1993q4

During this sub-sample period, the use of nominal M1 as the lone independent variable in the regression generates the smallest sum of squared residuals and the largest adjusted R-squared statistic of the variables considered. Further, the estimated coefficient for nominal M1 is negative, as is expected from the algebraic definition of velocity. Does this indicate that the decrease in the velocity of M1 during this sub-sample period is largely due to an increase in the growth rate of average quarterly nominal M1?

In terms of minimizing the sum of squared residuals and maximizing the adjusted R-squared statistic, nominal GDP was second best in this sub-sample period, followed in descending order of maximizing the adjusted R-squared statistic by real money supply, the ten-year rate, the deflator, real GDP, and the federal funds rate. A question for further study could be why the federal funds rate failed to perform as well as any other variable considered and why the ten year rate performed better than real GDP and the deflator as well as performing much better than the federal funds rate during this sub-sample period. Further, the methodology used may overstate how well nominal GDP, real GDP, and the deflator explain the velocity of M1 during this period because the estimated coefficients are negative rather than positive.

DATA DESCRIPTION: 1990q3-1993q4

While the velocity of M1 increased in each quarter from the third quarter of 1987 through the second quarter of 1990 except for the fourth quarter of 1989 (when there was a small decrease), M1 velocity fell each quarter from the third quarter of 1990 through the fourth quarter of 1993. What are some factors that could have caused a recession around the beginning of this sub-sample period that helped lead to velocity falling?

Burton and Lombra (2006, pp. 292-294, 315-316) discuss the Savings and Loans Crisis in the United States in the 1980s and the Financial Institutions Reform, Recovery, and Enforcement Act of 1989 in response to the Savings and Loans Crisis. Burton and Lombra (2006, p. 292) point out that one of the results of the crisis was that over 1,500 thrifts ceased operations. Additionally, Burton and Lombra (2006, pp. 235-236) point out that a surge in commercial bank failures also occurred in the late 1980s and the early 1990s, when the average number of bank failures per year increased from about five per year from 1955 to 1981 to an average of nearly 190 per year from 1987 to 1990.

Additionally, Dornbusch, Fischer, and Startz (2008, pp. 137) discuss an increase in the price of oil in the last two quarters of 1990 but note that a recession began before the price increased. Data from www.economagic.com and the author's calculations indicate that, although declining for four consecutive quarters from the third quarter of 1989 through the second quarter of 1990 (and beyond), the quarterly average federal funds rate increased by more than three percentage points from 6.65 per cent in the second quarter of 1987 to about 9.73 per cent in the second quarter of 1989. These events may have been at least partly responsible for a recession in the early 1990s. Real GDP started decreasing for three consecutive quarters in the third quarter of 1990, with a cumulative decrease of around 1.4 per cent of output.

In terms of other variables, the implicit deflator increased about 2.8 per cent from the second quarter of 1990 through the first quarter of 1991. Thus, nominal GDP increased in two of the three quarters (the exception being the fourth quarter of 1990) and was greater in the first quarter of 1991 than in the second quarter of 1990. So, although a decrease in *real* GDP could have caused the decrease in velocity, at least initially, a decrease in *nominal* GDP could have been a contributing factor in only one quarter (the fourth quarter of 1990) as nominal GDP continued to grow most quarters.

What about the money supply? The nominal M1 money supply grew at a quarterly rate in the third quarter of 1990 of about 1.11 per cent, very roughly the same as the rate from the first quarter of 1990 (about 1.17 per cent) and from the second quarter of 1990 (about 1.01 per cent). The quarterly money supply growth rate in the third quarter of 1990 was somewhat less than the rate in the fourth quarter of 1989 (approximately 1.25 per cent), but greater than the growth rate between the fourth quarter of 1988 and the third quarter of 1989, with the nominal money supply decreasing in the first and second quarters of 1989. The nominal M1 money supply grew at a somewhat slower rate in the fourth quarter of 1990 (approximately 0.85 per cent).

But, in the first quarter of 1991, the nominal money supply grew at a rate of nearly 1.29 per cent, the highest growth rate since the third quarter of 1988 (around 1.31 per cent). Afterward, the M1 money supply in nominal terms grew at a quarterly rate of greater than 1.9 per cent for eleven consecutive quarters and surpassed the four per cent growth mark in two of those quarters. In the second quarter of 1991, growth in real GDP resumed and the implicit deflator continued growing. Yet, the velocity of M1 continued falling through the fourth quarter of 1993, likely due to faster money supply growth.

In an earlier sub-sample period, the real money supply reached a local minimum in the third quarter of 1989 at roughly 1.1157 trillion dollars of buying power in the year 2005. After increasing to roughly 1.1223 trillion 2005-constant-buying-power dollars in the fourth quarter of 1989, the real money supply fell again to approximately 1.1218 trillion 2005-constant-buying-power dollars in the first quarter of 1990 and approximately 1.1201 trillion 2005-constant-buying-power dollars in the second quarter of 1990.

But starting with the third quarter of 1990 (the beginning of the sub-sample period of the main focus in this section), the real money supply began to increase each quarter until the fourth quarter of 1994, increasing into the next sub-sample period. By the fourth quarter of 1993 (the end of the sub-sample period), the real money supply, around 1.4225 trillion 2005-constant-buying-power dollars, was about twenty-seven per cent greater than in the second quarter of 1990. That represents an average increase of around 1.93 per cent per quarter over fourteen quarters. Although this is not the fastest quarterly growth in the real money supply among the various sub-sample periods considered in this study, it represents the third largest growth rate. The relatively rapid growth rate in the real money supply could be the factor most responsible for the decrease in the velocity of money from the second quarter of 1990 through the fourth quarter of 1993, when the cumulative decrease in the velocity of money (after the second quarter of 1990) reached approximately 15.6 per cent.

The importance of the increase in the real money supply leading to a decrease in the velocity of money was particularly strong starting with the second quarter of 1991. The real money supply levels during the third quarter of 1990 (roughly 1.1222 trillion 2005-constant-buying-power dollars), the fourth quarter of 1990 (roughly 1.1227 trillion 2005-constant-buying-power dollars), and the first quarter of 1991 (roughly 1.1251 trillion 2005-constant-buying-power dollars) were little changed compared with the level in the second quarter of 1990 (roughly 1.1201 trillion 2005-constant-buying-power dollars), yet the velocity of M1 began to decrease in the third quarter of 1990. Some of the decrease in velocity is attributable to the decrease in real GDP in the third quarter of 1990, the fourth quarter of 1990, and the first quarter of 1991. While the velocity of M1 fell by nearly 1.8 per cent from the second quarter of 1990 through the first quarter of 1991, real GDP also fell by about 1.36 per cent over the same time interval. From the equation of exchange, the remaining decrease in the velocity of money from the second quarter of 1990 through the first quarter of 1991 is attributable to an increase in the real money supply of approximately 0.45 per cent. But real GDP started growing in the second quarter of 1991 and grew through the fourth quarter of 1993 (the last quarter of the sub-sample period) and well beyond, while the implicit deflator continued increasing through the fourth quarter of 1993 and well beyond. Starting with the second quarter of 1991 in this sub-sample period, the faster growth in the nominal money supply dominated the growth rate of the implicit deflator by a wider margin and caused the real money supply to grow at a faster rate, thus explaining the continued decrease in velocity.

Due at least in part to the recession, average quarterly real GDP growth was slower than over the previous sub-sample period (approximately 0.52 per cent per quarter versus approximately 0.91 per cent per quarter). The average percentage growth in the implicit deflator (roughly 0.68 per cent per quarter) during this sub-sample period, was also less than during the previous sub-sample period (roughly 0.96 per cent).

The faster growth in the money supply may have been implemented to reduce interest rates and stimulate growth in real GDP. In the fourth quarter of 1993, the average federal funds rate was 2.99 per cent, well below the calculated value of approximately 8.243 per cent from the second quarter of

1990 and down even further from the value of roughly 9.73 per cent in the second quarter of 1989. By the fourth quarter of 1992, the average federal funds rate was about 3.04 per cent, having decreased every quarter after the second quarter of 1989. The average federal funds rate then fluctuated between 3.0 per cent and 3.6 per cent through the third quarter of 1993 before reaching a local minimum of 2.99 per cent in the fourth quarter of 1993. After the third quarter of 1990, the average U.S. Treasury ten-year rate declined in most quarters through the fourth quarter of 1993. In the second quarter of 1990, the average ten-year rate was nearly 8.68 per cent. By the fourth quarter of 1993, the average ten-year rate had fallen to about 5.61 per cent.

SEVENTH SUB-SAMPLE PERIOD: 1994Q1 THROUGH 2000Q4

	Coeffi.	Const.	R-Squ.	Adj. R-Squ.	Sum Squ. Res.
M1	-0.024238	34.43935	0.458884	0.438072	14.65963
GDP	0.001183	-4.149526	0.971597	0.970504	0.769492
Defl	0.343614	-21.38603	0.984738	0.984151	0.413458
FFR	0.661068	4.069963	0.212337	0.182042	21.33895
10YR	-0.846604	12.84441	0.384671	0.361004	16.67016
NomY	0.000999	-0.788252	0.976974	0.976089	0.623802
RealM	-0.013132	24.86743	0.891118	0.886930	2.949768

Table 6.7 Regression Results from Equations for Velocity as a Function of One Other Variable (listed at the beginning of each row of numbers) and a Constant
Seventh Sub-Sample Period (1994q1-2000q4)
Source: www.economagic.com and the author's calculations

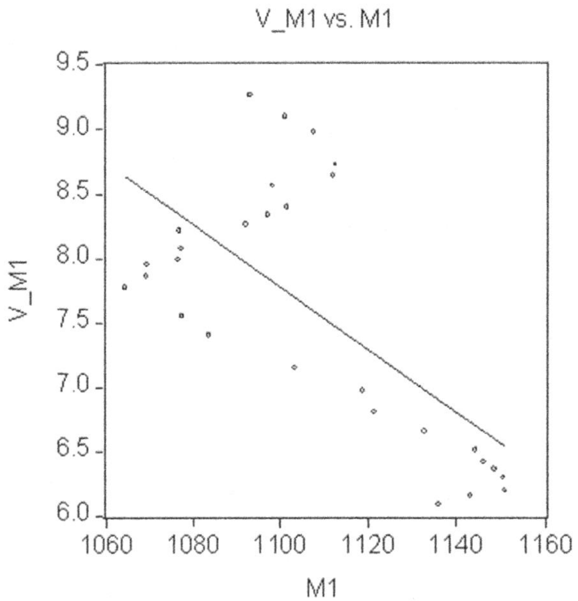

Figure 6.44 Scatter-Graph Plot of the Velocity of M1 (on the Vertical Axis) and Quarterly Average M1 (Nominal)
Regression Line Included
1994 quarter one through 2000 quarter four
Source: www.economagic.com and the author's calculations

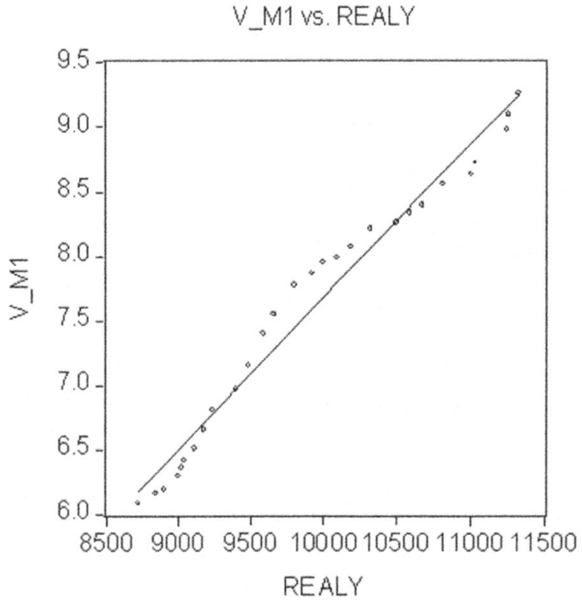

Figure 6.45 Scatter-Graph Plot of the Velocity of M1 (on the Vertical Axis) and Real GDP
Regression Line Included
1994 quarter one through 2000 quarter four
Source: www.economagic.com

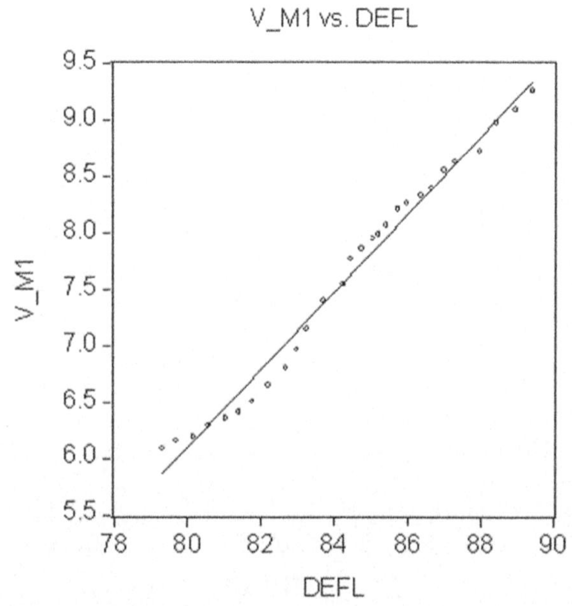

Figure 6.46 Scatter-Graph Plot of the Velocity of M1 (on the Vertical Axis) and the Deflator
Regression Line Included
1994 quarter one through 2000 quarter four
Source: www.economagic.com

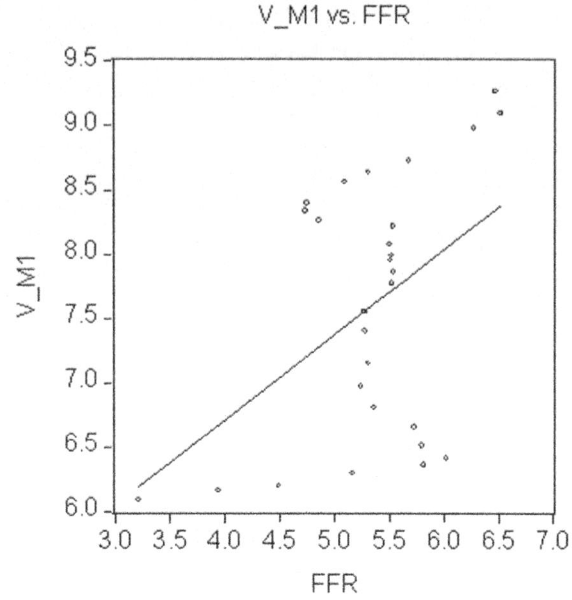

Figure 6.47 Scatter-Graph Plot of the Velocity of M1 (on the Vertical Axis) and the Quarterly Average Federal Funds Rate
Regression Line Included
1994 quarter one through 2000 quarter four
Source: www.economagic.com and the author's calculations

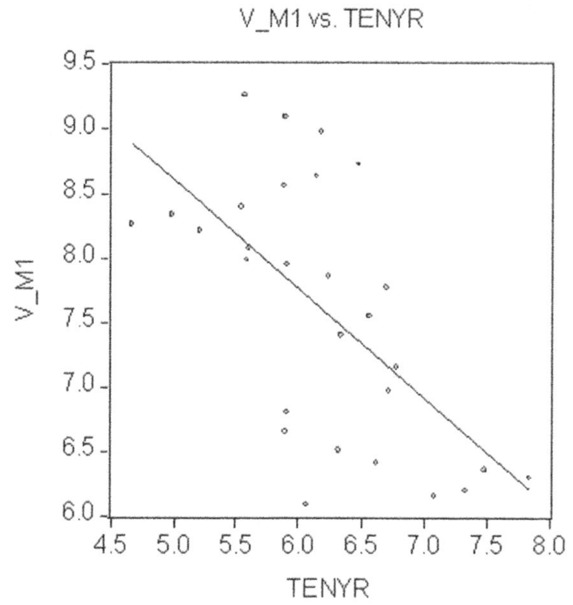

Figure 6.48 Scatter-Graph Plot of the Velocity of M1 (on the Vertical Axis) and the Quarterly Average Ten-Year Treasury Interest Rate
Regression Line Included
1994 quarter one through 2000 quarter four
Source: www.economagic.com and the author's calculations

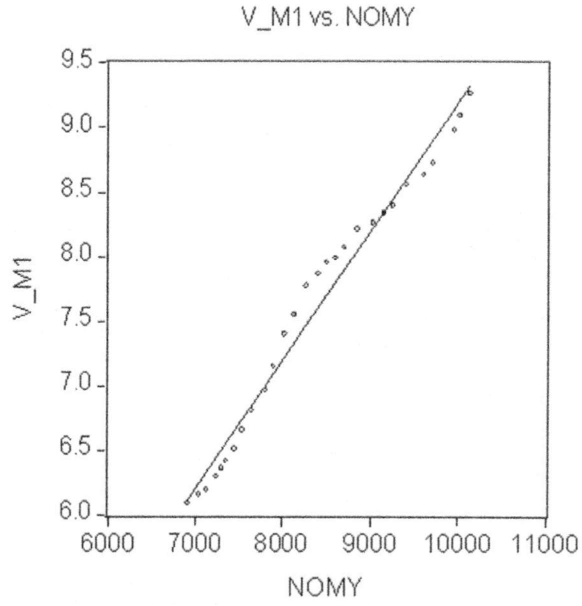

Figure 6.49 Scatter-Graph Plot of the Velocity of M1 (on the Vertical Axis) and Nominal GDP
Regression Line Included
1994 quarter one through 2000 quarter four
Source: www.economagic.com

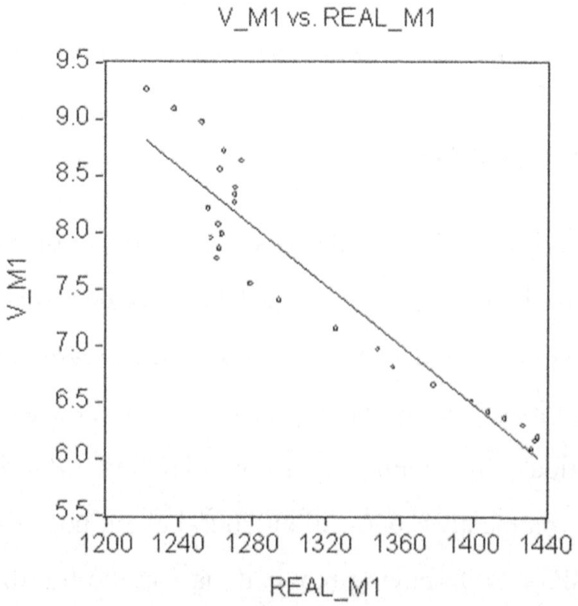

Figure 6.50 Scatter-Graph Plot of the Velocity of M1 (on the Vertical Axis) and Quarterly Average Real M1
Regression Line Included
1994 quarter one through 2000 quarter four
Source: www.economagic.com and the author's calculations

REGRESSION DISCUSSION: 1994q1-2000q4

Nominal M1 does not seem to perform well as the lone independent variable compared with the other variables considered in terms of producing the smallest sum of squared residuals and the greatest adjusted R-squared statistic in the sub-sample period running from the first quarter of 1994 through the fourth quarter of 2000. In this regard, nominal M1 is better than only the federal funds rate and the ten-year rate of the variables considered. Perhaps this is due to nominal M1 increasing and decreasing by relatively small amounts, as discussed below, while nominal GDP increased, perhaps more rapidly on average toward the end of the sub-sample period (but before the last two quarters of the sub-sample period). However, unlike some other sub-sample periods, the estimated coefficient for M1 is negative as may be expected from the algebraic definition of velocity.

The use of the implicit deflator as the sole independent variable generates the smallest sum of squared residuals and the largest adjusted R-squared. Nominal GDP is second-best, followed by real GDP, and then real M1. Although the sum of squared residuals from the regression with the ten-year rate is smaller than the sum from the regression with the federal funds rate, the estimated coefficient for the ten-year rate is negative, contrary to what one may expect and unlike the coefficient for the federal funds rate.

DATA DESCRIPTION: 1994q1-2000q4

The first quarter of 1994 'kicked off' a period when the velocity of money increased for twenty-eight consecutive quarters. In the fourth quarter of 1993, the velocity of M1 was roughly 6.07 times per year. By the fourth quarter of 2000, the velocity of M1 had increased to nearly 9.27 times per year. Thus, the velocity of M1 had increased by roughly 52.6 per cent, or nearly 1.9 per cent per quarter.

Given that this was a period of economic expansion when real GDP increased by approximately thirty-one per cent from approximately 8.636 trillion 2005-buying-power dollars in the fourth quarter of 1993 to nearly 11.325 trillion 2005-buying-power dollars in the fourth quarter of 2000, this study attributes much of the increase in velocity during this period to increasing real GDP. An increase in the price level was another important factor leading to the increase in velocity. In fact, in light of the results from the sums of squared residuals and adjusted R-squared statistics in the table above, the implicit deflator may have been somewhat more important than real GDP in explaining variation in the velocity of M1 during this sub-sample period. In the fourth quarter of 2000, the implicit deflator was 89.447, up approximately 13.4 per cent from its level in the fourth quarter of 1993, which was 78.897. Does the fact that the percentage increase in real GDP (roughly 31 per cent) was closer to the percentage increase in velocity (roughly 53 per cent) than the percentage increase in the deflator (roughly 13 per cent) imply that the increase in velocity over this sub-sample period was more due to the growth in real GDP than the growth in the deflator, despite the adjusted R-squared statistic and sum of squared residuals results?

The average nominal money supply in the fourth quarter of 2000, approximately 1.093 trillion dollars, was actually slightly less than in the fourth quarter of 1993, when it was roughly 1.122 trillion dollars. Although there was an overall decrease in the nominal M1 money supply of nearly 2.6 per cent during this period, there were 'ups and downs' in the nominal M1 data during this period. The greatest quarterly value for nominal M1 during the sub-sample period spanning from the first quarter of 1994 through the fourth quarter of 2000 was approximately 1.15097 trillion dollars in the third quarter of 1994. Nominal M1 then began to decrease each quarter until reaching a sub-sample period minimum of roughly 1.0646 trillion dollars in the second quarter of 1997. The average M1 nominal money supply then increased most quarters through the first quarter of 2000, when it reached approximately 1.113 trillion dollars. The average nominal M1 data then decreased again in the second quarter, the third quarter, and the fourth quarter of 2000, reaching roughly 1.093 trillion dollars in the fourth quarter of 2000.

Given that real GDP and the implicit deflator both increased each quarter during this period, it is highly likely that these two variables are more important in explaining the rise in the velocity of money during this period than relatively short-term decreases in the nominal money stock during the sub-sample period. Whether the nominal money supply was increasing or decreasing during this sub-sample period, the absolute value of the percentage change in the money supply from local maximum to local minimum or *vice versa* was smaller than the percentage growth in real GDP over the same time interval. This further shows that changes in real GDP were more important than changes in nominal money supply in determining growth in the velocity of money from 1994 through 2000.

Regarding the real money supply, the real quantity of money fell from 1.4225 trillion 2005-constant-buying-power dollars in the fourth quarter of 1993 to 1.2221 trillion 2005-constant-buying-power dollars in the fourth quarter of 2000, a decrease of about 14.1 per cent. The decrease in the real M1 money supply is explained by growth in the deflator of about 13.4 per cent plus a slight overall net decrease in the nominal M1 money supply of roughly 2.6 per cent over the period.

EIGHTH SUB-SAMPLE PERIOD: 2001Q1 THROUGH 2003Q2

	Coeffi.	Const.	R-Squ.	Adj. R-Squ.	Sum Squ. Res.
M1	-0.003010	12.48533	0.771711	0.743175	0.057474
GDP	-0.000705	17.02277	0.399316	0.324230	0.151229
Defl	-0.096158	17.75630	0.512985	0.452108	0.122611
FFR	0.094332	8.685874	0.707002	0.670378	0.073765
10YR	0.161468	8.175385	0.330567	0.246888	0.168537
NomY	-0.000406	13.20864	0.460158	0.392677	0.135911
RealM	-0.004244	14.38861	0.870523	0.854338	0.032597

Table 6.8 Regression Results from Equations for Velocity as a Function of One Other Variable (listed at the beginning of each row of numbers) and a Constant
Eighth Sub-Sample Period (2000q1-2003q2)
Source: www.economagic.com and the author's calculations

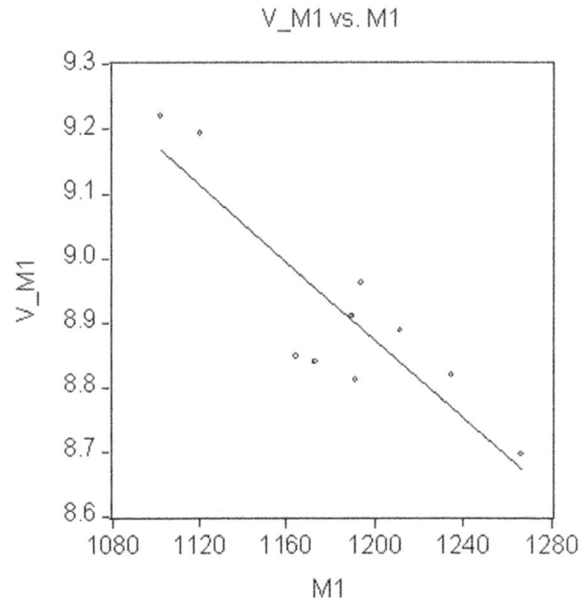

Figure 6.51 Scatter-Graph Plot of the Velocity of M1 (on the Vertical Axis) and Quarterly Average M1 (Nominal)
Regression Line Included
2001 quarter one through 2003 quarter two
Source: www.economagic.com and the author's calculations

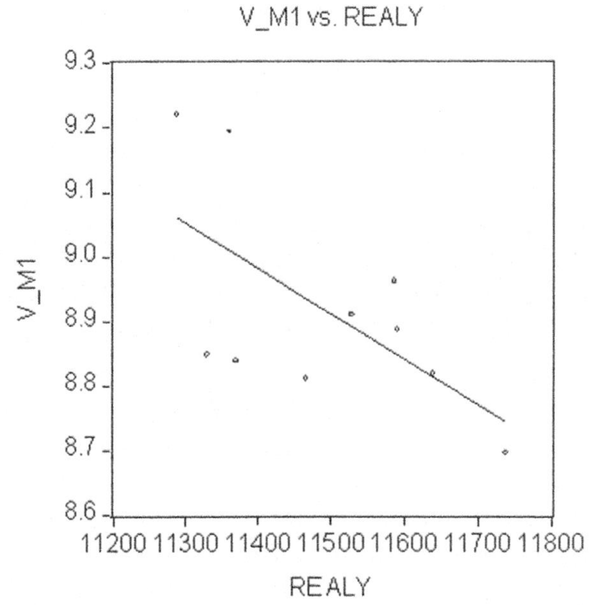

Figure 6.52 Scatter-Graph Plot of the Velocity of M1 (on the Vertical Axis) and Real GDP
Regression Line Included
2001 quarter one through 2003 quarter two
Source: www.economagic.com

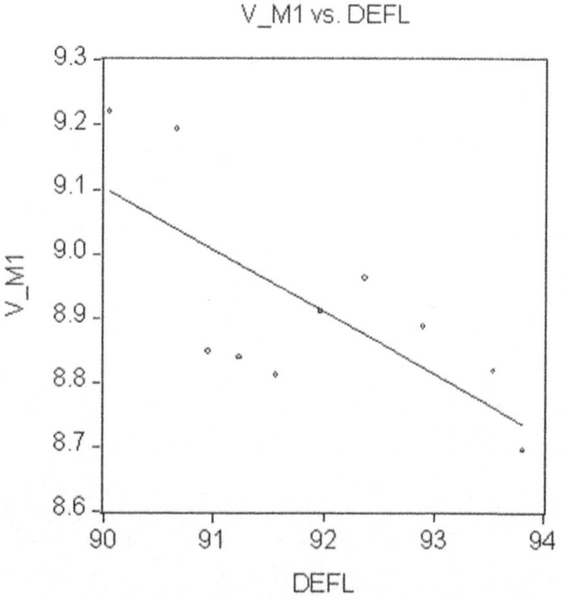

Figure 6.53 Scatter-Graph Plot of the Velocity of M1 (on the Vertical Axis) and the Deflator
Regression Line Included
2001 quarter one through 2003 quarter two
Source: www.economagic.com

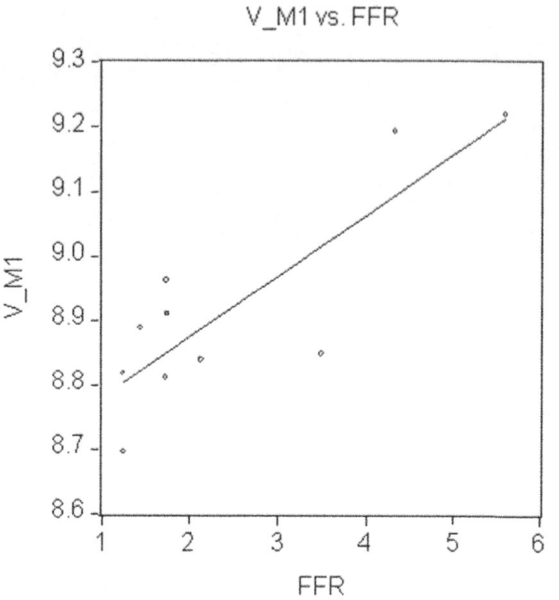

Figure 6.54 Scatter-Graph Plot of the Velocity of M1 (on the Vertical Axis) and the Quarterly Average Federal Funds Rate
Regression Line Included
2001 quarter one through 2003 quarter two
Source: www.economagic.com and the author's calculations

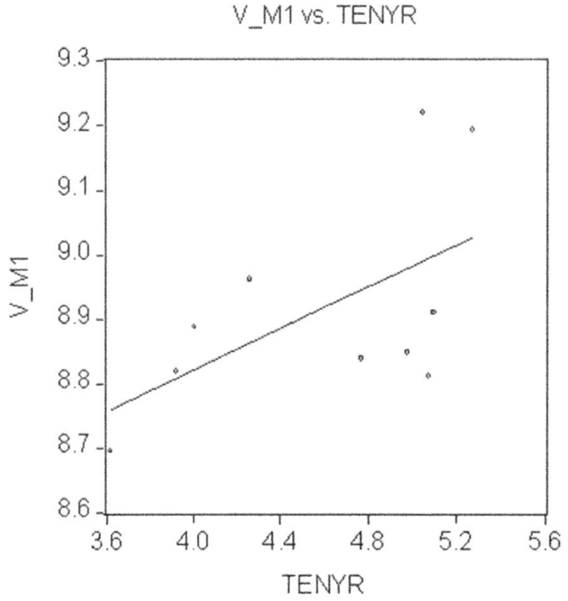

Figure 6.55 Scatter-Graph Plot of the Velocity of M1 (on the Vertical Axis) and the Quarterly Average Ten-Year Treasury Interest Rate
Regression Line Included
2001 quarter one through 2003 quarter two
Source: www.economagic.com and the author's calculations

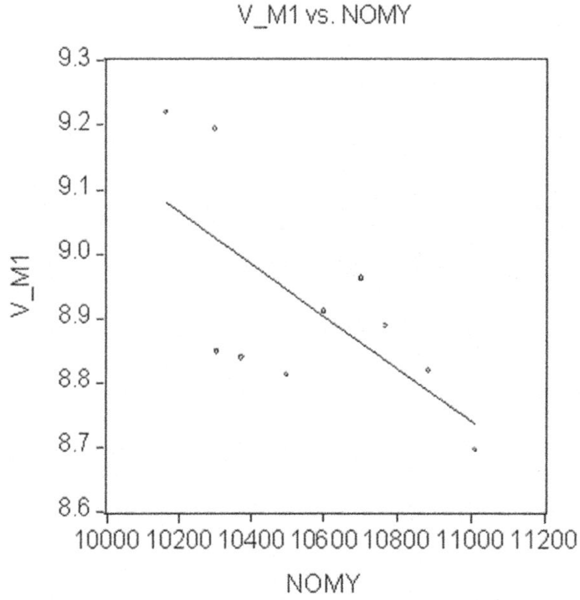

Figure 6.56 Scatter-Graph Plot of the Velocity of M1 (on the Vertical Axis) and Nominal GDP
Regression Line Included
2001 quarter one through 2003 quarter two
Source: www.economagic.com

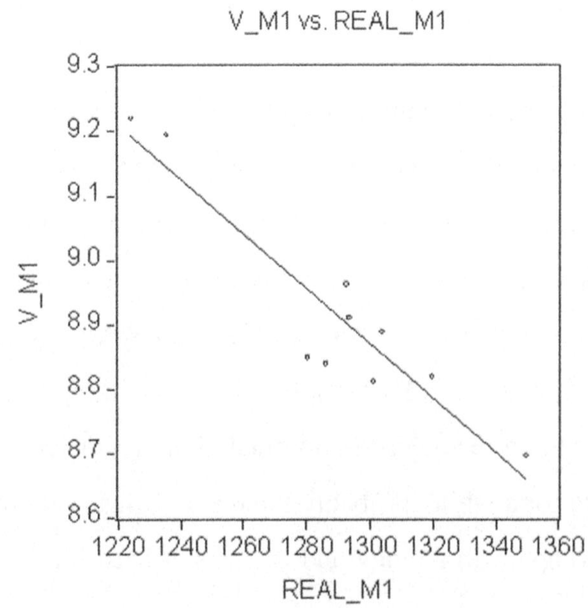

Figure 6.57 Scatter-Graph Plot of the Velocity of M1 (on the Vertical Axis) and Quarterly Average Real M1
Regression Line Included
2001 quarter one through 2003 quarter two
Source: www.economagic.com and the author's calculations

REGRESSION DISCUSSION: 2001q1-2003q2

While nominal M1 may not have faired well compared with the other variables considered in the prior sub-sample period, nominal M1 was topped by only real M1 in the sub-sample period running from the first quarter of 2001 through the second quarter of 2003. The estimated negative coefficient suggests that the increase in nominal M1 during this sub-sample period could have caused or at least contributed to the decrease in the velocity of M1 during this period. The federal funds rate was 'third best' at minimizing the sum of squared residuals and maximizing the adjusted R-squared statistic. In fact, that is the highest position in the relative rankings for the federal funds rate of all the sub-sample periods. The remaining variables in descending order of performance are: the deflator, nominal GDP, real GDP, and the ten-year rate.

The estimated coefficients for real GDP, the implicit deflator, and nominal GDP are less than zero – counter to what would be expected all other things equal from the algebraic definition of the velocity of money. As noted above, this also happened in the sub-sample periods running from the fourth quarter of 1981 through the second quarter of 1983, the first quarter of 1985 through the second quarter of 1987, and the third quarter of 1990 through the fourth quarter of 1993. In material to follow, this is also true of the last sub-sample period running from the first quarter of 2008 through the first quarter of 2013. In each of these sub-sample periods, rapid money supply growth occurred. Further, nominal M1 performed better in the regressions in terms of producing the smallest sum of squared residuals and the largest adjusted R-squared statistic than did nominal GDP or its components, real GDP and the implicit deflator (divided by 100) in these sub-sample periods. Moreover, with the exception of the sub-sample period from the first quarter of 1985 through the second quarter of 1987, each period had a recession and the beginning of a recovery. As nominal GDP and its components began to increase, velocity continued to decline for a while, probably the result of faster money supply growth spurring growth in nominal GDP perhaps with a delay and perhaps at least initially at a rate slower than the increase in the money supply.

DATA DESCRIPTION: 2001q1-2003q2

The velocity of M1 began to decrease most quarters from the first quarter of 2001 through the second quarter of 2003, declining from around 9.27 times per year in the fourth quarter of 2000 to about 8.70 times per year in the second quarter of 2003. The two exceptions were the second and third quarters of the year 2002, when the velocity of money exhibited relatively small increases. In the second quarter of 2002, the velocity of money increased to approximately 8.91 times per year, up from approximately 8.81 times per year the quarter before. In the third quarter of 2002, M1 velocity increased to roughly 8.96 times per year. But again, after the fourth quarter of 2000 through the second quarter of 2003, a clear downward trend in velocity resulted in a decrease in M1 velocity of roughly 6.16 per cent over ten quarters.

A relatively mild recession in terms of the real output lost contributed to the decline in velocity early during this sub-sample period, as real GDP declined in the first and third quarters of 2001. The loss in output between the fourth quarter of 2000 and the first quarter of 2001 was approximately 0.33 per cent, and the loss between the second quarter and the third quarter of 2001 was roughly 0.28 per cent. Like in many other quarters during this period, velocity fell during the first and third quarters of 2001. The percentage declines in velocity during these two quarters were larger than the percentage declines in real GDP in their respective quarters. Between the fourth quarter of 2000 and the first quarter of 2001, M1 velocity fell by slightly more than one-half percentage point, and between the second and third quarters of 2001, M1 velocity fell by roughly 3.75 per cent. Given that the deflator rose during these two quarters and that a higher deflator, all other things equal, would cause velocity to rise, the rising nominal money supply must have also contributed to the decline in velocity during these two quarters. M1 increased by nearly 0.86 per cent in the first quarter of 2001 and by roughly 3.94 per cent in the third quarter of 2001.

Over the sub-sample period, real GDP increased by about 3.64 per cent, and the deflator rose by approximately 4.88 per cent. Thus, during this sub-sample period, the decline in velocity of approximately 6.16 per cent was largely due to an increase in the nominal money supply of approximately 15.85 per cent. During this sub-sample period, the real money supply increased by nearly 10.45 per cent.

Rising interest rates could have led to the recession which began in 2001. Data from www.economagic.com and the author's calculations reveal that the quarterly average federal funds rate reached a local maximum of 6.52 per cent in the third quarter of 2000 and fell slightly to approximately 6.47 per cent in the fourth quarter of 2000. The quarterly average federal funds rate decreased most quarters in the eighth sub-sample period (and the first two quarters of the next sub-sample period), reaching about 1.247 per cent in the second quarter of 2003.

NINTH SUB-SAMPLE PERIOD: 2003Q3 THROUGH 2007Q4

	Coeffi.	Const.	R-Squ.	Adj. R-Squ.	Sum Squ. Res.
M1	0.013658	-9.142095	0.411192	0.374392	3.378881
GDP	0.001284	-6.857877	0.940557	0.936842	0.341114
Defl	0.136966	-4.394699	0.968977	0.967038	0.178027
FFR	0.309403	8.374064	0.856118	0.847125	0.825669
10YR	1.205930	4.018283	0.378247	0.339387	3.567939
NomY	0.000589	1.876008	0.964009	0.961760	0.206532
RealM	-0.014442	28.89255	0.922478	0.917633	0.444860

Table 6.9 Regression Results from Equations for Velocity as a Function of One Other Variable (listed at the beginning of each row of numbers) and a Constant
Ninth Sub-Sample Period (2003q3-2007q4)
Source: www.economagic.com and the author's calculations

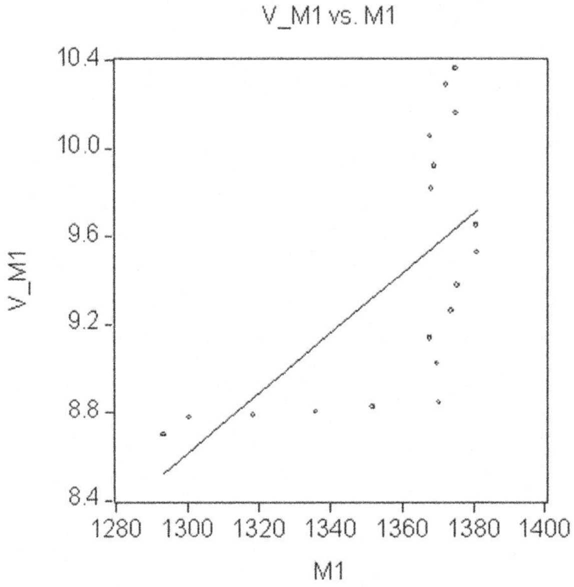

Figure 6.58 Scatter-Graph Plot of the Velocity of M1 (on the Vertical Axis) and Quarterly Average M1 (Nominal)
Regression Line Included
2003 quarter three through 2007 quarter four
Source: www.economagic.com and the author's calculations

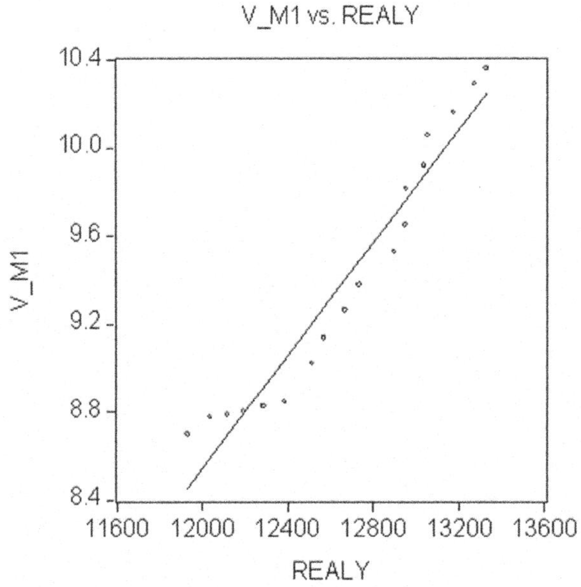

Figure 6.59 Scatter-Graph Plot of the Velocity of M1 (on the Vertical Axis) and Real GDP
Regression Line Included
2003 quarter three through 2007 quarter four
Source: www.economagic.com

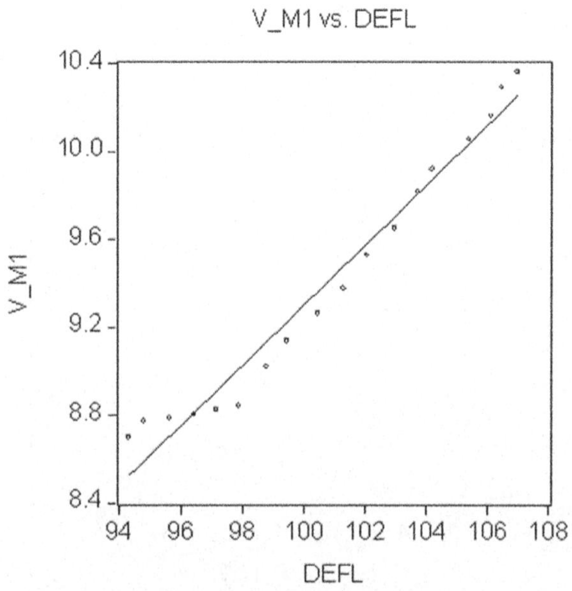

Figure 6.60 Scatter-Graph Plot of the Velocity of M1 (on the Vertical Axis) and the Deflator
Regression Line Included
2003 quarter three through 2007 quarter four
Source: www.economagic.com

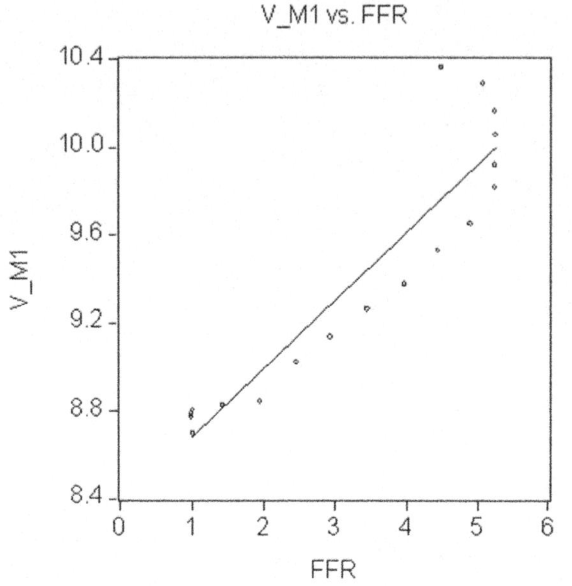

Figure 6.61 Scatter-Graph Plot of the Velocity of M1 (on the Vertical Axis) and the Quarterly Average Federal Funds Rate
Regression Line Included
2003 quarter three through 2007 quarter four
Source: www.economagic.com and the author's calculations

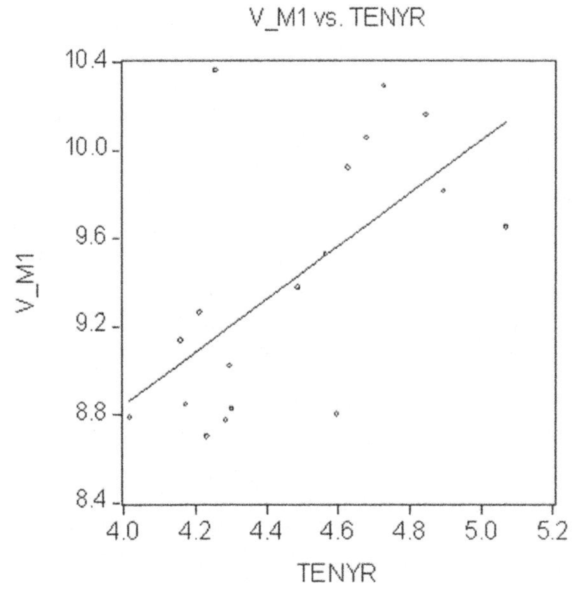

Figure 6.62 Scatter-Graph Plot of the Velocity of M1 (on the Vertical Axis) and the Quarterly Average Ten-Year Treasury Interest Rate
Regression Line Included
2003 quarter three through 2007 quarter four
Source: www.economagic.com and the author's calculations

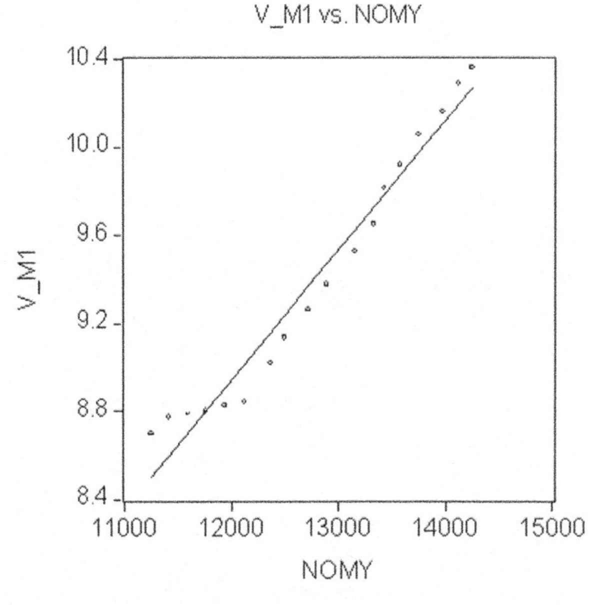

Figure 6.63 Scatter-Graph Plot of the Velocity of M1 (on the Vertical Axis) and Nominal GDP
Regression Line Included
2003 quarter three through 2007 quarter four
Source: www.economagic.com

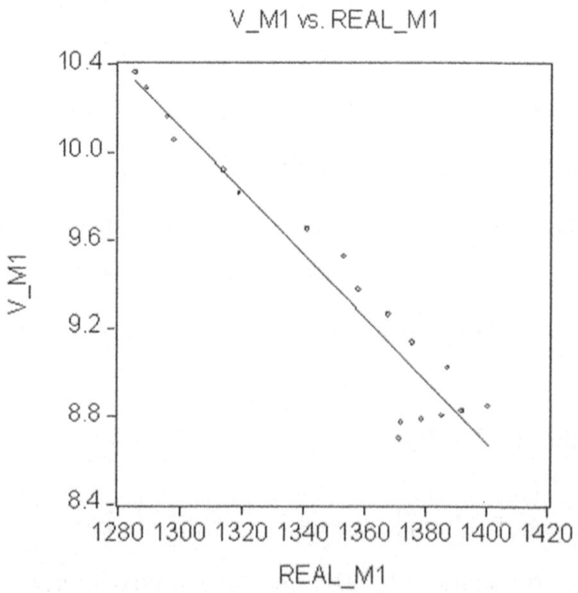

Figure 6.64 Scatter-Graph Plot of the Velocity of M1 (on the Vertical Axis) and Quarterly Average Real M1
Regression Line Included
2003 quarter three through 2007 quarter four
Source: www.economagic.com and the author's calculations

REGRESSION DISCUSSION: 2003q3-2007q4

In the sub-sample period from the third quarter of 2003 through the fourth quarter of 2007, nominal M1 returned to performing less favorably than many of the other variables considered in terms of minimizing the sum of squared residuals and maximizing the adjusted R-squared statistic. Not only did the use of real M1 produce better results than the use of nominal M1 (as was the case in the previous two sub-sample periods, although only real M1 topped nominal M1 in the previous sub-sample period), but real GDP, the implicit deflator, the federal funds rate, and nominal GDP also performed better from the third quarter of 2003 through the fourth quarter of 2007. During this sub-sample period, only the ten-year rate failed to perform at least as well as nominal M1. Further, the estimated coefficient for nominal M1 is positive, rather than negative as would be expected from the algebraic definition of velocity. Nominal M1 is the only one of the seven variables considered in this sub-sample period where the sign of the coefficient is probably not as expected. The estimated coefficient for real M1 is less than zero, as implied by the algebraic formula for velocity.

On the matter of ranking the variables in descending order in terms of producing the smallest sum of squared residuals and the largest adjusted R-squared statistic from regression equations for the velocity of M1, each with just one independent variable and a constant term, the implicit deflator ranks first, followed by nominal GDP, real GDP, real money supply, the federal funds rate, nominal M1, and the ten-year rate. Again, the deterioration in the performance of nominal M1 coincides with a period of slower growth in the nominal M1 money supply. The improved performance of the federal funds rate compared with the ten-year rate in this sub-sample period and the one immediately before could be a topic for further study.

DATA DESCRIPTION: 2003q3-2007q4

The velocity of M1 increased from about 8.7 times per year to about 10.4 times per year from the second quarter of 2003 through the fourth quarter of 2007. This was approximately a 19.2 percent increase in the velocity of M1, or an increase of about 1.07 per cent per quarter over eighteen quarters. The period could be characterized by economic expansion, slower money supply growth than the previous sub-sample period, but faster growth in the deflator than in the previous period. Clearly, an increase in real GDP and an increase in the deflator would contribute to an increase in velocity. Further, while an increase in nominal M1 would, all other things equal, lead to a decrease in the velocity of M1, a slower growth rate in nominal M1 than in the previous sub-sample period would, all other things equal, lead to a greater likelihood of an increase in M1 velocity, particularly when nominal GDP grows at a faster rate.

Over this sub-sample period, real GDP increased by about 13.5 per cent, from approximately 11.7375 trillion 2005-buying-power dollars in the second quarter of 2003 to about 13.3260 trillion 2005-buying-power dollars in the fourth quarter of 2007. This represents growth of roughly 0.75 per cent per quarter. The implicit deflator increased by about 14 per cent, approximately from 93.8 to 107.0 over this sub-sample period.

Nominal M1 increased from about 1.2663 trillion dollars to about 1.3751 trillion dollars, an increase of about 8.6 per cent or about 0.48 per cent per quarter. Given that the implicit GDP deflator as the measure of the price level increased by approximately 14 per cent but nominal M1 increased by only about 8.6 per cent, the real money supply decreased during this period. The real money supply in 2005-constant-buying-power dollars declined from approximately 1.3498 trillion dollars in the second quarter of 2003 to approximately 1.2856 trillion dollars in the fourth quarter of 2007, a decrease of about 4.8 per cent or about 0.26 per cent per quarter. An increase in real GDP of about

13.5 per cent combined with a decrease in the real money supply of around 4.8 per cent led to an increase in the velocity of M1 of roughly 19.2 per cent.

TENTH SUB-SAMPLE PERIOD: 2008Q1 THROUGH 2013Q1

	Coeffi.	Const.	R-Squ.	Adj. R-Squ.	Sum Squ. Res.
M1	-0.003288	14.25599	0.926805	0.922952	2.009651
GDP	-0.002106	35.95443	0.324895	0.289363	18.53569
Defl	-0.397733	52.61506	0.886197	0.880208	3.124561
FFR	1.068247	7.631115	0.578824	0.556657	11.56380
10YR	1.313601	4.341420	0.735432	0.721507	7.263976
NomY	-0.001374	28.43187	0.646814	0.628226	9.697061
RealM	-0.004296	15.25924	0.938023	0.934761	1.701643

Table 6.10 Regression Results from Equations for Velocity as a Function of One Other Variable (listed at the beginning of each row of numbers) and a Constant
Tenth Sub-Sample Period (2008q1-2013q1)
Source: www.economagic.com and the author's calculations

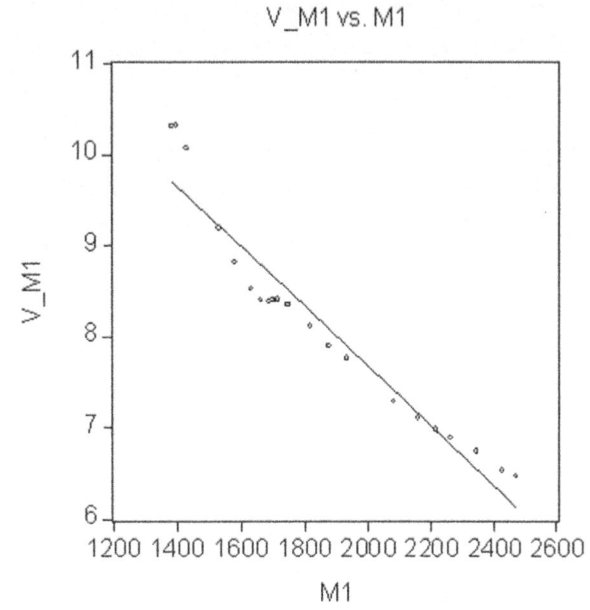

Figure 6.65 Scatter-Graph Plot of the Velocity of M1 (on the Vertical Axis) and Quarterly Average M1 (Nominal)
Regression Line Included
2008 quarter one through 2013 quarter one
Source: www.economagic.com and the author's calculations

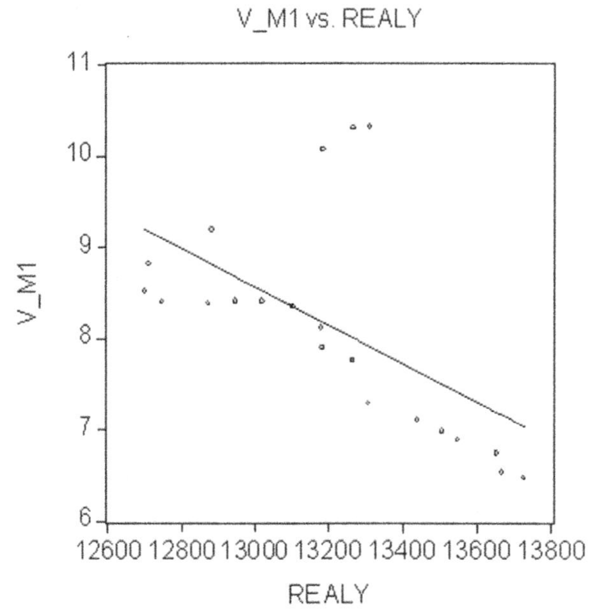

Figure 6.66 Scatter-Graph Plot of the Velocity of M1 (on the Vertical Axis) and Real GDP
Regression Line Included
2008 quarter one through 2013 quarter one
Source: www.economagic.com

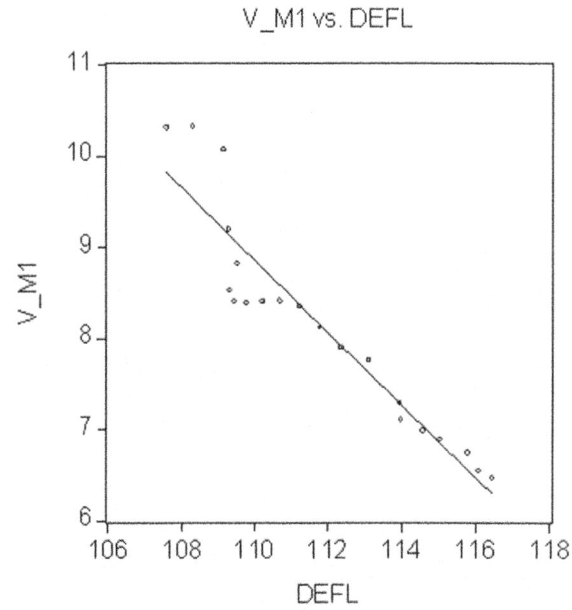

Figure 6.67 Scatter-Graph Plot of the Velocity of M1 (on the Vertical Axis) and the Deflator
Regression Line Included
2008 quarter one through 2013 quarter one
Source: www.economagic.com

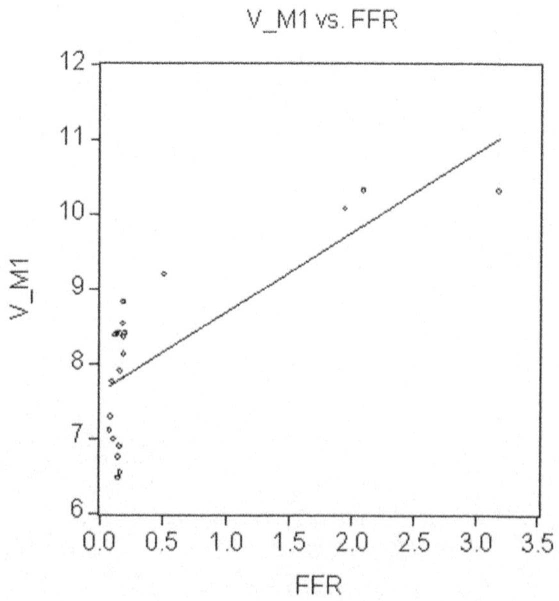

Figure 6.68 Scatter-Graph Plot of the Velocity of M1 (on the Vertical Axis) and the Quarterly Average Federal Funds Rate
Regression Line Included
2008 quarter one through 2013 quarter one
Source: www.economagic.com and the author's calculations

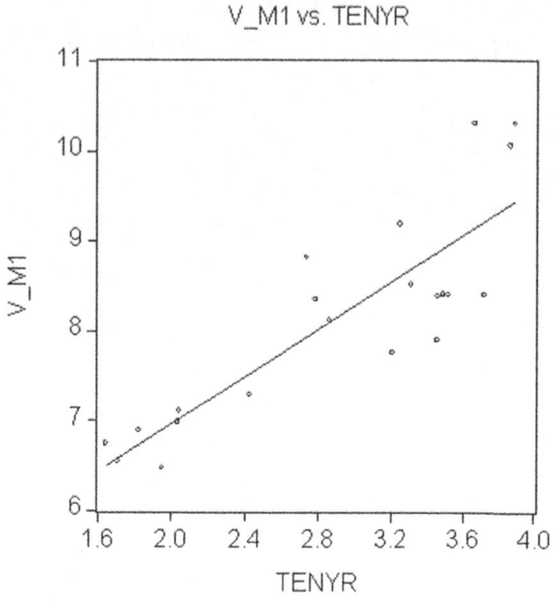

Figure 6.69 Scatter-Graph Plot of the Velocity of M1 (on the Vertical Axis) and the Quarterly Average Ten-Year Treasury Interest Rate
Regression Line Included
2008 quarter one through 2013 quarter one
Source: www.economagic.com and the author's calculations

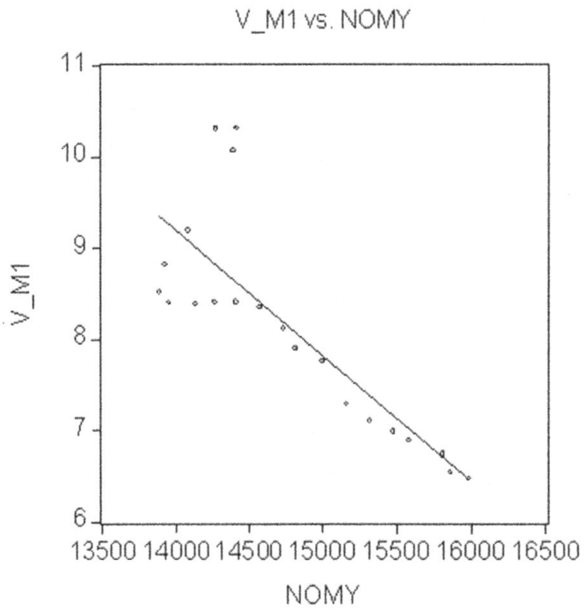

Figure 6.70 Scatter-Graph Plot of the Velocity of M1 (on the Vertical Axis) and Nominal GDP
Regression Line Included
2008 quarter one through 2013 quarter one
Source: www.economagic.com

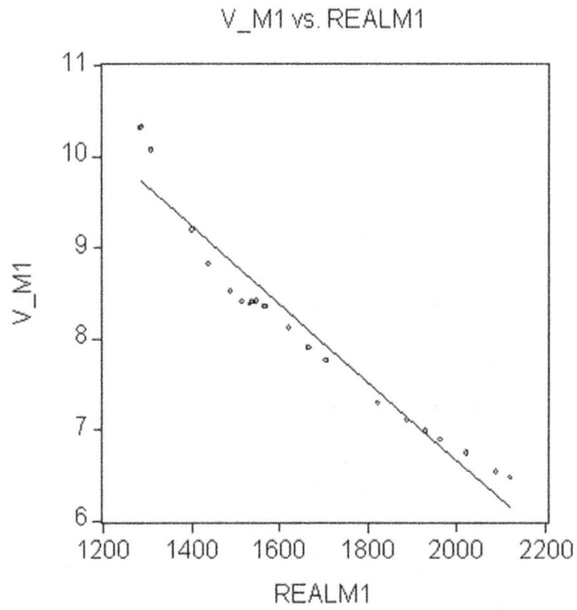

Figure 6.71 Scatter-Graph Plot of the Velocity of M1 (on the Vertical Axis) and Quarterly Average Real M1
Regression Line Included
2008 quarter one through 2013 quarter one
Source: www.economagic.com and the author's calculations

REGRESSION DISCUSSION: 2008q1-2013q1

The last sub-sample period is one in which the velocity of M1 in the United States has decreased by a greater percentage than any other period since the Great Depression and World War II era. The velocity of M1 has also decreased in nearly every quarter of this sub-sample period spanning twenty-one quarters (and continuing beyond the end of the sub-sample period). As discussed below, this sub-sample period which began with the first quarter of 2008 can be characterized as one of rapid growth rates of both nominal M1 and real M1. The surge in nominal M1 was likely in response to the most recent financial crisis in the U.S. and an effort to prevent the Great Recession from turning into another depression.

The pattern continues that in periods of more rapid nominal M1 growth, nominal M1 and real M1 perform well compared with other variables at generating large adjusted R-squared statistics and small sums of squared residuals from the regressions. In this sub-sample period, real M1 is the best and nominal M1 is second best (and seemingly not far behind). The remaining variables in descending order are the deflator, the ten-year rate, nominal GDP, the federal funds rate, and real GDP. The estimated coefficients for nominal M1 and real M1 are less than zero, as would be expected from the algebraic definition of velocity. However, the estimated coefficients for the deflator, real GDP, and nominal GDP are also less than zero which would not be expected, all other things equal. Thus, real M1 and nominal M1 are probably even better than the other variables considered (or better than at least the deflator, real GDP, and nominal GDP) in explaining the variation of the velocity of M1 during this sub-sample period than the adjusted R-squared statistics and sums of squared residuals would indicate.

DATA DESCRIPTION: 2008q1-2013q1

This sub-sample period is the only one in the sample period that is probably not yet complete. (The first sub-sample period, one of increasing velocity, probably would have begun before the first quarter of 1959, but quarterly velocity and quarterly money supply data from before 1959 were not readily available at the time of this writing.) The velocity of M1 had fallen from approximately 10.366 times per year in the fourth quarter of 2007 to approximately 6.474 times per year in the first quarter of 2013. This represents a decrease of more than 37.5 per cent, or a decrease of nearly 1.8 per cent per quarter over 21 quarters. This is the fastest quarterly decrease in M1 velocity in any of the sub-sample periods with quarterly data in which velocity decreased overall. The trend of declining M1 velocity will continue as long as rapid nominal money supply growth fails to be associated with a percentage increase in nominal GDP that is at least as large.

After decreasing sharply during most quarters early in this sub-sample period, real GDP rebounded but was only about three per cent greater at the end of the sample period than it was at the beginning. The quarterly average increase in the implicit deflator in this sub-sample period was only very roughly half as large as it was in the previous sub-sample period (2003q3 through 2007q4). Moreover, the percentage increase in M1 was much higher. With the nominal money supply growing much faster than the deflator, the real money supply also grew at its fastest rate of any sub-sample period (of quarterly data) in this study.

U.S. real GDP decreased in five out of six consecutive quarters starting in the first quarter of 2008 and going through the second quarter of 2009. During this period, real GDP fell by nearly 4.7 per cent from approximately 13.326 trillion 2005-buying-power dollars in the fourth quarter of 2007 to approximately 12.701 trillion 2005-buying-power dollars in the second quarter of 2009.

Inflation pressure appears to have been subdued during this period, as the implicit deflator rose from approximately 107.0 in the fourth quarter of 2007 to approximately 109.5 in the first quarter of 2009 before *de*creasing to roughly 109.3 in the second quarter of 2009. Before the slight decrease in the GDP deflator, inflation from the fourth quarter of 2007 through the *first* quarter of 2009 was about 2.4 per cent, and the cumulative increase in the GDP deflator from the fourth quarter of 2007 through the second quarter of 2009 was roughly 2.2 per cent.

Whether the calculation of inflation during the most recent U.S. recession ends with the GDP deflator data from the first quarter of 2009 or the second quarter of 2009, the approximate rate of inflation at either 2.2 per cent or 2.4 per cent seems quite low given that the quarterly-average M1 money supply increased by nearly 18.5 per cent between the fourth quarter of 2007 and the second quarter of 2009. This could be yet another example of the often relatively weak *short*-term correlation between the money supply growth rate and the rate of inflation discussed in Baumol and Blinder (2012, p. 300) and elsewhere. With a wave of mortgage defaults, an inability of some financial organizations to make contracted payments, and actual and potential bankruptcies, aggregate demand in the United States economy decreased substantially. The decrease in aggregate demand, perhaps combined with an increase in aggregate supply (where people in the economy as producers of labor and goods were willing to accept either decreases in, no change in, or smaller increases in wages, salaries, and goods prices due to the belief that other prices were going to increase at a slower rate or decrease or remain unchanged) likely kept inflation in check during this period.

One of the goals of the rapid money supply growth through the second quarter of 2009 was to drive down the federal funds rate. The quarterly average of monthly federal funds rates had reached a local maximum of nearly 5.26 per cent in the first quarter of 2007. By the fourth quarter of 2007, the quarterly average federal funds rate had fallen slightly below 4.5 per cent. In the first quarter of 2008, the quarterly average federal funds rate fell to around 3.18 per cent, a decrease of more than one percentage point in one quarter. In the second quarter of 2008, the average federal funds rate again fell by more than one full percentage point, to roughly 2.09 per cent, in just one quarter. After a relatively small decline in the third quarter of 2008 to 1.94 per cent, the quarterly average federal funds rate again fell by more than one full percentage point in the fourth quarter of 2008 to around 0.51 per cent.

In the first quarter of 2009, the average federal funds rate decreased to approximately 0.18 per cent. The quarterly average federal funds rate was below 0.195 per cent for each subsequent quarter in the sample period and was less than 0.10 per cent in the second, third, and fourth quarters of 2011.

At least some longer-term interest rates also decreased, although perhaps at a slower pace than the decrease in the average federal funds rate. The local maximum for the quarterly-average ten-year U.S. Treasury rate, 5.07 per cent, occurred in the second quarter of 2006, three quarters before the local maximum of the quarterly average federal funds rate, in the first quarter of 2007. In the fourth quarter of 2008, the average ten-year Treasury interest rate had decreased only approximately one percentage point since the fourth quarter of 2007 (from 4.26 per cent to roughly 3.253 per cent) while the average federal funds rate had decreased by nearly four percentage points over the same period.

From the first quarter of 2009 on, the quarterly average federal funds rate was consistently less than 0.20 percentage points. The quarterly average ten-year rate, on the other hand, increased most quarters from the second quarter of 2009 through the first quarter of 2010 (rising from about 2.74 per cent in the first quarter of 2009 to about 3.72 per cent in the first quarter of 2010) before continuing a general downward trend into the middle of 2012. Further, while the quarterly average federal funds rate posted small gains in the first two quarters of 2012 (from roughly 0.07 per cent in the fourth quarter of 2011 to roughly 0.10 per cent to roughly 0.15 per cent in the second quarter of 2012), the quarterly average ten-year rate continued declining toward its sample-period minimum, from approximately 2.05 per cent in the fourth quarter of 2011 to approximately 2.04 per cent to approximately 1.82 per cent in the second quarter of 2012. The quarterly average ten-year rate fell to its sample-period minimum, approximately 1.64 per cent, in the third quarter of 2012.

The goals of reducing interest rates have already been discussed. One goal would be to encourage firms to purchase physical capital (and perhaps also to encourage households to increase consumption) by reducing the cost of borrowing to finance such transactions. The reader may want to note that the lower interest rates also reduce the reward that households receive by postponing consumption and the revenue that firms can generate by buying bonds or by granting loans. The expansionary monetary policy also makes it easier for borrowers to repay loans. Borrowers with adjustable-rate mortgages can repay loans by paying fewer dollars as interest rates fall. To the extent that inflation is positive (perhaps due to the very expansionary monetary policy in recent years in the U.S.), all borrowers benefit by repaying dollars with less buying power than if inflation were less than or equal to zero. This avoids the debt deflation problem that Mishkin (2004, pp. 192-193), Burton and Lombra (2006, pp. 285-286), Krugman and Wells (2009, p. 463) and others discuss that Krugman and Wells (2009, p. 463) attribute to Irving Fisher. This could also be helping to bring a recovery to the housing market by raising asset prices and by preventing further defaults.

SUMMARY AND CONCLUDING REMARKS

To wrap up this chapter, first note that in each of four sub-sample periods when the quarterly growth rate (not compounded) of nominal M1 (compared to its value in the last quarter of the previous sub-sample period) exceeded 2.4 per cent (not annualized), velocity decreased in most quarters, if not all quarters, of the sub-sample period and clearly trended downward. Second, note that conversely, in five of six sub-sample periods when the quarterly growth rate of nominal M1 was less than 2.4 per cent (not annualized), velocity trended upward. Thus, regression results and descriptions of the data in this chapter have suggested that rapid increases in nominal M1 have often been associated with decreases in the velocity of M1, while periods of either slower nominal M1 growth or contractions in nominal M1 have been associated with increases in the velocity of M1.

Some may think that a possible exception to the pattern could have been periods in the 1970s when nominal M1 growth was rapid at times. Yet, velocity continued to increase many, if not most quarters through the third quarter of 1981. Also, the quarterly growth rate (not compounded or annualized) over either the full first sub-sample period or over the first part (1959q1-1973q1) and the second part (1973q2-1981q3 but using 1973q1 as the starting point for calculating the quarterly growth rate) was less than 2.4 per cent per quarter. Another possible exception was the first few years of the Great Depression in the United States (prior to the quarterly data sample period), as discussed in Chapter 3, when both nominal M1 and velocity simultaneously fell. For additional discussion of the U.S. economy after the first quarter of 2013 and early 2014 beyond this chapter, refer to Chapters 5 and 8 (and perhaps other chapters).

Although the 1970s have often been characterized as times of rapid money supply growth in the United States, using quarterly data from www.economagic.com and the author's calculations, quarter-to-quarter average nominal M1 growth exceeded three per cent for the first time in the relevant sample period (which began in 1959) in the third quarter of 1980. Further, quarter-to-quarter average nominal M1 growth exceeded four per cent for the first time in the fourth quarter of 1982. Moreover, of the ten sub-sample periods considered, the sub-sample period from the first quarter of 1985 through the second quarter of 1987 with a quarterly average growth rate of nearly 3.6 per cent had the second fastest quarterly growth rate of the average nominal money supply, topped by only the last sub-sample period (2008q1-2013q1).

However, data from www.economagic.com accessed after July 20, 2013 and the author's calculations show that the velocity of M1 has continued to decline most quarters, at least through the fourth quarter of 2013. Therefore, the last sub-sample period, with the fastest quarterly average growth rate of the nominal M1 money supply, could potentially wind up decreasing in the relative rankings of sub-sample periods with the fastest quarterly average M1 growth as more data become available (if velocity continued or continues to fall past the first quarter of 2013 but with slower growth in nominal M1).

This chapter has not dealt much with unemployment rates rate largely because (1) the unemployment rate is not in the algebraic definition of velocity, and (2) I am unaware of others paying much attention to the unemployment rate when discussing velocity. However, data from www.economagic.com accessed July 20, 2013 show that the unemployment rate (on a monthly basis) reached a high of ten per cent in October 2009 and has been relatively slow to decline in the Not-So-Great Recovery. This surge in the unemployment rate followed by a slow decline and perhaps some increases and slow declines in the unemployment rate during other recessions and recoveries could help explain falling velocity during some sub-sample periods.

Quarterly average nominal M1 growth exceeded seven per cent (and five and six per cent) for the first time in the sample period in the last sub-sample period, reaching about 7.1 per cent in the fourth quarter of 2008 and again in the third quarter of 2011 at roughly 7.6 per cent. Afterward, the percentage increase in nominal average M1 was slower. Further, given that the FOMC has started to taper its bond purchases that are part of QEIII, then the average growth rate of quarterly average M1 for the last sub-sample period could decrease below the average growth rate for this variable from the 1985q1-1987q2 sub-sample period (as implied above) if nominal M1 growth slows sufficiently while the velocity of M1 continues to decline. Slower nominal money supply growth, however, could coincide with a turnaround in the velocity of M1 and bring the beginning of another sub-sample period.

Given the data, the algebraic explanation for velocity usually increasing in the 1970s was because nominal M1 growth remained below nominal GDP growth during most quarters. This was true during most of the first sub-sample period running from the first quarter of 1959 through the third quarter of 1981.

In six of the ten sub-sample periods, the use of nominal M1 was either the most successful or second most successful of all seven variables considered at generating the smallest sum of squared residuals and the greatest adjusted R-squared statistic from regressions for the velocity of M1 on the left side of the equation and on the right side only one independent variable and a constant term. In the sub-sample periods where nominal M1 was second best, it trailed only real M1. Thus, it appears that, at times, much of the variation in the velocity of M1 is attributable to changes in the nominal money supply. (As noted above, this may not be true in the first sub-sample period because the estimated coefficient for nominal M1 is positive.)

In five of the six sub-sample periods in which nominal M1 was either best or second best in minimizing the sum of squared residuals, the estimated coefficient for nominal M1 was negative, as would be expected, all other things equal, from the algebraic definition of velocity. The negative coefficient implies that increases in the nominal money supply were associated with decreases in the velocity of M1 in those five sub-sample periods. This is certainly consistent with the existence of a non-decreasing-velocity money supply level (NDVMSL) and supports the theory of a NDVMSL, but it is not proof of NDVMSL theory. The one sub-sample period where nominal M1 performed very well compared with the other variables considered in terms of sums of squared residuals and adjusted R-squared statistics but the estimated coefficient was greater than zero was the first sub-sample period (1959q1-1981q3). Apparently, nominal GDP (which grew most quarters) dominated the impact of the rising quarterly average nominal M1 money supply most quarters during that sub-sample period.

Let's now return to thinking about Figure 2.1, a scatter-graph plot of the velocity of M1 on the vertical axis and the quarterly-average nominal M1 money supply on the horizontal axis. Figure 2.1 reappears below as Figure 6.72a for convenience. Recall the analogy at the beginning of the chapter between the demand function for lemonade and the velocity function of M1 as a function of the nominal M1 money supply. Just as factors such as changes in income and changes in the number of consumers cause shifts in the demand for lemonade as a function of the price per gallon, changes in nominal GDP (which can be thought of as changes in real GDP and/or changes in the implicit deflator) lead to shifts in the velocity function.

Recall that the velocity of M1 = Nominal GDP/Nominal M1. Assuming a fixed nominal GDP, continuous increases in nominal M1 approaching infinity would result in the velocity of M1 getting closer and closer to zero without ever reaching zero. This is called asymptotically approaching zero. If this is not clear, consider the function $y = 1/x$. As x approaches infinity, the function $y = 1/x$ asymptotically approaches zero.

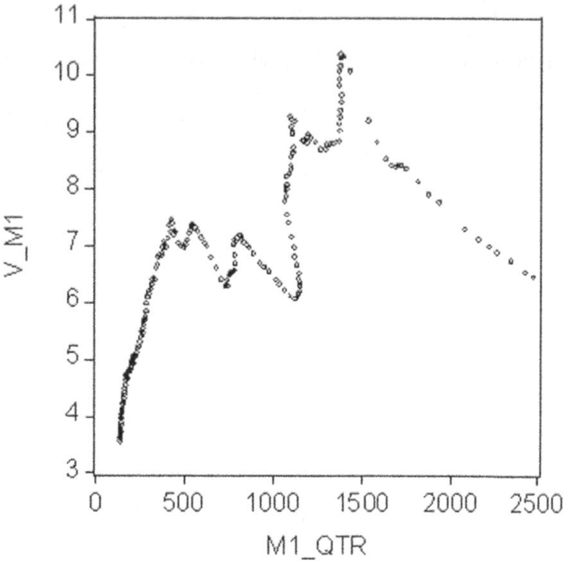

Figure 6.72a M1 Money Supply (quarterly) and the Velocity of the M1 Money Supply
1959 quarter one through 2013 quarter one, quarterly data
Source: www.economagic.com and the author's calculations

Examining data reveals that nominal GDP usually increases over time. Thus, just as increasing the numerator in the function $y = 1/x$ to $y = 2/x$ to $y = 3/x$ would cause the function for y to shift upward, increases in nominal GDP cause upward shifts in the velocity function, velocity = nominal GDP/ nominal M1, all other things equal. To simplify in constructing and understanding a diagram, periods of small percentage changes in nominal GDP compared to the percentage increase in nominal M1 can be thought of as negligible changes in nominal GDP with essentially no shift in the velocity function *in the diagram*. Thus, rising nominal M1 would lead to a move along a velocity function toward the horizontal axis as long as the percentage increase in nominal M1 dominates the percentage increase in nominal GDP.

In the first sub-sample period, with both nominal M1 and the velocity of M1 increasing most of the time, the impact of rising nominal GDP dominated the impact of increasing nominal M1 on the velocity of M1. Thus, the velocity function (as a function of nominal M1) shifted up most quarters during the first sub-sample period, and the fact that nominal GDP growth exceeded nominal M1 growth in most quarters from the first quarter of 1959 through the third quarter of 1981 evidently explains the rising velocity of M1 during this sub-sample period. However, a recession at the beginning of the second sub-sample period in the fourth quarter of 1981 (sometimes viewed as the second dip in a double dip recession) meant declining real GDP early on in this sub-sample period. Although nominal GDP continued to rise most quarters during the recession, increases in nominal M1 began to dominate rising nominal GDP and pushed velocity down during this period as velocity moved down along a velocity function. This continued through 1983q2 despite real GDP starting to grow again for consecutive quarters in the fourth quarter of 1982 and the first quarter of 1983.

This sequence then repeated itself, perhaps in slightly different forms, throughout the sample period. For example, from the third quarter of 1983 through the fourth quarter of 1984, growth in nominal GDP dominated growth in the nominal money supply as velocity increased. In this case, we can consider upward shifts in the velocity of money function occurring as nominal GDP rose from the third quarter of 1983 through the fourth quarter of 1984. This explains the increase in velocity at that time. However, from the first quarter of 1985 through the second quarter of 1987, the impact of rapid nominal M1 growth (exceeding nominal GDP growth) caused velocity to slide down a velocity function. (In reality, in addition to moving toward the horizontal axis along a velocity function, growth in nominal GDP from the first quarter of 1985 through the second quarter of 1987 (and other sub-sample periods) would cause upward shifts in the velocity function. However, from the first quarter of 1985 through the second quarter of 1987, the impact of growth in nominal M1 dominated the impact of growth in nominal GDP.)

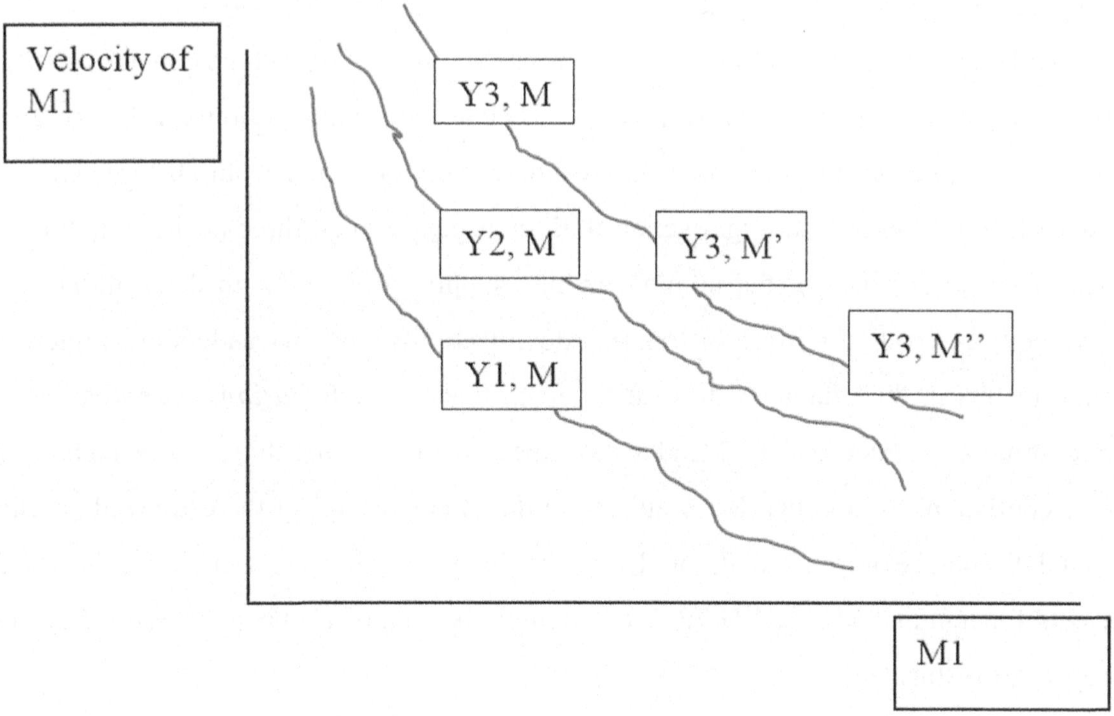

Figure 6.72b Shifts in the Velocity of Money Function Versus Movements Along a Velocity Function

Figure 6.72b shows the results of this 'knife-edge' thinking. If nominal GDP increases at a faster rate than the money supply, this simple model assumes that only nominal GDP increased, and if the money supply increased at a faster rate than nominal GDP, then the model assumes that only the money supply increased. Thus, in Figure 6.72b, the percentage increase in nominal GDP initially exceeded the percentage increase in the money supply, causing the velocity of money function to shift upward from when nominal GDP increased from Y1 to Y2 and from Y2 to Y3. Then, after reaching Y3, the percentage growth in the money supply dominated the percentage increase in nominal GDP, so that as the money supply increased from M to M' and from M' to M'' (ignoring possible earlier changes in the money supply as nominal GDP increased from Y1 to Y2 to Y3), the economy moved toward the horizontal axis along a velocity function. Note that in the previous figure, Figure 6.72a, when velocity is decreasing, the points in the diagram often appear farther apart than when velocity is increasing. Points farther apart in that figure represent larger dollar increases in M1.

Questions remain for further work. Given the econometric caveats, can the single-variable equations be thought of in a sense as predictors of velocity? And do changes in the other variables cause changes in velocity, or do changes in velocity cause changes in the other variables, or both?

Additionally, the estimated coefficients for nominal M1, real GDP, and the deflator usually have the same sign, either positive or negative, within the same sub-sample period. Further, when going from one sub-sample period to the next, the results usually go either from all three coefficients positive to all three coefficients negative, or all three negative to all three positive. Is this further evidence of the importance of the nominal money supply growth rate in determining whether money velocity is trending upward or trending downward? But again, readers must interpret the regression results in this chapter with caution given that a *ceteris paribus* interpretation of the algebraic formula for velocity would lead me to expect that if all other things were unchanged, the estimated coefficient for nominal M1 would have the opposite sign of the estimated coefficients for real GDP and the implicit deflator. However, in most sub-sample periods, the estimated coefficients for nominal M1, real GDP, and the implicit deflator all have the same sign. Future work can address this.

This chapter has not focused much on fiscal policy. However, in light of the apparently strong negative correlation between nominal M1 and its velocity in the last sub-sample period starting in the first quarter of 2008 and thinking about rapid increases in nominal M1 during the sub-par economic recovery, can we find ways to use newly-added dollars more productively?

The Appendix to this chapter has more information about the divided first sub-sample period. It also has correlations in the ten sub-sample periods between velocity and the variables from the right sides of regression equations in this chapter. Attention in Chapter Seven turns to the difference between nominal M1 and nominal M2 as measures of the money supply and money multipliers. This discussion will be applied to the velocity of money.

CHAPTER SIX REFERENCES

Baumol, W. J. and Blinder, A. S. (2012) *Macroeconomics: Principles and Policy*, twelfth edition. South-Western Cengage Learning, Mason, Ohio.

Brunner, K. and Meltzer, A. H. (1963) "Predicting Velocity: Implications for Theory and Policy." *Journal of Finance*, vol. 18, May, pp. 319-354.

Burton, M. and Lombra, R. (2006) *The Financial System and the Economy: Principles of Money and Banking*, fourth edition. Thomson South-Western, Mason, Ohio.

Dornbusch, R., Fischer, S., and Startz, R. (2008) *Macroeconomics*, tenth edition. McGraw-Hill Irwin, Boston, Massachusetts.

Dougherty, C. (2007) *Introduction to Econometrics*, third edition. Oxford University Press, New York, New York.

Hamilton, J. D. (1994) *Time Series Analysis*. Princeton University Press, Princeton, New Jersey.

Hartman, H. C. (2011) "The Decrease in the Velocity of Money in the United States: Some Possible Causes and Some Implications." *International Journal of Accounting Information Science and Leadership*, vol. 4, iss. 11, pp. 15-27.

Hartman, H. C. (2013) "More about the Decrease in the Velocity of Money in the United States: Some Potential Causes and Policy Implications." *Journal of International Business Management and Research*, vol. 3, iss. 10, pp. 116-138.

Krugman, P. and Wells, R. (2009) *Macroeconomics*, second edition. Worth Publishers, New York, New York.

Laidler, D. E. W. (1993) *The Demand for Money: Theories, Evidence, and Problems*, fourth edition. Harper Collins College Publishers, New York, New York.

Mishkin, F. S. (2004) *The Economics of Money, Banking, and Financial Markets*, seventh edition. Pearson Addison Wesley, Boston, Massachusetts.

www.economagic.com

APPENDIX TO CH. 6

The first sub-sample period is divided into two sections for some of the analysis in this chapter based on (1) a maximum of the real money supply *within* the first sub-sample period occurring in the first quarter of 1973 followed by periods of declining real money supply and (2) generally higher quarter-to-quarter inflation rates starting in the second quarter of 1973 and going at least through the end of the first sub-sample period (1981q3). Higher inflation implies that the implicit deflator is rising more rapidly. All other things equal, an increase in the price level leads to an increase in velocity.

One of the most important things to note when comparing the regressions and scatter graph plots from the two parts of the divided first sub-sample period is that the estimated slope of the best-fit line for the velocity of M1 as a function of the *real* money supply is positive in the first part (from the first quarter of 1959 through the first quarter of 1973) but negative in the second part (from the second quarter of 1973 through the third quarter of 1981). The fact that both velocity and the real money supply increased most quarters from the first quarter of 1959 through the first quarter of 1973 likely gave rise to the positive estimated coefficient in the first part of the first sub-sample period (through the first quarter of 1973). The estimated negative coefficient for the real money supply in the equation for the velocity of M1 in the second part of the first sub-sample period probably stems from decreasing real money supply (as nominal money supply growth failed to keep pace with growth in the implicit deflator in many quarters) while velocity continued to increase. The change in slope of the best-fit line from the first part of the first sub-sample period to the second could help explain why over the full first sub-sample period (from 1959q1 through 1981q3), the real money supply was the least successful of the seven variables in regressions at producing the smallest sum of squared residuals and the largest adjusted R-squared statistic.

From the algebraic definition of velocity, a decrease in the real money supply would lead to an increase in velocity, all other things equal. While decreasing real money supply helps in explaining velocity in the second part of the first sub-sample period (when periods of declining real M1 money supply occurred), this fails to explain how the real money supply trended upward through the first quarter of 1973 while velocity also trended upward. Apparently, real GDP increased at a faster rate than the real money supply most quarters from the first quarter of 1959 (and perhaps before) through the first quarter of 1973, so that the velocity of M1 and the real money supply both generally increased during this period, as noted above.

When further comparing scatter graphs from the first part of the first sub-sample period (through the first quarter of 1973) with those from the second part (the second quarter of 1973 through the third quarter of 1981), Figures 6.73 and 6.80 show that during the first part of the first sub-sample period, the relationship between nominal M1 and its velocity may have been more like that of an upward-sloping concave curve than the relationship between those same variables in the second part of the first sub-sample period. During the second part of the first sub-sample period, the relationship may have been more linear. This observation about the linearity of the scatter graph plots may also apply to the relationship between the deflator and the velocity of M1, as shown in Figures 6.75 and 6.82, and between nominal GDP and velocity as shown in Figures 6.78 and 6.85 (and briefly discussed below).

Regarding the relationship between real GDP and the velocity of M1, the data observations seem to be closer to the best-fit line in the scatter graph for the first part of the first sub-sample period than in the graph for the second part. In fact, the sum of squared residuals in the second part is more than five times as large as the sum of squared residuals in the first part, even though the second part has fewer observations than the first part.

The scatter graphs for (1) the quarterly average federal funds rate and the velocity of M1 and (2) the quarterly average ten-year Treasury rate and velocity seem to show that these two interest rates do not perform particularly well at minimizing the sum of squared residuals over either the first part of the first sub-sample period or the second part of the first sub-sample period. This may not be a surprise given that interest rates are not included directly in the algebraic definition of velocity.

As was the case with M1 (nominal) and the implicit deflator, the relationship between nominal GDP and velocity may be more concave (but upward-sloping) during the first part of the first sub-sample period and more linear (but still upward-sloping) during the second part. Perhaps this is to be expected given that the deflator, one of the components of nominal GDP, also exhibited the same pattern, as noted above.

Over the first part of the first sub-sample period (the first quarter of 1959 through the first quarter of 1973), real GDP performs the best at minimizing the sum of squared residuals of the seven potential independent variables used in regressions (with a constant) for the velocity of M1. However, in the second part (the second quarter of 1973 through the third quarter of 1981), the performance of real GDP was topped by nominal GDP, the deflator, and nominal M1.

Real M1 performed second best in minimizing the sum of squared residuals in the first part of the first sub-sample period, topped only by real GDP. However, the estimated coefficient was positive, in contrast with the negative coefficient implied by the algebraic definition of velocity, all other things constant. In the second part of the first sub-sample period, the estimated coefficient for real M1 is negative, but the sum of squared residuals is second-largest (or sixth best out of seven variables).

Nominal GDP was third best in minimizing the sum of squared residuals during the first part of the first sub-sample period (1959q1 through 1973q1) and first-best during the second part of the first sub-sample period (1973q2-1981q3). Nominal M1 was fourth best in minimizing the sum of squared residuals in the first part of the first sub-sample period and third-best in the second part but first-best in the full sub-sample period (although the signs of the estimated coefficients were positive for the full sub-sample period and its two subdivided parts, rather than negative as implied by a *ceteris paribus* interpretation of the algebraic definition of velocity). The deflator ranked fifth-best in the first part of the first sub-sample period but second-best in the second part.

Neither measure of the interest rate faired particularly well in minimizing the sum of squared residuals in the first sub-sample period. The ten-year rate was sixth-best in the first part and fifth-best in the second part, while the federal funds rate was seventh-best in both parts.

The following is a list of the seven variables used on the right side of equations for velocity in descending order from first-best at minimizing sums of squared residuals to seventh-best (or worst) over the full first sub-sample period: nominal M1, real GDP, nominal GDP, the deflator, the ten-year rate, the federal funds rate, and real M1. In terms of comparing the two divisions of the first sub-sample period, real M1 and real GDP had the largest declines in relative rankings between the two subdivisions (from second to sixth and from first to fourth, respectively). The deflator had the largest upward movement, from fifth to second, while nominal GDP, going form third to first, had the second largest upward movement. Does this indicate the importance of the two energy crises and other factors behind rising inflation in the mid-1970s through the early 1980s in explaining velocity and portfolio holdings?

	Coeffi.	Const.	R-Squ.	Adj. R-Squ.	Sum Squ. Res.
M1	0.014758	1.842143	0.894893	0.892982	1.570343
GDP	0.000806	1.479133	0.991152	0.990991	0.132194
Defl	0.172818	0.762893	0.849612	0.846878	2.246860
FFR	0.208558	3.525102	0.509559	0.500642	7.327417
10YR	0.381678	2.507544	0.724085	0.719068	4.122298
NomY	0.002077	2.783992	0.933387	0.932175	0.995235
RealM	0.010241	-3.973831	0.946422	0.945448	0.800480

Table 6a.1 Regression Results from Equations for Velocity as a Function of One Other Variable (listed at the beginning of each row of numbers) and a Constant
First Part of Divided First Sub-Sample Period (1959q1-1973q1)
Source: www.economagic.com and the author's calculations

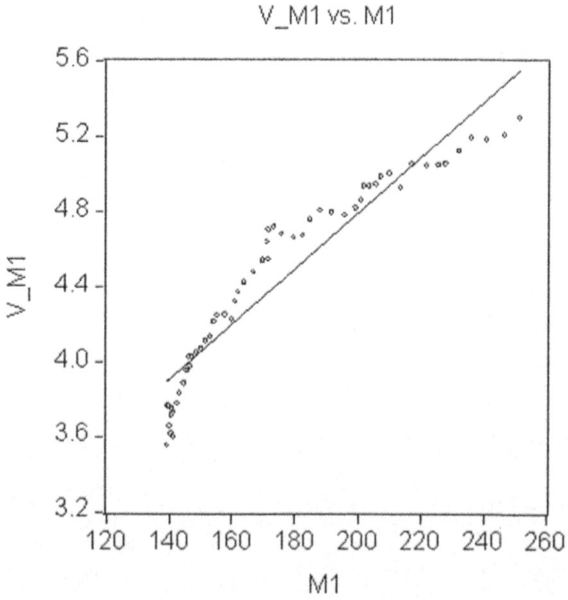

Figure 6.73 Scatter-Graph Plot of the Velocity of M1 (on the Vertical Axis) and Quarterly Average M1 (Nominal)
Regression Line Included
1959 quarter one through 1973 quarter one
Source: www.economagic.com and the author's calculations

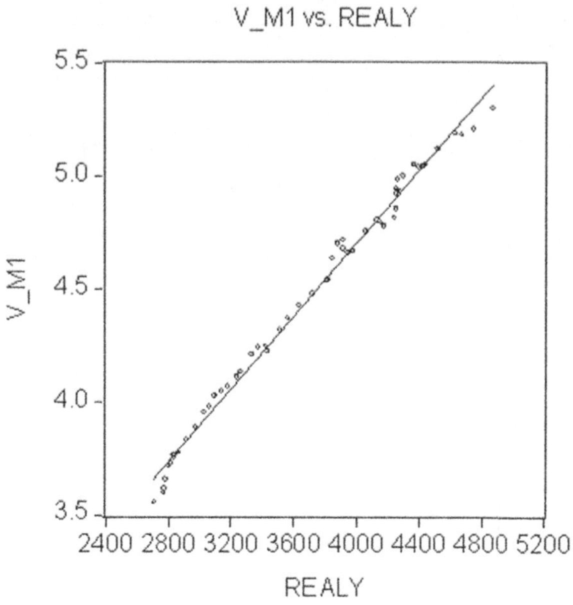

Figure 6.74 Scatter-Graph Plot of the Velocity of M1 (on the Vertical Axis) and Real GDP
Regression Line Included
1959 quarter one through 1973 quarter one
Source: www.economagic.com

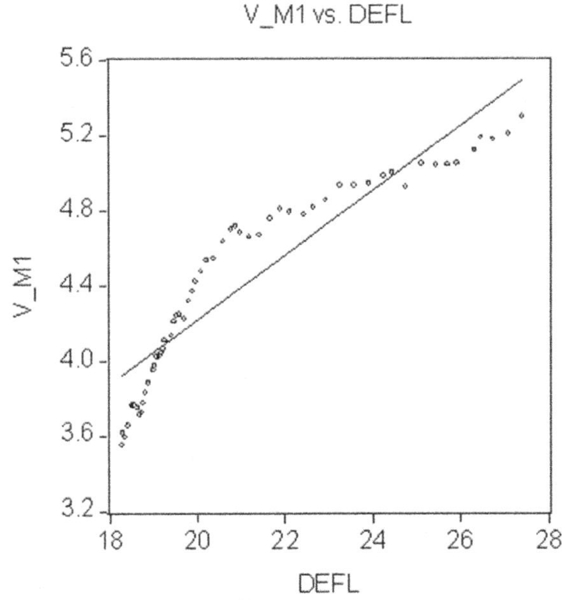

Figure 6.75 Scatter-Graph Plot of the Velocity of M1 (on the Vertical Axis) and the Deflator
Regression Line Included
1959 quarter one through 1973 quarter one
Source: www.economagic.com

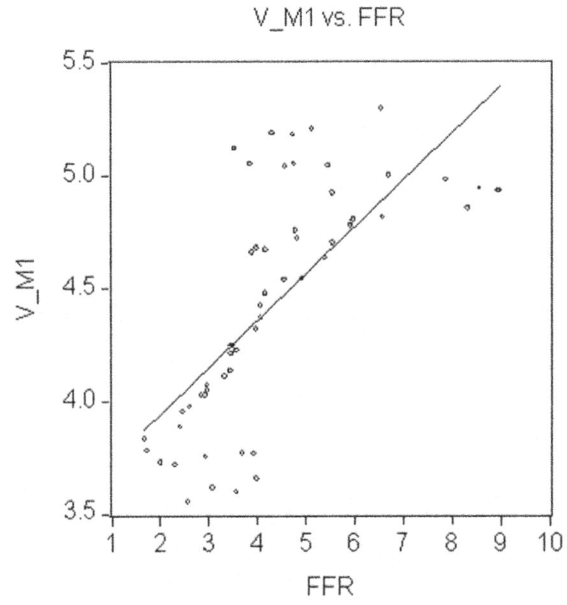

Figure 6.76 Scatter-Graph Plot of the Velocity of M1 (on the Vertical Axis) and the Quarterly Average Federal Funds Rate
Regression Line Included
1959 quarter one through 1973 quarter one
Source: www.economagic.com and the author's calculations

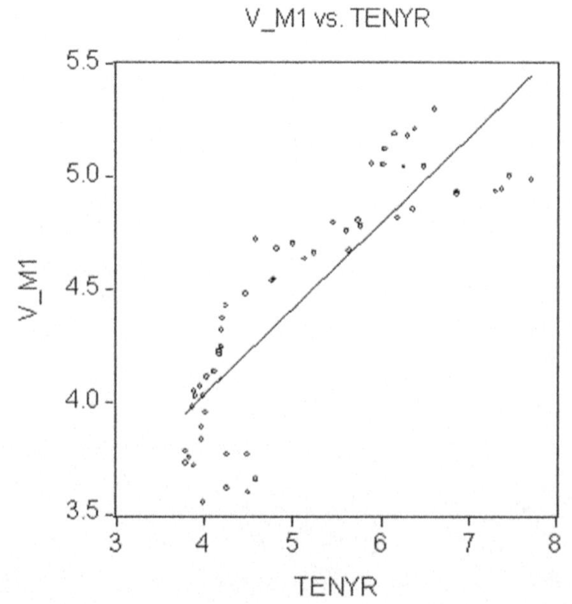

Figure 6.77 Scatter-Graph Plot of the Velocity of M1 (on the Vertical Axis) and the Quarterly Average Ten-Year Treasury Interest Rate
Regression Line Included
1959 quarter one through 1973 quarter one
Source: www.economagic.com and the author's calculations

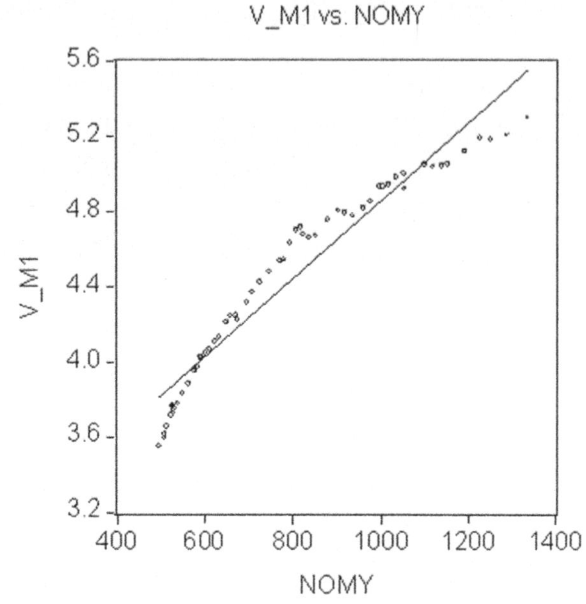

Figure 6.78 Scatter-Graph Plot of the Velocity of M1 (on the Vertical Axis) and Nominal GDP
Regression Line Included
1959 quarter one through 1973 quarter one
Source: www.economagic.com

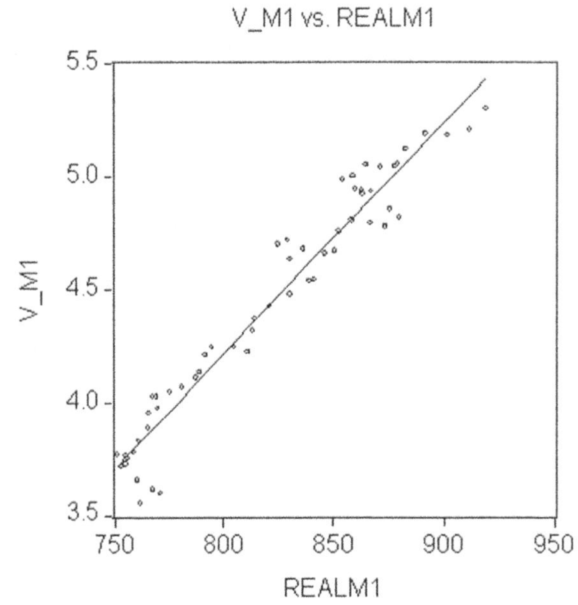

Figure 6.79 Scatter-Graph Plot of the Velocity of M1 (on the Vertical Axis) and Quarterly Average Real M1
Regression Line Included
1959 quarter one through 1973 quarter one
Source: www.economagic.com and the author's calculations

	Coeffi.	Const.	R-Squ.	Adj. R-Squ.	Sum Squ. Res.
M1	0.011334	2.629146	0.969004	0.968035	0.399136
GDP	0.001400	-1.192735	0.938170	0.936238	0.796187
Defl	0.085452	3.037864	0.969690	0.968743	0.390299
FFR	0.090055	5.510505	0.322050	0.300864	8.729959
10YR	0.244592	4.180743	0.681311	0.671352	4.103750
NomY	0.001113	3.993033	0.976797	0.976071	0.298791
RealM	-0.016994	20.80178	0.495297	0.479525	6.499051

Table 6a.2 Regression Results from Equations for Velocity as a Function of One Other Variable (listed at the beginning of each row of numbers) and a Constant
Divided First Sub-Sample Period (1973q2-1981q3)
Source: www.economagic.com and the author's calculations

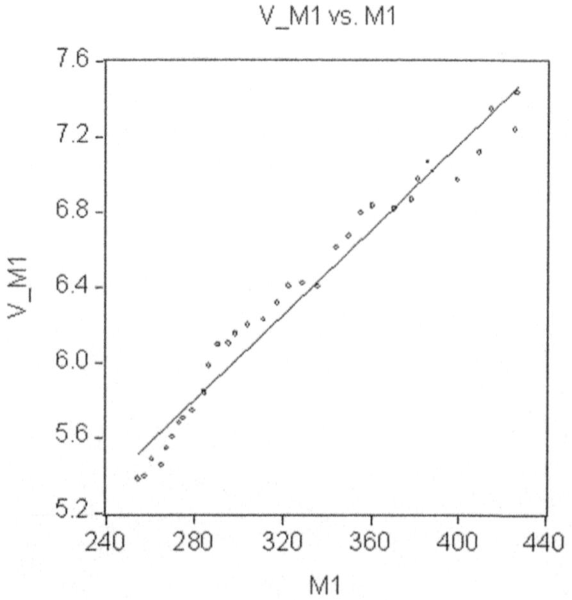

Figure 6.80 Scatter-Graph Plot of the Velocity of M1 (on the Vertical Axis) and Quarterly Average M1 (Nominal)
Regression Line Included
1973 quarter two through 1981 quarter three
Source: www.economagic.com and the author's calculations

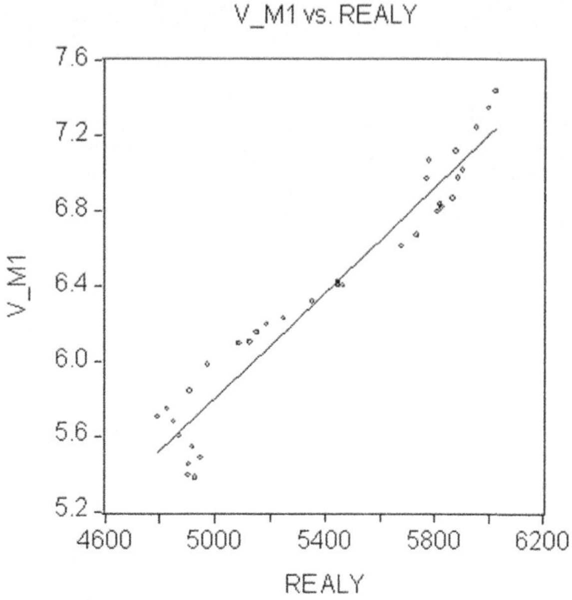

Figure 6.81 Scatter-Graph Plot of the Velocity of M1 (on the Vertical Axis) and Real GDP
Regression Line Included
1973 quarter two through 1981 quarter three
Source: www.economagic.com

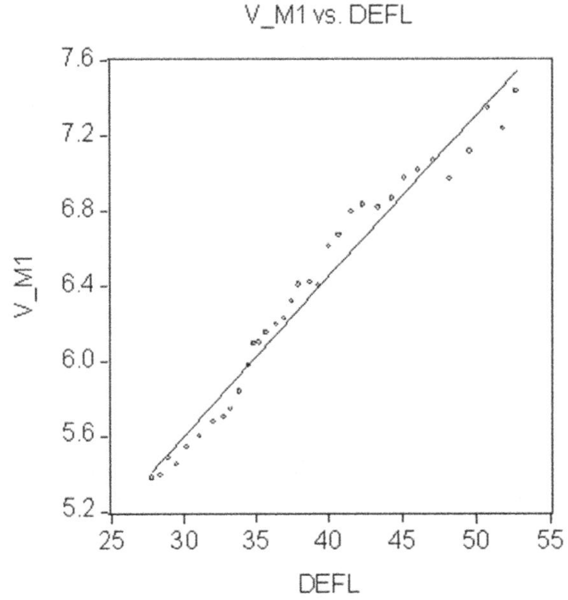

Figure 6.82 Scatter-Graph Plot of the Velocity of M1 (on the Vertical Axis) and the Deflator
Regression Line Included
1973 quarter two through 1981 quarter three
Source: www.economagic.com

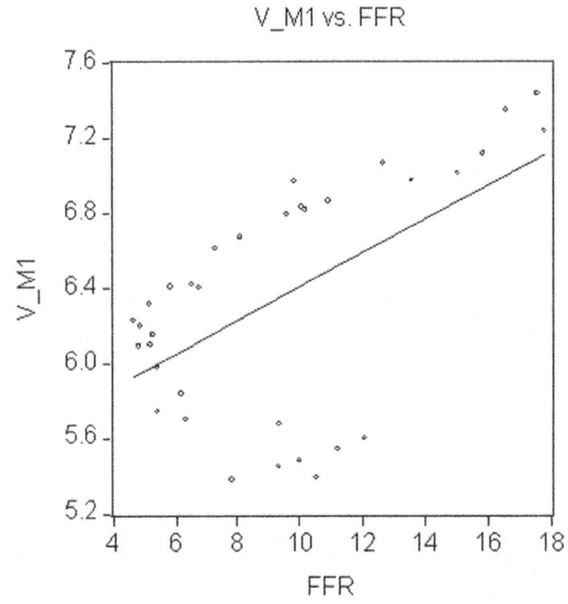

Figure 6.83 Scatter-Graph Plot of the Velocity of M1 (on the Vertical Axis) and the Quarterly Average Federal Funds Rate
Regression Line Included
1973 quarter two through 1981 quarter three
Source: www.economagic.com and the author's calculations

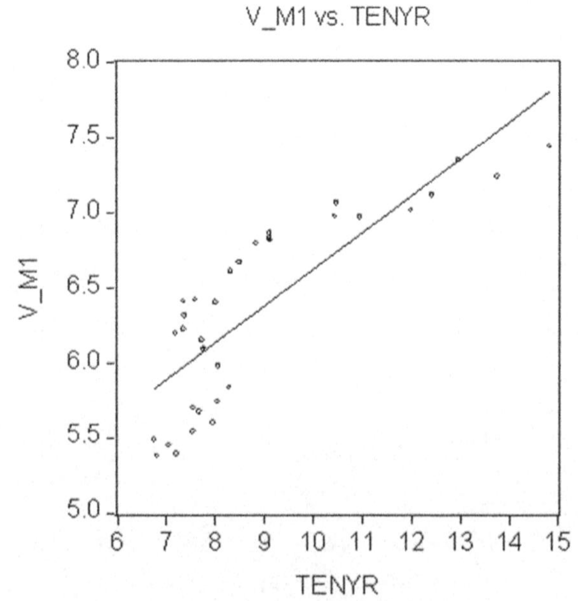

Figure 6.84 Scatter-Graph Plot of the Velocity of M1 (on the Vertical Axis) and the Quarterly Average Ten-Year Treasury Interest Rate
Regression Line Included
1973 quarter two through 1981 quarter three
Source: www.economagic.com and the author's calculations

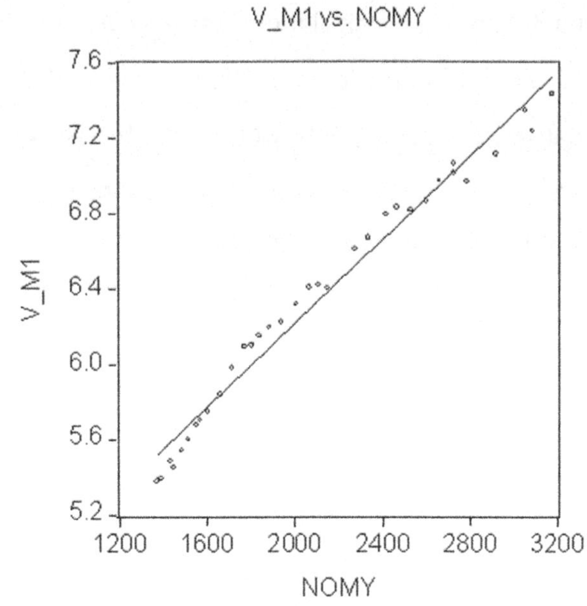

Figure 6.85 Scatter-Graph Plot of the Velocity of M1 (on the Vertical Axis) and Nominal GDP
Regression Line Included
1973 quarter two through 1981 quarter three
Source: www.economagic.com

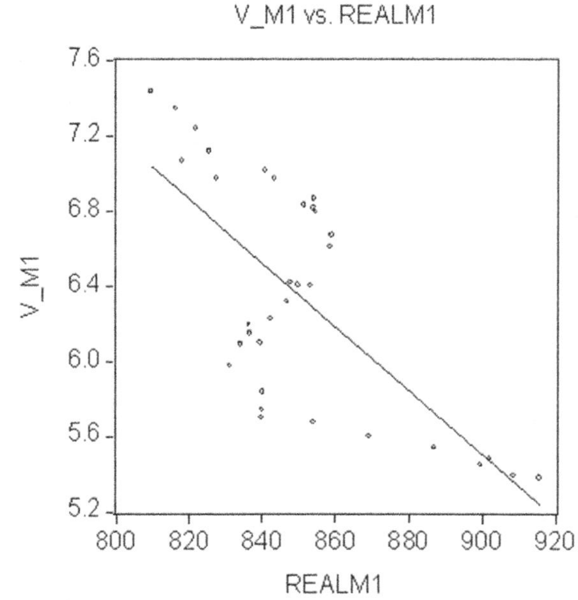

Figure 6.86 Scatter-Graph Plot of the Velocity of M1 (on the Vertical Axis) and Quarterly Average Real M1
Regression Line Included
1973 quarter two through 1981 quarter three
Source: www.economagic.com and the author's calculations

On the next page, Table 6a.3 shows the correlation between the velocity of M1 and each of the seven potentially explanatory variables considered in Chapter Six in the ten sub-sample periods. As noted in Chapter Six, the relative rankings of how well a variable performs in minimizing the sum of squared residuals in regressions are the same as the relative rankings of the absolute value of the correlation between each variable and the velocity of money.

	59q1-81q3	81q4-83q2	83q3-84q4	85q1-87q2	87q3-90q2
M1	0.988456	-0.941834	0.994788	-0.997058	0.810143
GDP	0.984219	-0.388587	0.997051	-0.965265	0.974500
Defl	0.974470	-0.917641	0.996050	-0.986977	0.975029
FFR	0.794128	0.834735	0.467571	0.925964	0.732565
10YR	0.926508	0.907731	0.519707	0.867670	-0.569425
NomY	0.982403	-0.849844	0.998019	-0.979912	0.977780
RealM	0.501135	-0.906949	0.976208	-0.998229	-0.891848
	90q3-93q4	94q1-00q4	01q1-03q2	03q3-07q4	08q1-13q1
M1	-0.998130	-0.677410	-0.878471	0.641243	-0.962707
GDP	-0.977399	0.985696	-0.631914	0.969823	-0.569995
Defl	-0.979846	0.992340	-0.716230	0.984366	-0.941381
FFR	0.910986	0.460800	0.840834	0.925266	0.760805
10YR	0.983656	-0.620219	0.574950	0.615018	0.857573
NomY	-0.995934	0.988420	-0.678349	0.981840	-0.804248
RealM	-0.995579	-0.943991	-0.933018	-0.960457	-0.968516

Table 6a.3
Correlations between the Velocity of M1 and Other Variables
Source: www.economagic.com and the author's calculations

CHAPTER 7

MONEY MULTIPLIERS, THE MONEY SUPPLY PROCESS, AND VELOCITY

INTRODUCTION

The last chapter examined some of the variables probably most responsible for impacting the velocity of money during the various sub-sample periods in the quarterly-data period beginning with the first quarter of 1959. The evidence suggests, at least to me, that during *some* sub-sample periods, changes in the M1 money supply (both nominal and real) do much to account for changes in the velocity of M1. Thus, further study of the M1 money supply process could be useful for understanding movements in the velocity of money. Given that the data for many of the variables in this chapter are available on a monthly basis (as found on www.economagic.com on July 31, 2013), this chapter often uses the monthly data for those variables rather than converting the monthly data to quarterly data.

After the introduction, this chapter notes that depository institutions such as banks hold reserves to guard against unforeseen withdrawals. This gives rise to an elementary model called the simple money multiplier. Assuming that banks lend a large percentage of their deposits (perhaps unlike the recent experience in the U.S.), if borrowed funds wind up being re-deposited in the banking system, then banks can lend most, if not all, of the funds again. At least until recently, many banks were awash with reserves. This study draws an analogy with the simple multiplier in the income-expenditure model in macroeconomics to make the simple money multiplier more readily understandable for those not familiar. A model of the multiple expansion of credit or the multiple expansion of deposits helps to explain how a purchase of debt by the Federal Reserve can increase the money supply by more than the size of the initial debt purchase.

Attention then turns to a somewhat more realistic version of the money multiplier where (1) banks voluntarily hold some excess reserves and (2) the general public holds some funds in the form of currency rather than in the form of checkable deposits. The discussion of data includes at least some of the components of the money multipliers, such as currency and checkable deposits, both individually and in ratio form (currency divided by checkable deposits). Based on the analysis of the data, this study raises the question of whether a transfer of funds between different methods of storing purchasing power occurred as the result of the most recent financial crisis and the Great Recession, and what the impact of these changes would be on the money multipliers. A very simple method for calculating possible ranges of values for the velocity of M1 based on the levels of M1 and M2 and on possible ranges of values for the velocity of M2 follows the money multiplier discussion.

Afterward, the study compares the money multiplier during the Great Depression in the U.S. with the money multiplier during the Great Recession and the Not-So-Great Recovery in the U.S. Next, this chapter briefly discusses differences in the timing of turning points in the general movements of the velocity of M1 and the velocity of M2 from usually increasing to usually decreasing and *vice versa*. The differences in timing show that the sizes of the monetary aggregates M1 and M2 *must* have an impact on the velocities of M1 and M2. The end of the chapter once again calls for expansionary fiscal policy to increase real GDP and employment in light of the declining velocity of M1 (and M2).

RESERVES AND SOLVENCY

Depository institutions such as commercial banks need to have some concern that depositors may want to withdraw funds. In addition to the need for funds for spending, some depositors may withdraw funds to receive a higher expected return from another institution, or from another method of storing purchasing power, if other depository institutions, bonds, stocks, and/or other assets offer a greater expected return. But, at the present time, if a depository institution faces an unexpected surge in withdrawals for any reason and thus needs to borrow funds to meet reserve requirements (given that depository institutions normally lend a very large percentage of their deposits), then many, if not most, depository institutions can borrow on a short-term basis from other depository institutions at an interest rate that is as of this writing less than 0.20 per cent per year. The interest rate that one bank charges another bank on a short-term loan (perhaps only overnight) is called the federal funds rate. By comparison, data from www.economagic.com and the author's calculations show that in 2007, the quarterly average of monthly federal funds rate data on an annual basis varied from approximately 4.49 per cent to roughly 5.26 per cent. Thus, all other things equal, it is as of this writing less costly than it was a few years ago for depository institutions to have to borrow on a short-term basis from other banks.

In the recent past if not the present environment, perhaps a depository institution had less reason to offer higher interest rates in an effort to make sure that depositors keep funds with the institution due to greatly reduced borrowing costs and a drastic surge in reserves in the federal funds market. A depository institution short on reserves could potentially borrow in the federal funds market at an interest rate currently less than 0.20 per cent per year. A depository institution seeking profit opportunities could possibly buy federal government debt with a term to maturity long enough so that the rate of interest, at least presently, is much greater than the rate that the institution has to pay either depositors or other depository institutions.

One of the results of the quantitative easing (QE) measures of the Federal Reserve and at least some of the Troubled Assets Relief Program (TARP) is that many commercial banks and other depository institutions are awash with reserves, as I inferred from Baumol and Blinder (2012, pp. 254-255, 270-271, 281-282, 290-291). Presumably, one of the goals of at least some of these policy measures was to shore up solvency concerns. Whether banks are reluctant about lending due to a perceived much higher default risk, whether loan applications are down, or whether banks need the reserves to preserve their solvency, the sharp increase in reserves has likely reduced something called 'the money multiplier.'

MONEY MULTIPLIERS AND THE MONEY SUPPLY PROCESS

AN ANALOGY BETWEEN THE SIMPLE MULTIPLIER AND THE SIMPLE MONEY MULTIPLIER

Recall the simple multiplier in the model for finding equilibrium real GDP from Chapter One. In the assumptions of that model, an increase in spending that has nothing to do with a change in income leads to new income for others and subsequent spending increases, with each round of new spending smaller than the previous round because some of the new income in each round is saved. Because of this, an increase in spending in the model can lead to an increase in real GDP greater than the original increase in spending.

As we will see, the simple money multiplier model has some similarities with the simple multiplier model. Just as an increase in spending can lead to further spending, an increase in bank reserves can lead to new loans and funds being re-deposited into the banking system. Further, each subsequent round of loans is smaller than the previous round, much in the same way that each subsequent round of spending decreased in the income-expenditure model discussed in Chapter One. Moreover, similar to the process of an increase in spending leading to an increase in real GDP that is larger than the initial increase in spending, an initial purchase of debt by the Federal Reserve can lead to an increase in the money supply by an amount greater than the initial debt purchase.

THE MULTIPLE EXPANSION OF CREDIT OR DEPOSITS

Above, we noted that banks and other depository institutions need to guard against unforeseen withdrawals given that depository institutions normally lend a large percentage of the deposits they attract. The Federal Reserve sets a required reserve ratio, or a fraction of certain types of deposits, that banks must keep either as cash in their vaults or in a separate account with the Federal Reserve which they are not allowed to lend. To ease the analysis, the present study assumes in a simple model discussed below one constant required reserve ratio. Some more detailed information about the required reserve ratio appears a few pages later under the subheading 'required reserve ratio' in a section titled 'Component Parts of M1 And M2 Multipliers: Why is M1 Growing So Fast?'.

In a simple model, we can suppose that the required reserve ratio is simply ten per cent of all dollars in checking accounts in depository institutions. Then, we can further suppose that the Federal Reserve buys $1,000,000 of T-bills issued by the United States Treasury from Bank A. Bank A would have $1 million dollars less in an asset called 'T-bills,' but Bank A would gain $1 million of new reserves, another type of asset. (The reader may benefit from a review of the brief discussion of assets, liabilities, and equity in Chapter Four.) Because the $1,000,000 of new reserves are not the result of new deposit liabilities, all $1,000,000 of the new reserves are excess reserves. This simple model assumes, among other things, that banks lend all excess reserves. Assuming that the loans are repaid in full (with a positive interest rate), banks' lending of all excess reserves enables the greatest profit.

Suppose that Company One is seeking a loan for $1,000,000, and Bank A approves the loan. Under these assumptions, we can summarize the impact on the various categories of assets on the balance sheet for Bank A in the T-account below. (In our analysis, we will ignore subsequent increases in assets all other things equal that depository institutions hope to receive when loans are repaid. These assets, if held by the depository institutions, would also increase equity.)

Bank A		
	Assets	Liabilities and Equity
-	$1,000,000 T-bills	
+	$1,000,000 excess reserves	
-	$1,000,000 excess reserves	
+	$1,000,000 loans	

Table 7.1 T-Account Summary of the Impact of a $1 million T-bill Purchase by the Federal Reserve on the Balance Sheet for Bank A

Note that U.S. Treasury bills held by Bank A, excess reserves held by Bank A, and loans granted by Bank A are all assets from the perspective of Bank A. Thus, no activity has been recorded under the Liabilities and Equity heading. Note further that the + $1 million entry for the one million dollar increase in excess reserves in a sense cancels out with the one million dollar decrease in the total value of T-bills held by Bank A, and the + $1 million entry for one million dollars more in loans with the loan made to Company One in a sense cancels out with the entry - $ 1 million excess reserves for the decrease of one million dollars worth of excess reserves when lending those funds.

Thus, at this point, there is no change in the *total* amount of assets held by Bank A, just a change in the categorizations of assets held. Therefore, if the balance sheet for Bank A was in balance (with total assets equaling total liabilities plus total equity) before Bank A sold the $1 million of T-bills to the Fed, the balance sheet would remain in balance to this point. If Bank A hypothetically had $10 million of Treasury bills and $5 million of loans as assets before the $1 million sale to the Fed, Bank A would have $9 million of T-bills (the initial $10 million minus the $1 million sold to the Fed) and $6 million of loans (the initial $5 million prior to the T-bill sale plus the new loan of $1 million funded by the proceeds from the T-bill sale) as assets afterward.

What happens to the $1 million borrowed by Company One? This simple model assumes not only that banks lend all excess reserves (as noted above), but that all loan proceeds are re-deposited in the banking system, and that the loan proceeds are re-deposited in a fully checkable account at a different depository institution (not the institution that granted the loan). As Baumol and Blinder (2012, p. 248-252) and many others note (although perhaps in simplified examples), when banks lend money, borrowers often place the loan proceeds at least temporarily in a bank account until they are ready to spend the funds. Although the reader should expect that in reality there would be instances where (1) depository institutions would want to hold excess reserves (with depository institutions having held a combined quantity of excess reserves likely more than 1.85 trillion dollars in May 2013 according to data from www.economagic.com), (2) borrowers would want to hold at least part of the proceeds as currency (so that not all loan proceeds are re-deposited in the banking system), and (3) loan proceeds that are re-deposited would likely be re-deposited in an account with the lending institution; the assumptions made in this model simplify the analysis to illustrate key concepts. (Modifications to the model regarding excess reserves and the public's desire to convert checkable deposits to currency making the model somewhat more realistic will follow.)

Returning to the specific hypothetical example of Company One, suppose that Company One does not need the funds right away, so the company deposits the funds in a checking account. Moreover, suppose that Company One deposits the $1 million that it borrowed from Bank A into a checking account at Bank B. The assumption about borrowers depositing funds at a bank different from the lending institution helps to simplify the T-account analysis showing changes in categories of balance sheet items by keeping the length of each T-account in this simple model relatively short. The assumption may also make the analysis more like the case where borrowers spend the funds right away and the recipients of those expenditures deposit the funds at a different institution.

If Company One deposits the $1 million in a checking account at Bank B, what is the impact on required reserves, deposit liabilities, and loans for Bank B? Bank B is responsible for paying Company One any or all of these funds any time that Company One wants the funds if the funds are deposited in an account having no limits on check-writing. Thus, Bank B would have $1 million of new deposit liabilities. If the required reserve ratio was 0.10, Bank B would need to hold $100,000 (0.10 * $1 million) of these funds as required reserves. If Bank B holds the remaining $900,000 of funds ($1 million of new deposits from Company One less the $100,000 of required reserves), then the $900,000 of remaining funds would be categorized as excess reserves. But, recall that the model assumes that the banks lend the maximum amount possible. Thus, suppose that Company Two seeks a loan for $900,000, and Bank B approves the $900,000 loan to Company Two. The T-account analysis below summarizes the balance sheet impact for Bank B of these events.

Bank B

	Assets		Liabilities and Equity
+	$ 100,000 required reserves	+	$1,000,000 checkable deposits
+	$ 900,000 excess reserves		
-	$ 900,000 excess reserves		
+	$ 900,000 loans		

Table 7.2 T-Account Summary of the Impact of a $1 million Deposit by Company One on the Balance Sheet for Bank B

Now suppose that Company Two does not need the loan proceeds right away, and Company Two deposits the $900,000 of loan proceeds at Bank C. What impact will this have at Bank C? Bank C will have an additional $900,000 of deposit liabilities and will be required to keep $90,000 of these funds as required reserves. If Bank C does not lend out the remaining $810,000 of funds, they will contribute $810,000 toward excess reserves on the balance sheet of Bank C. If Bank C lends the $810,000 of excess reserves, then the entry for $810,000 of additional excess reserves would need to be canceled out and an entry for $810,000 of additional loans would be recorded. The T-account below summarizes the impact on the balance sheet for Bank C.

Bank C

	Assets		Liabilities and Equity
+	$ 90,000 required reserves	+	$900,000 checkable deposits
+	$ 810,000 excess reserves		
-	$ 810,000 excess reserves		
+	$ 810,000 loans		

Table 7.3 T-Account Summary of the Impact of a $900,000 Deposit by Company Two on the Balance Sheet for Bank C

The reader may want to note that the activities above starting with the Fed's purchase of $1 million worth of T-bills from Bank A wind up increasing the money supply, and these activities wind up increasing the money supply by more than $1 million. Many modern-era texts (for example, Mishkin (2004, p. 44-47) and Burton and Lombra (2006, p. 24-25)) use a functional definition of what money is: money stores or preserves value, money provides a measurement unit, and money is nearly universally accepted as a means of payment in the economy in which the item is considered 'money.' According to Burton and Lombra (2006, p. 29), at least at the time of their writing, M1 was the monetary aggregate that best fit the definition of money. The components of M1 are travelers' checks, funds in checking accounts where the owner or owners of the account can write any number of checks per month desired (as long as the account has sufficient funds for the check to clear), and the public's holdings of currency. Such funds keep a substantial portion of their worth over time, provide a measurement quantity, and are generally acceptable for making payments.

Technically speaking, if the Federal Reserve had purchased $1 million of Treasury bills from Bank A but Bank A had *not* granted any loans from the $1 million of reserves that it received from the Fed in exchange for the T-bills, then the money supply would *not* have increased at all just from that transaction. The loan from Bank A to Company One, however, increases the money supply by at least $1 million depending on what happens to the loan proceeds. If the loan proceeds are held as currency and not re-deposited in the banking system, then the increase in the money supply is $1 million.

Alternatively, if the $1 million of proceeds from this loan and all loans are re-deposited in full and depository institutions lend the maximum amount allowed (both assumptions in this simple model), then the money supply increases by *more* than $1 million. The reason why in our example is because the $1 million of checkable deposits held by Company One at Bank B count as part of the money supply, and so do the $900,000 of checkable deposits held by Company Two at Bank C. Assuming the borrower of $810,000 from Bank C re-deposits the funds into a checkable account, those funds will also count toward the money supply. (Although this simple version of the model abstracts away from the possibility of borrowers holding loan proceeds as cash, such borrowed funds held as cash also count toward the money supply.)

THE SIMPLE MONEY MULTIPLIER

In this simplified model, by how much would the money supply grow? Given the unrealistic but simplifying assumptions, the \$1 million purchase of Treasury bills would increase the money supply by \$10 million eventually. To obtain that result, economists use the formula below.

(7.1) Change in Deposits = (Initial Change in Total Reserves)*(1/*rr*)

In the formula above, Total Reserves = Required Reserves + Excess Reserves, and *rr* is the required reserve ratio. The required reserve ratio in this model is similar to the marginal propensity to save (*mps*) or (1 – *mpc*), where *mpc* is the marginal propensity to consume, in the simple multiplier model used to find equilibrium GDP (or the equilibrium change in real GDP). Just as the *mps* limited growth in spending because a fraction of each dollar of additional income was saved, the required reserve ratio limits the amount that depository institutions can lend. Both the *mps* and the *rr* must be greater than zero in order for the models to provide solutions for equilibrium GDP or changes in equilibrium GDP and changes in the money supply, respectively.

Because checkable deposits are part of the money supply, the Change in Deposits (which can be assumed for now to be checkable deposits) represents the change in the money supply. In addition to each listing a formula similar the one above for the *change* in deposits, both Burton and Lombra (2006, p. 478) and Mishkin (2004, p. 370) list a variation of the above formula similar to the one below, showing the *level* of deposits as a function of the level of *total* reserves.

(7.2) Deposits = (Total Reserves)*(1/*rr*)

Thus, *rr* must also be greater than zero to find the level of deposits as well as the change in deposits.

FORMULAE FOR THE (MODIFIED) MONEY MULTIPLIERS

The above analysis assumed that all loan proceeds are re-deposited in the banking system. In other words, the model above assumes that no funds that are borrowed wind up being held as currency by the public. Additionally, the analysis above assumed that depository institutions keep no excess reserves and thus lend the maximum allowed. In reality, however, the reader should expect that the public will hold some borrowed funds as currency (or that when borrowed funds are spent by borrowers, the recipients may want to hold some of the funds as currency), and depository institutions will hold some excess reserves. Both of these complicating factors reduce the size of the actual money multiplier process at work in the economy.

Burton and Lombra (2006, p. 484), Mishkin (2004, p. 377) and likely others list a modified version of the money multiplier where the modified version below adjusts for the public's desire to hold some borrowed funds as currency and depository institutions' desire to hold some deposit liabilities as excess reserves. The modified money multiplier captures how the Federal Reserve's purchases and sales of U.S. Treasury debt (which impact the monetary base (also known as high-powered money, as Mishkin (2004, p. 359) notes), which is total reserves plus currency), the general public's decision of what ratio of currency to checkable deposits to hold, the required reserve ratio set by the Federal Reserve, and the fraction of excess reserves to total checkable deposits that banks want to hold; all impact the total quantity of M1 in circulation.

(7.3) Change in M1 Money Supply =
(Initial Change in Monetary Base)*[(1 + c)/(rr + e + c)]

In equation (7.3) above, c equals C/D, the ratio of currency held by the public to checkable deposits, e equals ER/D, the ratio of excess reserves held by banks to checkable deposits, and rr equals RR/D, the ratio of required reserves held by banks to checkable deposits, as noted earlier. For our purposes, we can consider rr as essentially the same as the required reserve ratio. The equation above is specifically for the change in the M1 money supply. Burton and Lombra (2006, p. 484) list a formula for not only the change in M1, but also the level of M1. While Mishkin (2004, p. 377) may not list the formula in change form but in level form only, the analysis in his text is clearly applicable for calculating the change in the money supply also. An analog for the formula for the level of M1 is below, where [(1 + c)/(rr + e + c)] is the M1 money multiplier.

(7.4) M1 Money Supply = (Monetary Base)*[(1 + c)/(rr + e + c)]

Deriving the M2 money multiplier requires further modifications because M2 includes not only all of the components of M1 but also assets not counted in M1 such as money market deposit accounts, money market mutual funds accounts not owned by institutions, small time deposits, and small savings deposits. Burton and Lombra (2006, p. 495) and likely many others have equations similar to the equation below that includes the M2 money multiplier.

(7.5) M2 Money Supply = (Monetary Base)*[(1 + c + d + m)/(rr + e + c)]

According to information in Burton and Lombra (2006, p. 495), in the equation above, d equals D'/D, the ratio of the sum of small time and savings deposits part of M2 to the checkable deposits counted in M1 (and M2), m equals the ratio of individual money market mutual funds, money market deposit accounts, and other non-M1 components of M2 not included in D (such as overnight Eurodollars (probably U.S. dollar-denominated assets held in European banks) and overnight repurchase agreements) to checkable deposits, the latter counted in M1 and M2. The variables c, rr, and e are as defined above.

If data for the M1 money supply and the monetary base in the same period are available, then the reader can calculate the M1 money multiplier for that period simply by dividing the M1 money supply by the monetary base. The reader can do the same for the M2 money multiplier if data for the M2 money supply and the monetary base in the same period are available. Alternatively, the reader can use data if available for the components of the money multiplier to calculate the ratios that are part of the multiplier (c, rr, and e (and d and m for the M2 multiplier)) and substitute them into the formula.

COMPONENT PARTS OF M1 AND M2 MULTIPLIERS: WHY IS M1 GROWING SO FAST?

The understanding about the money multipliers for M1 and M2 and the money supply process developed above will help in analyzing the recent sharp decline in the velocity of M1, given that in three out of five sub-sample periods when the velocity of M1 decreased, the percentage growth rate of M1 was greater than the percentage growth rate of M2. Additionally, in each of four sub-sample periods when the percentage growth rate of M2 exceeded the percentage growth rate of M1 by at least seven percentage points, the velocity of M1 increased.

Could these findings support the view that a non-decreasing-velocity money supply level (NDVMSL) exists? As discussed in the previous chapter, is there a negative relationship, at least at times, between the percentage growth rate of nominal M1 and the velocity of M1? Does faster growth in the nominal M1 money supply suggest that if a NDVMSL exists, then it is more likely that either the level of nominal M1 is already beyond the NDVMSL or the level is about to cross the threshold? Below, we begin data descriptions with the components of money multipliers that are part of both the M1 and M2 money multipliers. (Earlier, I started looking at factors such as currency, the monetary base, and total reserves in Hartman (2012).)

Required Reserve Ratio

Burton and Lombra (2006, p. 75) note that at least in the year 2004, the Fed could choose any required reserve ratio that is at least eight per cent but at most fourteen per cent, and the required reserve ratio was graduated. (The ability for the Fed to choose the required reserve ratio probably comes from Congress.) The following information is from Burton and Lombra (2006, p. 75). In the year 2004, up to $7 million of checkable deposits at an institution were not subject to any requirement. For checkable deposits above $7 million dollars but smaller than $47.6 million in that year, the required reserve ratio was three per cent. Ten per cent was the required reserve ratio for checkable deposits greater than (and probably equal to) $47.6 million in 2004.

According to Baumol and Blinder (2012, p. 270), the Fed has not adjusted the required reserve ratio since 1992. Burton and Lombra (2006, p. 75) observe that the Fed reduced the required reserve ratio in December 1990 and December 1992. While the required reserve ratio did not apply either to savings deposits or to time deposits as of the writing of Burton and Lombra (2006, p. 75), the required reserve ratio did apply in the past to those forms of deposits.

Checkable Deposits, Currency and the Ratio of Currency to Checkable Deposits

In January 1959, currency in the hands of the public amounted to $28.5 billion according to www.economagic.com (accessed July 31, 2013), while checkable deposits totaled $110 billion. For decades, checkable deposits exceeded currency, but in most months currency grew or at least held steady. Checkable deposits, on the other hand, reached a local maximum of nearly $801 billion in March 1994. At this point, checkable deposits were less than eight times as large as they were in January 1959, but currency, at approximately $331 billion, had increased to be more than eleven times its size in January 1959.

After March 1994, checkable deposits declined most months through December 2000, when checkable deposits reached a local minimum of roughly $548 billion. Currency continued to trend upward, standing at approximately $531 billion in that month, nearly as large as checkable deposits. Checkable deposits then had some 'ups and downs' including a relatively minor one-month spike in September 2001 but clearly trended upward most months, reaching a local maximum of about $671 billion in December 2004 before trending downward again, reaching a local minimum around $602 billion in November 2007. Checkable deposits then increased most months after November 2007, reaching a local maximum around $1.415 trillion in May 2013 (although checkable deposits probably continued increasing most months into the year 2014). Thus, checkable deposits, which are part of both M1 and M2, exhibited rapid growth over the last few years. In fact, checkable deposits more than doubled from November 2007 through May 2013. From June 2007 through May 2013, the growth in checkable deposits was more than $800 billion.

Currency eventually surpassed checkable deposits for the first time in the sample period in March 2002 (about $595 billion for currency and $589 billion for checkable deposits that month). Currency then exceeded checkable deposits each month through December 2010, with the listing from www.economagic.com showing currency at $919.1 billion and checkable deposits as $912.9 billion for that month. Afterward, checkable deposits have exceeded currency, with checkable deposits amounting to almost $300 billion more than currency in May 2013. It is probably safe to say that the upward trend in currency has been less volatile overall during the quarterly-data sample period than the upward trend in checkable deposits.

Like checkable deposits, the public's holdings of currency have also increased in recent years. However, as implied above, the increase in currency was at a slower rate than checkable deposits between December 2007 and March 2013 and beyond. Data from www.economagic.com indicate that from December 2007 to March 2013, currency increased from about $760.3 billion to about $1.103 trillion, an increase of roughly $342 billion. In May 2013, the public held roughly $1.12 trillion of currency, amounting to an increase of roughly 48 per cent compared with June 2007 rather than roughly 135 per cent as was the case with checkable deposits. In fact, checkable deposits grew nearly three times as fast on a percentage basis (about 2.8 times as fast) as currency during this period in the U.S.

The ratio of currency to checkable deposits reached a maximum within the sample period of roughly 1.266 in November of 2007. This ratio, which is part of the money multipliers for both M1 and M2, generally decreased afterward, reaching values below 0.800 in February, April, and May 2013. Prior to December 2007, the ratio of currency to checkable deposits had frequently increased from one month to the next, with some exceptions. In each month of the year 1959, the ratio was slightly less than 0.26.

As suggested above, despite some months of decline, the general trend in the ratio of the public's holding of currency to checkable deposits was clearly upward, exceeding 0.30 for the first time in the sample period in September 1973 and not decreasing below 0.30 since then. In May 1982, the ratio of currency to checkable deposits surpassed 0.40 for the first time and then varied between 0.380 and 0.406 through October 1985. A local minimum around 0.335 was reached in December 1986 before trending upward again. (The reader may want to recall that the velocity of M1 declined from roughly 7.37 times per year in the fourth quarter of 1984 to about 6.30 times per year in the second quarter of 1987. This was also a period of relatively rapid growth in the M1 money supply.) The decrease in the ratio of currency to checkable deposits was due to rapid growth in checkable deposits, increasing from around $436 billion in October 1985 to around $538 billion in December 1986, an increase of roughly 23.4 per cent, while over the same period, currency increased by only about 8.6 per cent, from about $166 billion to about $180 billion.

The ratio of currency to checkable deposits again surpassed 0.40 in March 1990, this time not declining below 0.40 through the end of the sample period. The ratio was at least 0.50 for the first time in December 1995. Currency divided by checkable deposits for the first time in the sample period exceeded 0.60 in March 1997 and exceeded 0.70 for the first time in July 1998. In July 1999, the ratio was greater than 0.80 for the first time and was greater than 0.90 for the first time in June 2000.

Some of the more rapid growth in currency divided by checkable deposits was due to *decreasing* checkable deposits. Currency continued to grow from December 1995 when it was roughly $373 billion through June 2000 when it was approximately $521 billion, an increase around forty per cent. Checkable deposits fell from about $746 billion in December 1995 to around $573 billion in June 2000. That is a decrease of roughly twenty-three per cent. (For completeness, the reader may wish to note that the local maximum for checkable deposits did *not* occur in December 1995. The public held nearly $801 billion of checkable deposits, the local maximum, in March 1994. The public held only about $548 billion of checkable deposits, the local minimum, in December 2000, six months after the ratio of currency to checkable deposits surpassed 0.90.)

Currency to checkable deposits surpassed 1.0 in March 2002, surpassed 1.1 for the first time in October 2005, and surpassed 1.20 for the first time in September 2006. As noted above, the maximum within the sample period is approximately 1.266 in November 2007. The ratio then fell precipitously to less than 0.80 in February 2013. Thus, the ratio was roughly 37 per cent lower in February 2013 than it was a bit more than five years earlier at its peak in the sample period. As was the case with the rapid decrease in the velocity of M1 after the fourth quarter of 1984 through the second quarter of 1987, the decline in the ratio of currency to checkable deposits was largely due to a surge in the public's holdings of checkable deposits, which have more than doubled since the end of 2007.

Estimates for ranges of values of the money multipliers at some points in time appear later in this chapter under 'The Money Multiplier in Recent Years Versus the Great Depression.' The estimates show downward trending M1 and M2 money multipliers (although the declines started before the Great Recession). Did funds flow out of other forms of storing purchasing power and into currency, and is that one of the main reasons for a decline in the money multipliers in the U.S. in recent years?

The following data help answer that question. From December 2008 through November 2012, currency increased by roughly 33 per cent. From May 1989 through April 1993, from April 1993 through March 1997, from March 1997 through February 2001, from February 2001 through January 2005, and from January 2005 through December 2008, the percentage growth rates of currency were approximately 39 per cent, 33 per cent, 34 per cent, 30 per cent, and 17 per cent, respectively. Thus, the 33 per cent growth in currency from December 2008 through November 2012 seems perhaps normal or average, with the percentage growth rate very similar to most of these other periods of the same length except for the period immediately before it (January 2005 through December 2008). To the extent that the growth in currency from December 2008 through November 2012 was simply normal or average, it may not be accurate to think about extraordinarily large sums of money flowing out of both time deposits and individual money market mutual funds and into currency. Checkable deposits, the much more volatile series, more likely absorbed some of the amounts released from time deposits and individual money market mutual funds. Further discussion of possible movements of funds is below under the heading 'Portfolio Readjustments.'

Based on material presented above and material to follow, the rapid increase in M1 does not appear to be mainly the result of a rise in currency. Data from www.economagic.com accessed in July 2013 show that the percentage of currency in M1 was around 20.5 per cent in January 1959. Despite some decreases, the percentage of currency in M1 trended upward for most of the sample period. In November 2007, the share of currency in M1 reached an in-sample maximum of roughly 55.6 per cent. This is just before the velocity of M1 started to decline most quarters beginning with the first quarter of 2008. Currency fell slightly below 44 per cent of M1 in April 2013 before rebounding to about 44.5 per cent in June 2013. Thus, as M1 was growing rapidly, the share of currency in M1 was generally declining. This further underscores the importance of the growth in checkable deposits when trying to explain the surge in M1 that started in 2008, particularly in the second half. (The reader should realize that travelers' checks are part of the M1 measure of the money supply but during the sample period have been less than one per cent of M1. Thus, at times, the current study ignores the negligible share of travelers' checks in M1.)

Excess Reserves

Starting in September 2008, depository institutions' holdings of excess reserves jumped up in a fashion unprecedented in the sample period of monthly data (which began in January 1959). (The reader may want to note that this series is not seasonally adjusted.) In January 1959, excess reserves were just below half of one billion dollars. The next few years brought some 'ups and downs,' reaching a local maximum of about $0.77 billion in January 1961 after dipping to a local minimum around $0.41 billion in June 1959. After reaching the aforementioned local maximum in January 1961, despite some 'ups and downs' and shorter-term erratic movements, the clear trend for excess reserves was downward, at least into 1974. In October 1974, excess reserves held by depository institutions decreased to $0.12 billion (or $120 million), a minimum within the sample period soon after a mini-surge from around $0.13 billion in March 1974 to around $0.20 billion by June 1974.

Depository institutions held more than one billion dollars of excess reserves for the first time in the sample period and perhaps since the 1930s (based in part on information from Burton and Lombra (2006, p. 485)) in December 1985. Excess reserves then dipped back below $0.70 billion in September 1986 before reaching a local maximum around $1.25 billion in January 1988. From February 1988 through November 1990, excess reserves fluctuated between $0.78 billion and $1.18 billion. In December 1990 and January 1991, excess reserves spiked up to roughly $1.67 billion and $2.14 billion, respectively.

However, excess reserves were below $2 billion each month afterward until January 2000, when excess reserves surged to roughly $2.01 billion. In most months between January 1991 and January 2000, excess reserves were less than $1.5 billion, with excess reserves below $1 billion in some months, reaching a local minimum in April 1995 of about $0.76 billion. Starting in February 2000, excess reserves were again below $1.5 billion but above $0.95 billion each month through August 2001. In September 2001, excess reserves surged to approximately $19 billion likely as the result of September 11. In October 2011, excess reserves fell again to around $1.33 billion. From October 2001 through July 2003, excess reserves varied between $1.2 billion and $2.1 billion, before surging again in August 2003 to around $3.76 billion. The surge in excess reserves of August 2003 subsided for a while, with excess reserves dropping below $2 billion each month from September 2003 through July 2007 (and even below $1 billion in January 2004).

Another surge in depository institutions' holdings of excess reserves occurred in August 2007, when excess reserves totaled approximately $4.83 billion after totaling only about $1.63 billion the month before. In September 2007, excess reserves fell to around $1.73 billion and hovered between $1.4 billion and $2.7 billion each month through August 2008, when depository institutions held roughly $1.88 billion of excess reserves. The reader may note that the second greatest quantity of excess reserves in a month between January 1959 and August 2008 occurred in August 2007, when depository institutions held roughly $4.8 billion dollars of excess reserves. The third greatest surge in excess reserves in percentage terms after January 1959 but before September 2008 occurred in November 1980, when excess reserves rose from about $0.21 billion to roughly $0.52 billion but declined back to approximately $0.37 billion in January 1981 (and around $0.17 billion in April 1981).

The surge in excess reserves that started in September 2008 dramatically towers over all previous surges, at least within the sample period which began in January 1959. In September 2008, excess reserves jumped to nearly $59.5 billion, followed by another jump in October 2008 to more than $267 billion, and another jump to nearly $559 billion in November 2008, and yet another jump in December 2008 to roughly $767 billion. After that, the acceleration in excess reserves became more subdued at least temporarily, with excess reserves fluctuating between $642 billion and $860 billion through September 2009, when excess reserves totaled about $859.9 billion, although excess reserves grew by about $94 billion dollars in that month.

More rapid growth in excess reserves resumed temporarily in October 2009, with the figure rising to nearly $995 billion, and the estimate was roughly $1,077 billion (or $1.077 trillion) just one month later. After that, excess reserves had 'ups and downs,' but the overall trend was upward through July 2011, when excess reserves amounted to approximately $1.618 trillion. From August 2011 through September 2012, excess reserves exhibited an overall decline, with the local minimum over that period approximately $1.41 trillion in September 2012. But, after hovering between $1.409 trillion and $1.618 trillion from August 2011 through February 2013, excess reserves grew to nearly $1.70 trillion in March 2013. In fact, growth in excess reserves started to accelerate again in February 2013 and in May of 2013 stood at more than $1.863 trillion.

The gargantuan increase in excess reserves that began in September 2008 not only in dollar terms but also in percentage terms dominated any other increase within the monthly-data sample period (which began January 1959), far surpassing any other increase during that time (and perhaps in the history of the United States). Within the sample period, the largest surge in excess reserves (in dollar terms) before September 2008 was from about $1.2 billion in August 2001 to roughly $19.0 billion in September 2001 but then back down to around $1.3 billion in October 2001. The next largest monthly increases in dollar terms within the sample period were (1) from about $1.6 billion to about $4.8 billion but then back to about $1.7 billion over July, August, and September of 2007, and (2) approximately $1.9 billion to approximately $3.8 billion but then falling to roughly $1.5 billion over July, August, and September of 2003.

Regarding the time before the sample period began, information in Burton and Lombra (2006, p. 485) suggests that early in the Great Depression, excess reserves increased very roughly eighty-fold, exceeding $2 billion in 1933 after being only about $25 million in 1929. (Additional discussion of the surge in excess reserves during the Great Depression follows near the end of the chapter.) For a few months before the rapid rise in excess reserves that commenced in September 2008, excess reserves hovered at approximately $2 billion, according to data from www.economagic.com. Then, in July 2011, with depository institutions holding more than $1.6 trillion in excess reserves, the increase to that point was approximately eight *hundred*-fold. Using data from www.economagic.com, I calculate that the percentage increase in excess reserves was almost 86,200 per cent from August 2008 through July 2011 (and a larger cumulative increase through May 2013). Using data from Burton and Lombra (2006, p. 485), I calculate that the percentage increase in excess reserves between 1929 and 1933 was roughly 7,900 per cent. The data from www.economagic.com and the author's calculations indicate that over the sample period, the greatest percentage increase in excess reserves before September 2008 was about 1,481 per cent around the time of September 11, 2001.

The comparison of the surge that began in September 2008 and other surges in excess reserves prior to September 2008 may not be the most accurate comparison because the percentage calculated is over years, rather than one month. However, the other surges in 1980, 2001, 2003, and 2007 lasted either only one month or a few months, while it took nearly three years for excess reserves to reach their local maximum (through 2011) after the surge began in 2008 and more than four-and-a-half years to reach approximately 1.86 trillion dollars in May 2013 (roughly a 99,000 per cent cumulative increase). Moreover, the monthly percentage change in September 2008 was more than 3,070 per cent.

The rapid rise in excess reserves from September 2008 through July 2011 and relatively slow partial decline afterward but followed by another surge in excess reserves starting in early 2013 could contain the most important data in explaining the decrease in both the M1 money multiplier and the M2 money multiplier discussed later in the chapter. As noted above, the ratio of excess reserves to checkable deposits e is in the denominator of the money multipliers. Thus, all other things equal, an increase in excess reserves leads to an increase in e but a decrease in both the M1 and M2 money multipliers. Data from www.economagic.com and the author's calculations indicate that in the sample period (which began in January 1959) but before September 2008, the monthly value for e was less than 0.008 in each month except September 2001, when it increased to approximately 0.030. The second greatest value during that period for e occurred in August 2007 when e was roughly 0.0079, and in the third greatest value in this period, it was approximately 0.0069 in January 1961.

In the sample period but before September 2008, the value for e was below 0.003 in well over half of the months. In September 2008, the ratio increased to roughly 0.088, then to nearly 0.40 in October 2008, and to nearly 0.80 in November 2008 and nearly 0.98 in December 2008. From then through May 2013, e was no lower than 0.88 with a local minimum of about 0.884 in February 2009. In most months between January 2009 and May 2013, e was greater than 1.0, reaching a maximum (at least within the sample period) of roughly 1.61 in June 2011 and exceeding 1.0 each month from September 2009 through May 2013 and perhaps beyond. (A value of e greater than one could indicate banks voluntarily holding reserves from time deposits and other deposits not currently subject to reserve requirements. Thus, under the present system, all reserves held from these deposits would be excess reserves.)

The rapid surge in the ratio of excess reserves to checkable deposits that started in September 2008 is perhaps more dramatic when realizing that checkable deposits, the denominator of *e*, roughly doubled between September 2008 and December 2012, rising from about $675 billion to $1,351 billion, and exceeded $1.4 trillion in April and May of 2013. With depository institutions holding such large quantities of excess reserves (well over one trillion dollars worth), the institutions are not lending those funds, thus leading to a reduction in lending and the potential for re-depositing and re-lending, and so on. This intuitively explains part of the decrease in the money multiplier.

Why did depository institutions start holding such large quantities of excess reserves in September 2008? Since then, depository institutions could have grown much more concerned that any loans that they make may not be repaid, thus not only adversely impacting profitability but also threatening the solvency of a depository institution with too great a quantity of loans that wind up going into default. A similar explanation for vast holdings of excess reserves is that depository institutions have been holding (and are presently holding) a much greater quantity of reserves starting in September 2008 due to *past* portfolio strategies. Perhaps depository institutions are concerned about loans made in the past going into default, or perhaps depository institutions are concerned about real estate and equity holdings plummeting in value (the latter of which is potentially much more relevant since the Financial Modernization Act of 1999 ended the separation of commercial banking and investment banking, thus allowing depository institutions to hold common stocks). Perhaps depository institutions are guarding against a surge in withdrawals and feel that required reserves are insufficient. Someone suggested to me that maybe depository institutions are holding much greater balances of excess reserves to ensure passage of recently created stress tests.

Regardless of the reason, Baumol and Blinder (2012, pp. 254-255, 289) point out that if a surge in excess reserves occurs, the money supply would decrease without expansionary policy from the central bank. Unless it is essential for depository institutions to hold all of these excess reserves, think of the benefits that could be realized if some of the excess reserves left the banking system (at least temporarily) in production-related transactions as so many now are either unemployed or working for much less pay in the United States.

Small Time Deposits and Individual Money Market Mutual Funds

Another possible explanation for the surge in excess reserves deals in part with the plummeting sums in time deposits and money market mutual funds. (Dramatic withdrawals from money market mutual funds may have ended or at least decreased when economic conditions stabilized at least to some extent. Further, longer-term interest rates have risen, although longer-term rates remain depressed as of this writing.) It seems like people in the U.S. economy pulled funds out of money market mutual funds and certificates of deposit, the latter perhaps mainly at maturity, and this could be in part due to dramatically lower returns from holding those assets, as many if not most interest rates have fallen sharply.

From the perspective of depository institutions that issue certificates of deposit, other deposits that they issue give depositors more flexibility in the timing of their withdrawals. Thus, depository institutions may be guarding against unforeseen withdrawals. Given the increase in unemployment rates in the Great Recession and a relatively slow decrease in unemployment rates in the Not-So-Great Recovery, companies going out of business, defaults in recent years, and budgetary concerns both domestically and abroad in the European Union, a dramatic rise in withdrawals at a depository institution could have occurred.

Another factor helping to explain astronomically higher holdings of excess reserves could be that the Federal Reserve began paying interest on excess reserves in October of 2008 as per Baumol and Blinder (2012, p. 264), although the interest rate is probably very low. Yet another factor could be that as checkable deposits (part of M1 and M2), savings deposits, and money market account deposits (the latter two both part of M2 but not M1) increased, depository institutions in the aggregate had a greater ability to hold reserves. However, this does not explain why depository institutions suddenly voluntarily held a much greater percentage of deposits as excess reserves in addition to holding more required reserves. The data from www.economagic.com described in the next paragraph show the outflow of funds from small time deposits and money market mutual funds.

The series showing total small time deposits found on www.economagic.com shows that total small time deposits first passed 1.2 trillion dollars in December of 2006 (after varying between only 11.4 billion dollars and 12.4 billion dollars each month in the year 1959 and after being greater than one trillion dollars at times in the late 1980s, the early 1990s, the early 2000s, and earlier in the year

2006). Total small time deposits continued to trend upward most months for two more years, first surpassing the 1.3 trillion dollar mark in August 2008 and reaching a maximum of nearly 1.457 trillion dollars in December 2008. Total small time deposits then decreased every month afterward, at least through June 2013, when it was approximately 0.57 trillion dollars, falling by more than fifty per cent over approximately four-and-one-half years. In October 2012, with total small time deposits standing around $656 billion, this series had fallen by more than $800 billion in just under four years.

Individual money market mutual funds (from a series named retail money funds that began in 1973) reached a peak of roughly 1.025 trillion dollars in October 2008, before decreasing most months thereafter, at least through September 2012. In that month, individual money market mutual funds were about 0.625 trillion dollars, a decrease of roughly $400 billion (or $0.40 trillion) since October 2008, a decrease of roughly 39 per cent in slightly less than four years. Although individual money market mutual funds have rebounded somewhat since then, the total value has still been less than $652 billion each month, at least through June 2013.

Clearly, most time deposits impose a notable loss of liquidity on the owners of the funds, with the owners of the accounts likely subject to penalties for withdrawing the funds prior to a certain point in time. I am not sure whether deposits in money market mutual funds are subject to early withdrawal penalties. However, such deposits are subject to capital losses (depending on market conditions and the decisions made by the mutual fund managers) and are not FDIC insured. Further, money market mutual fund accounts, like money market deposit accounts, likely have a maximum number of checks per period permissible. The relatively rapid decline in both small time deposits and money market mutual funds deposits may possibly suggest greater concern that savers have.

With regard to the depletion of funds in small time deposits, savers may have more concern about tying up their funds and an increased desire for liquidity. Further, savers may not want to renew funds in maturing certificates of deposit or bring funds from other sources to place in new certificates at very low interest rates if they can get a return that is as large or nearly as large (or at least equal to some minimal value) from a savings account or a money market deposit without sacrificing as much liquidity as the loss imposed by a certificate of deposit. With regard to lessening sums in money market mutual funds, savers could be concerned about possible defaults and the potential for losses. Savers may believe that a reduced expected return from money market mutual funds may not be worth the risks.

Money Market Deposit Accounts and Savings Accounts

The sum of money market deposit accounts and savings deposits, which are much more liquid than time deposits in that the owner or owners of the account can withdraw funds at any time without penalty, surged while time deposits and individual money market mutual fund balances plummeted. In May of 2008, data from www.economagic.com show that the sum of savings deposits and money market deposit accounts surpassed $4 trillion for the first time (having been only around $136 billion in January 1959). The sum of savings deposits and money market deposit accounts continued growing most months since then, surpassing $5 trillion in May 2010, surpassing $6 trillion in November 2011, reaching nearly $6.62 trillion in November 2012 and passing $6.7 trillion by January 2013 while passing $6.8 trillion by May 2013. This represents an increase in total money market deposit accounts and savings accounts of roughly sixty-five per cent from May 2008 through November 2012 while money market mutual funds and time deposits fell sharply (and the velocity of both M2 and especially M1 fell).

Recall that total small time deposits fell by more than fifty per cent and individual money market mutual funds lost more than thirty-five per cent of their total value in a span of less than four years. The sum of small time deposits and individual money market mutual funds may have fallen by more than one trillion dollars (roughly $1.2 trillion) over a span of time rather similar to the time span when the sum of savings deposits and money market deposit accounts rose by more than two trillion dollars.

PORTFOLIO READJUSTMENTS?

As mentioned earlier, data from www.economagic.com and the author's calculations show that total small time deposits fell by roughly $800 billion and individual money market mutual funds fell by approximately $400 billion over similar, but not identical, spans of time. The combined decrease is very roughly $1.2 trillion. Where did all of that approximately $1.2 trillion go? It is not possible with the information available to answer the question in terms of each individual person as a depositor, but we can say at least a little about a possible transfer of funds in the aggregate or from the perspective of the economy as a whole.

As noted earlier, checkable deposits and the sum of total savings deposits plus money market deposit accounts (MMDAs) soared in terms of total asset values. Between December 2008 and November

2012, the sum of MMDAs and savings deposits soared by more than $2.5 trillion. Checkable M1 deposits rose by more than $700 billion from November 2007 through October 2012. Thus, at a macroeconomic level, perhaps some or most or all of the approximately $1.2 trillion less combined in small time deposits and individual money market mutual funds could have gone to savings accounts, money market deposit accounts (MMDAs), checkable M1 deposits, or some combination of these.

Depositors could have opted to shift funds away from time deposits for the increased liquidity offered by MMDAs, savings accounts, and checkable accounts. Those with funds in individual money market mutual funds could have transferred at least some of the funds in those accounts because they became more concerned about potential capital losses and sought the safety of FDIC-insured deposits. The increased concern over possible capital losses could have come from the quarterly average federal funds rate reaching near zero by the first quarter of 2009.

Using data from www.economagic.com, the author calculates that the quarterly average federal funds rate fell from approximately 0.51 per cent to around 0.18 per cent between the fourth quarter of 2008 and the first quarter of 2009. (Chapter 5 has more information about federal funds rate targets.) Assuming a zero bound, with the quarterly average federal funds rate being able to decline possibly only about 0.18 percentage points more, people in the economy could have become wary of leaving funds in individual money market mutual funds which use customers' funds to purchase assets with short terms to maturity. The thinking could have been that if other short-term assets would experience increasing interest rates in the future (as could have been a greater risk than falling short-term interest rates with short-term rates already quite low), higher short-term interest rates, all other things equal, imply that previously issued assets with short terms to maturity would decline in value.

Another problem could have been the commercial paper market. If individual money market mutual funds placed customers' funds in the commercial paper market, people in the economy could have been concerned about the possibility of defaults, thus expediting the exit of some of the funds placed in individual money market mutual funds. (Commercial paper rates rose rapidly in the financial crisis in the U.S. if I am inferring correctly from Baumol and Blinder (2012, p. 269). This could have indicated lenders requiring a higher risk premium when lending in the commercial paper market.) Furthermore, savers could have been concerned about placing funds in equity shares, real estate, and bonds.

Regardless of whether the money came out of individual money market mutual funds and small time deposits, one potential factor that could have increased the desire to hold funds as checkable deposits was a temporary elimination of the ceiling for FDIC-insured deposits per person per institution if the funds were held in non-interest-bearing accounts. According to www.fdic.gov/deposit/deposits/unlimited/expiration.html (accessed December 18, 2012), the Dodd-Frank Wall Street Reform and Consumer Protection Act removed the insurance ceiling on such transaction deposits from December 31, 2010 through December 31, 2012, so this could explain some of the surge in checkable deposits during this two-year period. As of this writing, it is not completely clear what will be the full impact on checkable deposits now that an insurance ceiling will again be imposed on demand deposits per person at each institution, although the limit will be higher than it was before the financial crisis. Further portfolio adjustments could be forthcoming.

Readers should note that checkable deposits have continued to trend upward most months through May 2013 despite a deposit insurance ceiling being imposed again. At any rate, the rapid rise of checkable deposits appears largely responsible for the percentage growth rate of nominal M1 exceeding the percentage growth rate of nominal M2 after the fourth quarter of 2007 (although the total number of dollars in M2 has increased by more than the total number of dollars in M1), and the percentage decrease of the velocity of M1 exceeding the percentage decrease in the velocity of M2. The surge in excess reserves appears largely, if not solely responsible for the decrease in money multiplier values shown near the end of the chapter.

PREDICTING POSSIBLE VALUES FOR THE VELOCITY OF M1 USING MONETARY AGGREGATES AND (FORECASTED) VALUES OF THE VELOCITY OF M2

WITH M1 AND M2 AS CONTROL VARIABLES

The attention to further consideration of both the M1 and M2 money multipliers could prove well worth the effort. Many assume that the central bank in the U.S., the Federal Reserve, can exert very large influence over the quantity of U.S. dollars in both the M1 and M2 monetary aggregates if it so desires but cannot completely control them. However, even if the Federal Reserve could control the sizes of monetary aggregates, factors listed under the next sub-heading 'With M1 and M2 Not as Control Variables' below require readers to interpret the results with a healthy degree of skepticism.

The substantial influence of the Federal Reserve on the monetary aggregates via the money multiplier process comes through three main policy tools. First in terms of importance in modern times (at least before the most recent financial crisis) would be the Fed's open market operations (purchases and sales of U.S. Treasury debt) to impact the quantity of total reserves in the banking system. The Washington D.C.-based Federal Open Market Committee of the Federal Reserve could instruct the New York Federal Reserve Bank to purchase U.S. federal government debt instruments not only to reduce interest rates (or to keep interest rates from rising or to keep rates from rising as much) but also to increase total reserves and the money supply. Likewise, an instruction for the New York Fed to sell U.S. Treasuries could be implemented not only to increase interest rates (or to keep interest rates from falling or to keep rates from falling as much) but also to decrease total reserves and the money supply (or the growth rates of total reserves and the money supply). (Readers should realize that if the money multiplier holds constant, an increase in total reserves will lead to an increase in the money supply, and a decrease in total reserves will lead to a decrease in the money supply.)

Second, the FOMC can change its discount rate, the rate that banks pay when they borrow from the Fed, so that a lower discount rate encourages more borrowing from the Fed and increases the money supply, all other things equal. A higher discount rate reduces the money supply or the growth rate in the money supply by making it more difficult for banks to borrow, all other things equal. A third way that the Federal Reserve can influence the money supply would be through the required reserve ratio, where higher ratios require banks to hold more reserves and thus, all other things the same, lead to a reduction in the money supply. Likewise, all other things the same, a lower required reserve ratio allows greater expansion of credit and an increase in the money supply. As noted above, the Federal Reserve has not altered the required reserve ratio often in recent decades.

But, how is this information useful for understanding the decrease in the velocity of money, particularly the velocity of M1, in the United States? The reader may recall that, from the algebraic definitions of the velocities of M1 and M2, the only difference in the two is the difference in the monetary aggregates in the denominators, as the velocity of M1 = (nominal GDP)/(M1) = (P^*Y)/(M1) and the velocity of M2 = (nominal GDP)/(M2) = (P^*Y)/(M2), where Y is real GDP and P equals the implicit deflator divided by 100. Therefore, if we divide the velocity of M1 by the velocity of M2, the fraction simplifies to M2 divided by M1, as shown below. So, the ratio constructed by dividing the velocity of M1 by the velocity of M2 equals the level of M2 divided by the level of M1.

$$
\begin{aligned}
(7.6)\ V(M1)/V(M2) &= [(\text{nominal GDP})/(M1)]/[(\text{nominal GDP})/(M2)] \\
&= [(P^*Y)/(M1)]/[(P^*Y)/(M2)] \\
&= [1/(M1)]/[1/(M2)] \\
&= (M2)/(M1)
\end{aligned}
$$

The general public has 'control' over how much of its purchasing power it wants to hold in the form of currency, how much it wants to hold as checkable deposits, how much it wants to hold in the form of travelers' checks, how much it wants to hold as assets not part of M1 but part of M2, and how much it wants to hold in other forms not part of either M1 or M2. Depository institutions in the banking system have 'control' over the quantity of excess reserves they want to hold (subject to the condition that excess reserves cannot exceed total assets). However, these decisions by the public and depository institutions likely depend on interest rates in the economy at least to some extent, and the Federal Reserve has influence over interest rates in the United States. Hence, I placed the word 'control' above in this paragraph in single quotes to note that the portfolio decisions made by the general public and depository institutions probably depend in part on economic conditions.

In light of these points about factors that influence the money multipliers, I assume that the Federal Reserve cannot completely control either M1 or M2. But, to help illustrate a point, suppose that the Federal Reserve could completely control both M1 and M2 (given that the components of the money multipliers over which the Fed has less direct control could still be influenced indirectly by the Federal Reserve through interest rates). As implied by the algebraic steps shown above, if we assume that the Federal Reserve can completely control the quantities of both monetary aggregates, M1 and M2, then not only could the Federal Reserve control the ratio of one monetary aggregate to the other (by controlling, for example, (M2)/(M1)), but the Federal Reserve could then control the ratio of the velocities V(M1)/V(M2).

Now, suppose further that one takes the view that the velocity of money is highly predictable. This would likely be consistent with a monetarist view of the velocity of money. It may also be consistent with the original classical view of velocity where according to Mishkin (2004, pp. 518-519), the classical school of thought assumed that the velocity of money was usually nearly constant in the short term. If we know the levels of both M1 and M2 assuming that they can be controlled by the Federal Reserve, and if we know the velocity of one of the two monetary aggregates, then we can solve for the velocity of the other aggregate. More specifically, if we know the sizes of the monetary aggregates M1 and M2, and if we know the velocity of M2, then we can determine the velocity of M1.

The assumptions in the analysis above may seem a bit extreme. With less severe assumptions, we can still determine ranges of possible values. At least since the beginning of the sample period (the first quarter of 1959), the velocity of M2 has perhaps experienced less volatility in terms of changes in the number of times per year that each dollar of M2 was traded in GDP transactions. Thus, suppose that we can assume that the velocity of M2 will be between 0.8 and 2.5. Then, we can make predictions about possible ranges of values for the velocity of M1.

For example, suppose that we know the values of the monetary aggregates M1 and M2, and the ratio of M2 to M1 in this hypothetical example equals 2/1, or 2. If M2 is twice as large as M1, then the velocity of M1 must be twice as large as the velocity of M2. From the first quarter of 1959 through the first quarter of 2013, the velocity of M2 has varied between roughly 1.53 times per year and roughly 2.14 times per year. This range of variability of approximately 0.61 times per year is much less than the variability in the velocity of M1, which varied between approximately 3.5 times per year and approximately 10.4 times per year, a range of variability of nearly 7.0 times per year.

So, if there was a period between the first quarter of 1959 and the first quarter of 2013 when M2 happened to be twice as large as M1, we know not only that the velocity of M1 must have been twice as large as the velocity of M2 during that period, but we can also use the relatively narrow range of values for the velocity of M2 to determine possible values for the velocity of M1 without further data. Because the velocity of M2 was never less than 1.50 times per year during the period, if the velocity of M1 is twice as large as the velocity of M2 in this hypothetical example, then we know that the velocity of M1 must have been at least 3.0 times per year. Likewise, because the velocity of M2 was never more than 2.14 times per year, then the velocity of M1 must have been no greater than 4.28 times per year if the velocity of M1 must have been twice the velocity of M2.

On the other hand, if M2 happens to be five times as large as M1, then we know that the velocity of M1 must be five times as large as the velocity of M2. With the velocity of M2 being no less than 1.50 times per year in the period discussed above, then the velocity of M1 must be no less than 7.5

times per year. Since we know that the velocity of M2 was less than 2.14 times per year during the aforementioned sample period, then we know that the velocity of M1 must have been less than 10.70 times per year.

WITH M1 AND M2 NOT AS CONTROL VARIABLES

Much of the analysis holds even if the Federal Reserve cannot completely control the size of either monetary aggregate. Just the knowledge of the values for M1 and M2 within a period without assuming that the Fed can set values for either monetary aggregate still provides sufficient information to determine the ratio of the velocities of the two aggregates. Without assuming a fairly high degree in the predictability of the velocity of money as ascribed to the monetarist school of thought by Burton and Lombra (2006, p. 516-517), we can narrow down possible values for the velocity of M1 by simply calculating what the velocity of M1 would be given the values for M1, M2, and maximum and minimum values for the velocity of M2 which was less volatile than the velocity of M1.

Without knowledge of the exact values of M1, M2, and their velocities, policymakers could forecast the values of M1 and M2 (over which most would probably assume the central bank has at least some control) and forecast the velocity of M2 (which may be more stable than the velocity of M1) as part of the process in forecasting the velocity of M1. Obviously, rather than using maximum and minimum values over the entire sample period for the velocity of M2, a narrower spread of forecasted values for M2 (which did not vary as much over the sample period) for a short time horizon would enable a narrower range of values that could be predicted for the velocity of M1.

One could take the view, however, that the general public has considerable influence, if not outright control, over the sizes of the monetary aggregates. In order for a dollar to be part of either M1 or M2, the general public must decide to hold that dollar as an asset that would count either (1) toward M2 but not M1 (if the asset is part of M2 but not M1) or (2) toward both M1 and M2 (if the asset is part of both M1 and M2). In this view, the Federal Reserve can attempt to influence the general public's decision of how many dollars to hold by trying to alter interest rates, but ultimately the decision of how purchasing power is stored, be it in methods part of M1 and M2, part of M2 but not M1, or not part of either M1 or M2, is the general public's. If one takes the view that the general public has the final say over how large 'the money supply' is through its decision of how to hold purchasing power, then suppose further that decisions made by the general public are not always very predictable with a high degree of accuracy.

The reader should also interpret the results for finding possible ranges of values for M1 velocity with appropriate caution, given that according to Mishkin (2004, p. 426), the Federal Open Market Committee (FOMC) deemphasized monetary aggregate targets for M2 (and other possible target variables) starting in or around 1993 due to a weakened link between M2 and other macroeconomic variables. Mishkin (2004, p. 426) also points out that in 1987, the Fed publicly dropped targets for M1 for reasons at least partially similar. Mishkin (2004, pp. 425-426) notes that in late 1982 the FOMC switched back to a practice more similar to interest-rate smoothing than to the nonborrowed reserves targeting and (at least nominal) monetary-aggregate targeting practice employed from late 1979 through late 1982. (Baumol and Blinder (2012, p. 298) have time series graphs for the velocity of M1 and the velocity of M2. The graphs show the velocity of M1 detrending in the early 1980s and the velocity of M2 abruptly beginning to trend upward either in the late 1980s or the early 1990s. These changes in the velocities of M1 and M2 likely deal with the deteriorations in linkages between each of the aggregates and other economic variables of interest, such as real GDP, price levels, inflation, and nominal GDP.)

If the velocities of both M1 and M2 and the money supply levels for both M1 and M2 are at least at times not predictable, then movements in money velocities and the monetary aggregates could provide useful information for policymakers and others about changes in economic conditions. The information may be particularly useful when the changes are not extremely short term. For example, the recent surge in M1 (especially checkable deposits) which began in 2008 (particularly in the second half of that year) where the M1 money supply grew at a faster percentage rate than the M2 money supply (which has important implications for the velocity of both M1 and M2) could provide important information about the financial crisis or at least the general public's reaction to the financial crisis and the public's reaction to the recession and the sluggish recovery.

It could potentially also provide useful information about why the recovery has been so lackluster and what is likely to happen next. The information provided could be so useful that it is perhaps surprising that more attention is not paid either to money velocity or to the sizes of the monetary aggregates, at least outside of some policy circles, academic circles, and financial circles. (Many in academic circles may pay much more attention to money supply levels than to the velocity of those monetary aggregates. Information in Dornbusch, Fischer, and Startz (2008, pp. 386-387) leads me to believe that some in financial circles may possibly pay much more attention to the velocity of M2 than to the velocity of M1.) However, in light of the caveats in the previous paragraph, appropriate skepticism will be helpful.

To give an example of the impact of changes that may have been unexpected, the reader should realize that the decline in M2 velocity from about 2.14 times per year in the second quarter and the third quarter of 1997 (or even from very roughly around 1.9 times per year in each quarter of the year 2007) to about 1.5 times per year means that nominal GDP is substantially lower than it would have been had the velocity of M2 remained around 2.0 times per year because of the large size of M2 – more than 10 trillion dollars as of this writing. People may not have expected a sharp decrease in the velocity of M1 either. However, the velocity of M1 began to decrease nearly every quarter starting in the first quarter of 2008. Had the velocity of M1 remained at around 10.3 or 10.4 times per year, expansionary monetary policy would have been much more successful at keeping aggregate demand growth and employment growth on track without the need for such a rapid increase in the money supply.

THE MONEY MULTIPLIER IN RECENT YEARS VERSUS THE GREAT DEPRESSION

As pointed out earlier, information in Burton and Lombra (2006, p.485) notes that during the Great Depression, excess reserves soared past the $2 billion mark after totaling only $25 million a few years earlier. Something similar also happened following the most recent financial crisis and Great Recession in the United States. During both periods, the ratio of excess reserves to checkable deposits increased. However, according to Burton and Lombra (2006, p, 485), the ratio of currency to checkable deposits almost doubled during the Great Depression to about 33 per cent (up from roughly 17 per cent). On the other hand, as noted above, the ratio decreased in the aftermath of the most recent U.S. financial crisis.

As Burton and Lombra (2006, p. 485) note, defaults on loans from banks (that probably increased sharply early in the Great Depression) led to depositors growing more concerned about bank solvency and thus resulted in withdrawals from banks. Therefore, it is nearly certain that U.S. checkable deposits declined early in the Great Depression. A decrease in checkable deposits early during the

Great Depression would be consistent with a decrease in nominal M1. From 1929 to 1933 in the U.S., nominal M1 decreased by more than twenty-five per cent, as implied by Dornbusch, Fischer, and Startz (2008, p. 462), and noted by Burton and Lombra (2006, p. 485) and others. (The reader should realize that prior to 1933, no deposit insurance existed in the United States, as per Burton and Lombra (2006, p. 234).) With excess reserves skyrocketing and checkable deposits almost surely falling, the ratio of excess reserves to checkable deposits e almost certainly rose early in the Great Depression. Assuming that both e and c rose, the money multiplier would have fallen during the Great Depression in the United States.

Although the money multiplier also fell in the recent downturn and sluggish recovery in the U.S., it may be worth emphasizing that checkable deposits increased after the velocity of M1 reached its peak. Decades after the successful implementation of deposit insurance, people in the economy may view insured checkable deposits as a safe way of storing purchasing power. The aforementioned temporary removal of the ceiling of deposit insurance on certain types of highly liquid deposits may have nearly guaranteed continued growth in checkable deposits. Thus, c, the ratio of currency to checkable deposits, was likely below values that it would have taken had deposit insurance not existed in the United States during the most recent financial crisis and its aftermath. In turn, the money multiplier in the U.S. exhibited values higher than they likely would have been without deposit insurance, despite declining as e soared. In other words, although the M1 money multiplier declined in the Great Recession and the Not-So-Great Recovery as e skyrocketed, the decline in the M1 money multiplier would have been larger had c risen as it did in the Great Depression rather than having fallen.

Recently, both the M1 money multiplier and the M2 money multiplier in the United States fell. Using data from www.economagic.com, I calculate the M1 money multiplier as M1 divided by the monetary base (total reserves plus currency) and the M2 money multiplier as M2 divided by the monetary base. (The monetary base, M1, and M2 data are seasonally adjusted.) The M1 money multiplier has generally trended downward over the sample period which begins in January 1959, when the M1 multiplier was about 3.4. The M1 multiplier fell below 3.0 (but barely below) for the first time in the sample period in November 1977. After reaching a local maximum around 3.25 in April 1987, the general downward trend in the M1 money multiplier resumed. April 1989 was the last month in the sample period when the M1 money multiplier was greater than 3.0, while August 1999 was the last month when the M1 multiplier was greater than 2.0.

In August 2008, the M1 money multiplier declined from about 1.69 the month before to roughly 1.67. Then, a more rapid decline ensued. In September 2008, the money multiplier fell to roughly 1.62, then to approximately 1.30 in October 2008, about 1.05 in November 2008, and approximately 0.97 in December 2008 (the first month (at least in the sample period beginning in 1959) when the money multiplier was less than 1.0). After February 2009, the M1 money multiplier was below 1.0 for the remainder of the sample period. Given that it took two years (April 1987 to April 1989) for the M1 money multiplier to trend downward from around 3.25 to approximately 3.00 and it took about a decade (April 1989 to approximately September 1999) for the M1 money multiplier to fall from 3.00 to 2.00 in approximate numbers, the decrease in the M1 money multiplier from around 1.62 to roughly 0.97 in three months (from September 2008 through December 2008) seems very rapid, relatively speaking.

The M1 money multiplier reached a minimum within the sample period of about 0.74 in June 2011. Afterward, the money multiplier increased to about 0.93 in October 2012, but this is only a little more than half of the value of the M1 money multiplier in August 2008. At the minimum of approximately 0.74, the M1 money multiplier was less than half of its value in August 2008. After the rebound in October 2012, the M1 multiplier fell somewhat to around 0.82 in May 2013. Could the decline in the M1 money multiplier over most of the sample period have been due in part to increases in excess reserves and currency to guard against potential risks due to greater leveraging?

While the general trend of the M1 money multiplier is clearly downward over the sample period (despite some periods when the M1 money multiplier increased somewhat), initially the M2 money multiplier generally trended upward (despite some periods when the M2 multiplier decreased) from January 1959, when it was approximately 7.09, through March 1985, when it was roughly 12.43. After that, the general trend for the M2 money multiplier was clearly downward. June 1987 was the last month in the sample period in which the M2 money multiplier exceeded 12.0. April 1991 was the last month in which the M2 money multiplier was at least 11.0 (after briefly dipping below 11.0 in February 1991 and March 1991). September 1992 was the last month where the M2 money multiplier was at least 10.0. December 1993 was the first month since the mid-1960s in which the M2 money multiplier was less than 9.0.

From December 1993 through November 1999, the M2 money multiplier fluctuated between 8.04 and 8.98. This represented relative stability in the M2 multiplier, varying by less than 0.95 over more than five years. By contrast, in the early 1990s and the early part of the mid-1990s, data from www.economagic.com and the author's calculations indicate that, as implied above, it took less than two years for the M2 money multiplier to fall from 11 to 10 and from 10 to 9 in the 1990s. From November 1999 through November 2007, the M2 money multiplier fluctuated between 7.78 and 8.98. The M2 money multiplier rose back above 9.0 from December 2007, when it was roughly 9.03, through August 2008, when it was approximately 9.17, reaching a local maximum of approximately 9.33 in April 2008.

Just as the rapid decline in the M1 money multiplier began in September 2008, the M2 multiplier started plummeting in the same month, when the M2 multiplier fell to about 8.65. Over the next three months (October 2008, November 2008, and December 2008), approximations of the M2 money multiplier fell in rough numbers to approximately 7.03, 5.57, and 4.94. Afterward, the M2 money multiplier fluctuated between 4.67 and 5.33 through September 2009 before falling further. The last month in the sample period when the M2 money multiplier was at least 4.0 was February 2011. The M2 money multiplier reached a local minimum in June 2011 at roughly 3.43. In October 2012, the M2 money multiplier was about 3.92 as the M1 money multiplier was approaching, although remaining below, 1.0. The M2 money multiplier started declining again in November 2012 and was around 3.39, the minimum in the sample period, in May 2013.

Both the M1 money multiplier and the M2 money multiplier started much more rapid decline in the same month, September 2008 (and even faster decline in October 2008), and they both reached at least local minimum values in the same month, June 2011. From August 2008 (just before the faster decline) through June 2011, the M1 money multiplier fell from about 1.67 to about 0.74, a decrease of about 0.93 'units.' The M2 money multiplier fell from approximately 9.17 to roughly 3.43, a decrease of roughly 5.74 'units.' The percentage decreases in the M1 money multiplier and the M2 money multiplier during these periods are approximately 55.7 per cent and approximately 62.6 per cent. Could the fact that the calculated percentage decrease in the M2 money multiplier exceeded the calculated percentage decrease in the M1 money multiplier help in our analysis?

It may be useful to note that the calculations for the money multiplier presented above could be thought of as average money multipliers rather than marginal money multipliers. When little volatility exists in the ratio of currency to checkable deposits, the ratio of excess reserves to checkable deposits, the ratio of required reserves to checkable deposits, the ratio of the sum of time deposits and savings deposits in M2 to checkable deposits, and the ratio of the sum of individual money market mutual funds, money market deposit accounts, and all remaining components of M2 to checkable deposits; then the average money multiplier and the marginal money multiplier are essentially the same for our purposes.

However, when considerable variation in any of these ratios exists, then a substantial difference could exist between the marginal and average money multipliers. The average money multiplier is simply the ratio of the money supply (either M1 or M2) divided by the monetary base, while the marginal money multiplier is the change in the monetary aggregate (either M1 or M2) divided by the change in the monetary base, ideally over a relatively short time period. In other words, the appropriate marginal money multiplier would very likely come *much* closer than the corresponding average money multiplier in showing the impact on either M1 or M2 resulting from a decision by the Federal Reserve either to increase or decrease the monetary base through open market operations when the ratios mentioned above are *not* approximately constant. (The marginal money multiplier for a period may not be known with high accuracy before a change in the monetary base is implemented.)

I am not aware if others have worked on marginal money multipliers. Early work on calculating monthly marginal money multipliers for both M1 and M2 shows that the marginal multipliers are much more volatile than the monthly average money multipliers. For example, the marginal M1 money multiplier values from February 1959 through November 2012 range from a low of roughly -53.9 to a high of nearly +117, while the average M1 money multipliers range only from a low of about +0.74 to a high of about +3.50. Likewise, the marginal M2 money multipliers range from a low of nearly -762.8 to a high of about +265.1, while the average M2 money multipliers vary much less, from a low of roughly +3.39 to a high of roughly +12.43. Note that the average multipliers must be greater than zero if the monetary aggregates are greater than zero and the monetary base is greater than zero.

Perhaps the greater volatility for the marginal money multipliers when compared with the average money multipliers is to be expected because it could take some time for the general public to adjust its portfolio to its desired holdings of M1 components, non-M1 components of M2, and other assets not part of either M1 or M2 following a change in the monetary base initiated by the Federal Reserve (although we may question how long it takes to adjust between non-M1 components of M2 and components of M1 which are also part of M2). It could also take time for commercial banks and other depository institutions to adjust to the desired amount of excess reserves.

Future work could calculate marginal money multipliers with data converted from monthly data either to quarterly or annual data. This would smooth out some of the short-term fluctuations in the monthly calculations for marginal money multipliers. The Federal Reserve should be well aware that the multiple expansion of credit process of lending, funds being re-deposited in the banking system, more lending and re-depositing takes time. More work could be done on how changes in the monetary base have had an impact months, quarters, or years later on the money supply.

TURNING POINTS IN THE TREND OF THE MOVEMENT IN M2 VELOCITY

If there are any 'hard sells' left who still need more convincing that the growth rate of the money supply can have a potential impact on the velocity of money (some of whom may believe that the velocity of money is essentially constant in the short term and thus does not depend on the money supply), consider re-dividing the quarterly-data sample period into sub-sample periods based on when the velocity of M2 changes from generally increasing to generally decreasing or from generally decreasing to generally increasing rather than basing the divisions on when the general direction of M1 velocity changes from generally increasing to generally decreasing or *vice versa.* Although the sub-sample periods using data for the velocity of M1 were first identified in Chapter 3, the discussion of possible sub-sample periods using the velocity of M2 appears in this chapter because the distinction between M1 versus M2 could be clearer following the discussions of the money supply process, the money multipliers, and possible portfolio changes appearing in the present chapter. Further, this book emphasizes the use of M1 to represent 'money' most of the time.

Early in the overall quarterly-data sample period, a potentially important difference emerges when looking at data from www.economagic.com. Comparing values of velocity from the first quarter of 1960 and the fourth quarter of 1964, the velocity of M2 decreased from about 1.76 times per year to roughly 1.60 times per year, with M2 velocity decreasing in thirteen quarters out of the nineteen quarters from the second quarter of 1960 through the fourth quarter of 1964. Over the same time period, the velocity of M1 trended upward from roughly 3.77 times per year in the first quarter of 1960 to roughly 4.23 times per year in the fourth quarter of 1964. (The reader may want to note that the velocity of M1 was almost 4.25 times per year in the third quarter of 1964, one quarter before when it was about 4.23 times per year.) The velocity of M1 increased for sixteen out of nineteen quarters after the first quarter of 1960 through the fourth quarter of 1964, while the velocity of M2 was generally decreasing, falling in thirteen of nineteen quarters.

Perhaps the fourth quarter of 1964, a clear local minimum for the velocity of M2, would have been the last quarter of a sub-sample period had this study focused on M2 as the main monetary aggregate rather than M1. By focusing on M1, the fourth quarter of 1964 did not mark the end of a sub-sample period because the velocity of M1 had increased the previous fifteen quarters and increased the following nine quarters. Further, the decrease in the velocity of M1 in the fourth quarter of 1964 was relatively small.

The reader must recall that the only difference in the equation used to calculate the velocity of M1 and the equation used to calculate the velocity of M2 is the value for either M1 or M2 in the denominator. The numerator, nominal GDP, is exactly the same when calculating the velocity of either M1 or M2 for a particular time period. Obviously, then, the money supply level must have an impact on velocity. But, the divergent directions of the velocity of M1 (generally increasing) and the velocity of M2 (generally decreasing) after the first quarter of 1960 through the fourth quarter of 1964 show that the *growth rate* of the money supply can have an important impact on the velocity of money.

Data from www.economagic.com and the author's calculations show that the quarterly average M2 money supply grew at a faster rate than the quarterly average M1 money supply over this time period, roughly 41 per cent versus about 14 per cent. Again, because the numerators for M1 velocity and M2 velocity in all of the calculations of velocity are identical in each period whether the velocity of M1 or the velocity of M2 is being calculated, the difference in growth rates of M1 versus M2 explains why the velocity of M1 increased most of the time after the first quarter of 1960 through the fourth quarter of 1964 while the velocity of M2 decreased most of the time. Both M1 and M2 increased in general throughout the period in question, with quarterly average M1 increasing most quarters and quarterly average M2 increasing every quarter. But, with the substantially different growth rates, quarterly average M1 grew at a slower rate than nominal GDP over the period, resulting in an increase in M1 velocity, while quarterly average M2 increased at a faster rate than nominal GDP, thus decreasing M2 velocity.

Throughout the rest of the sample period, the turning point in the velocity of M2 usually occurs in a different quarter than the occurrence of the turning point in the velocity of M1. For example, a local maximum for the velocity of M2 occurs in the first quarter of 1981, two quarters before a local maximum for the velocity of M1 in the third quarter of 1981. A subsequent local minimum for the velocity of M2, in the first quarter of 1983, occurs one quarter before a local minimum for the velocity of M1. Another local maximum for the velocity of M2 occurred in the third quarter of 1984, which was one quarter before a local maximum for the velocity of M1 in the fourth quarter of 1984. The next local minimum for the velocity of M2 was in the first quarter of 1987, one quarter before the corresponding local minimum of the velocity of M1. (While M1 velocity reached a local maximum in the second quarter of 1990 marking a clear turning point with M1 velocity falling the next fourteen quarters, the decline in M2 velocity after the second quarter of 1990 lasted only three quarters and was relatively small.)

The next clear turning point after which M2 velocity would decrease for eighteen out of the next twenty-three quarters was the third quarter of 1997, also the maximum for the sample period, when M2 velocity reached roughly 2.14 times per year. This maximum occurred thirteen quarters prior to the local maximum for the velocity of M1, at about 9.27, in the fourth quarter of 2000. The next turning point for the velocity of both M1 and M2 occurred in the same quarter, the second quarter of 2003, after which both velocities were increasing for at least three consecutive quarters. The following turning point for the velocity of M2 occurred in the second quarter of 2006, at roughly 1.96. This was six quarters prior to the maximum value of the velocity of M1 within the sample period at roughly 10.37 times per year, in the fourth quarter of 2007. Because the denominators are the only difference in the fractions used to calculate the velocity of money for M1 and for M2 in a period, the different growth rates of the two measures of the money supply must be causing the turning points in the velocity of M1 and the velocity of M2 usually to happen in different quarters.

APPLICATION TO NDVMSL THEORY AND THE ROLE FOR FISCAL POLICY

The finding that the growth rate in the money supply can have an impact on the velocity of money as discussed above is certainly consistent with a non-decreasing-velocity money supply level (NDVMSL) as discussed elsewhere in this book. Recall that the NDVMSL postulates that a money supply level exists beyond which further increases in the money supply *must* cause the velocity of that measure of the money supply to fall. The thinking behind a NDVMSL is based on the ideas of (1) a maximum amount of real GDP that an economy can produce in the short term, (2) some prices not being able to adjust rapidly to long-run equilibrium levels following an increase in the money supply due to contracts and other sources of rigidities, (3) at least some in the economy willing to hold more dollars in their portfolios but not for the purpose of increasing nominal GDP spending in the current quarter, and (4) a possibility that, in the short run, nominal GDP may increase by a smaller percentage than the money supply, in light of the first three ideas.

The idea that a maximum money supply level (the NDVMSL) may exist in the short term beyond which any further increase in the money supply will result in a decrease in the velocity of money may seem trivial for someone who assumes that the velocity of money is not necessarily constant in the short term. However, the theory of a NDVMSL, if it is true, could be important for policymakers and others interested in monetary policy and more generally stabilization policy to consider when trying to offset the negative impact of the most recent financial crisis in the United States on production as measured by real GDP and on employment. Since stimulus measures passed in 2008 (near the end of the second term of President George W. Bush) and in 2009 (at the beginning of the first term of President Barack Obama) as discussed in Krugman and Wells (2009, pp. 351, 362-363), Baumol and Blinder (2012, p. 222) and elsewhere, much of the effort to further stimulate the economy has been in the form of expansionary monetary policy by keeping interest rates low. Wiseman (2012) points out that at least one measure of total government spending actually decreased 4.5 per cent from the second quarter of 2009 through the second quarter of 2012.

If a NDVMSL does exist, then the existence of a NDVMSL may imply a limit to how much further additions to the money supply can stimulate spending and production in the economy in the short term. In turn, then, the possible existence of a NDVMSL seems to fit the data well in the U.S. economy post-2007 (and during some other periods) where the U.S. economy was above the NDVMSL most quarters since then, if such a level exists. The possibility of a NDVMSL serves as a call for further expansionary fiscal policy in the form of tax cuts and increases in government spending to promote increases in employment and production. Now that the payroll tax holiday has expired (noted by many including Schwartz (2013) and others), that leads to an increase in taxes paid by most working people who, as a result, have less available to spend, all other things equal. The expiration of the payroll tax holiday comes after decreases in total government spending discussed above. Moreover, phasing in sequestration spending cuts (noted by Malewitz (2013) and others) also implies a decrease in incomes for at least some in the economy. Thus, fiscal policy may actually be moving in the wrong direction for stimulating the economy.

While it is true that increases in government spending and tax reductions, all other things equal, lead to an increase in the budget deficit, note that based on information from CNBC (2014) on August

6, 2014, the federal government can borrow money for ten years at an interest rate of around 2.5 per cent. Thus, the federal government running a deficit at such a low interest rate would lead to little, if any, crowding out of private sector economic activity. Strategic fiscal policy could be the best bet for trying to stimulate the U.S. economy in the short term. After all, if a NDVMSL does exist, then following the rapid increase in the money supply starting in 2008, the U.S. economy has plenty of dollars. Now, it is time to get the dollars moving faster again!

CHAPTER SEVEN REFERENCES

Baumol, W. J. and Blinder, A. S. (2012) *Macroeconomics: Principles and Policy*, twelfth edition. South-Western Cengage Learning, Mason, Ohio

Burton, M. and Lombra, R. (2006) *The Financial System and the Economy: Principles of Money and Banking*, fourth edition. Thomson South-Western, Mason, Ohio.

CNBC. (2014) Ten-Year U.S. Treasury Interest Rate Data. August 6, 2014.

Dornbusch, R., Fischer, S., and Startz, R. (2008) *Macroeconomics*, tenth edition, McGraw-Hill Irwin, Boston, Massachusetts.

Hartman, H. C. (2012) "Questions about the Changing Relationship between Total Reserves (or the Monetary Base), M1, and Real GDP in the U.S." *International Journal of Accounting Information Science and Leadership*, vol. 5, iss. 13, pp. 47-59.

Krugman, P. and Wells, R. (2009) *Macroeconomics*, second edition. Worth Publishers, New York, New York.

Malewitz, J. (2013) "Universities Scale Back Research." *Atlanta Journal-Constitution*, April 14, 2013, p. A16.

Mishkin, F. S. (2004) *The Economics of Money, Banking, and Financial Markets*, seventh edition. Pearson Addison Wesley, Boston, Massachusetts.

Schwartz, N. D. (2013) "Higher Payroll Tax Saps Buying Power." *Atlanta Journal- Constitution*, February 10, 2013, p. A2.

Wiseman, P. (2012) "Weak Recovery Marked." *Atlanta Journal-Constitution*, August 16, 2012, p. A8.

www.economagic.com

www.fdic.gov/deposit/deposits/unlimited/expiration.html

CHAPTER 8

VELOCITY - A REVIEW AND A PREVIEW

OVERVIEW

Much work remains to improve our understanding of fluctuations in the velocity of money. But, the first part of that journey in this book (i.e., delving into the recent sharp decline in the velocity of money in the United States as well as other fluctuations in velocity) is nearly complete. Before finishing, let's take some time to review briefly some of the highlights and findings of this study. Afterward, with the benefit of the material covered in the first seven chapters and the brief review, this chapter raises questions about the velocity of money in the main schools of macroeconomic thought. Then, with the review and additional comments in mind, we can better address future work.

A RECAP

The first part of this chapter is primarily a review, followed by a section focusing more on work to be done. This book is among the works noting the recent, rapid plummeting of the velocity of money in the United States, as discussed in Chapter 1 and elsewhere. If the velocity of money falls sufficiently, then expansionary monetary policy alone may accompany either no change in nominal GDP or even a decrease in nominal GDP. In either case, it is unlikely that real GDP would increase, contrary to one of the probable goals of the monetary expansion. (For completeness, if velocity falls but does not fall sufficiently, nominal GDP will increase following an increase in the money supply, but growth may be inadequate. This situation can describe the U.S. economy most, if not all, quarters from the third quarter of 2009 through the fourth quarter of 2013, while the possibility of rising money supply but falling nominal GDP due to falling velocity characterized the U.S. economy during part of 2008 and part of 2009 based on data from www.economagic.com.)

With many interest rates in the United States being relatively low, the U.S. appears to be in a situation close to a liquidity trap (discussed in Chapters 2 and 4), but not in a complete liquidity trap.

In this scenario, large percentage increases in the money supply, all other things equal, are currently accompanied by relatively small percentage increases in both real GDP and nominal GDP (and the deflator).

At least some macroeconomic theory discussed in this study and many others suggests that expansionary fiscal policies, meaning tax reductions and increases in government spending, can be near their greatest effectiveness (compared to expansionary monetary policies) in this type of economy. Chapter 2 noted that expansionary monetary policy can be used to keep interest rates low to minimize the burden of greater budget deficits resulting from expansionary fiscal policy. But when an economy is either in a liquidity trap or near a liquidity trap, monetary policy would be largely, if not exclusively, in a support role of keeping interest rates low.

Chapters 2 and 4 also discussed spending capacity, which deals with the amount of GDP (in nominal terms) that could be purchased. Chapter 2 clearly distinguishes spending capacity from actual aggregate demand, measured by nominal GDP. (Baumol and Blinder (2012, pp. 298-299) use nominal GDP as a measure of aggregate demand.) Sometimes actual aggregate demand fails to keep pace with spending capacity when the money supply increases, resulting in a decrease in velocity.

A review of data suggests that rapid increases in the M1 money supply in the U.S. are often associated with decreases in the velocity of M1. Does this imply that a money supply level exists (at least at some points in time) where further increases in the money supply automatically lead to decreases in velocity? In other words, does a non-decreasing-velocity money supply level (NDVMSL) exist as discussed above? The evidence considered thus far suggests, at least to me, that a NDVMSL could have existed during at least some periods in the United States. If a NDVMSL does exist, then the M1 money supply in the U.S. has been at levels greater than the NDVMSL during nearly every quarter of the last six years, which would help to explain why the velocity of M1 has been decreasing. Readers may refer back to Chapters 3, 4, and 6 for a review. (Readers may also refer back to Chapter 3 for discussion of U.S. data from the Great Depression/World War II era and identification of sub-sample periods beginning with the year 1959.) A possible first step in finding the NDVMSL appears in the 'In-Chapter Appendix' toward the end of this chapter.

Financial crises have often been associated with sizable decreases in the velocity of money. Thus, some likely causes of financial crises were discussed in Chapter 5, as well as the presentation of a timeline of events that may be causes of and responses to the most recent financial crisis in the United

States. Chapter 5 also notes that innovation and changes in financial regulation can cause changes in velocity.

The theory of a NDVMSL assumes that the money supply level itself can influence the velocity of money. Therefore, the study considers the velocity of money as a function of the nominal money supply and other variables, one at a time, in Chapter 6. When compared with other variables such as the price level, real GDP, and the real money supply, changes in the nominal money supply perform best or second-best of the seven variables considered during many of the sub-sample periods identified in terms of minimizing the sum of squared residuals in regression equations with only one independent variable and a constant on the right side of the equation. Thus, it appears likely that during a subset of these sub-sample periods (in five of the six sub-sample periods in which nominal M1 was best or second-best of the seven variables considered at minimizing the sum of squared residuals) where in this subset the estimated coefficient for nominal M1 was less than zero in the equation for the velocity of M1, changes in the nominal money supply could be explaining much of the variability of the velocity of M1.

The exception not in the subset is the first sub-sample period, where the estimated coefficient for M1 was positive, despite the use of nominal M1 minimizing the sum of squared residuals of the seven variables considered. The first sub-sample period was also by far the longest sub-sample period, spanning more than twenty years. A negative estimated coefficient for the nominal M1 money supply implies that an increase in the money supply would, all other things equal, be associated with a decrease in the velocity of M1. This is consistent with the NDVMSL theory, but does not prove the theory.

Chapter 6 also observed that when the average quarterly growth rate of nominal M1 (as calculated in that chapter) was greater than or equal to 2.4 per cent, as it was in four sub-sample periods, the velocity of M1 trended downward during these sub-sample periods.

In five of the other six sub-sample periods when the average nominal money supply growth rate was less than 2.4 per cent, the velocity of M1 trended upward. (Recall that the growth rates of nominal M1 are not annualized.)

This book also provides information about the money multipliers and the money supply process in Chapter 7. In so doing, it discusses the relationship between the M1 money supply and the M2 money supply. One reason for considering the money multipliers and the money supply process is that such an examination can show how aggregate movements between different forms of holding purchasing power can impact the sizes of the monetary aggregates. Chapter 7 noted that surging excess reserves would, all other things equal, cause the money multiplier to decrease.

Chapter 7 showed that movements between holdings of assets in M2, but not M1, and assets in both M1 and M2 could have an impact on the velocity of M1. That chapter observed that the timing of switching from a period of generally increasing velocity to generally decreasing velocity and *vice versa* for both M1 velocity and M2 velocity in the quarterly data sample often occurred in different quarters. In other words, if we would focus on M2 velocity, then the starting and ending quarters for sub-sample periods of M2 velocity would often differ from those of M1 velocity. That must be due to differences in percentage changes in M1 and M2, because the numerator, nominal GDP, is identical each quarter in the algebraic definitions of the velocity of both M1 and M2 in each quarter. A method for estimating possible ranges of values for the velocity of M1 given values for M1 and M2 and likely values for the velocity of M2 was also discussed.

Chapter 7 also distinguished between the average money multiplier and the marginal money multiplier, where the average money multiplier is the ratio of the total monetary aggregate divided by the total monetary base, while the marginal money multiplier is the change in the monetary aggregate divided by the change in the monetary base. Early results suggest that the marginal money multipliers for both M1 and M2 are *much* more volatile than the average money multipliers.

ADDITIONAL COMMENTS ON VELOCITY IN THE THREE MAJOR SCHOOLS

The study also considered in Chapters 2 and 3 the velocity of money within the context of the three major schools of macroeconomic thought: the classical school, the Keynesian school, and the monetarist school. If the NDVMSL theory holds, it is perhaps the antithesis of the classical view of the velocity of money, which views velocity as being either constant or nearly constant in the short term in most cases. By contrast, if the NDVMSL exists, and if the money supply level is greater than the NDVMSL, then the velocity of money must decrease. But, in that case, the velocity of money is not constant in the short term.

Information in Mishkin (2004, p. 524, 533) implies that the velocity of money is unpredictable in Keynesian analysis due to changes in the quantity of money demanded resulting from changes in interest rates. By contrast, velocity is predictable in monetarist analysis, at least to some extent, according to Baumol and Blinder (2012, p. 298) and Burton and Lombra (2006, pp. 516-517). In a sense, the NDVMSL theory can be thought of as being in between the monetarist view of velocity and the Keynesian view of velocity. Can NDVMSL theory help to bridge the chasm between monetarist and Keynesian macroeconomic analysis?

The NDVMSL theory assumes like the Keynesian school (and the monetarist school) that the velocity of money is not necessarily constant in the short term. However, the NDVMSL theory assumes a degree of predictability in the velocity of money (at least within a sub-sample period) that is probably greater than in the Keynesian view, although less predictable than in the monetarist view. Information in Baumol and Blinder (2012, pp. 298-299) and Burton and Lombra (2006, pp. 516-517) suggests, at least to me, that at least one form of monetarism viewed the velocity of money to be predictable to such a degree that it may have been sufficient to use a forecast of velocity, a target for nominal GDP, and the equation of exchange as the only guides for monetary policy. NDVMSL theory does not necessarily assume that much predictability in velocity.

However, results from showing the velocity of M1 as a function of the money supply seem to indicate that some degree of predictability in the velocity of money often exists, at least within a sub-sample period. The assumption of at least some degree of predictability in the velocity of money within at least some sub-sample periods was one of the reasons for the regressions in Chapter 6 for the velocity of M1 with one variable and a constant on the right side of each equation. Moreover, part of Chapter 7 dealt with using the ratio of M1 to M2 and possible ranges of values for the velocity of M2 to find a possible range of values for the velocity of M1.

A change in the velocity of money implies a change in the ratio of GDP spending (nominal GDP) to the quantity of money held (and perhaps a whole lot more). But why would such a ratio change? If money is held strictly for transaction purposes and if most transactions were planned in advance, then it may well be reasonable to assume that velocity would be nearly constant in the short term, as in the classical school of macroeconomic thought. However, this study notes that, based on data from www.economagic.com accessed October 15, 2014 and the author's calculations, the velocity of M1 has fallen by approximately forty-two per cent after the fourth quarter of 2007 as the M1 money supply has surged in the U.S.

The classical school as described by Mishkin (2004, pp. 518-519) allows for changes in velocity due to changes in technology applied to the payments system. These may also include institutional factors (such as the use of credit cards versus cash). However, improvements in technology (or at least those applied to the payments system) would likely increase velocity, all other things equal, as it would be easier for dollars to trade. Recently, the velocities of M1 and M2 have plummeted in the U.S., and it is difficult to imagine a deterioration in technology consistent with the classical school of macroeconomic thought that could have produced such a large decrease in the velocity of money in recent years. As Chapter 5 noted, the velocity of money often decreases during or after financial crises. Could that have been a factor in the recent sharp downturn in the velocity of M1 in the U.S.?

Mishkin (2004, p. 521 and 524) observed that Keynes stopped assuming that the velocity of money is nearly constant in the short term, instead at least implicitly assuming that increases in real GDP and interest rates individually, all other things equal, would be associated with an increase in the velocity of money. As might be expected in a recession or a depression, decreases in real GDP and/or interest rates, all other things equal, would be associated with decreases in the velocity of money.

According to Mishkin (2004, p. 528-532), Friedman found that money demand depended little, if at all, on interest rates, echoing classical analysis of Irving Fisher, according to Mishkin (2004, pp. 519, 523). Thus, interest rates do not play an important role in determining velocity in the work of Milton Friedman, according to Mishkin (2004, p. 531). (Laidler (1993, p. 144) notes that Brunner and Meltzer (1963) (who many classify as monetarists) find that interest rates can impact velocity.)

If my reading of Mishkin (2004, p. 531) is correct, real money demand in the work of Milton Friedman is mainly a function of permanent income, and velocity is mainly a function of permanent income and current real GDP (after substituting a general functional form of permanent income for real money demand (*M*/*P*) in the algebraic definition of velocity). More specifically, Mishkin's (2004, p. 531) equation for velocity in the work of Milton Friedman is

$$(8.1)\ V = Y/\mathrm{f}(\mathrm{Yp}),$$

where Yp is permanent income (although Mishkin (2004, p. 531) uses a subscript for the 'p' in permanent income, and Mishkin has a different equation number for this equation). Mishkin (2004, p. 532) notes that in Milton Friedman's analysis, velocity is positively correlated with real GDP, because permanent income in the denominator (in a general functional form) of the equation for velocity fails to increase as much in an expansion as real GDP, which is in the numerator of the expression for velocity.

Also, if my understanding of Mishkin (2004, p. 523) is accurate, in Keynesian analysis, the main determinants of velocity are income (or real GDP) and interest rates. After substituting the general functional form for Keynes' real money demand into the algebraic definition for velocity, Mishkin (2004, p. 523) finds equation (8.2) below, but with a different equation number.

(8.2) $V = Y/\mathrm{f}(i, Y)$,

where i represents an interest rate.

All other things equal, it is assumed that lower interest rates lead to an increase in the real quantity of money demanded, thus giving rise to velocity being positively correlated with interest rates, as lower interest rates increase the denominator in equation (8.2) above. As per Mishkin (2004, pp. 523- 524, 531-532), Keynesian analysis (like Friedman's analysis) often assumes that velocity is procyclical, or that when the economy is expanding, velocity is also rising, and downturns in the economy are associated with decreases in velocity. This implies that the impact of an increase in real GDP on velocity in the numerator of equation (8.2) dominates the impact of an increase in real GDP on $\mathrm{f}(i, Y)$ in the denominator. Higher interest rates, all other things equal, resulting from growing real GDP would reduce the quantity of real money demanded in the denominator and increase velocity.

THE ROAD AHEAD

QUESTIONS FOR MONETARIST AND KEYNESIAN ANALYSIS

In light of equation (8.1) above, does this mean that in monetarist analysis (or at least Milton Friedman's analysis), the impact of the nominal money supply on velocity comes mainly through permanent income and current real GDP? How does monetarist analysis, particularly that of Milton Friedman as discussed by Mishkin (2004, pp. 528-532), explain real GDP increasing for fifteen consecutive quarters in the recovery from the Great Recession but velocity continuing to decline in most of those quarters according to data from www.economagic.com accessed July 20, 2013? Is permanent income rising faster than current real GDP?

Based on equation (8.2) above, does this imply that the nominal money supply impacts velocity in Keynesian analysis mainly through real income (or real GDP) and interest rates? Real and nominal GDP and the deflator have been increasing in the U.S. each quarter after the second quarter of 2009 through the first quarter of 2013 (and beyond) based on data from www.economagic.com accessed July 20, 2013. Further, data accessed later suggest that some interest rates, such as the ten-year rate, have trended upward from mid-July 2012 through the end of 2013 (although the sizes of the increases in interest rates in terms of percentage-point increases have been relatively small). All of these seem to point to rising velocity in Keynesian analysis. However, velocity has continued to decrease most quarters. How does the Keynesian school of thought explain this?

According to Baumol and Blinder (2012, p. 298), as noted before, an increase in the money supply leads to a decrease in the velocity of money through its effect on interest rates. However, does this match the experience of the first sub-sample period (1959q1-1981q3), when both the M1 money supply and the velocity of M1 were usually increasing? Further, a footnote in Dornbusch, Fischer, and Startz (2008, p. 386) states that money demand and velocity are used in academia perhaps synonymously. My interpretation of this statement is that the two variables are inversely related via the algebraic definition of velocity. Is this consistent with the first sub-sample period?

While the Keynesian school and the monetarist school could point back to the algebraic definition of velocity with the huge surge in M1 in the U.S. after the year 2007, why does the impact of nominal money supply on velocity seem to be deemphasized, if not absent, in the textbook synopses of the work of Keynes and Milton Friedman from Mishkin (2004, pp. 523, 531-532)? (More may be available in other editions of textbooks from Mishkin and/or others.) Given the potential impact that the nominal money supply can have on velocity as shown in this book, why has the nominal money supply been algebraically removed from equations (8.1) and (8.2) above? Has at least some Keynesian analysis and at least some monetarist analysis understated the impact of the nominal money supply on velocity, particularly related to economies near liquidity traps or in complete liquidity traps? Can NDVMSL theory and the difference between spending capacity and aggregate demand add to the analysis? Can NDVMSL theory help to fill in a gap between monetarist and Keynesian analysis?

Can specifying a real money demand function help our understanding? And, although Keynesian analysis often assumes that velocity is procyclical, does this automatically follow from the equation of exchange? Consider Dornbusch, Fischer, and Startz's (2008, p. 234) real money demand equation as shown below as equation (8.3).

(8.3) $M^D/P = k^*Y - h^*i$

The coefficients k and h could be estimated through econometric analysis. This seems to be an appropriate functional form for Mishkin's (2004, p. 523) general equation for real money demand, f(i, Y). After substituting the right side of equation (8.3) for P/M in the algebraic definition of velocity ($V=P^*Y/M$), equation (8.2) can be written as equation (8.4) below.

(8.4) $V = Y/(k^*Y - h^*i)$

An increase in real income (interpreted in this case as real GDP) would increase not only the numerator of the right side of equation (8.4) but also the denominator, through k^*Y. Does Keynesian analysis assume that, all other things equal, the impact of the increase in real GDP on velocity dominates the impact of an increase in k^*Y on velocity, all other things equal? Does the assumption that a growing economy, all other things equal, leads to higher interest rates increase the likelihood that as Y increases, the impact of higher real GDP in the numerator of equation (8.4) and the impact of increasing h^*i in the denominator (reducing the overall denominator) dominate the impact of an increase in k^*Y in the denominator and thus increase velocity? Does that fit the U.S. economy experience in the Not-So-Great Recovery?

At least to me, velocity seems to be much more than just a ratio of nominal GDP to a measure of the money supply, either M1 or M2. Velocity seems to have information about beliefs and plans of people in the economy. Why then has Keynesian analysis paid relatively little attention (at least explicitly) to velocity, a potentially important economic variable, even if velocity is only the result rather than the cause? Does it make sense for Keynesian economic work to assume that velocity is not necessarily constant in the short term, but then, at least implicitly, ignore the velocity of money most of the time by failing to study velocity directly sufficiently? If one takes the view that a dollar (in either nominal or real terms) held by the general public must be part of the public's quantity of money demanded because money must be held by the general public, then does Dornbusch, Fischer, and Startz' (2008,

p. 234) real money demand equation in equation (8.3) above assume a change in either k or h or both to explain how the real money supply can grow in a complete liquidity trap while real GDP and interest rates would remain unchanged?

MORE ABOUT MONEY DEMAND

In explaining the surge in real money demand starting in 2008, Keynesian analysis could possibly maintain that the quantity of real money demanded started surging in the U.S. in late 2008, given falling interest rates followed by low interest rates and in the third quarter of 2009 a return to increasing real GDP. The quantity of real money demanded soared, increasing at a faster rate than nominal GDP and causing velocity to fall. However, as noted, some longer term interest rates trended upward from around the third quarter of 2012 through the fourth quarter of 2013, and yet velocity continued to trend downward. Furthermore, the relatively sluggish growth of real GDP (and nominal GDP) in most quarters of the Not-So-Great Recovery suggests that the greater money holdings are mainly not for GDP spending (at least in the near term). Keynesian analysis often assumes that velocity is procyclical, but velocity has continued to decline most quarters in the expansion. Is this consistent with an economy near a liquidity trap? Even if complete liquidity traps do not exist outside of economic theory, is the concept of a liquidity trap as an extreme still very helpful in explaining the U.S. economy in the Not-So-Great Recovery?

According to Mishkin (2004, pp. 522, 524), Keynes' speculative motive for holding money suggests that if people expect that interest rates will be higher in the future, real money balances at the present will be more lucrative and other assets such as bonds will be less lucrative due to the anticipated capital loss. The result will be an increase in the quantity of real money demanded. Could this explain why velocity has continued to decrease most quarters in the United States in the Not-So-Great Recovery?

Does the plummeting of velocity combined with the surging of the M1 money supply (or the surging quantity of M1 demanded) indicate that some of the M1 dollars that people are holding are held in M1 forms for reasons other than planned transactions in the current quarter? Does it imply that a rather sharp increase in precautionary money holdings has occurred? If so, what does this indicate about views of the lackluster economic recovery? Why might people be so concerned? Why are people holding these M1 balances when they can receive higher returns by holding the buying power in the form of non-M1 components of M2, especially if the funds are not going to be spent in the current quarter?

Are people concerned about the possibility of another financial crisis, thus leading to an increased desire to hold cash and cash equivalents? Could there be another explanation for why M1 has risen so rapidly in recent years, and by a faster percentage than M2 (although M2 has risen by a larger dollar amount)? Although information from www.fdic.gov/deposit/deposits/unlimited/expiration.html (accessed December 18, 2012) suggested that deposit insurance limits went into effect again but at a higher insured limit either December 31, 2012 or January 1, 2013 (after the suspension of a limit on certain types of checking accounts for two years), checkable deposits part of M1 continued to grow thereafter. Thus, the temporary suspension of deposit insurance limits does not appear to be the *only* factor explaining why M1 has grown so rapidly starting in 2008.

The federal funds rate has been near zero per cent for more than five years, and at least until a few months prior to this writing if not up through this writing, other longer-term interest rates in the U.S., although having risen somewhat, have been quite low compared with recent historic values. Could there be validity to the speculative motive for holding money, where people may want to limit purchases of newly issued debt at very low interest rates to guard against capital losses that would arise if buyers of debt issued with lower coupon rates would need to resell these debt instruments after interest rates had risen? With interest rates in the U.S. still relatively low, it is very likely that interest rates will rise at some point in the future. It could be more a question of 'when' rather than a question of 'if.' Could this have led to hesitancy regarding buying long-term debt, particularly debt from some private issuers?

Are the non-M1 assets part of M2 paying returns that are in a sense 'too low' so that the premium they offer relative to M1 assets is insufficient to keep M2 growing at the same rate as M1? Has the presence of extremely low interest rates led to an increase in the asset motive for holding money that Laidler (1993, p. 182) attributes to Marty (1961) and Cagan and Schwartz (1975)? Is there possibly another motive for holding money besides the transactions motive, the precautionary motive, and perhaps the speculative and asset motives, the first three of which were discussed by Keynes according to Mishkin (2004, pp. 521-522)? Is the asset motive for holding money balances related to the speculative motive or one of the other motives?

Many studies have been conducted dealing with money demand, and the topic certainly is not new. For example, Hamilton's (1994, p. 1) time series econometrics text mentions a money demand equation estimated by Goldfeld (1973). However, could further study of money demand specifically within the context of NDVMSL theory be helpful (particularly if such a study has not been conducted)? What is certain is that the much greater holdings of nominal M1 balances starting in the first quarter of 2008, combined with either the contractions of nominal GDP in some quarters or the modest increases of nominal GDP in many quarters in the U.S., have resulted in a sharp decrease in the velocity of M1. In my opinion, the topic is worth further study.

VERIFYING AND FINDING THE NDVMSL

With the topic having returned to NDVMSL theory, this study suggests that should a NDVMSL *not* exist at any point in time, future work could explain this and refute the evidence presented herein. If a NDVMSL *does* exist, then future work could identify how we could approximate this money supply level.

Policymakers could benefit from additional information about the NDVMSL if it exists (even if only at times) or about the refutation of a NDVMSL if it does not exist under any circumstance. The reason is that in the event of expansionary monetary policy, the change in the velocity of money helps show how effective the monetary expansion is in stimulating additional spending. For example, if an increase in the money supply aimed at increasing nominal GDP results in no change in spending and is thus completely ineffective, then the velocity of money must fall from the algebraic definition of velocity. (This certainly does *not* imply that if an increase in the money supply and a decrease in velocity occur in the same quarter, then nominal GDP spending must have either decreased or remained constant. In order for nominal GDP to remain constant or to decrease after monetary expansion, velocity would have to fall by at least a certain amount to offset the increase in the money supply.) But what factors could impact the NDVMSL, if it exists? (The 'In-Chapter Appendix' has discussion beyond what follows below.)

Nominal GDP and Its Components

Because velocity deals with the ratio of nominal GDP to a monetary aggregate, the change in nominal GDP that would arise in association with a change in the nominal money supply is critical for a possible NDVMSL. It follows that real GDP and the price level individually and together as nominal GDP (or the changes in those variables) could impact the NDVMSL. (Recall that if a NDVMSL exists, it is not necessarily constant and can either increase or decrease.) If nominal GDP spending is decreasing, then velocity must fall unless the money supply falls by a percentage at least as large as the percentage decrease in nominal GDP. In the case that nominal GDP falls and velocity falls, the money supply is at a point greater than the NDVMSL, if a NDVMSL exists. On the other hand, if nominal GDP spending is increasing, then velocity is increasing unless the money supply increases at a rate at least as large as the rate of increase in nominal GDP. In the event that nominal GDP and velocity both increase, then the money supply must have been less than any NDVMSL that may have existed.

Because the change in nominal GDP is so important to where the economy is in relation to the NDVMSL, let's consider some of the factors that can impact nominal GDP, because these factors can potentially impact the NDVMSL (if a NDVMSL exists), and many likely do. Obviously, the nominal money supply has an impact on nominal GDP (at some point in the future if not in the current quarter) unless the economy is in a complete liquidity trap. But, the current discussion is about how nominal GDP is related to the NDVMSL. If a NDVMSL does exist, and if the money supply is less than or equal to the NDVMSL, then the velocity of money will either increase or remain unchanged. Likewise, if the money supply is greater than the NDVMSL, then the velocity of money will decrease. If a NDVMSL exists, then the *current* nominal money supply either does not impact the NDVMSL or impacts the NDVMSL indirectly via its effect on nominal GDP (because the NDVMSL is the maximum money supply level consistent with either no change in or an increase in velocity) or other variables that impact nominal GDP.

Past money supply levels, however, could have an impact on the NDVMSL of the present. To see this possibility, consider a brief thought experiment where we have data from an economy from two quarters ago (the first quarter), one quarter ago (the second quarter), and the current quarter (the third quarter). Suppose the money supply level in an economy surged ahead last quarter, but nominal GDP stayed the same. This would have caused a decrease in the velocity of money in the last quarter, the second quarter. Now suppose further that the money supply and nominal GDP remain unchanged in the current quarter. In this case, velocity would remain constant in the current quarter, the third quarter. Would this represent an increase in the NDVMSL given no change in velocity in the current quarter? The money supply, which is at the same level in the second and third quarters, caused a decrease in velocity in the second quarter by surging. Given that the money supply surged in the second quarter, the previous quarter, when velocity fell, an even greater money supply in the third quarter (the current quarter) would be required to further depress velocity given the assumption that nominal GDP was at the same level in the current quarter and the previous two quarters.

If a NDVMSL exists, does an increase in either the precautionary motive, the speculative motive, or the possible fourth motive (for example, the asset motive) lead, all other things equal, to a decrease in the NDVMSL by having either (1) more dollars in circulation without an increase in nominal GDP, or (2) the same number of dollars in circulation with a decrease in nominal GDP? Because nominal GDP is a complex variable that could be influenced by many different variables and factors, the NDVMSL (if it exists) could also be influenced by many different variables. Below, I list some of the other variables and factors that may impact them.

Given that GDP can be broken down into consumption, investment, government purchases, and net exports, any factor that affects spending on consumption, investment, government purchases, and/or net exports could possibly impact the velocity of money. Therefore, a stronger desire by households, firms, government sectors, and/or those in other countries to spend on U.S.-made goods could increase both the velocity of money and also the NDVMSL. The thinking is that a stronger desire to spend leads to an increase in spending, unless something is preventing it. This means that nominal GDP would probably increase. Assuming no change in the money supply, velocity would also increase. This suggests an increase in the NDVMSL. The reasoning is that it would take a greater money supply for velocity to fall if nominal GDP spending per period picks up. The financing of a larger nominal GDP per period without an increase in the nominal money supply requires that each dollar trades more frequently in GDP transactions.

A weaker desire to spend by households, firms, government sectors, and/or those in other countries, all other things equal, would depress nominal GDP, velocity, and the NDVMSL. It is possible to finance a reduced amount of spending with a smaller money supply assuming no change in velocity.

But, if a smaller amount of spending on GDP goods per period is accompanied by a constant money supply, then velocity must decrease. This suggests a decrease in the NDVMSL. Given that nominal GDP equals real GDP multiplied by a measure of the price level, an increase in either real GDP or the price level could increase the NDVMSL, all other things equal.

Unemployment Rates and Interest Rates

The unemployment rate could have an impact on the NDVMSL. A higher unemployment rate, all other things equal, depresses spending in an economy. Further, an economy may not be capable of producing as many goods at a higher unemployment rate than at a lower unemployment rate. Thus, for any quantity of money in circulation, a higher unemployment rate, all other things equal, would imply a lower velocity of money if nominal GDP is lower. In turn, a higher unemployment rate would, all other things equal, lead to a lower NDVMSL because of a likely lower level of spending associated with a higher unemployment rate, all other things equal. Conversely, a lower unemployment rate would, all other things equal, lead to more spending and an increase in the NDVMSL.

Interest rates are another factor. All other things equal, a higher interest rate paid to assets which are not part of M1 causes the opportunity cost of holding each dollar in an M1 form to rise. Thus, we expect at a higher interest rate, the velocity of money would increase, all other things equal, as people would hold fewer M1 components that pay little or no interest and more non-M1 assets paying a higher return. A greater percentage of the M1 assets held could be held in such forms just for spending. And therefore, a higher interest rate could imply an increase in the NDVMSL to the extent that a higher interest rate increases velocity, all other things equal, with more planned and actual spending per dollar of M1, although not necessarily more total spending. Likewise, all other things equal, lower interest rates could lead to greater M1 balances held and a decrease in the NDVMSL.

Financial Crises, Leveraging, and Asset Values

Financial crises seem to be associated with decreases in the velocity of money. Early in the Great Depression in the United States, both the money supply and the velocity of money fell substantially. Needless to say, nominal GDP fell sharply. By contrast, the money supply increased substantially in the aftermath of the most recent financial crisis and the Great Recession, but the velocity of money fell sharply. Following and/or during the Savings and Loans Crisis and the bursting of the dot-com bubble, money supply also grew while the velocity of money decreased. Intuitively, financial crises can put a damper on spending plans, thus causing the velocity of money to decrease. The loss of income and wealth associated with financial crises prevents some from spending as much as before, and those fortunate enough to avoid a loss of either income and/or wealth are often less in a mood to spend due to the overall economic environment. Additionally, the Federal Reserve may increase the money supply growth rate to try to promote increases in real GDP and employment, both of which are in danger of falling after a financial crisis hits.

In terms of NDVMSL theory, a financial crisis likely decreases the ability to spend. Rises in bankruptcies and defaults and decreases in asset values would likely cause reductions in spending. Thus, it is possible that a decrease in the NDVMSL could occur. Furthermore, if the Federal Reserve tries to offset the likely decrease in aggregate demand that arises due to a financial crisis by increasing the money supply growth rate, then regardless of whether NDVMSL theory holds, the higher money supply growth rate increases the likelihood that nominal GDP growth will fail to keep pace with the money supply growth (at least initially), thus leading to a decrease in velocity. If NDVMSL theory holds, the higher money supply growth is more likely to cause the money supply level to be greater than the NDVMSL.

Increasing leveraging, a factor that may increase the likelihood of financial crises and may also increase the damage of a financial crisis if such a crisis occurs, may also impact the NDVMSL. Greater leveraging has likely been associated with increasing M1 velocity in the mid-2000s (from the third quarter of 2003 through the fourth quarter of 2007), in the 1990s (from first quarter of 1994 through the fourth quarter of 2000), and likely other periods. When people and non-financial organizations borrow money, the purpose is usually for spending the money. Financial organizations such as banks often borrow money for the purpose of generating revenue from borrowed funds. The revenues could be in the form of fees from financial activities or interest revenue from loans made by the financial organizations. If the funds borrowed from banks and other financial organizations are spent on GDP items, then the result could be an increase in the velocity of money. If the NDVMSL theory holds, then greater leveraging could possibly increase the NDVMSL if greater leveraging leads to more spending of the dollars that are already in the money supply.

Access to credit could be a factor that helps to determine the NDVMSL. With greater access to credit, people or organizations with insufficient funds without the credit can increase spending. Because the credit is coming from people or organizations who did not spend but rather lent the funds, the result would be a greater velocity, all other things equal (if the lenders would not have spent the funds and thus would have saved them had they not granted the loans). Assuming that greater access to credit leads to more GDP spending and greater velocity with perhaps no change in the money supply, a larger money supply would be needed to cause velocity to fall. Thus, the NDVMSL would increase. For this study, access to credit is very similar to, if not the same as, leveraging. Readers should note that credit and debt are opposite sides of the same transaction.

Many in the United States have been involved in deleveraging, or reducing their indebtedness, in recent years. Paying back the principal of debt is not counted as part of GDP, and debtors may be forced to reduce spending in order to pay off debts. Thus, all other things equal, deleveraging could be associated with a decrease in the NDVMSL, as deleveraging may be associated with a decrease in velocity, assuming no change in the money supply.

Asset values would likely impact any NDVMSL that may exist. Of course, asset values (1) can change given the health of the overall economy and the financial system, and (2) were discussed briefly above when discussing financial crises. Higher asset values, for example higher stock and bond values and higher home values, give people in the economy more confidence about economic prospects in the future. They also enable people to borrow larger sums of money for expenditures and thus enhance access to credit, which was discussed above. Therefore, all other things equal, higher asset values would likely increase any NDVMSL that may exist, while lower asset values would decrease it.

Animal Spirits and Permanent Income – Back to Keynes and Milton Friedman

Related to asset values and expenditures, Keynes' "animal spirits" (noted by Krugman and Wells (2009, pp. 473-474) and likely many others) that affect asset values and spending plans could influence the velocity of money and the NDVMSL. Refer to the discussion of consumption, investment, and asset values above for the impact of these on the NDVMSL. Consumption and investment are covered under 'Nominal GDP and its Components' and asset values are discussed under 'Financial Crises, Leveraging, and Asset Values.'

Friedman's permanent income (as discussed by Mishkin (2004, pp. 528-532)) could also impact velocity and the NDVMSL. For example, if permanent income increases, spending would likely also increase given that the increase in income is expected to be permanent. This assumes that at the individual or household level, if permanent income increases, then when a dollar is spent, the person or family expects to be able to recoup the dollar spent in future income because the higher income level is expected to continue each year over a person's lifetime. If the money supply stays the same following an increase in permanent income, velocity also increases, although it may be predictable. However, with dollars changing hands more frequently as a result of the increase in permanent income, the NDVMSL may also rise. With people planning an increase in expenditures (the nominal GDP part of which is in the numerator for velocity), a greater money supply (in the denominator of velocity) would be 'required' to keep velocity constant, and an even slightly greater money supply would be required to force a decrease in velocity. Hence, the anticipated result, all other things equal, would be an increase in the NDVMSL. A decrease in permanent income would have the opposite effect.

Exchange Rates, Expected Inflation, and Income Taxes

Changes in exchange rates, all other things equal, can impact the desire to buy domestically-produced goods versus those made abroad. All other things constant, a stronger U.S. dollar leads to an increase in imports into the U.S. which are not counted in U.S. GDP and decreases in U.S. exports and other domestically produced goods which are counted in U.S. GDP, as U.S.-made goods become relatively more expensive compared with goods from other countries. Assuming no change in the U.S. money supply, the velocity of the U.S. dollar would decrease due to the strengthening of the U.S. dollar. Thus, we might expect a decrease in the NDVMSL. (Recall that this is GDP velocity, not transactions velocity.) By similar reasoning, a weaker U.S. dollar, assuming no change in the number of U.S. dollars in circulation, leads to an increase in the velocity of the U.S. dollar and the NDVMSL due to greater spending on U.S.-made goods.

Expected inflation in the future can also impact velocity and the NDVMSL at the present. If expected inflation increases, all other things constant, people in the economy may be more apt to buy today at what are believed to be lower prices. This would increase nominal GDP, velocity, and the NDVMSL, all other things equal. Lower expected inflation would have the opposite effects, all other things equal.

Income taxes represent an example of something that is likely negatively correlated with velocity. The thinking is that higher income taxes, all other things equal, decrease nominal GDP by taking buying power away from spenders and leading to a decrease in nominal GDP. Barring a decrease in the money supply, velocity would decrease, as would the NDVMSL. Lower income taxes would lead, all other things constant, to increases in nominal GDP, velocity, and the NDVMSL.

Population and Distributional Factors

Population may also affect the NDVMSL. An increase in population, all other things equal, would likely increase spending. Without an increase in the money supply, velocity would also increase, and so would the NDVMSL.

The distributions of both income and wealth could impact velocity and the NDVMSL. Stated simply, all other things equal, when income and wealth go to those less likely to spend following an increase in their income and/or wealth, velocity would probably fall, all other things equal. Thus, a lower money supply level would be needed to keep velocity constant, in turn decreasing the NDVMSL. Likewise, all other things the same, when income and wealth go to those more likely to spend following an increase in their financial resources, velocity and the NDVMSL would likely rise by similar reasoning.

Other Factors

Regarding some other factors, it may be more difficult to determine how they may impact the velocity of money. Political stability could be a factor. Political stability may be positively associated with velocity and an NDVMSL due to higher spending under stability. However, if instability (or a decrease in stability) is expected in the future, spending could increase at the present time if, for example, people are concerned about being unable to buy some items in the future but can buy the items now.

An energy crisis has a theoretically ambiguous effect on velocity. While higher inflation rates associated with an energy crisis would make the price level component of velocity increase, the likely decrease in real GDP due to an energy crisis leaves the net impact on nominal GDP indeterminate, all other things equal, without further information. Although the velocity of M1 increased at least some quarters around the time of the energy crises in the U.S. in the 1970s (and perhaps spilling into the early 1980s), this is based on analysis of data, not on theoretical reasoning.

While technological improvements applied to the payments system would likely increase the velocity of money, all other things constant, more general technological improvements not applicable to the payments system may possibly have an ambiguous impact on velocity. Although an improvement in technology, all other things equal, would lead to an increase in real GDP, it would also lead to a decrease in the equilibrium price level, all other things equal. (If all other things are not equal, the impact of an improvement in technology may show up in the data as a decrease in the rate of inflation but not the price level.) Thus, although the impact of a technological improvement all other things equal on real GDP would be an increase, the impact of a technological improvement on nominal GDP could be ambiguous without further information.

POSSIBLE GAUNTLETS OR CHALLENGES RELATED TO THE NDVMSL

Having reviewed several factors that could impact the velocity of money and the NDVMSL, several questions remain. Is this list of factors accurate and complete? That is, should any factors on the list be removed, and should any factors not on the list be added? And, is the analysis about the effect of an increase or an improvement in each one of the variables listed above on velocity and the NDVMSL correct (as to whether velocity and the NDVMSL would increase or decrease)? Even if the list is complete and accurate with correct analysis, then by how much does each factor on the list impact the NDVMSL? Is it possible that some factors impact the NDVMSL continuously, while others have only an intermittent impact on the NDVMSL? If an NDVMSL does exist, then is a gauntlet or a challenge to try to estimate the impact of each of these, or at least the most important factors, on the NDVMSL and to find or at least approximate the NDVMSL? If a NDVMSL does not exist in any case, then the challenge is to prove that it does not exist under any circumstance.

Obviously, any conclusions about a possible NDVMSL are extremely tentative at this point and should be treated with appropriate skepticism. The 'In-Chapter Appendix' in this chapter offers very tentative, preliminary thoughts on approximating the NDVMSL.

Further, if some factors impact the NDVMSL only from time to time, and/or if the NDVMSL exists only intermittently, identifying those times will be important. Assuming that the NDVMSL exists at least at some points in time, then improving our understanding of the nominal GDP process and nominal money demand (or perhaps the real GDP process and real money demand) could provide valuable help in approximating the NDVMSL in the future. Could another challenge be that if a NDVMSL does exist, then can we estimate by how much velocity will decline if the money supply grows by a certain amount beyond the NDVMSL? Would velocity fall by a little or a lot? In other words, can the slope of the velocity function (with the velocity of money as a function of the money supply) be estimated? FOMC policy discussions could be improved with this knowledge if it is attainable. As noted before, if the NDVMSL does not exist at any point in time, then the evidence supporting the likelihood of the existence of a NDVMSL at least at some points in time should be refuted.

THE WHOLE BALLGAME?

Recently, when discussing some of the concepts in this book with someone, this person said to me, "velocity is the whole ballgame" in macroeconomics. Even if that turns out to be an exaggeration, the velocity of money is very important, because it shows the relationship between the money supply and nominal GDP in the economy, where nominal GDP equals real GDP multiplied by the implicit deflator (divided by 100). The percentage change in the price level is the inflation rate, something of interest to policymakers.

Burton and Lombra (2006, p. 589) list the Employment Act and the Humphrey-Hawkins Full Employment and Balanced Growth Act (the former of 1946 and the latter of 1978) as guiding monetary policymakers to implement policies to promote economic growth consistent with full employment but also consistent with low inflation. The change in the unemployment rate and real GDP growth may be empirically inversely interrelated via an Okun's Law relationship as discussed by Dornbusch, Fischer, and Startz (2008, pp. 148-149) and many others. All other things constant, monetary policies that would promote growth in real GDP and employment (both Federal Reserve goals) at least in the short run would also increase the rate of inflation (often contrary to one of the Federal Reserve's goals, unless inflation is negative or below its targeted level). Likewise, monetary policies to reduce inflation rates would, all other things equal, also lower real GDP and employment, at least in the short run. Thus, trying to improve monetary policy is a worthwhile goal.

During a period of expansionary monetary policy, as in the present U.S. economy, the change in the velocity of money provides some feedback to policymakers regarding the success of the expansionary policy. While the recent expansionary monetary policy has been successful at preventing or helping to prevent a depression and greatly reducing the costs of federal budget deficits, the policy has not returned real GDP to its potential or trend from before the most recent financial crisis in the U.S. The relatively steep decline in the velocity of M1 in the U.S. casts doubt on the ability of monetary policy alone to finish the economic recovery in returning real GDP to trend, especially very quickly.

MACROECONOMIC POLICY IMPLICATIONS OF DECLINING VELOCITY AND THE NDVMSL

What is the recent, sharp decline in the velocity of M1 in the United States telling us? Further addressing this question could prove well worth the effort. Is the abrupt drop in the velocity of M1 merely the result of a coincidental coupling of very slow nominal GDP growth and rapid nominal money supply growth (following a period of declining nominal GDP and increasing nominal M1)? Alternatively, can policymakers, researchers, and others glean useful information from the well-documented decline in the velocity of U.S. M1?

Based on the information presented to this point, my inclination is to think that the latter is much more likely. But, even if that is correct, further work will be necessary to understand more fully the information content that is waiting to be put to use by policymakers and researchers. Does a money supply level exist at least at *some* points in time (such as the United States economy during most of the last five-plus years) where any further increase in the money supply will automatically result in a decrease in the velocity of money? That is, does a NDVMSL exist at least at some points in time? Again, based on the evidence presented above, my belief is that it is likely that such a NDVMSL exists at least during *some* periods.

Some of the ramifications of the possible existence of a NDVMSL in the U.S. economy now include that expansionary monetary policy alone is unlikely to hasten the sluggish, lackluster recovery in which the U.S. economy has been languishing now for approximately five years after a sharp decline in real GDP. (This is not necessarily true of a more normal downturn when interest rates are higher.) If a NDVMSL currently exists in the U.S., and if the U.S. economy is currently at a money supply level greater than the NDVMSL, then the velocity of money will decline as long as the money supply level is above the NDVMSL. Further, additional increases in the money supply in such a context will be associated with either further sluggish growth in nominal GDP or no change in nominal GDP or contraction in nominal GDP. (This is in contrast with the sub-sample period from the first quarter of

1985 through the second quarter of 1987, when it appears that economic growth was generally higher than during the Not-So-Great Recovery, but rapid money supply growth still forced the velocity of M1 down from 1985q1 through 1987q2.)

Above, the case has been made for expansionary fiscal policy (*both* reductions in taxes and increases in government spending) in an effort to accelerate growth in aggregate demand. Further expansionary monetary policy would likely greatly reduce, if not altogether eliminate, any harmful long-term effects on economic growth that could result from expanding budget deficits arising from further expansionary fiscal policy by making interest rates lower than they would otherwise be. Keeping interest rates low would reduce the crowding out problem where expansionary fiscal policy prevents businesses from acquiring physical capital when interest rates rise, all other things equal, as the government borrows to finance the deficit. Higher interest rates, all other things equal, discourage business investment in physical capital by making it harder for firms to borrow, all other things equal, and also by increasing the reward for lending, all other things the same, for firms with additional cash (so that they would not need to borrow to buy more capital). At least until just a few months before this writing, it would be difficult to argue that high interest rates on ten-year loans were discouraging firms with strong credit ratings from borrowing.

If the fragile economic recovery weakens, it could be because some data suggest that fiscal policy has actually become more contractionary recently. According to Wiseman (2012), a measure of total U.S. government spending (federal, state, and local) decreased between 2009 and 2012. Further, with sequestration cuts (noted by Malewitz (2013) and many others) going into effect and the expiration of the payroll tax holiday (mentioned by Schwartz (2013) among others), many households have less income to spend. Combining expansionary fiscal policy with expansionary monetary policy would be most likely to reverse the trend the most quickly, and at less of a cost to long-term growth. Expansionary monetary policy alone may lead to little additional spending when velocity is declining, *even if a NDVMSL does not exist*!

SOME ADDITIONAL AREAS FOR FURTHER WORK

Questions about the 1980s

A reading of Baumol and Blinder (2012, pp. 297-299) may possibly suggest that M1 velocity stopped following its trend in 1981 due to financial innovations. Future work could determine if interest rates on M1 checking accounts became more volatile following the elimination of interest rate ceilings with the passage of the Depository Institutions Deregulation and Monetary Control Act of 1980, as discussed in Chapter 5, and if so, whether that played a role in the detrending of the velocity of M1.

Additionally, data from www.economagic.com suggest to me that the rapid money supply growth rate from the first quarter of 1985 through the second quarter of 1987 was the main reason why the velocity of money decreased during this period. Why did the money supply grow so rapidly during this sub-sample period? Was it to bring down the federal funds rate and other interest rates? Why was nominal GDP growth positive but restrained enough despite rapidly rising money supply to result in a relatively sharp drop in the velocity of M1?

Data Revisions

A perusal of data available on www.economagic.com shows that recently, a change in the base year for measuring real GDP and the implicit deflator was made. Also planned was the addition to the measurement of GDP items such as at least some artistic works and at least some R&D expenditures, according to Sommer (2013), to past, current, and future GDP data. The latest estimates of real GDP, nominal GDP, and velocity at www.economagic.com probably also reflect these revisions of additional expenditures being counted toward GDP. To share results as soon as possible and to use economic variables that are the same as or more similar to those used by decision-makers during the most recent U.S. financial crisis, the Great Recession, and much of the Not-So-Great Recovery in terms of both (1) the productive activities reflected and (2) the units of measurement used; the current study emphasizes data that were found on www.economagic.com before the conversion to the new base year and before the most recent additions to GDP items. Future work could see if the results of the current study hold with the new base year and other data revisions.

Other Countries

While the focus of this book has been on the United States, future work could investigate the velocity of money in other countries. For example, according to Dornbusch, Fischer, and Startz (2008, p. 253), Paul Krugman and others have described the economy of Japan as being in a liquidity trap (at least at times) for a while. What happened to the velocity of money in Japan, and has that impacted real GDP growth in Japan? Further, the *Atlanta Journal-Constitution* ("European Bank Leaves Key Rate Unchanged," author not specified, 2014) and others have noted that the European Central Bank has begun or is about to begin its version of expansionary unconventional monetary policy, rather than QE. What will happen to the velocity of the euro and growth in real GDP in the part of the EU using the euro?

IN-CHAPTER APPENDIX

INTRODUCTION

Much of what follows in this In-Chapter Appendix may be most beneficial for economists and graduate students in economics. Readers should feel free either to continue reading or to skip ahead to the 'Concluding Remarks' section.

This book raises the theoretical possibility of a non-decreasing-velocity money supply level (NDVMSL). But, does such a NDVMSL exist, and if so, how can we approximate that particular money supply level?

While this book may not be able to provide a definitive answer to that question, the first step in verifying whether the NDVMSL exists and, if so, the money supply level consistent with that level, could begin with going back to the equation of exchange and modified versions of the equation of exchange and remembering what the NDVMSL implies. Afterward, the relationship between the change in nominal GDP and the change in M1, both in natural log form, can be considered, recalling that no change in velocity occurs at the NDVMSL if an NDVMSL exists. Four main cases regarding the sensitivity (or lack thereof) of nominal GDP to M1 within the same period are considered, two of which appear to be consistent with the possible existence of a NDVMSL, but two of which apparently do not. (A fifth possible case where increases in the money supply appear to be associated with (and perhaps somehow causing) decreases in nominal GDP, can be considered more carefully if statistical evidence warrants such consideration.) Next, algebraic analysis is presented for one of the four cases to find the NDVMSL. Finally, regressions estimating the change in the natural log of nominal GDP under different assumptions are discussed briefly, with emphasis on the relationship between the change in the natural log of M1 and the change in the natural log of nominal GDP within the same quarter.

REARRANGING THE EQUATION OF EXCHANGE TO SHOW THE RELATIONSHIP BETWEEN THE CHANGE IN THE NATURAL LOG OF NOMINAL GDP AND THE CHANGE IN THE NATURAL LOG OF M1 AT THE NDVMSL

Recall the equation of exchange below listed in Mishkin (2004, p. 518) and many other places, where the money supply multiplied by the income velocity of money equals the price level times real GDP.

(ICA 8.1) $M*V = P*Y$

Let's restate the equation above, (ICA 8.1), by noting that all of the variables are in the same time period, quarter *t*, with the subscript *t* representing the quarter in the equations below.

(ICA 8.2a) $M1_t*V_t = P_t*Y_t$

In the equation above, $M1_t$ is the M1 money supply in quarter *t*, V_t represents the income velocity of M1 in quarter *t*, P_t represents the price level in quarter *t*, and Y_t stands for real GDP in quarter *t*. Because the price level (in this case the implicit deflator divided by 100) times real GDP equals nominal GDP, we can rewrite equation (ICA 8.2a) above in quarter *t* as below in equation (ICA 8.2b).

(ICA 8.2b) $M1_t*V_t = NOMY_t$

In the equation above, $NOMY_t$ stands for nominal GDP in quarter *t* and the other variables are as defined above. Given the mathematical properties of natural logarithms (natural logs) and the number *e* in Appendix A.3 in Hamilton (1994, pp. 715-718) and many other places, the equation above can be rewritten in the natural-log form below.

(ICA 8.3) $LN\_M1_t + LN\_V_t = LN\_NOMY_t$

Suppose that the notation LN_X_t represents the natural log of the variable X in quarter *t*. Thus, equation (ICA 8.3) above states that the natural log of M1 plus the natural log of velocity equals the natural log of nominal GDP, all in quarter *t*. Dornbusch, Fischer, and Startz (2008, p. 470), Baumol and Blinder (2012, p. 297) and likely many others have an equation similar to the equation above. (The equations in Dornbusch, Fischer, and Startz (2008, p. 470) and Baumol and Blinder (2012, p. 297) imply that the percentage change in the money supply plus the percentage change in velocity equals the percentage change in real GDP plus the percentage change in the price level.) The equation above could be written as $LN\_M1_t + LN\_V_t = LN\_P_t + LN\_Y_t$. However, the discussion to follow about the NDVMSL may be clearer if the equation uses the natural log of nominal GDP as above in equation (ICA 8.3) rather than the natural logs of real GDP and the price level.

Subtracting the natural log of M1 in quarter *t* from both sides of the equation suggests that the natural log of velocity in quarter *t* equals the natural log of nominal GDP in quarter *t* minus the natural log of M1 in quarter *t*.

$$\text{(ICA 8.4) } LN\_V_t = LN\_NOMY_t - LN\_M1_t.$$

If $LN\_V_t = LN\_NOMY_t - LN\_M1_t$ for each quarter *t*, then in the quarter *t-1* (the quarter immediately before quarter *t*), the following equation must also hold.

$$\text{(ICA 8.5) } LN\_V_{t-1} = LN\_NOMY_{t-1} - LN\_M1_{t-1}.$$

Subtracting the rearranged equation of exchange from period *t-1* shown in equation (ICA 8.5) from the rearranged equation of exchange from period *t* shown in equation (ICA 8.4) produces

$$\text{(ICA 8.6a) } LN\_V_t - LN\_V_{t-1} = (LN\_NOMY_t - LN\_NOMY_{t-1}) - (LN\_M1_t - LN\_M1_{t-1}),$$

or

$$\text{(ICA 8.6b) } D\_LN\_V_t = D\_LN\_NOMY_t - D\_LN\_M1_t.$$

In the equation above, the notation 'D_' in the names of the variables represents the first difference in the variable in quarter *t*, or the change in the variable in quarter *t* from one quarter before, quarter *t-1*. For example, $D\_LN\_V_t$ is simply equal to LN_V_t - LN_V_{t-1}. If a NDVMSL exists and if the money supply is at the NDVMSL in a quarter, then $D\_LN\_V_t$ equals zero at the NDVMSL because velocity in quarter *t* will be equal to velocity in quarter *t-1*. Substituting zero for the change in the natural log of velocity in quarter *t*, the equation becomes $0 = D\_LN\_NOMY_t - D\_LN\_M1_t$, so that

(ICA 8.7) $D\_LN\_NOMY_t = D\_LN\_M1_t$,

or the change in the natural log of nominal GDP equals the change in the natural log of the M1 money supply at the NDVMSL. Similarly, the percentage change in nominal GDP equals the percentage change in M1 at the NDVMSL.

THE IMPACT OF THE CHANGE IN THE NATURAL LOG OF M1 ON THE CHANGE IN THE NATURAL LOG OF NOMINAL GDP IN A QUARTER

An important matter for the possibility of a NDVMSL at least within one particular quarter is the possible impact of the money supply in a quarter on nominal GDP spending within the same quarter, and this In-Chapter Appendix considers four main cases. In one case, consider the possibility that the change in the natural log of M1, all other things equal, leads to a change in the natural log of nominal GDP that is larger within the same quarter. This is very similar to considering the possibility of an increase in the money supply by a certain percentage leading all other things equal to an increase in nominal GDP by a percentage that is greater than the percentage increase in the money supply. Let's consider the possibility of an increase in M1 associated with an increase in nominal GDP by an equal percentage separately from the possibility where an increase in M1 is associated with an increase in nominal GDP of a greater percentage. If the ratio of the percentage change in nominal GDP to the percentage change in nominal M1 is always more than 'one to one,' the matter of whether the change in nominal M1 or other factors cause the change in nominal GDP may possibly not be important for our analysis.

If the percentage change in the nominal money supply in a quarter is always equal to the percentage change in nominal GDP within the same quarter (so that nominal money supply and nominal GDP always move 'one to one' percentagewise), then velocity is constant (which is perhaps the most extreme interpretation of the classical view of velocity). If for example nominal GDP and the nominal money supply both rise by ten per cent in a quarter, then velocity remains unchanged. On the other hand (for a second example), if nominal GDP and the nominal money supply both decrease by five per cent within the same quarter, then velocity is also unchanged. In this case, velocity cannot fall, so velocity is constant at any money supply level (greater than zero or some extremely small quantity). It is not possible to find a money supply level that will lead to velocity falling if nominal GDP and the nominal money supply always move 'one to one' percentagewise within the same quarter.

If a certain growth rate in the nominal money supply is always accompanied by an increase in nominal GDP that is greater than the percentage increase in the nominal money supply within the same quarter, then an increase in the nominal money supply will always produce an increase in velocity because any increase in the money supply is accompanied by an increase in nominal GDP that is larger. Thus, velocity cannot decline just because the money supply rises above some level. However, velocity may possibly decrease in this case even if the percentage change in nominal GDP rises more than 'one to one' with the percentage change in M1 within the same quarter, but decreasing velocity in this case would be due to a decrease in the money supply in a quarter leading to a decrease in nominal GDP by a larger percentage within the same quarter (if the ratio still holds for decreases in the money supply). If nominal GDP increases either 'one to one' or more than 'one to one' with nominal money supply, then it makes little sense to seek a NDVMSL as money supply growth fails to cause velocity to fall.

But what if an increase in the money supply of a certain percentage in a quarter, all other things equal, leads to an increase in nominal GDP within the same quarter but by a smaller percentage than the percentage increase in the money supply? And what if the percentage increase in the money supply in a quarter has *no* impact on the percentage change in nominal GDP in the current quarter (but may impact the percentage change in nominal GDP in future quarters)? In the latter case where the percentage change in nominal GDP is independent of the percentage change in the money supply (at least within the same quarter), then the NDVMSL is simply the money supply level where the percentage change in the money supply from the previous period to the next period equals the percentage change in nominal GDP between the two periods (or the money supply level such that the changes in the natural logs of M1 and nominal GDP are equal). Heading into a quarter before the value of nominal GDP is known, the NDVMSL can be forecasted by using a forecast of nominal GDP growth and also a forecast of the money supply if the money supply for the quarter is not known. (Forecasting the money supply may be required if the central bank cannot completely control the money supply due to factors such as depository institutions' desires to hold excess reserves and the general public's desire to change the ratio of currency to checkable deposits.)

ALGEBRAIC ANALYSIS

Regarding the former case where the percentage increase in nominal M1 in a quarter causes nominal GDP to increase in the same quarter but by a smaller percentage and where other factors also influence the percentage change in nominal GDP in the quarter, algebraic analysis will help to find the NDVMSL. We seek a level of the money supply (M1 in this case) such that both equations (ICA 8.7) (from above) and (ICA 8.8) below both hold true. Equation (ICA 8.7) must hold at the NDVMSL.

(ICA 8.7) $D\_LN\_NOMY_t = D\_LN\_M1_t$

(ICA 8.8) $D\_LN\_NOMY_t = \beta_1 * D\_LN\_M1_t + \text{Other Variables} + C + \varepsilon_t$.

Suppose that equation (ICA 8.8) is the process determining values of the change in the natural log of nominal GDP (approximately equal to the percentage change in nominal GDP divided by 100 for small percentage changes in nominal GDP). β_1 is a coefficient that can be estimated, and C is a constant that can be estimated. ε_t is an error term for time period *t*, and if serial correlation is not present, then the error term in one period is not correlated with the error terms from any other period. (Future work could determine whether the error terms are correlated with any variables on the right side of the equation and whether the error terms have constant variance. Recall that this is preliminary analysis.)

The term 'Other Variables' refers to past changes in the natural log of M1, past changes in the natural log of nominal GDP, and current and past changes in additional variables, where each of these changes in a variable (including the changes in the natural logs of M1 and nominal GDP) is multiplied by a coefficient that can be estimated. For example, suppose for illustration purposes that except for the constant and the error term, the time-series variables in the equation giving the change in the natural log of nominal GDP are the change in the natural log of nominal GDP (obviously), the change in the natural log of M1, the change in the federal funds rate, the change in the ten-year Treasury rate, and the change in the unemployment rate.

If a model with two lagged values of variables from the previous two quarters (with values also in the current period) was judged to be appropriate, then the right side of the equation for the change in the natural log of nominal GDP would have values from the current quarter (multiplied by coefficients) of all variables in the equation except for the change in the natural log of nominal GDP and the values from the previous two quarters (multiplied by coefficients) of the changes in the natural log of M1, the natural log of nominal GDP, the federal funds rate, the ten-year rate, and the unemployment rate, plus a constant term and an error term. In that case, we could write the following equation, equation (ICA 8.9), an equation for Other Variables. We could substitute the terms on the right side of equation (ICA 8.9) for Other Variables in equation (ICA 8.8). The values of the 'β-variables' in equation (ICA 8.9), β_2 through β_{14}, are simply coefficients that can be estimated.

$$\text{(ICA 8.9) Other Variables} = \beta_2{*}D\_LN\_M1_{t-1} + \beta_3{*}D\_LN\_M1_{t-2} + \beta_4{*}D\_LN\_NOMY_{t-1} + \beta_5{*}D\_LN\_NOMY_{t-2} + \beta_6{*}D\_FFR_t + \beta_7{*}D\_FFR_{t-1} + \beta_8{*}D\_FFR_{t-2} + \beta_9{*}D\_TENYR_t + \beta_{10}{*}D\_TENYR_{t-1} + \beta_{11}{*}D\_TENYR_{t-2} + \beta_{12}{*}D\_U_t + \beta_{13}{*}D\_U_{t-1} + \beta_{14}{*}D\_U_{t-2}$$

Returning focus to the NDVMSL under the assumptions made, if we substitute $D\_LN\_M1_t$ for $D\_LN\_NOMY_t$ in equation (ICA 8.8) (because the change in the natural log of nominal GDP must equal the change in the natural log of M1 at the NDVMSL), we get

$$\text{(ICA 8.10) } D\_LN\_M1_t = \beta_1{*}D\_LN\_M1_t + \text{Other Variables} + C + \varepsilon_t.$$

Subtracting $\beta_1{*}D\_LN\_M1_t$ from both sides of the equation generates

$$\text{(ICA 8.11) } (1-\beta_1){*}D\_LN\_M1_t = \text{Other Variables} + C + \varepsilon_t.$$

Dividing both sides by $(1-\beta_1)$ produces

$$\text{(ICA 8.12) } D\_LN\_M1_t = [1/(1-\beta_1)]{*}[\text{Other Variables} + C + \varepsilon_t].$$

The above equation is equivalent to

$$\text{(ICA 8.13) } LN\_M1_t - LN\_M1_{t-1} = [1/(1-\beta_1)]{*}[\text{Other Variables} + C + \varepsilon_t].$$

Thus, adding LN_M1_{t-1} to both sides,

$$\text{(ICA 8.14) } LN\_M1_t = LN\_M1_{t-1} + [1/(1-\beta_1)]{*}[\text{Other Variables} + C + \varepsilon_t],$$

where LN_M1_t is the natural log of the NDVMSL in quarter *t*. Finally, to solve for the NDVMSL, we can apply the exponential function (the number *e*, which is the inverse of the natural log) to both sides of the equation to get

$$\text{(ICA 8.15) } \exp(LN\_M1_t) = \exp\{LN\_M1_{t-1} + [1/(1-\beta_1)]*[\text{Other Variables} + C + \varepsilon_t]\}, \text{ or}$$

$$e^{LN\_M1_t} = e^{\{LN\_M1_{t-1} + [1/(1-\beta_1)]*[\text{Other Variables} + C + \varepsilon_t]\}}$$

but $\exp(LN\_M1_t) = M1_t$, so

$$\text{(ICA 8.16) } NDVMSL_t = M1_t = e^{\{LN\_M1_{t-1} + [1/(1-\beta_1)]*[\text{Other Variables} + C + \varepsilon_t]\}}$$

$$= \exp\{LN\_M1_{t-1} + [1/(1-\beta_1)]*[\text{Other Variables} + C + \varepsilon_t]\},$$

REGRESSION ANALYSIS

Overview

What then is the impact of the change in the natural log of M1 on the change in the natural log of nominal GDP within the same quarter? The answer could be largely an empirical matter.

Over the full sample period with quarterly data from www.economagic.com from the first quarter of 1959 through the first quarter of 2013, very tentative results from regression analysis suggest that most likely, the change in the natural log of M1 in a quarter does not have a statistically significant impact on the change in the natural log of nominal GDP *within the same quarter*. More technically, the t-statistics and associated probabilities from regressions in EViews 5.1 software over the full sample period presented below fail to reject the null hypothesis that the value for β_1 equals zero. In some cases, the estimate of β_1 is less than zero but is small in absolute value and is not statistically different from zero.

If the first difference of the natural log of nominal GDP is not impacted by the first difference of the natural log of M1 within the same quarter, then the NDVMSL is simply the money supply level where the percentage change in the two variables (nominal GDP and M1) or the changes in the natural logs of the two variables are equal but independent of each other in one particular quarter. For example, if the percentage changes in nominal GDP and M1 are independent of each other in the current quarter, and if the percentage change in nominal GDP in a quarter is three per cent, then the NDVMSL for that quarter is simply 1.03 multiplied by the M1 money supply from the previous quarter. On the other hand, if nominal GDP growth for the current quarter is not known but can be forecasted and is forecasted to be three per cent, then the forecasted NDVMSL would simply be three per cent higher than the actual money supply from the previous quarter.

However, changes in the relationships between M1, nominal GDP, and other variables over the sample period have very likely occurred. According to Burton and Lombra (2006, pp. 51-53), the ability of the Federal Reserve to influence the amount of credit extended (and perhaps gross domestic product) in the U.S. economy has decreased at least after the late 1980s but perhaps beginning in the early 1980s as a greater percentage of loans were granted by entities that are not domestic depository institutions. Could this be related to the end of the first sub-sample period (1981q3), with the velocity of M1 in the U.S. decreasing for six out of seven quarters starting with the fourth quarter of 1981? At any rate, the generally declining velocity of M1 in the second sub-sample period could indicate a change in the relationship between nominal GDP and M1 compared to the relationship between these two variables in the first sub-sample period.

Using data from www.economagic.com, if we focus on regressions over just the first sub-sample period (1959q1 through 1981q3), then most of the regressions that will be considered in this Appendix suggest that during this period, the first difference in the natural log of M1 had a statistically significant impact on the first difference of the natural log of nominal GDP within the same period, and the impact was positive. The estimated coefficients for β_1 were also much larger over the first sub-sample period than over the full sample period (between 0.20 and 0.40 rather than all less than 0.035). Thus, a tentative conclusion is that the percentage growth in the money supply had a positive impact on the percentage growth in nominal GDP in the same quarter over the first sub-sample period but not over the full sample period. In the first sub-sample period, it appears that the higher the growth in M1, the higher the growth in nominal GDP, all other things equal, but the estimated values for β_1 were clearly less than one. Thus, given the algebra above, it is possible in the framework considered to solve for the NDVMSL over the first sub-sample period because β_1 is probably less than one.

Some Issues in Modeling the Change in the Natural Log of Nominal GDP

What is the best way to model the change in the natural log of nominal GDP? The answer to this question is very important for trying to determine whether the change in the natural log of M1 has an impact on the change in the natural log of nominal GDP within the same period. Yet, a definitive answer to this question does not appear in this book.

First, realize that many variables may impact the change in the natural log of nominal GDP in a quarter, but partly in the interest of saving time to make the findings available as soon as possible, this book considers only the factors listed above. For example, according to Dornbusch, Fischer, and Startz (2008, p. 409), Benjamin Friedman (1983) found a closer relationship between a measure of debt and a measure of output than the relationship between money and a measure of output. Should other variables like a measure of credit extended or debt also be included in the regressions for the change in the natural log of nominal GDP? Second, the possibility that the change in the natural log of nominal GDP could impact the change in the natural log of M1 within the same quarter while the change in the natural log of M1 also impacts the change in the natural log of nominal GDP is not addressed in the econometric analysis in this In-Chapter Appendix but could be a topic for future work.

There are additional criticisms of or questions about the econometric analysis in this Appendix that can be raised. Some of them will be addressed. However, the purpose of this Appendix is *not* to offer the definitive model for determining the percentage change in nominal GDP or the change in the natural log of nominal GDP in the United States. Also, the purpose is *not* to offer absolute proof of the existence of a NDVMSL. Rather, the purpose is to *begin* to investigate the relationship between M1 growth and nominal GDP growth within the same quarter and to *begin* to identify where the NDVMSL *may* lie if it exists, and to share these tentative, preliminary findings in a timely manner. Thus, this In-Chapter Appendix leaves to future work expanding on what is presented in this In-Chapter Appendix and supporting, modifying, or refuting the work herein as appropriate.

An additional question regarding the econometric analysis in the Appendix is even if all of the variables impacting the change in the natural log of nominal GDP in a quarter are included as variables on the right side of regression equations, how many lags of each variable should be used? Consensus regarding that question likely does not exist. Thus, in the interest of trying to achieve some robustness of results to different modeling strategies, at least three different methods for selecting the number of lags of variables on the right sides of regression equations are used. For simplicity, this Appendix uses the same number of lagged values of each variable from previous quarters in each regression. For example, using this approach, a regression in this Appendix can*not* have on the right side of the regression equation the change in the natural log of nominal GDP from each of the six previous quarters but only one lagged value of the change in the natural log of M1 from the previous quarter.

EViews 5.1 software includes the Akaike (1974) Information Criterion (or the AIC) and the Schwarz (1978) Criterion (or the SC) for regressions, with the smaller or smallest values of each criterion from regressions with different numbers of lagged values of variables from previous periods on the right side of regression equations representing the better or best model of the models considered. As regressions in this study show, the AIC and SC often give different answers for the optimal number of lagged values to include in a regression.

Because of the importance of trying to determine whether statistical evidence exists as to whether the percentage change in M1 in a quarter has an impact on the percentage change in nominal GDP in the same quarter, another method is to select the smallest number of lags that produces regressions without evidence of serial correlation in Breusch-Godfrey tests available in EViews 5.1 software. The regression equation for the change in the natural log of nominal GDP with one lagged value (from the previous quarter) of each variable on the right side of the equation would count as a separate model from the regression equation with two lagged values (from the previous two quarters) of each variable. I am not clear on how many lagged errors to include in the serial correlation tests for each model. Therefore, I perform the Breusch-Godfrey test for each regression model (with all variables having the same number of lagged values) ten times, one time with one lagged error in the test equation, a second time with two lagged errors in the test equation, a third time with three lagged errors, and so on.

Without being in differenced form (or 'change in' form), nominal GDP, the M1 money supply, and perhaps other variables in the regressions in this appendix would likely show signs of being unit root processes in augmented Dickey-Fuller (1979) tests and other unit root tests. Hamilton (1994, pp. 435-451) provides background information on unit roots and references. Regressions with variables having unit roots can produce spurious results that could reduce or nullify the validity of statistical inference, as noted by Hamilton (1994, p. 557-562) and many others. Thus, not only does the specification of models for nominal GDP in this Appendix using both nominal GDP and M1 in the 'change in the natural log' form align well with the theory of the NDVMSL (where the changes in the natural logs of nominal GDP and M1 would be equal at the NDVMSL), but such specifications combined with the other variables in differenced form also reduce the chance of spurious regressions.

However, the unemployment rate probably does not have a unit root in un-differenced form, and consensus may not exist as to whether the federal funds rate and the ten-year Treasury rate have a unit root in un-differenced form. Hamilton (1994, p. 562) notes the use of differenced data may not be correct when variables may be near unit-root processes. Thus, in addition to regressions with all variables in differenced form, some regressions are considered with the unemployment rate in un-differenced form, and some regressions have the unemployment rate and both interest rate variables in un-differenced form. Hamilton (1994, p. 562) also raises the possibility of a vector error correction model with a cointegrating vector when two or more variables have unit roots. Testing for cointegration between nominal GDP, M1, and the other variables in regressions as they relate to the NDVMSL is beyond the scope of this book but may be a topic for future work.

Regression Results

In Table ICA 8.1 below, the column with the heading β_1 contains the estimates of β_1 from different regressions for equation (ICA 8.8) above. Estimates over the full sample period ending with the first quarter of 2013 appear first, followed by estimates over just the first sub-sample period ending with the third quarter of 1981. In both regressions over the full sample period and over just the first sub-sample period, regressions with all time-series variables in differenced form appear first, followed by regressions with only the unemployment rate *not* in differenced form, followed in turn by regressions with only the changes in the natural logs of nominal GDP and M1 in differenced form. The number of lags of each time series variable is specified in each row in Table ICA 8.1. In both Table ICA 8.1 and Table ICA 8.2, 'S.E.' represents the standard error, 'T-Stat' represents the t-statistic, and 'P-value' represents the level of statistical significance associated with each t-statistic. For significance at the five per cent level, the p-value must be less than or equal to 0.0500.

Table ICA 8.2 below has regression results from EViews 5.1 software over the full sample period with all variables in differenced or 'change in' form for the model with two lags of each time series variable on the right side of the regression. Thus, in Table ICA 8.2, the regression for equation (ICA 8.8) has Other Variables as in equation (ICA 8.9) above. The column labeled 'Variable' has the name of each time series variable (and 'C' for the constant term) in the row in the table showing regression estimates including coefficients (the β_1 through β_{14}). With an R-squared value of nearly 0.48 and an adjusted R-squared value of roughly 0.44, the equation explains somewhat less than half of the change in the natural log of nominal GDP. In all cases considered, the R-squared and adjusted R-squared statistics are greater than 0.40, and in more than half of the cases, they are greater than 0.50. Given that many of the time series variables if not all of them are in differenced form in the various cases, it seems like the regressions explain a relatively large degree of the variation in nominal GDP. However, the caveats in Chapter 6 about R-squared and adjusted R-squared statistics would likely still apply.

Over the full sample period with all variables in differenced form and also with only the unemployment rate not differenced; two lags minimize the SC, while five lags minimize the AIC, and eight lags is the lowest number of lags generating no evidence of serial correlation in the errors in the procedure used in this study. With only the changes in the natural logs of nominal GDP and M1 in differenced form, five lags minimize the AIC but one lag minimizes the SC. Also, with four lags of each variable with the federal funds rate, the ten-year Treasury rate, and the unemployment rate not in differenced form; no serial correlation is found in any trial (using the methodology of this study) of the Breusch-Godfrey test at the five per cent level, but the test with nine lagged errors is close to showing serial correlation at the five per cent level. Thus, the study will also consider eight lags of each time series variable – the shortest lag structure with no evidence of serial correlation when using trials with one lagged error term through ten lagged error terms in the test equation. Let me emphasize that this is a preliminary effort, so that any possible conclusions are tentative and should be interpreted accordingly.

Regardless of whether two lags, five lags, or eight lags are used; as shown in the table below, the t-statistics and associated probabilities indicate that the over the full sample period with all variables in differenced form, the change in the natural log of M1 does not have a statistically significant impact on the change in the natural log of nominal GDP within the same period. The estimated values for β_1 are found in the first column of numbers in Table ICA 8.1 below, which summarizes results from various regressions over the full sample period and the first sub-sample period. Notice that not only can we not reject the null hypothesis in the full-sample-period regressions that the value of β_1 in each regression is actually zero, but the estimated coefficients are all rather close to zero, since D_LN_NOMY and D_LN_M1 are measured on the same scale (the change in the natural log of each variable, which is approximately the percentage change of each variable divided by 100). The lack of statistical significance also holds over the full sample period if the unemployment rate is un-differenced (in 'levels') but the other variables are in differenced form, and if the unemployment rate, the federal funds rate, and the ten-year Treasury rate are all in un-differenced form.

However, over the first sub-sample period ending in the third quarter of 1981, most of the regression models considered find that the first difference in the natural log of M1 has a statistically significant impact on the first difference of the natural log of nominal GDP within the same quarter. In all regressions for the first sub-sample period considered in this In-Chapter Appendix, the estimates of β_1 imply that a one per cent increase in M1 in a quarter, all other things equal, leads to an increase in nominal GDP within the same quarter of between 0.20 per cent and 0.40 per cent. Thus, it is possible to solve for the NDVMSL with the algebraic approach above.

For the first sub-sample period with all variables in differenced form, one lag minimizes the SC, while eight lags minimize the AIC. While the model with three lags is the shortest lag structure where the Breusch-Godfrey test finds no serial correlation at the five per cent level, in the test (for three lagged variable values) with four lagged errors, serial correlation is present at the six per cent level. Thus, the study also uses the model with four lags (of each variable) which does not have evidence of serial correlation. With only the unemployment rate un-differenced in the first sub-sample period, the use of one lag of each variable minimizes the SC and the use of three lags minimizes the AIC and also provides the shortest lag structure with no evidence of serial correlation. With only the natural logs of the change in nominal GDP and M1 differenced when the sample period is restricted to the first sub-sample period, one lag minimizes the SC and five lags minimize the AIC while also being the shortest lag structure with no evidence of serial correlation.

Results in Table ICA 8.2 show that the change in the natural log of M1 is the only variable on the right side of the regression equation where neither lagged values from the previous period nor contemporaneous values (except for the change in the natural log of nominal GDP which is the variable on the left side of the equation) are statistically significant at either the five per cent level or the ten per cent level. However, Table ICA 8.1 shows that in regressions over the first sub-sample period, the change in the natural log of M1 in a quarter has a statistically significant impact on the change in the natural log of nominal GDP at the ten per cent level within the same quarter in seven of the eight regressions considered. Of those seven cases, the impact is statistically significant at the five per cent level in six of those cases. Further, results not included here suggest that in several regressions over the full sample period, one or more lagged values of the change in the natural log of M1 may be statistically significant at the ten per cent level. Thus, using the five time series variables in the regression equations for the change in the natural log of nominal GDP may be well justified, and perhaps more should be added in future work to try to account more fully for changes in nominal GDP.

Figures ICA 8.1 and ICA 8.2 show scatter graphs for the change in the natural log of nominal GDP (on the vertical axis) and the change in the natural log of M1 (on the horizontal axis) with regression lines, although the regression lines shown are not for any of the cases covered in Tables ICA 8.1 and ICA 8.2. The cases in the tables have lagged variable values for those two variables and other variables also on the right side of regression equations. Figure ICA 8.1 shows data for the full quarterly data sample period, while Figure ICA 8.2 shows data for the first sub-sample period. Although the regression lines in the figures do not directly correspond to any cases from the results in the tables, these figures help to show why estimates of β_1 are not statistically different from zero over the full sample period but in most cases considered are statistically different from zero in the first sub-sample period. Table ICA 8.3 showing the correlations between the changes in the natural logs of M1 and nominal GDP also tells a similar story about the relationship between the changes in the natural logs of nominal GDP and nominal M1 over the full sample period versus over only the first sub-sample period.

In sum, whether considering regressions for the change in the natural log of nominal GDP over the full sample period or just the first sub-sample period ending with the first quarter of 1981, the estimated impact of a one per cent increase in M1 in a quarter is an increase in nominal GDP by less than one per cent (and over the full sample period would probably be essentially be zero per cent). Thus, it appears possible to estimate a NDVMSL. Future work can consider sub-sample periods other than the first sub-sample period. Future work can also improve the model for estimating growth in nominal GDP. Future work can also address whether changes in nominal GDP lead to increases in M1 within the same quarter. Perhaps more importantly, a time horizon longer than just one quarter for a possible NDVMSL may be quite helpful for policymakers. For example, if the money supply increases in one quarter, what happens to nominal GDP (and velocity) not only in the current quarter but also future quarters? Of course, before more confidence can be placed in the theory of a NDVMSL, the analytical framework (for example, the use of natural logs in the equation for the change in the natural log of nominal GDP) and econometric analysis should be verified. More work on robustness of results to different models would also help. Also, if structural changes occur (for example, maybe further work would reveal the U.S. economy went from periods when the change in M1 impacts the change in nominal GDP within the same quarter to periods when no impact occurs in the current quarter and *vice versa*), future work could attempt to address what causes this and predict periods of structural change.

	β_1	S.E.	T-Stat	P-value
Full Sample Period				
All Variables Diff				
Two Lags	0.023238	0.057458	0.404435	0.6863
Five Lags	0.007744	0.055477	0.139594	0.8891
Eight Lags	-0.011930	0.058407	-0.204257	0.8384
U NOT Diff				
Two Lags	0.023058	0.058716	0.392700	0.6950
Five Lags	-0.000992	0.055937	-0.017740	0.9859
Eight Lags	-0.008708	0.058456	-0.148965	0.8818
FFR, TenYr, U NOT Diff				
One Lag	0.031947	0.055304	0.577658	0.5641
Four Lags	0.034864	0.055454	0.628701	0.5303
Five Lags	0.007465	0.055855	0.133644	0.8938
Eight Lags	-0.010253	0.058787	-0.174413	0.8618
End 1981q3				
All Variables Diff				
One Lag	0.295842	0.141201	2.095185	0.0394
Three Lags	0.377814	0.147193	2.566785	0.0125
Four Lags	0.361376	0.165129	2.188450	0.0325
Eight Lags	0.233052	0.222896	1.045564	0.3025
U NOT Diff				
One Lag	0.367796	0.142010	2.589926	0.0114
Three Lags	0.397763	0.140401	2.833044	0.0061
FFR, TenYr, U NOT Diff				
One Lag	0.243109	0.140539	1.729838	0.0876
Five Lags	0.377201	0.174187	2.165491	0.0347

Table ICA8.1
Estimated Values for the Coefficient (β_1) on the Change in the Natural Log of M1 in Regression Equations for the Change in the Natural Log of Nominal GDP
Full Sample Period (through 2013q1) Regressions Presented above those for First Sub-Sample Period (ending 1981q3)
Either (1) All Variables (except the constant and the error term) in Differenced Form or (2) Only the Unemployment Rate (U) Is Not Differenced or (3) Only the Changes in the Natural Logs of Nominal GDP and M1 Are Differenced
Number of Previous Quarters of Lagged Dependent Variables Listed in Each Row

Variable	Coefficient	S.E.	T-Stat	P-value
D_LN_M1	0.023238	0.057458	0.404435	0.6863
D_LN_M1(-1)	-0.045471	0.062857	-0.723392	0.4703
D_LN_M1(-2)	0.032855	0.056165	0.584968	0.5592
D_LN_NOMY(-1)	0.243769	0.066983	3.639266	0.0003
D_LN_NOMY(-2)	0.319920	0.066741	4.793472	0.0000
D_FFR	-9.79E-05	0.000736	-0.132959	0.8944
D_FFR(-1)	0.000522	0.000727	0.717709	0.4738
D_FFR(-2)	-0.001580	0.000703	-2.245988	0.0258
D_TENYR	0.002649	0.001287	2.058876	0.0408
D_TENYR(-1)	0.000595	0.001399	0.425240	0.6711
D_TENYR(-2)	0.000479	0.001374	0.348957	0.7275
D_U	-0.012864	0.002213	-5.812732	0.0000
D_U(-1)	0.003898	0.002783	1.400966	0.1628
D_U(-2)	0.005747	0.002318	2.479441	0.0140
C	0.006941	0.001452	4.779805	0.0000
R-squared	0.478009			
Adjusted R-squared	0.441286			

Table ICA8.2
Equation for the Change in Natural Log of Nominal GDP as a Function of the Current and Past Changes in the Natural Log of M1, Past Changes in the Natural Log of Nominal GDP, Current and Past Values of Other Variables and a Constant Term
Sample Ending 2013q1
Two Lags, All Variables in Differenced Form

Full Sample Period	First Sub-Sample Period (ending 1981q3)
-0.010698	0.461289

Table ICA 8.3 Correlation Between Change in the Natural Log of Nominal GDP and Change in the Natural Log of M1

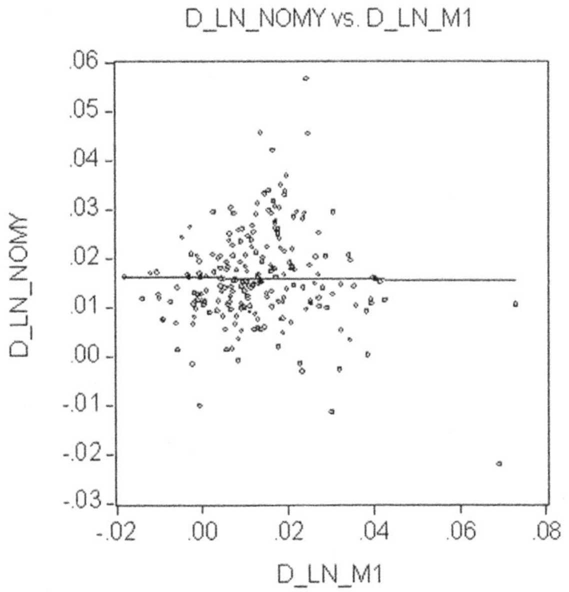

Figure ICA 8.1
Change in the Natural Log of Nominal GDP (on the Vertical Axis) and Change in the Natural Log of M1
Full Sample Period
Source www.economagic.com and the author's calculations

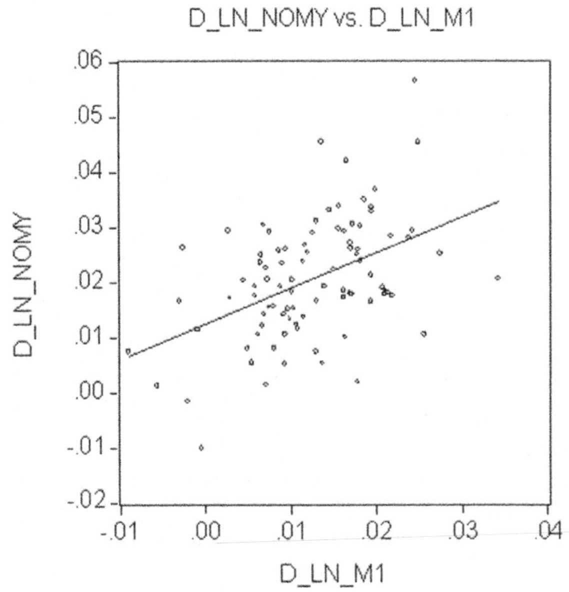

Figure ICA 8.2
Change in the Natural Log of Nominal GDP (on the Vertical Axis) and Change in the Natural Log of M1
First Sub-Sample Period (1959q1-1981q3)
Source www.economagic.com and the author's calculations

CONCLUDING REMARKS

The Federal Reserve has started to taper its purchases of longer-term federal debt, while trying to keep the federal funds rate quite low. The tapering began at the end of Ben Bernanke's term as Chair. Many expected tapering to continue into Janet Yellen's term as Chair, according to Crutsinger (2014, a). If my memory and understanding are correct, however, the FOMC has given itself leeway to put tapering on hold if not reverse course should economic conditions warrant such a reversal, as discussed in Crutsinger (2014, b). Although many may believe that monetary policy in the U.S. is still extremely expansionary, the commencement of tapering represents at least a minor shift toward tighter monetary policy.

While tighter monetary policy may be necessary in the future to stave off higher inflation rates, is it possible that inflation will not accelerate in the United States until after the velocity of M1 and the velocity of M2 begin to increase again? Also, would a combination of tighter monetary policy and tighter fiscal policy in the near future in the United States be akin to an automobile driver hitting the break too soon before the journey is over?

Again, with the velocity of money falling and many interest rates in the United States still relatively low, further expansionary monetary policy may be in more of a support role to federal budget deficits. Still, if the economy is not in a complete liquidity trap, further increases in the money supply may increase real GDP somewhat. But with money velocity continuing to fall, interest rates remaining relatively low, and the U.S. economy seemingly close to a liquidity trap, it is likely that expansionary fiscal policy would be more helpful for the road ahead in accelerating the journey to full employment and completing the journey away from the Great Recession. Some macroeconomic theory as described in Dornbusch, Fischer, and Startz (2008, pp.253, 261) and elsewhere seems to support this view when the slope of the LM curve is rather flat, as evidently is the case in the United States today. Many dollars newly added to the U.S. economy seem to be held rather than being spent, thus giving rise to the decline in velocity. Future work could identify which types of tax reductions and increases in government spending would generate the greatest increases in real GDP and employment. Political considerations would also need to be considered given that tax reductions and increases in government spending, all other things equal, lead to greater budget deficits.

Expansionary monetary policy in the United States has increased the nominal M1 money supply by more than one hundred per cent after the fourth quarter of 2007 based on data from www.economagic.com accessed September 2014 and the author's calculations. The U.S. has plenty of dollars to enable a noticeably larger amount of spending on nominal GDP (with the goal of generating a larger real GDP). However, if a NDVMSL exists, then in nearly every quarter starting with the first quarter of 2008, either the money supply level in the U.S. has been greater than the NDVMSL or the growth in the money supply has pushed the money supply level above the NDVMSL. The result has been a startling drop in the velocity of money. That provides a statistical fact explainable to the general public which shows the diminished effectiveness of monetary policy in stimulating spending when the economy is near a liquidity trap, as well as providing food for thought for economists.

Data from www.economagic.com accessed September 28, 2014 and the author's calculations have recently indicated that real GDP in the U.S. economy *de*creased by more than two per cent (on an annualized, seasonally adjusted basis) in the first quarter of 2014. Was this a hiccup in the Not-So-Great Recovery, or the beginning of another recession? Only time will tell. Some (for example, Appelbaum (2014) note that the FOMC may end its tapering in October 2014 rather than in December 2014. Although as noted above, the completion of tapering may be essential to prevent inflation from soaring, what will probably happen to nominal GDP spending, already growing at a rate that many find too slow, if monetary policy tightens and the U.S. economy is not in a complete liquidity trap?

An early October 2014 column written by Paul Krugman (2014) suggests that the U.S. economy, in his view, is still in a liquidity trap (at least as of his writing). Further, my interpretation of Krugman (2014) tells me that in his view, the rapid jumps in interest rates and inflation that many thought would arise due to expansionary stabilization policy have not yet materialized. Regarding interest rates, I noticed on the morning of October 8, 2014, CNBC (2014) showed on the screen trades of ten-year U.S. Treasury debt at a rate of 2.336 per cent and thirty-year U.S. Treasury debt at a rate of 3.046 per cent. Budget deficits to stimulate economic growth at such low interest rates would not necessitate a large decrease in business spending on buildings, machines, and inventories. Further, these interest rates in early October 2014 represent decreases compared with data measured on a daily basis from late December 2013 and early January 2014 available at www.economagic.com accessed October 8, 2014. Also, I seem to recall gold prices and silver prices much higher just a few years ago. If my memory is correct about precious metal prices, do these price decreases and a return to a downward trend in U.S. interest rates indicate something about inflation expectations?

With a large increase in the number of dollars in the economy but sub-par economic growth, the study reiterates that the time has come to get the dollars moving again at a faster rate. Could completing the recovery from the Great Recession require the stabilization of the velocity of money (or at least a clear slowdown in its decline), if not at least a small increase in velocity? Barring a noticeable increase in inflation, could a small increase in velocity possibly be harmful? An apparent lack of sufficient demand from households, businesses, and non-profit organizations leads me to call on the government sectors to use fiscal policies (again, tax reductions and increases in government spending) to increase aggregate demand. Increasing the money supply alone appears insufficient to return the economy to a level of real GDP consistent with 'full employment' or trend real GDP any time soon. The short explanation, which has been discussed in more detail in this book and elsewhere, is, as I keep thinking while working on this book, 'it's velocity, 'stupid!"

CHAPTER EIGHT REFERENCES (INCLUDING THE IN-CHAPTER APPENDIX)

Akaike, H. (1974) "A New Look at the Statistical Model Identification." *IEEE Transactions on Automatic Control*, vol. 19, iss. 6, pp. 716-723.

Appelbaum, B. (2014) "Fed, Confident in Economy, Details End of Bond-Buying Program." July 9, 2014, accessed October 4, 2014, available online at: www.nytimes.com/2014/07/10/business/federal-reserve-june-minutes-detail-end-of-bond-buying-program-.html?_r=0

Atlanta Journal-Constitution. (2014) "European Bank Leaves Key Rate Unchanged." author not specified, October 3, 2014, p. A8.

Baumol, W. J. and Blinder, A. S. (2012) *Macroeconomics: Principles and Policy*, twelfth edition. South-Western Cengage Learning, Mason, Ohio.

Brunner, K. and Meltzer, A. H. (1963) "Predicting Velocity: Implications for Theory and Policy." *Journal of Finance*, vol. 18, May, pp. 319-354.

Burton, M. and Lombra, R. (2006) *The Financial System and the Economy: Principles of Money and Banking*, fourth edition. Thomson South-Western, Mason, Ohio.

Cagan, P. and Schwartz, A. J. (1975) "Has the Growth of Money Substitutes Hindered Monetary Policy?" *Journal of Money, Credit, and Banking*, vol. 7, May, pp. 137-160.

CNBC. (2014) Ten-Year U.S. Treasury Interest Rate Data and Thirty-Year U.S. Treasury Interest Rate Data. October 8, 2014.

Crutsinger, M. (2014, a) "Fed Stays Course, Cuts Bond Buying." *Atlanta Journal- Constitution*, January 30, 2014, p. A13.

Crutsinger, M. (2014, b) "Yellen: Fed Monitoring 'Soft Data.'" *Atlanta Journal- Constitution*, February 28, 2014, pp. A9, A11.

Dickey, D. A. and Fuller, W. A. (1979) "Distribution of Estimators for Autoregressive Time Series with a Unit Root." *Journal of the American Statistical Association*, vol. 74, pp. 427-431.

Dornbusch, R., Fischer, S., and Startz, R. (2008) *Macroeconomics*, tenth edition. McGraw-Hill Irwin, Boston, Massachusetts.

Friedman, B. (1983) "The Roles of Money and Credit in Macroeconomic Analysis". In James Tobin (editor) *Macroeconomics, Prices, and Quantities*. The Brookings Institution, Washington, D. C.

Goldfeld, S. M. (1973) "The Demand for Money Revisited." *Brookings Papers on Economic Activity*, vol. 3, pp. 577-638.

Hamilton, J. D. (1994) *Time Series Analysis*. Princeton University Press, Princeton, New Jersey.

Krugman, P. (2014) "Depression Denial Syndrome." October 2, 2014, accessed October 8, 2014, available online at: www.nytimes.com/2014/10/03/opinion/paul-krugman-depression-denial-syndrome.html

Krugman, P. and Wells, R. (2009) *Macroeconomics*, second edition. Worth Publishers, New York, New York.

Laidler, D. E. W. (1993) *The Demand for Money: Theories, Evidence, and Problems*, fourth edition. Harper Collins College Publishers, New York, New York.

Malewitz, J. (2013) "Universities Scale Back Research." *Atlanta Journal-Constitution*, April 14, 2013, p. A16.

Marty, A. (1961) "Gurley and Shaw on Money in a Theory of Finance." *Journal of Political Economy*, vol. 69, February, pp. 56-62.

Mishkin, F. S. (2004) *The Economics of Money, Banking, and Financial Markets*, seventh edition. Pearson Addison Wesley, Boston, Massachusetts.

Schwartz, N. D. (2013) "Higher Payroll Tax Saps Buying Power." *Atlanta Journal- Constitution*, February 10, 2013, p. A2.

Schwarz, G. (1978) "Estimating the Dimension of a Model." *Annals of Statistics*, vol. 6, pp. 461-464.

Sommer, J. (2013) "Getting Creative with the G.D.P." July 27, 2013, accessed April 24, 2014, available online at: www.nytimes.com/2013/07/28/your-money/getting-creative-with-the-gdp.html?r_=0

Wiseman, P. (2012) "Weak Recovery Marked." *Atlanta Journal-Constitution*, August 16, 2012, p. A8.

www.economagic.com

www.fdic.gov/deposit/deposits/unlimited/expiration.html

INDEX

Note:

(net) = appears only in an internet address on that page and it is not in a reference list
(ref) = appears in reference list (but not necessarily as an author) on that page
(s) = identified as a source (author or co-author) on that page
(tr) = included in a table and also in reference list on that page
(*) = may not have pages that do not identify the Great Recession by name
(**) = may not have pages that discuss 'per cent' changes in money supply

Made in the USA
Monee, IL
25 April 2022

95373195R00195